Social Class, Race, and Psychological Development

Edited by

MARTIN DEUTSCH

New York University

IRWIN KATZ

University of Michigan

ARTHUR R. JENSEN

University of California

HOLT, RINEHART and WINSTON, INC.

New York   Chicago   San Francisco   Atlanta   Dallas
Montreal   Toronto   London

This book

is

dedicated

to

the memory

of

Dr. Martin Luther King, Jr.

*And I assert at this time that once again
we must reaffirm our belief in building a democratic society, in which blacks and whites can live
together as brothers, where we will all come to see
that integration is not a problem, but an opportunity to participate in the beauty of diversity.*

From the address of Dr. Martin Luther
King, Jr., to the American Psychological
Association, Washington, D.C.,
September 1967.

Preface

The conscience of America has become aroused by problems of inequality. Why we should have been so laggard in the public recognition of these problems, which have been with us all along, is a task to trouble the social historian. Perhaps our pervasive optimism and the doctrine of inevitable progress made us feel that all would soon be better. Perhaps a certain smugness and self-righteousness allowed us to enjoy "the highest standard of living in the world" without being aware that many among us have not had, and do not now have, access to their just share of the world's goods and opportunities. The social scientists were not unaware of these problems. We need think only of *Recent Social Trends* (1938) or Gunnar Myrdal's *American Dilemma* (1944). Still, it took the events of the last decade—sit-down strikes, marches, violent protests, even the tragic death of Dr. Martin Luther King—to move an aroused public to want to do something important, and soon, to relieve the inequities with which we had learned to live all too complacently.

What is the role of the behavioral and social scientist at the present time? Obviously social inequality lies within the areas of inquiry of these fields of knowledge, but it does not necessarily follow that the behavioral scientist has workable solutions to the problems of inequality, or that, if he has the solutions, he knows how to get them adopted. The government has stepped in to aid him, however, granting funds through the Office of Education, the Office of Economic Opportunity, the Department of Housing and Urban Development, and other agencies. These funds, and those from private foundations, provide an opportunity for the behavioral and social scientist to be of service, if he is ready.

There are essentially three things that he can do: First, he can contribute to an understanding of the situation as it exists, examining our social structure, social classes, social mobility, the causes and consequences of poverty. Second, he can look to his research data and his theories to see what might be done to correct the effects of poverty on children, and he might also look for ways in which his science might help to ameliorate conditions that have resulted in poverty in the first place. Thus he looks to the body of theory and data in his science for suggestions that are relevant to the problems at hand. Third, he can move directly toward the solution of the problem in steps that are the equivalent of research and development in other sciences. That is, he takes his laboratory directly to the field (as in Head Start programs) and does a kind of "quality control" study to see whether his ideas, when put into practice, do indeed achieve the intended results.

All this seems so obvious that obstacles in the way of following it are not likely to be appreciated by those who have not faced them. In recent years there has been such a celebration of "basic research" that the criterion of relevance to important problems has receded, and many behavioral and social scientists find satisfaction in building elaborate theoretical models around precise but somewhat irrelevant data. Hence when colleagues who attempt to face up to social problems look for relevant data and hypotheses, they often do not find much that they can use. Not unrelated to the emphasis upon basic science is the tendency to specialize. Even within psychology, the subspecialties of behavior genetics, physiology of learning, social psychology, clinical psychology, and educational psychology become encapsulated and thus less accessible to the kind of team effort that is essential to the solving of social problems. Finally, actual applications in the field meet with a number of barriers to proper science—particularly prejudice, romanticism, and haste.

The present book is timely in its bearing on all the foregoing considerations. It is at once analytical with regard to the underlying problems, hence avoiding the urgency that something be done now; scientific, in that it seeks for laboratory evidence regarding development; and practical, in that it looks toward actual educational procedures that may correct deficiencies due to poverty in early childhood.

We see here all the dilemmas of current behavioral and social science. There are points at which the authors cry out for new data, in order to be sure that their conjectures are applicable. There are occasions to complain that educational reforms have not gone far enough. Throughout, however, there is a high concern for relevance—a useful corrective of the plea for indulgence until psychology evolves more highly.

The contributors cover a wide range of the subdisciplines within psychology, including behavior genetics, experimental psychology, social psychology, and educational psychology. That all are psychologists is somewhat to be regretted, in that the problems faced are anthropological, sociological, psychiatric, political, and economic, as well, and we need to learn the full interdisciplinary approach to them. The limitation of the book to psychologists is not a severe handicap, however, in part because psychologists of such diverse interests are included, and in part because the developmental emphasis belongs more to psychology than to its sister disciplines.

The text is not easy; it is not watered down to make psychology palatable to the activists. As scientists, we need to avoid the stance of the "expert witness" who gives immediate solutions to pressing problems. The authors of this book keep a proper perspective on the problems they treat, and they know the difficulties of solution, so that the scientist here plays his proper role of treating answerable problems with the tools at his disposal rather than making premature prescriptions. Still there is no retreat from responsibility, and this is perhaps the book's greatest lesson: it is possible for the behavioral scientist today to deal responsibly with pressing social problems without relinquishing his role as an objective investigator.

The Society for the Psychological Study of Social Issues was wise to undertake this venture, and its members can take satisfaction in this book produced by their editors and authors.

Ernest R. Hilgard

April 1968

The editors acknowledge with gratitude the goodwill of all the contributors to this volume. Not only have they worked diligently and willingly revised their contributions, but they have waited patiently for the final production of this volume. The contributions reflect the thinking of their authors; the editors have seen their role as one of checking for errors of fact, omissions, logical coherence, and stylistic clarity. In this we have been encouraged by the editorial staff of Holt, Rinehart and Winston. We are particularly grateful to Carol Stanwood and Peggy Newton, who coordinated the compilation of the manuscript and carried on an extensive correspondence and discussion with all the contributors and editors.

Contents

INTRODUCTION

Martin Deutsch

Irwin Katz

Perhaps the most fundamental domestic problem of latter twentieth-century America is the persistence of gross inequalities in the life opportunities of youth from different social classes and racial groups. A critical component of the problem is the failure of most poor children to master the basic knowledge and skills that are necessary for assimilation into a highly technical and industrialized economy. The scholastic achievement gap that separates pupils in the slums from those in affluent neighborhoods remains tragically wide. This was shown in a recent nationwide survey conducted by James Coleman and others (1966) for the United States Office of Education. In every region of the country about 85 percent of Negro elementary and high school students scored below white averages on objective tests of scholastic ability and achievement.

Identifying the causes of academic failure in depressed-area schools is an issue of intense controversy among school officials, political leaders, spokesmen for minority group parents, and other interested groups. Even the views of social scientists concerned with the problem are widely divergent—ranging from Kenneth Clark's (1965) telling criticism of black ghetto schools to Bruno Bettelheim's (1964) psychoanalytically inspired contention that lower-class homes inflict irreversible damage upon the personalities of children even before they enter kindergarten or first grade. Unfortunately, in the current national debate over the causes of unequal opportunity, basic assumptions about class and race differences in psychological development continue to rest more upon conjecture and subjective impressions than upon the findings of scientific research.

1

Accordingly, it is altogether fitting that the Society for the Psychological Study of Social Issues, an affiliate of the American Psychological Association, should sponsor a book which seeks to clarify the present state of knowledge about social and biological influences on intellectual development. Most of the chapters that follow were written specifically for this volume; the rest are more or less extensive revisions of significant papers that were first published elsewhere. Each of them makes a unique contribution to an understanding of the larger subject.

Part One on "Biogenetic Perspectives" offers an objective exposition of research dealing with the traditional nature-nurture problem, particularly as it impinges on the issues of social-class and racial differences in intelligence. As Arthur Jensen observes in his introduction, many of the polemics in the field have issued from misconceptions about genetics and failure to think in terms of interactive effects of heredity and environment. "When the wrong questions are posed," he remarks, "the answers tend to be sought in the realm of argument rather than in scientific research, which by its very nature does not lend itself to answering ill-framed questions." It is hoped that the discussion of genetics will indicate to social scientists and educators both the legitimacy and importance of this topic, and the need for greater theoretical and methodological sophistication in research on biological factors in class and ethnic characteristics.

Until the 1960's very little scientific research was done on the causes and types of intellectual impairment of children coming from low-income homes, and most of it was narrowly concerned with the description of group differences in IQ. There has recently developed in American psychology a trend toward studies of the processes that underlie children's intellectual growth.

In Part Two, three chapters dealing with the topic of "Basic Processes in Intellectual Development" delineate various specific processes whereby the home environment influences psychological development. The discussions reflect recent efforts by behavioral scientists to move beyond simple correlational studies of indicators of socioeconomic status, on the one hand, and such global characteristics as general intelligence and academic achievement, on the other. In the past, most of the social-class variables examined, such as income, occupation, and physical condition of the home, were essentially nonpsychological in nature and thus did little to expose the causal factors underlying observed differences in the measured intelligence of poor and affluent children.

One of the chapters in this part analyzes recent theory and research on the developmental aspects of perceptual functions, the role of experience in their formation, and their relation to reading and problem-solving skills. Another contribution reports early findings from an extensive survey of linguistic skills, intelligence test scores, and social background factors in a balanced sample of Negro and white boys of both middle-class and lower-class status. The study concentrates on those aspects of environment which are most likely to be causally linked to language ability and mental proficiency, that is, on qualities of the parent-child interaction and the family constellation. An empirically derived "Deprivation Index" predicts more of the variance in educationally relevant traits than do the usual indices of socioeconomic status. Current thinking gives language a central place in problem solving and in cognitive processes generally. Bernstein's work in England highlighted a general relationship between language structure and particular social milieus. The third paper in this part employs a wealth of data from verbal learning experiments to suggest numerous ways in which social-class variations in language usage, hence in the early verbal stimulation of children, inexorably shape children's later intellectual ability.

Social factors that influence the disadvantaged pupil's will to learn are emphasized in Part Three, titled "Social and Psychological Perspectives." Certain characteristic deficiencies in the academic motivation of minority group children are glaringly obvious to anyone who observes typical fourth- or fifth-grade classrooms in urban ghetto schools. At the same time, it is equally clear that there are gross inadequacies in the educational services offered in nearly all these schools. Elsewhere, one of the present authors (Deutsch, 1960) has reported observations made in predominantly Negro public schools in Harlem which revealed that 50 to 80 percent of all classroom time was devoted to disciplinary and other essentially nonacademic tasks, as compared with only 30 percent of classroom time given to such activities in schools attended mainly by white children of roughly similar economic status. What the comparison conveys about the behavior and attitudes of socially disadvantaged students is poignantly elaborated in a recent article by a young, Harvard-trained teacher in a Negro ghetto school (Levy, 1966). She writes:

> What impressed me most was the fact that my children (9–10 years old) are already cynical and disillusioned about school, themselves, and life-in-general. They are hostile, rebellious, and bitter. . . . They are hyperactive and are constantly in motion. In many ways they can be compared with wild horses that are suddenly fenced in (pp. 430–431).

A common theme of the chapters in this part is that discrimination tends to create in its victims those very traits of "inferiority" that are mentioned to rationalize its practice. Even in the absence of the more blatant forms of discrimination, traditional stereotypes about the low ability and apathy of Negroes and other ethnic minorities can operate as self-fulfilling prophecies. Thus the belief that Negroes are intellectually incompetent can cause both whites and Negroes to behave in such manner as to yield confirmatory evidence.

The ways in which expectancies about others and about oneself develop, and their relation to academic performance, are explored from various perspectives. There is a review of studies dealing with the general topic of Negro self-concepts. Another contribution reports a series of intriguing experiments on human and animal subjects which support the hypothesis that the expectations of power figures, regarding the behavior of those whom they control, importantly influence the latter's behavior. The main experiment utilized an entire elementary school as a natural laboratory for a full academic year. Pupils from whom teachers were arbitrarily led to expect strong intellectual growth (the teachers were given fictitiously high intelligence test scores for the children involved) actually showed such growth during the ensuing year.

The primary thrust of the third paper on "Social and Psychological Perspectives" is toward motivational factors that favorably or adversely influence the achievement behavior of minority group children in biracial classrooms. Drawing upon evidence from a wide range of studies on the effects of stress and isolation, as well as from several experiments on Negro adolescents, the author suggests a model for predicting Negro performance in desegregated schools. The reactions—both real and anticipated—of white peers and teachers, and the Negro child's expectancies of success or failure on particular scholastic tasks, figure prominently in the conceptual scheme that is outlined. It is proposed that the racially mixed environment has greater potentiality both for academic success and failure than does the all-Negro environment. Whether the outcome for the individual pupil will be favorable or detrimental depends in large measure upon the specific social conditions that prevail in the classroom.

Part Four, the final section of the book, "On The Education of the Disadvantaged," describes the recent contributions of psychology to educational theory and practice, contributions that have been stimulated in part by the overturning of the concept of fixed intelligence and the concomitant rediscovery of the importance of experiential factors in cognitive development. The opening chapter elaborates the notion of intrinsic motivation, conceived as an autonomous urge toward novel experiences, and toward the exploration and manipulation of the physical environment. Presumably intrinsic motivation, which is essential for cognitive growth, requires for its own development variety of stimulation in early life. As Piaget has put it, "the more a child has seen and heard, the more he wants to see and hear." The obverse of this—that monotonous and restricted environments produce apathy—appears also to be true, though systematic evidence as yet is scarce. It is suggested that by the third year of life the physical and social conditions of low-income homes—with their crowding, dearth of manipulable objects, and restricted adult language patterns—are no longer adequate for the proper growth of intrinsic motivation. Hence, early enrichment of the disadvantaged child's environment is essential for satisfactory cognitive growth.

All the chapters in the final part discuss new or recently rediscovered approaches to the education of the disadvantaged. In a few instances the methods and rationales of particular enrichment programs—for example, those of Montessori and Bereiter—are discussed in some detail. In addition, fairly comprehensive surveys of compensatory projects for children of different ages are presented. Regrettably, few of the efforts that have been instituted above the preschool level have been genuinely innovative with respect either to instructional methods or curriculum content. Nor have these efforts usually been based upon well-established pedagogical principles. Moreover, very few of the programs have had evaluations of sufficient scope and objectivity to establish whether they were really effective over the long run.

While each chapter in this book has a specific focus, and each was written independently of the others, several themes emerge from the book as a whole. One such theme is the complexity and multiplicity of factors that influence psychological traits and govern their development. While emphasis is mostly on social and interpersonal influences, biological factors are not neglected. But those factors related to negative living conditions receive the most emphasis. In one way or another, all the chapters of the book are concerned with the deleterious effects of poverty on children's development. Another major theme is the search for psychological variables which mediate between the child's social background and his intellectual and school performance. One might begin with race or class as a kind of encompassing description of a social milieu, and one might end with academic competence as a criterion measure. But unless the intervening processes are specified, so that cause-and-effect relationships can be understood, sound bases for social and educational action programs will not result.

This book illustrates the current involvement of behavioral scientists with important social problems, especially in the field of education. Its contents show that, contrary to the tenets of some psychological systems which were influential in the past, research on urgent practical problems can also have basic scientific value, by providing effective tests of existing theories and by generating new ones. The editors hope that the volume will provide a useful assessment of what is known, and what still needs to be known—from the standpoint of providing equal educational opportunities—about the biological, psychological, and social factors governing the achievement of students from different types of home background.

References

Bettelheim, B. Review of B. S. Bloom's *Stability and change in human characteristics. New York Review of Books,* Sept. 10, 1964, **3**, 1–4.

Clark, K. B. *Dark ghetto.* New York: Harper & Row, 1965.

Coleman, J. S., *et al. Equality of educational opportunity,* United States Department of Health, Education, and Welfare. Washington, D.C.: United States Government Printing Office, 1966.

Deutsch, M. *Minority group and class status as related to social and personality factors in scholastic achievement.* Monograph No. 2, Ithaca, N. Y.: The Society for Applied Anthropology, 1960.

Levy, B. "An urban teacher speaks out." In S. W. Webster (ed.), *The disadvantaged learner.* San Francisco: Chandler, 1966.

PART ONE

Biogenetic Perspectives

INTRODUCTION—*Arthur R. Jensen*

The present volume, which deals so largely with environmental determinants of behavior, would leave the reader with an unbalanced picture indeed were it not for the following chapter. The fact that only one chapter out of the eleven in this book deals with the genetic basis of individual, class, and race differences should by no means be construed as belittlement of the importance of biological inheritance as a source of variance in psychological traits. The presentation of a balanced, objective exposition of the research dealing with the so-called nature-nurture problem—particularly as it impinges on the issues of social class and racial differences—has been a rare achievement throughout most of the history of American psychology. American social scientists have traditionally approached the subject less dispassionately than Europeans, except perhaps in the Soviet Union, where both behavior genetics and intelligence testing have been officially opposed by Marxist dogma.

A history of American psychology would not be complete without an account of the vicissitudes of the nature-nurture controversy. Many of the traditional polemics in this field have issued from early misconceptions about genetics and failure to think in terms of the interactive effects of heredity and environment. When the wrong questions are posed, the answers tend to be sought in the realm of argument rather than in scientific research, which by its very nature does not lend itself to answering ill-framed questions. A classic example of such a question is: (*a*) Which is more important in the development of intelligence—heredity or environment? Unfortunately, too many psychology textbooks, even recent ones, have tried to answer this question, with the result that they never get around to asking the question to which we would really like to know the answer and which, in fact, is empirically answerable. The customary answer to Question *a* is: Neither heredity nor environment is more important, since both are absolutely essential for the organism to come into existence and to survive. Therefore, it is impossible to say one is more important than the other; it is like saying that length or width is more important in determining the area of a rectangle. All this, of course, is both obvious and trivial. But it does not answer the very different (and answerable) question asked by geneticists and differential psychologists: (*b*) What are the relative contributions of genetic and nongenetic factors to *individual differences* in measured intelligence? Or, to be more technical, what proportion of the variance among phenotypes is attributable to variance among genotypes?

The second most common polemic has been the result of an unwarranted and misconceived expectation that there should be some absolute or "true" answer to Question *b,* like the answer to "What is the ratio of a circle's circumference to its diameter?" The researches of investigators such as E. L. Thorndike, Sir Cyril Burt, Newman, Freeman, Holzinger, and others, have yielded answers to Question *b*. Though the answers to this question arrived at by most investigators are not in perfect agreement, they are in close agreement. But the reason for this agreement is not that all these investigators are trying, more or less successfully, to discover *the* true *nature-nurture* ratio or other quantitative expression of the relative importance of heredity and environment. There is no single correct answer. This is not to say however, that the answers that have been obtained in various studies are not without importance, both theoretical and practical. The very nature of the problem precludes the possibility of an answer of the type "The ratio of the circumference to the diameter of a circle is 3.1416."

It is axiomatic in genetics that the relative contributions of heredity and environment to the variability of a given trait in the population are a joint function of the genetic variability and the variability of trait-relevant environmental factors. By and large, studies of the inheritance of intelligence have not been based on samples from populations that include the greatest possible extremes of trait-relevant environmental variation. Part of the problem is that we are not yet certain what the most relevant environmental influences are, and, therefore we cannot measure environmental variation satisfactorily. Researchers have studied the inheritance of intelligence in populations as they actually exist, rather than as they might be if relevant environmental influences varied over a wider range than normally occurs in the bulk of the population. It should be noted, however, that the lowest end of the socioeconomic scale is greatly underrepresented in studies of the heritability of intelligence. The largest and methodologically most adequate studies conducted in England and the United States have yielded heritability estimates for intelligence in the range from 0.70 to 0.90. This means that in the various populations studied, between 70 and 90 percent of the variability in measured intelligence is attributable to genetic factors and between 5 and 25 percent to environmental factors (including prenatal and perinatal biological factors). The remaining 5 percent of the variance is due to errors of measurement.

If one accepts the evidence for the hereditary determination of individual differences in intellectual ability, which indicates that genetic factors account for some 80 percent of the phenotypic variance, it is then hard to reject the hypothesis that social classes, as defined by occupational level and similar indices, differ in frequency distributions of genotypes for intelligence. If 20 percent of phenotypic variation is attributable to environment, then the excess of this percentage of the total variance in IQ in the population that is predictable from indices of socioeconomic status must have a genetic basis. This should not be surprising, since the occupational hierarchy and its correlated educational requirements act as an intellectual screening device. Therefore, in a society that permits a high degree of social mobility, socioeconomic status inevitably becomes correlated with intelligence and with its genetic basis.

The situation with respect to race is more ambiguous, since racially distinguishing characteristics, such as skin color, which are irrelevant to intellectual ability, are often barriers to social mobility. To the degree that a racial minority is restricted in its social mobility, the socioeconomic status of the group will fail to reflect genetic intellectual potential. Data that would permit firm conclusions about the genetic basis of differences among ethnic groups in measured intelligence do not yet exist. The question, however, is worthy of rigorous scientific research. It is unfortunate that so much of the past research on Negro-white differences, for example, has done so little to delineate either the genetic or environmental sources of these differences. Considerably greater methodological sophistication, both psychologic and genetic, will be required to answer the important questions in this area.

It may be hoped that Gottesman's introduction to the genetics of social class and racial differences will serve as a reminder that man's intelligence and social adaptability are the products of biological evolution as well as of individual experience. To fail to recognize the biological basis of human differences in psychological characteristics is to limit understanding to only half of reality.

CHAPTER ONE

Biogenetics
of Race and Class

I. I. GOTTESMAN[1]

This chapter will introduce the reader to some of the facts and interpretations advanced by scientists who study race and class with the concepts of human genetics as a guide.[2] A chapter which has as its thesis the idea that social classes as well as races may profitably be construed as Mendelian populations or *relatively* isolated groups in terms of reproduction, whose variation may be associated with genetic sources, is least likely to be rejected in the context of this particular book. In this context checks and balances from the viewpoints of more sociologically oriented colleagues give the reader an opportunity to arrive at his own dialectic and save the writer the awkwardness of constant qualification. Arguments in the past about the contributions of nature and nurture to a particular behavior have obscured the clarifying potential of biology, especially human genetics, to the problems inundating our understanding of race and class differences. In addition to the sources of variation in measured intelligence and personality,

---

[1] University of Minnesota.

[2] Earlier versions of this chapter were read and criticized by Sheldon C. Reed and William S. Pollitzer. Any errors that remain are the sole responsibility of the author.

some of the contemporary evidence relevant to adaptation and natural selection, and dysgenic trends[3] in intelligence, will be examined.

Race Taxonomy

All living men belong to one species, *Homo sapiens*. Our species is differentiated into subspecies, or races, who represent genetically open systems; that is, they are mutually interfertile. Reproductive isolating mechanisms either prevent crosses between species or reduce their full success (Mayr, 1963). It is only when genetically effective race crossing does not work that different species, rather than subspecies, emerge. Neither physical anthropologists nor human geneticists can agree on a preferred taxonomy for our polytypic species. In the history of race naming there have been extremes ranging from a simple dichotomy, straight versus woolly hair, to calling any difference in gene frequencies between two Mendelian populations a sign of racial distinctiveness. The latter are facts of nature easily established by such procedures as blood typing.

The choice of a convenient race taxonomy will depend on the particular purpose of the investigator. Blumenbach, a contemporary of Linnaeus, categorized men as Caucasians, Mongolians (yellow), Ethiopians (black), Malayans (brown), and Americans (red). All this, based only on skin color, in 1775, the year of the Revolutionary War. With advances in serological genetics that permitted the recognition of specific genes by chemical reactions with the components of human blood, populations could be objectively grouped so as to bring the study of races into the broader and more important area of evolution. Boyd (1950) defined a race as a population which differs significantly from other human populations in regard to the frequency of one or more of the genes it possesses. On this basis he described six races, one of which was a hypothetical early European group; the five remaining races conformed in a broad way with the earth's continents and did not differ in results from that of Blumenbach.

Crucial differences between the historical and contemporary methods of race taxonomy are that the latter avoids the subjectivity of older physical anthropology and shuns the fallacious thinking of the typological approach (Hunt, 1959) in favor of the population concept. By 1958 enough new blood-group genes had been discovered to force Boyd to amend his number of different races to thirteen. Coon *et al.* (1950) described a system of thirty races which took into consideration geography, various morphological characteristics, and, to some degree, the

---

[3] See Glossary at the end of the chapter for this and other terms.

size of the breeding population. Garn (1961), in an important synthesis of genetic and anthropological thinking on race, expanded the thirty to thirty-two, and Dobzhansky (1962) combined the latter two works and emerged with thirty-four which are named and located in Figure 1.1.

The apparent disagreements among taxonomists can be almost completely resolved by applying the term *race* at three different levels according to the purpose of the investigator. The first level describes the largest unit observed and is termed a *geographical race;* it corresponds with the races recognized by Blumenbach and Boyd. There are no more than ten geographical races (Garn, 1961) at the present time. Each such race comprises a collection of populations within geographical limits bounded by formerly insurmountable barriers to outbreeding, such as deserts, oceans, and mountains. Each shares a degree of homogeneity for blood-group genes and some morphological features, but still retains a considerable degree of heterogeneity for various characteristics. Some examples of geographical races are the Amerindians ranging from Alaska to Tierra del Fuego, with very low incidences of the genes for Type B blood and Rh-negative blood (r), and the African geographical race which occupies sub-Sahara Africa and which is characterized by extremely high frequency of the rhesus group gene R^0 and of the sickling gene associated with a type of anemia (Mourant, 1954). The presence of blood-group genes is easily inferred from chemical tests that clot samples of blood.

A second level of usage of the term *race* is *local race*. This term is necessitated by the fact that subordinate to a geographical race are the different breeding populations themselves, the groups which anthropologists and geneticists study when they speak of a sample of Navajos, Bantu, or Eskimos. Local races may be separated by physical or social obstacles, they mate chiefly within their group (endogamy), and they are most like their nearest neighbors in gene frequencies. They number in the hundreds as contrasted with the six to ten geographical races, even though only thirty-four are singled out in Figure 1.1 as representative of the utility of the concept.

Even when looking at the genetic characteristics of a local race, one can observe significant pockets of variation. The populations are statistically distinct from neighboring pockets in some gene frequencies in the absence of geographical barriers or extensive cultural prohibitions. With high population density, mating tends to occur as a function of distance. Future geneticists may have to take note of the routes of buses and subway systems to understand their data. This phenomenon gives rise to our final level for the race concept, which is termed *micro-geographical race* or *micro race* to avoid confusion with the first level above. An example of micro races, which number in the thousands, is provided by a survey of blood types for the ABO blood groups in

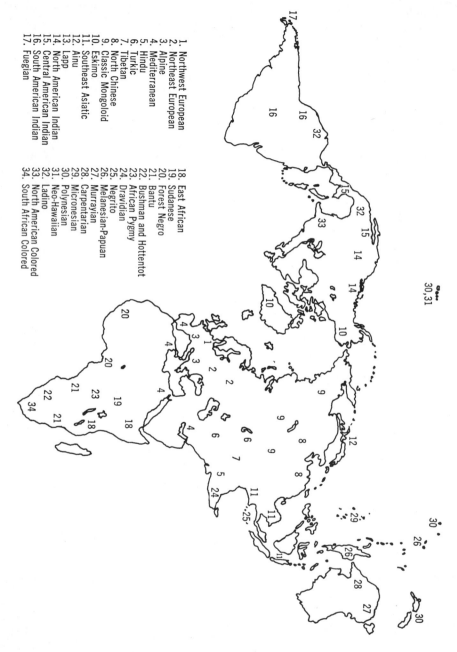

1. Northwest European
2. Northeast European
3. Alpine
4. Mediterranean
5. Hindu
6. Turkic
7. Tibetan
8. North Chinese
9. Classic Mongoloid
10. Eskimo
11. Southeast Asiatic
12. Ainu
13. Lapp
14. North American Indian
15. Central American Indian
16. South American Indian
17. Fuegian
18. East African
19. Sudanese
20. Forest Negro
21. Bantu
22. Bushman and Hottentot
23. African Pygmy
24. Dravidian
25. Negrito
26. Melanesian-Papuan
27. Murrayian
28. Carpentarian
29. Micronesian
30. Polynesian
31. Neo-Hawaiian
32. Ladino
33. North American Colored
34. South African Colored

Figure 1.1   The geographic occurrence of some of the more important local races of man. (After Dobzhansky, 1962)

14

Wales (Mourant and Watkin, 1952). As illustrated in Figure 1.2, there were significant local variations in the gene frequencies even though Wales is a small country. If the maps included lines of communication for the past few centuries, they might add to our understanding of the formation of micro races.

The most important concept to emphasize after this discussion of the taxonomy of races is one which bears repetition. Races are Mendelian or breeding populations which change as gene frequencies change. The sources of change will be discussed later in the chapter. Four of the local races in Figure 1.1 are the result of recent mixtures of other local races; they are no less deserving of a separate name. As Mayr (1963) pointed out,

> Biologically it is immaterial how many subspecies and races of man one wants to recognize. The essential point is to recognize the genetic and biological continuity of all these gene pools, localized in time and space, and to recognize the biological meaning of their adaptations and specializations. (p. 644)

Race naming may be somewhat arbitrary, but race differences are facts of nature which can be studied to help us understand the *continuing* evolution of man.

Who Is the Negro American?

Hybridization of the Europeans who colonized America with the slaves from western Africa imported to work in the American colonies initiated the hybrid race we now call the North American Negro. Although some Negroes convincingly described the existence of American Indian ancestry in their families to anthropologists (for example, Herskovits, 1930), more recent knowledge of the blood-group gene frequencies has enabled workers to discount the likelihood of significant admixture from the Indians to the slaves (Glass, 1955); Pollitzer *et al.* (1962), Donnan (1935), and Herskovits (1941) have studied the sources of the slaves imported to various colonies and concluded that the vast majority came from the west coast of Africa and from not much more than two hundred miles inland. The most accurate records of the slave trade, which were kept for Charleston, South Carolina, for the period 1733 to 1807, form the basis of an important study of the serology and morphology of today's Charleston Negroes (Gullah) by Pollitzer (1958). His map of Africa showing the origins of the over 72,000 slaves imported from 1733 to 1807 is reproduced in Figure 1.3. Percentages were computed after some 9000 individuals from such areas as "Africa" and the West Indies had been subtracted from the total; only 473 originated from East Africa, and those from the West

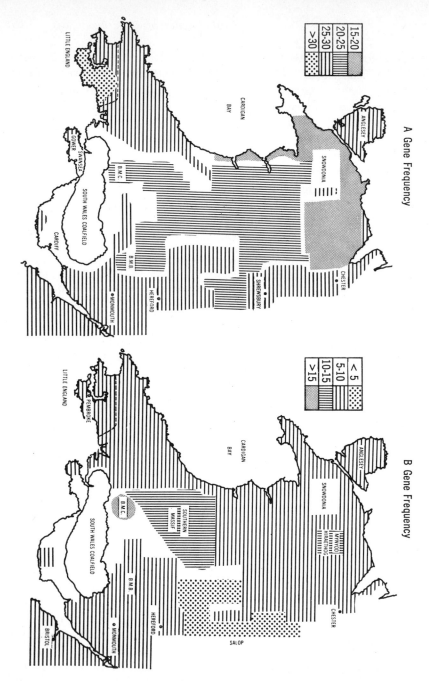

Figure 1.2 The frequencies of the genes for A and for B blood types in the populations of different parts of Wales. X = places where serological studies have been conducted, O = places where morphological studies have been conducted. (After Mourant and Watkins, 1952, *Heredity*, **6**)

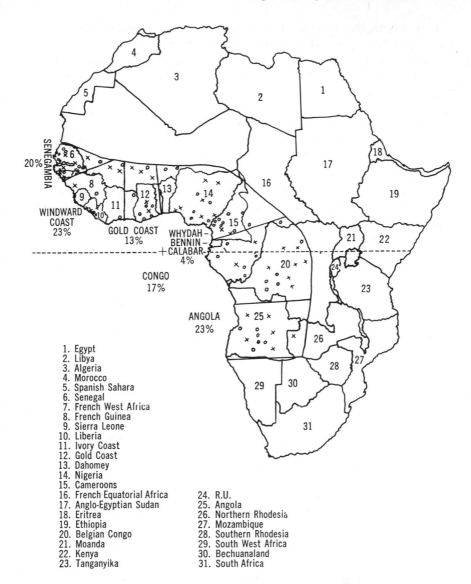

Figure 1.3   African origins of the slaves imported to Charleston from 1733 to 1807. (After W. S. Pollitzer, *American Journal of Physical Anthropology,* **16,** 245)

Indies were probably imported from the areas in Figure 1.3, arriving after a stay of acclimatization. The importance of the true sources of the African Negro ancestors of the North American Negro cannot be exaggerated, since calculations of the degree of hybridization or gene flow from whites to Negroes in the United States is based on gene frequencies of the current inhabitants of Western Africa.

It is informative to study the dynamics of racial intermixture from both a psychological and an anthropological point of view. The former has been inadequately studied; the latter is a matter of record but far from definitive. Glass and Li (1953) estimated that the accumulated amount of white admixture in the North American Negro was 30.56 percent and that the rate of gene flow from the white to Negro gene pool was 3.58 percent per generation. They assumed that the process started by 1675, reasoning that although the first shipload of slaves arrived in 1619, these slaves were males; the females did not arrive in significant numbers until after 1650. Among other assumptions in their estimates of m, gene flow, were these: that the average length of a generation was 27.5 years and that a minimum of ten generations had elapsed. The R^0 gene in the rhesus group was used because of its marked difference in frequency between the white and West African populations. In an admittedly speculative extrapolation, Glass and Li calculated that, *ceteris paribus*, the R^0 gene frequencies in the two populations would be matched in 60.7 generations or 1669 more years (A.D. 3622). Of course the populations would become practically indistinguishable in perhaps thirty-nine generations or about A.D. 3025.

Following upon the availability of knowledge about the gene frequencies of tribes in Nigeria and the Gold Coast, Roberts (1955) was able to improve on the estimates of m by Glass and Li, which had used data pertaining to the Bantu, East Africans, and Sudanese. Using five genes or chromosomes that give the clearest discrimination between the parental populations, Roberts' figures for m had a modal value between 0.02 and 0.025 for a total admixture of white genes in the present day North American Negro of 25 percent. At this rate it would take some 120 generations instead of 60.7 to reach equilibrium. Glass (1955) in revising his own estimates of m reached essentially the same values as Roberts.

By using a multivariate model, first with nine morphological characteristics and then with fifteen serological ones, Pollitzer was able to estimate the "biological distance" among Charleston, West African, and non-Charleston United States Negroes, and United States whites. His results, illustrated in Figure 1.4, reveal that the Gullah around Charleston have remained quite isolated compared to Negroes in such places as Baltimore or New York City.

Although descriptions of the gene differences among races are now on a firmer footing, they are only the first step in the more important process of understanding the reason for the differences. That is, the scientific study of races can lead to valid perspectives on man's continuing evolution. In one of the most sophisticated attempts so far to elucidate the meaning of different gene frequencies, Workman *et al.* (1963) examined the frequencies of more than fifteen polymorphic traits in southern Negro Americans. A polymorphism is simply defined as the simultaneous occurrence of two or more discontinuous phenotypes in a population; the frequency of even the rarest form is high enough so that it cannot be accounted for by recurrent mutation. Probably the ABO blood-group polymorphism is the most widely known. Six different phenotypes are associated with this locus (ten genotypes). Workman *et al.* compared the trait frequencies of Negroes and whites living in the same community with those of contemporary West Africans. They hoped to evaluate the relative roles of natural selection, race hybridization or gene migration, and chance in producing the observed trait frequencies in Georgia Negroes.

For various reasons, the frequency differences between the Georgia and West African Negroes could be almost totally attributed to the effects of admixture between white and Negro Americans and to differences in the adaptive values of the traits for the African and American environments. It will be recalled that the essence of natural selection is

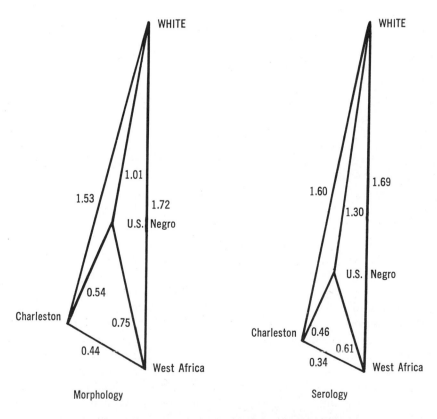

Figure 1.4   Schematic representations of the genetical distances among white and Negro populations. (After W. S. Pollitzer, *American Journal of Physical Anthropology*, **16,** 253)

differential reproduction and that the better adapted individuals leave proportionately more offspring. Thus traits conferring adaptive value increase in frequency in succeeding generations.

In order to estimate the relative effects of the two forces, selection and hybridization, the authors first assumed that the differences were solely due to hybridization. They estimated the amount of admixture (m) from the white to the Negro gene pool from the absolute value of the following:

$$m = \frac{q_N - q_{Af}}{q_W - q_{Af}}$$

where q_N, q_W, and q_{Af} are the frequencies of any particular gene in the samples of Negro, white, and West African Negro samples, respectively. By using white and Negro samples from the same area of Georgia, Workman *et al.* controlled for sources of variation which may have led earlier workers to less accurate solutions. The values of m for the different traits sorted themselves out into two distinct groups: for the red blood cell antigens (for example, Rhesus and ABO) the values ranged from 0.094 to 0.218; for the second group, which contained sickle-cell hemoglobin and phenylthiocarbamide (PTC) taste sensitivity, m ranged from 0.34 to 0.70. From these data the authors concluded that the m values for Group I genes reflect primarily the effects of hybridization with a mean value of 0.104, that is, half of Roberts' estimate. For the Group II polymorphisms the best explanation was that the traits have significantly different adaptive values in West Africa from Georgia and thus reflect a transient state of affairs wherein the environment will ensure an eventual convergence to the white gene frequencies. In the next section the example of sickle-cell hemoglobin will be used to illustrate this phenomenon of adaptation in detail.

By applying the above formula to the gene frequencies reported by Pollitzer (1958) for his Charleston Negroes we obtain still different and lower values for the amount of admixture. The variation observed in the studies reviewed in this section are probably valid and reflect the genetic heterogeneity of Negro Americans living different geographical and social distances away from their white neighbors. Such heterogeneity prevents us from speaking validly of an "average Negro American" with x percent of white genes.

The definition of a Negro has become a social and cultural one for the most part based almost entirely on skin color. As part of the vicious *apartheid* policy of South Africa, an official board certifies your race as white, African, or colored (any mixture of African and white). Since the genetics of skin color are determined on a polygenic basis, *apartheid* often results in brothers and sisters being assigned to different races and in children being certified as belonging to a different race from their parents. In the United States we have no accurate count of the so-called Negro population, because of inconsistent instructions in the past and the current rule that census-takers may not ask the race of the interviewee. The interviewers are required to make a clinical judgment concerning race which a trained physical anthropologist would hesitate to make. When the census-taker is in doubt, he is directed to assign race according to the prevailing racial composition of the neighborhood.

From a biological point of view, it is nonsensical to label someone with the remotest trace of Negro ancestry as a member of the Negro American local race. Geneticists do have a straightforward method for estimating the most probable number of genes one has in common with any particular relative. The coefficient of relationship is actually the most probable proportion of genes derived from a common ancestor and is sometimes referred to as the genetic correlation coefficient. Identical or one-egg twins have all their genes in common; no other two humans exceed 50 percent gene communality except in rare cases (offspring from incestuous matings). The various degrees of relationships are set out in Table 1.1.

If, for example, you are the great-grandchild of a man known to have only Negro ancestry, and he married your great-grandmother who was only of non-Negro ancestry, and all subsequent matings were with non-Negroes, 12.5 percent of your genes would theoretically be expected to be of Negro origin. However, most of these genes would have already been in the white gene pool, or, more accurately, in the human species gene pool. You will recall that earlier in this chapter it was shown that, depending on geography, Negro American gene pools contain from 10 to 25 percent white genes. Another way of viewing this is by looking at Table 1.1 and seeing that this range roughly corresponds to having a white great-grandfather or a white grandfather. If you

TABLE 1.1

Percentage of Genetic Communality
with Different Relatives

Relationship to Mr. X	Genes in Common (%)
Parent, child, fraternal twin, brother, sister	50
Grandparent, grandchild, half-sib, uncle, aunt, nephew, niece, double-first-cousin	25
Great-grandparent, great-grandchild, first cousin, half-uncle, half-aunt, half-niece, half-nephew	12.5
First cousin once removed, half-first-cousin	6.25
Second cousin	3.12

choose to call the white individual with a Negro grandfather a Negro, then logic would require you to call the "average" Negro in New York or Baltimore white. The science of human genetics cannot tell you whom to call Negro or white; it can only provide the biological facts as we now know them.

Natural Selection and the Origin of Race Differences

Since the time required for the observation of the processes of human evolution far exceeds that of man's longevity, we have had to resort to the rapid breeding Drosophila or fruit fly for many of our insights about our own evolution. In an important experiment designed to illustrate the formation of races (Dobzhansky and Pavlovsky, 1957), ten groups of twenty flies each were taken at random from a fairly heterogeneous population and used as founders of ten colonies. Each was maintained under uniform laboratory environmental conditions for about eighteen months, during which time twenty generations were produced. Each group of twenty founders yielded populations ranging from one thousand to four thousand adults after twenty generations. The point of this illustration is that the ten populations diverged genetically and would not have been recognizable as descendants from the same stock unless the conditions of the experiment were made known. Twenty human generations would cover a period of 550 years.

Why should a genetic divergence occur among populations derived originally from the same source and kept in a uniform environment? The answer is that each of the ten groups of twenty founder individuals contained a somewhat different assortment of genes. Natural selection did, so to speak, its best with the genetic materials at its disposal in each population. Since these materials were diverse, so were the results of the evolutionary changes induced by natural selection. Such a divergence may have easily been important in human evolution. (Dobzhansky, 1962, p. 283)

The preceding is primarily an example of genetic *drift* followed by natural selection. Genetic drift refers to changes in gene frequency in *small* breeding populations due to chance fluctuations. It is just as easy to demonstrate the directed effect of the environment in eliciting genetic diversity. The varieties which emerge then become fixed by natural selection if they are adaptive in the specific environment. The process of drift was probably very important at the beginning of *Homo sapiens'* dispersion. Selection assumed major importance after man had encountered a diversity of environmental challenges. If the chromosomes of Drosophila living at different elevations along the Sierra Nevada mountains are studied (Dobzhansky, 1963), they are seen to contain different frequencies of three kinds of chromosomes; that is, the populations are racially distinct. In a horizontal distance of just sixty miles the frequency of one chromosome goes up 400 percent. As pointed out earlier, these kinds of racial differences are quantitative and not qualitative. It is worth repeating that races are composed of Mendelian populations, and race differences are differences between populations.

At the human level an illustration of a race difference maintained by adaptation to particular environments is given by the example of hemoglobin *S* and sickle-cell anemia. Sickle-cell anemia is determined by a recessive gene, *si*. If an individual has received this gene from each of his parents, he is homozygous for this gene and will probably die of severe anemia before maturity. The heterozygote, *Si si,* has received the gene from only one parent, is free from anemia, but is a carrier for it, and has the sickling trait. The other possible homozygote, *Si Si,* has only the normal gene at this locus. After Neel's (1949) demonstration that the mode of inheritance was that of a recessive gene with a recognizable heterozygote, Allison (1954), with brilliant detective work, linked falciparum malaria to the maintenance of a gene which the logic of natural selection dictated should be eliminated. He showed that there is an advantage of resistance to malaria parasitization conferred upon heterozygotes for *si* which balances the loss of the gene through death in the homozygote with anemia. Since the normal homozygotes had little immunity from malaria, fewer of them survived to the age of maturity than the *Si si,* and they hence contributed fewer children to the next generation. Such a state of affairs accounts for the continued appearance of the three different genotypes and is termed a *balanced polymorphism*. Allison and others found that this particular genetic trait varied as a function of malaria prevalence and was independent of race per se.

Among many African Negro tribes 20 percent or more of the population have the sickling trait, and frequencies of 40 percent have been reported. In Greece frequencies of 17 percent are known. In the Charleston Negroes studied by Pollitzer (1958), about 16 percent showed sickling compared to a 7 to 10 percent frequency in other Negro American samples. As recently as 1944 positive malaria smears were found among Negro school children along the South Carolina coast where malaria persisted as a cause of death for a longer period of time than in other parts of the United States. While much of the reduction in trait frequency is associated with white hybridization, a larger part is due to the different adaptive values of the gene in a nonmalaria environment. Hence some of the difference between the Charleston and more northern or inland Negroes. The research of Workman *et al.* referred to earlier further documents this polymorphism. An important point to note in connection with a discussion on adaptation and natural selection is that many of the characteristics observed in current races are the results of adaptation to ancient environments. The *si* gene represents a transient polymorphism among Negro Americans which, in time, will disappear in a malaria-free environment.

More obvious physical differences among the human races are less easily accounted for by their adaptive values, but no other reasons seem more plausible at this stage of our knowledge. Garn (1960), Dobzhansky (1962), and Mayr (1963) have discussions and references to the detailed literature which can be pursued on this topic. Skin color is more intense in the humid tropics and lighter in the cool and dry areas of the earth. Darker colors protect from sunburn and radiation and decrease the probability of skin cancers. White skin may be advantageous in increasing the production of Vitamin D in areas with long winters and overcast skies. Another suggestion has it that darker skin evolved as a camouflage in the shade of tropical rain forests. It should be obvious that these ideas are not necessarily mutually exclusive. With respect to body build, it appears that protruding body parts and body surfaces as a whole are reduced in areas with severe winters. Small and/or long bodies are characteristic of subtropical and tropical savannahs. When a single racial group occupies diverse climatic zones, as with our Drosophila examples, selection works to make them similar to groups of men or animals already adapted to that kind of environment. Examples are the converging of the features of the Lapps, who are essentially European, with those of Mongoloid races after they occupied northern Scandinavia; the lung capacity of American Indians in the Andes Mountains; and the higher basal metabolism rates among the American Indians who occupy Tierra del Fuego. A good start has been made on the comparative physiology of human races (Baker, 1958; Barnicot, 1959; and Newman, 1956). Among the findings was the fact that Negro soldiers had a higher tolerance to humid heat than white soldiers, but did not fare so well as the whites under dry heat conditions. The practical application of such findings could increase manpower efficiency in the armed forces by influencing the training sites and field assignments of personnel. Perhaps the teams training for a landing on the moon should include a few American Eskimos.

Genetic racial differences are facts of nature and not signs of inferiority or superiority in themselves. Differences observed appear to be, for the most part, the results of selection for adaptation to ancient or contemporary environmental diversity, especially climatic and disease factors.

GENETIC ASPECTS OF RACE DIFFERENCES

IN INTELLECTUAL PERFORMANCE

If the difficulties of defining a race or of assigning a person to a particular race, such as the Negro, seem formidable from what has been said so far, it is an accurate reflection of our incomplete knowledge. Similar difficulties are encountered when psychologists attempt to define a concept of intelligence (Liverant, 1960; Maher, 1963). Such a concept is necessary for an understanding of human behavior since individuals differ in their rate of acquisition of responses under similar learning conditions. Caution is required when anyone tries to explain the differences observed between mean IQs of whites and Negroes when the only variables in their study are IQ and race. Intelligent behavior, as with every response, is multiply determined, and unless all the *relevant* variables are matched except race, no valid explanations can be made. Even a cursory glance at the literature about changes in IQ (for example, Anastasi, 1958; Tyler, 1965) reveals a vast number of statistically significant correlates of IQ. Among them are basal metabolism rate, EEG alpha frequency, height, weight, anxiety level, race and warmth of examiner, father's occupation and years of schooling, mother's attitude toward achievement, home cultural level, mother's concern with language development, degree of anoxia at birth, the desire to master intellectual skills, and others too numerous to mention. It should be obvious that IQ tests do not directly measure innate gene-determined intellectual capacity but do measure current intellectual performance as defined by a particular culture or at least by its psychologists.

In looking at the literature on Negro-white differences in measured IQ (for example, Kennedy *et al.,* 1963) in children from the same area, one will rarely find the Negroes higher, sometimes find them no different, but most often find them lower. It is a well-known fact that when tested on Army Alpha, some groups of northern Negroes made higher averages than some groups of southern whites, but that white soldiers consistently scored higher than Negro soldiers from the same region. Evidence from the classical studies by Klineberg and Lee shows that educational opportunity and not selective migration accounts for these kinds of results. A typical finding is that samples of northern Negro children have a mean IQ of 90 on the Stanford-Binet (Higgins and Sivers, 1958) compared to the normative sample (which excluded Negroes) mean of 100. In a well-designed study of 1800 elementary school Negro children representative of all those in Florida, Georgia, Alabama, Tennessee, and South Carolina (Kennedy *et al.,* 1963), a mean IQ on the 1960 revision of the Stanford-Binet of 80.7 was obtained. The distributions of the Negro and Binet normative samples are given in Figure 1.5.

What kinds of concrete meanings can be attached to the observed differences of 10 IQ points between northern Negroes and whites and 20 IQ points between southeastern Negroes and whites? As a result of a kind of overselling of the practical uses of IQ tests, professionals and laymen alike appear to invest test scores with an undeserved aura of permanence and profound significance. An ex-

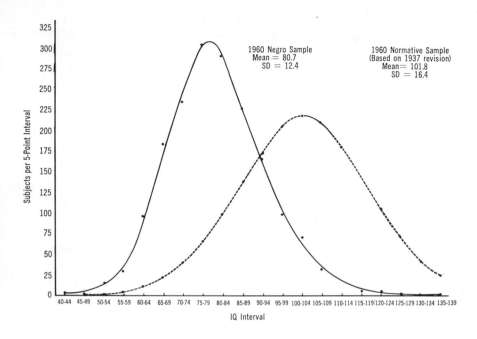

Figure 1.5   The IQ distributions of normative white and southeastern Negro school children. (After Kennedy *et al.*, 1963)

posure to data on the construct validity of intelligence tests and susceptibility to change of IQs (Maher, 1963; Hunt, 1961) would help temper this naive enthusiasm. It is too easy to forget the operations by which an IQ is computed. For example, on the 1937 Binet test the answer to a question is most often worth two months of mental-age credit; the answer to one question is thus good for 2 or 3 IQ points. Given two eight-year-old children with IQs of 90 and 100, the latter has been able to answer five more questions correctly than his classmate. It should be obvious that when an IQ test has fewer total questions than the Binet, each correct answer is worth proportionately more than 2 or 3 IQ points.

Another way to gain perspective on the practical meaning of 10 or 20 IQ points is to look at the means for certain physically handicapped groups. In a survey of the results of intelligence test results with deaf children, Louttit (1957) recognizes that an over-all generalization may not be justifiable in the light of the unknown sampling errors; Pintner's conclusion is apparently endorsed; that is, the most probable average IQ is 86 on specially designed nonlanguage group tests. Some studies are reported where the mean IQs are in the 70s and 80s.

Louttit also reports Hayes' survey of intelligence in blind children attending residential schools. Mean IQs measured on a special test ranged from 92 to 108, but the percentage of children with IQs 70 and below ranged from 4 percent to 19 percent. Only 2 percent of normal children on the Binet score less than IQ 70. In the Kennedy *et al.* sample of Negro school children 18.4 percent of the total group had Binet IQs less than 70. That such discrepancies primarily represent a form of over-all stimulus deprivation, somewhat like the sensorily handicapped rather than "genetic inferiority," is strongly suggested by the manner in which the mean IQs drop solely as a function of age (read exposure to an inadequate environment). While the mean IQ of the six-year-old group was 84, that of the thirteen-year-olds has dropped to 65; the proportion of IQs below 70 in these two extremes of the Kennedy *et al.* sample was 8.8 percent and 66.7 percent respectively.

A vast clinical and experimental literature has grown up documenting the importance of early experience for later development for both animals and man (Hunt, 1961; Brackbill, 1964). This literature strongly suggests that perceptual and stimulus deprivation of a rather subtle nature is capable of handicapping subsequent development. None of these statements should be taken to mean that true mental deficiency can be *cured* by a program of enriched education. One of the goals of this section is to explain Negro-white differences in IQ, rather than to explain them away.

Another way to gain perspective about the meaning of a 10 or 20 IQ point difference is to look at the data on within-pair differences in intelligence for identical (*MZ*) and fraternal (*DZ*) twins. The reason why these data are important to the issue of race differences in intelligence is that some people have interpreted the mean differences observed between white and Negro American samples as sufficient evidence of "genetic inferiority" or of differential capacity for intelligence. Since identical twins have no difference in their genes (they come from one egg which has split in two) any differences between them must be due to the environment, either prenatally or postnatally. If we construct two samples of identical genetic constitution by taking the brighter of each pair of identical twins in one group and the less bright in the other, what kind of mean IQ difference do we find? Even though the gene pools do not differ and even though each of the two groups has been raised under more or less the same regime, the mean difference amounts to 6 IQ points for the sample of fifty pairs studied by Newman *et al.* (1937). The range of within-pair differences was 0 to 20 points. Thus, even when gene pools are *known* to be matched, appreciable differences in mean IQ can be observed that could only have been associated with environmental differences.

A better appreciation of the influence of the environment on IQ can be gained from looking at the two unique samples of thoroughly described identical twins who have been reared apart and thus in discriminably different environments. Such data are crucial to understanding the range of intelligence which can be manifested by persons of the same genetic background. In the nineteen pairs of identical twins reared apart studied by Newman *et al.* (1937), the average intrapair difference on the Binet was 8 IQ points. The range of differences was 1 to 24 points! A very similar picture is given in a remarkably large sample of thirty-eight pairs of identical twins reared apart and studied by Shields (1962). When the tests used in this larger study are converted into IQ point equivalents (Shields and Gottesman, 1965), the average intrapair difference for the identicals is 14 points on a verbal IQ test and 10 points on a nonverbal test. The corresponding differences for a control sample of thirty-four identical pairs reared together, which Shields studied with the same instruments, were 9 IQ points for both tests. At least 25 percent of the sample of identicals reared apart had within-pair IQ point differences exceeding 16 points on at least one of the tests.[4]

It is obvious from looking at the data on identical twins that individuals with exactly the same genetic constitution can differ widely on the phenotypic trait we measure with IQ tests and label intelligence. The differences observed so far between whites and Negroes can hardly be accepted as sufficient evidence that with respect to intelligence, the Negro American is genetically less endowed. Should anyone choose to apply in a practical fashion the data obtained thus far on race differences in IQ, the procedure would be extremely inaccurate. From a consideration of the problems of overlapping distributions and different "base rates" of Negroes and whites in the United States population (compare Meehl and Rosen, 1955), it is possible to illustrate the practical futility of predicting race from a knowledge of IQ.

Let us use in our example the facts that 2 percent of the white standardization sample on the Binet obtain scores less than IQ 70 as contrasted with the 18 percent reported for the large representative sample of southeastern Negro elementary-school children described above. There are approximately 180 million whites and 20 million so-called Negroes in the United States at this time. If we choose to blindly label all individuals with tested IQs under 70 as Negro, the consequences are as follows: 3.6 million Negroes are accurately classified as to their race, but 3.6 million whites are misclassified as Negroes. In the United States, using IQ under 70 as a criterion, you

---

[4] Some of the differences across experiments are the result of differing numbers of items in the tests. The fewer the items, the more IQ points an answer is worth.

would be wrong 50 percent of the time if you were to use IQ as an indicator of race. You would be wrong more frequently than this if you were to use a higher cutting score, such as IQ 80. With this score you could accurately identify 10.4 million Negroes, but you would also label 14.4 million whites as members of the Negro race. Inasmuch as an individual's IQ does not permit you to identify his race accurately, so also his race does not permit you to estimate his intelligence with sufficient accuracy.

The Dialectics of Heredity and Environment

If the reader wishes to conclude at this point that the contribution of genetics to variation in IQ is negligible, he has read too much into the above attempts at explaining Negro-white differences in IQ. The complexities of the issues involved in a satisfactory understanding of how nature works together with nurture to produce a trait and trait variability can only be broached in this chapter. More complete introductions can be found in the writings of the behavior geneticists (Fuller and Thompson, 1960; Gottesman, 1963*b;* Hirsch, 1962; and McClearn, 1964). Such authors make clear a crucial distinction between the concepts of *genotype* and *phenotype.* Genotype refers to the totality of factors that make up the genetic complement of an individual. Phenotype refers to the totality of physically or chemically observable characteristics of an individual that result from the interaction of his genotype with his environment. Environment must be broadly defined to include not only intrauterine and postnatal conditions but also a host of molecular factors within and between the embryonic cells (Waddington, 1957).

Different genotypes may have the same phenotype, and different phenotypes may be displayed by the same genotypes. A lack of clarity is perpetuated in discussions of individual differences by a failure to specify the environmental circumstances when describing the phenotype of genes. And conversely, the attribution of an effect to an environmental manipulation may be misleading unless the genotype is specified.

Genetically identical Himalayan rabbits, for example, reared under ordinary conditions have a white body with black extremities. When reared in a warm cage, they do not show the black pigment (Sinnott *et al.,* 1958). Phenotypically white rabbits and phenotypically white-plus-black rabbits look different, while having the same genetic constitution, just because the environments to which they have been exposed were different. In an experiment by Freedman (1958) we have a very informative example of the interaction of heredity and environment in four breeds of dogs. Half of each litter was reared under "indulgent" conditions and the other half, "disciplined." Members of these highly inbred litters were as similar to each other as identical twins. At eight weeks of age each pup was tested for inhibition of eating after the person who had reared it had punished it for eating and then left the room. Basenjis ate as soon as the trainer left the room regardless of whether they had been raised in the indulged or disciplined environment. Both groups of Shetland sheep dogs refused the food over the whole test period of eight days. For these two genotypes then, the method of training had no effect, but the two breeds responded in opposite fashion. Beagles and fox terriers, however, divided themselves up neatly according to the method of training; the indulged beagles and terriers were more easily inhibited by the punishment. Freedman concluded that it was the strong constitutional attraction to the trainer interacting with the indulgent treatment that enhanced the effectiveness of later punishment for the beagles and terriers.

One further example from the experimental animal psychology literature emphasizes the crucial need to specify both environments and genotypes. The experiment will also serve as a bridge to a conceptual model of when it is appropriate to emphasize heredity, when it is appropriate to emphasize environment, and when it is appropriate to emphasize their interaction with respect to variability in a trait. Cooper and Zubek (1958) reared six groups of rats who were the thirteenth-generation descendants of animals selected for their ability to solve maze problems. One group each of genetically bright and genetically dull rats (as inferred from their breeding) were reared under three markedly different early environmental regimes.[5] An *enriched* environment was provided by slides, tunnels, balls, bells, and so on, and the cages faced a design-covered wall. A *restricted* environment was provided for the two genotypes by only a food box and water pan with the cages facing a gray wall. Control groups of the brights and dulls were reared in the *natural habitat* of a laboratory rat. At 65 days of age each of the six groups were tested for their problem-solving ability on the Hebb-Williams maze. The results are given in Figure 1.6. An enriched early environment led to a considerable improvement over the natural-habitat performance of the dulls but had little noticeable effect upon the brights. [A similar phenomenon has been observed in comparing the effects of preschool attendance on lower- and middle-class children (McNemar,

---

[5] Analogous experiments with children cannot ethically be done. Those few children reported in the literature who have been severely neglected cannot be assumed to have been like the average child *before* their exposure to deprivation, for example, feral children.

1945).] A restricted early environment increased the errors of the brights by about 44 percent, but had little or no effect on the dulls.

Under the restricted conditions the results were what might have been expected. Even the animals with the genetic potential for superior performance were prevented from developing their potential by the environmental handicaps. The dull animals were already performing poorly in what was for other animals an adequate environment and had no room for an even poorer performance. It is more difficult to account for the failure of the brights to improve their performance under the enriched conditions. The bright animals would be expected to make better use of the stimulation (Hebb, 1949) with their presumably better cerebral functioning. The authors suggest that the maze test may have been inappropriate for discriminating among levels of superior functioning. That is, if an IQ test had a ceiling of 120, individuals who might score higher than that still obtain scores of 120. Another possibility was that there was not a linear relationship between error reduction and environment. In other words, it might have been much more difficult for the brights to reduce their errors from 120 to 100 than for the dulls to reduce their errors from 165 to 145 even though the absolute reduction was 20 points in each case.

These three experiments with rabbits, dogs, and rats permit us to make some important theoretical generalizations. Given uniformity

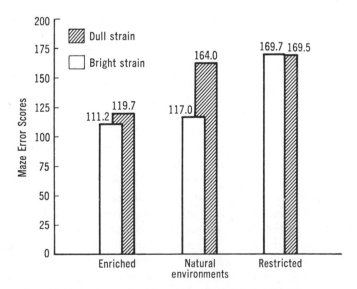

Figure 1.6   Maze error scores of genetically bright and dull rats reared in three different environments. (After Pettigrew, 1964)

of trait-relevant environment, almost all the observed phenotypical variance in a trait must stem from variability in the genotypes. Given uniformity in that part of the genotype relevant to the trait under consideration, almost all the observed phenotypical trait variance must stem from variability in the environments. Given heterogeneity for both genotypes and environments—the situation which prevails for human populations—the observed trait variability must be attributed to some combination of genetic and environmental variances.

The question of how much of intelligence is due to heredity and how much to environment is meaningless since neither agent alone can produce the trait. Such phrasing of the question is an important cause of the stalemate that has stifled progress in psychology over the past fifty years. Two answerable questions should be posed in the contemporary concern with the roles played by nature *and* nurture in human behavior: (1) How much of the variability observed within a group of individuals in a specified environment on a particular trait measure is attributable to hereditary differences among them, and (2) how modifiable by systematic environmental manipulation is the phenotypic expression of a trait. A further question is of crucial importance to the basic understanding of human behavior, but it must be deferred until such time as molecular geneticists, developmental biologists, and developmental psychologists are ready to collaborate. This is the question of *how* heredity interacts with the environment to produce trait variation (see Anastasi, 1958b). There are no genes *for* any behavior or other phenotypic trait. Genes exert their influence on behavior through their effects at the molecular level of organization. Enzymes, hormones, and neurons may be considered as the sequence of complex path markers between the genes and a behavioral characteristic (Fuller, 1957; Thompson, 1957).

For our purposes then, the best way to conceptualize the contribution of heredity to a trait such as intelligence is to think of heredity as determining a norm of reaction (Dobzhansky, 1955), or of heredity fixing a reaction range. Within this framework, a genotype determines an indefinite but nonetheless circumscribed assortment of phenotypes. Each phenotype corresponds to one of the possible environmental regimes to which the genotype could be exposed. Fuller (1954) has said that heredity is the capacity to utilize an environment in a particular way. Figure 1.7 is a schematic presentation of the concept of reaction range for the phenotypic trait of IQ.

Each curve in Figure 1.7 can be thought of as representing the response of samples of individuals homogeneous for four different levels of genetic potential who have been exposed to environments ranging from restricted through "natural" to enriched. Allen (1961) has noted that the most probable phenotype of some genotypes may

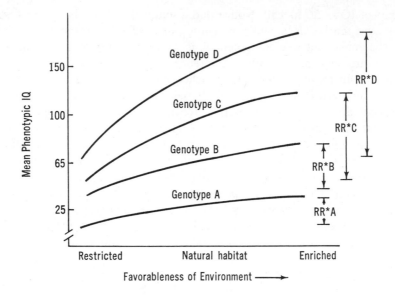

Figure 1.7 Scheme of the reaction-range (RR*) concept showing the interaction of heredity and environment. (From *Handbook of Mental Deficiency,* edited by N. Ellis. Copyright © 1963 McGraw-Hill, Inc. Used by permission of McGraw-Hill Book Company)

be a deviant one. These genotypes, for example Down's syndrome (Mongolism), phenylketonuria, and Huntington's chorea, would produce individuals of normal intellect only in unusual environments, if at all. Such genotypes are associated with autosomal chromosomal aberrations, a pair of recessive genes, and a dominant gene, respectively (Penrose, 1963). Curve Type *A* with a natural habitat mean IQ less than 40 is intended to represent roughly these classes of individuals who cannot be accounted for by the polygenic model (Gottesman, 1963*b;* Roberts, 1952).[6] The IQ distribution of very large and unselected samples of school children shows a "bump" at the low end; the severely retarded are overrepresented. Curve *A* individuals are in this bump. Much more frequent, and thus of more importance to the current discussion, are Curves *B* and *C*. An infinite number of such curves could be drawn to represent the continuous gradation of genetic potential for intelligence within the continuous

---

[6] The taxonomy of mental retardation is intimately tied to IQ testing of white children and adults. Generalizations to other races or to whites from atypical backgrounds are unwarranted without great caution. Generally, persons with tested IQs under 70 are labeled retarded, and those under 50 as severe or low-grade retarded. IQs under 40 are almost always associated with pathogenic simple dominant or recessive genes, chromosomal errors, and traumatic or infectious brain injury.

range of IQs—50 to 150. Notice that a major difference between *A* and the other curves is a wider reaction range (*RR*) for the latter; that is, the innate intellectual potential is more susceptible to upward or downward changes. Another difference is that Curves *B, C,* and *D* rise with increasing rates with enriched environments. The first difference is inferred from human and animal data, but the second is largely a speculation. From the overlap in reaction ranges it should be apparent that with no other information than an individual's IQ score, you could not tell whether he was of Genotype *B, C,* or *D*. Similarly three individuals with IQs of 80, 100, and 120 could theoretically all be of Genotype *C*. These two examples are merely a concrete way of saying again that the same phenotype may have different genotypes, and different phenotypes may have the same genotype.

Within the broad range of continuous variation in measured IQ, two aspects of the environment, *favorableness* and *commonness,* are important to the concept of reaction range. By this we mean to imply that each genotype has its own more or less natural habitat, at least in a society that fosters social mobility using ability as the sole criterion. In the light of what has been said in the introduction to this book and the literature on the effects of stimulation in early infancy (Casler, 1961; Riesen, 1961; Thompson and Schaefer, 1961), there is every reason to doubt that a typical Negro infant is reared in a typical white infant's natural habitat. In regard to the character intelligence, a natural habitat would include a normal delivery and freedom from organic impairment, an adequate diet, home rearing by both parents or adequate surrogates, exposure to adequate sensory stimulation, and exposure to an adequate system of compulsory education. One of the assumptions underlying the reaction-range concept is that marked deviation from the natural habitat occurs with a low probability. It is only when two individuals or two groups come from equally favorable environments (the horizontal axis in Figure 1.7) that a difference in measured IQ can be interpreted to indicate a difference in genetic potential.

Studies on identical twins reared apart, as mentioned earlier, afford us some insight into the effects of differing environments on the same genotype. This information can permit a rough estimate of the reaction range for average individuals under natural conditions. It is probably not more than 12 IQ points in either direction and most probably less; that is, the vertical distance in the middle part of *RR C* in our Figure 1.7 covers 24 points. Thus, IQs from 88 to 112 indicate the phenotype of equivalent genotypes under the conditions specified. The data from *MZ* twins reared apart (Shields, 1962) do not correspond to environmental differences much more extreme than those indicated by upper and lower limits of natural habitat in the reaction-range scheme. Only fourteen of Shields' forty-four *MZ* pairs reared apart were brought up in unrelated families, and in seven of these fourteen pairs one of the twins was reared by a relative.

Despite the length of this chapter, it still constitutes only an introduction to the dialectics of heredity and environment. Hopefully the ideas presented have introduced enough information to facilitate a valid perspective on the controversial issues.

GENETIC ASPECTS OF SOCIAL-CLASS

DIFFERENCES

Are there any parallels between the formation of races described earlier and the formation of social classes? There appear to be a number of important similarities and these have genetic consequences. In the prehistory of man, a class system probably evolved after food gathering had been replaced by food producing. An efficient agriculture then elicited the need for labor organization which involved a stratification into leaders and laborers. Sir Cyril Burt, an eminent English psychologist, has made an intensive analysis and a spirited defense of the idea that class differences in intelligence are largely due to genetic variation (1959; 1961). Much stronger views on the subject are advanced by Darlington (1963). It should be possible to examine the merits and degrees of validity of such positions without subscribing to social Darwinism or to the sickness of race and class prejudice (Gottesman, 1963*a;* 1965).

Support for the view that the structure of modern societies is at least in part dependent on biological phenomena rests on the demonstration that stratification is based on ability and, further, that individual differences in ability are partially genetically conditioned. In a truly democratic system an open-class society (Lerner, 1957) permits the formation of differentiated social classes and, most importantly, fosters class change and mobility. Thus a migration from one class to another based on presence or absence of ability is the final essential requirement for a biologically based model of social structure.

Burt (1959, pp. 23–24) said,

Roughly speaking . . . the formation of an elite or upper class is determined, in the course of a nation's evolution, chiefly by physical force at the outset, then by blood-relationship, and later by property or wealth, and finally by mental efficiency. Most of the time no doubt each of these factors is operative simultaneously though in varying proportions, and at every stage mental efficiency must have played *some* part; but its importance must have steadily increased until at the present time it now preponderates over the others.

TABLE 1.2

Distribution of Intelligence According to Occupational

Class: Adults (from Burt, 1961)

IQ	Professional		Clerical III	Skilled IV	Semiskilled V	Unskilled VI	Total
	Higher I	Lower II					
50–60						1	1
60–70					5	18	23
70–80				2	15	52	69
80–90			1	11	31	117	160
90–100			8	51	135	53	247
100–110			16	101	120	11	248
110–120		2	56	78	17	9	162
120–130		13	38	14	2		67
130–140	2	15	3	1			21
140+	1	1					2
Total	3	31	122	258	325	261	1000
Mean IQ	139.7	130.6	115.9	108.2	97.8	84.9	100

Some degree of class mobility has gone on for the past nine hundred years or so in Great Britain. Wherever class differences in intelligence, as measured by IQ tests, have been examined, a spread between the means of the highest and lowest class has been found. It is very important to specify whether the means are obtained from children classified on the basis of their fathers' occupations or from the adult members of a social class. And if the latter, whether they are the parents of children and thus a group selected for higher intelligence than the childless or unmarried adults in a stratum of the occupational hierarchy (Reed and Reed, 1965).

Data collected by Burt (1961) on intelligence in some 40,000 adults and their children as a function of occupational status are presented in Tables 1.2 and 1.3. The information was collected in the Greater London area during the the period 1913 to 1960. Sample sizes have been made proportional to a base of 1000; the N of 3 (per 1000) for Higher Professionals represents 120 fathers. The row totals reflect the estimated proportions for the total population, for example, only 3 per 1000 adults are actually employed in the Higher Professional category.

Notice that the mean IQs for adults (Table 1.2) range from 139.7 for Class I to 84.9 for Class VI. Those for the children of these adults (Table 1.3) show the expected regressions toward the population mean and only range from 120.8 to 92.6. In the United States, military testing in the 1940's of adults classified by occupation showed a range of mean IQs from 120 for Class I to 95 for the lowest class. Mean IQs for the white children used in the 1937 standardization of the Stanford-Binet, classified by their fathers' occupation, ranged from 116 to 96 (Johnson, 1948). The definitions of the occupational classes differ somewhat in the two countries, and Burt's subjects were largely urban.

Tables 1.2 and 1.3 provide a great deal of food for thought. It is apparent that the mean IQ of the children in each class is closer to the population mean of 100 than their fathers', and the IQs of the children vary much more than their fathers'. Within the occupational classes the standard deviation for adults is 9.6 contrasted with 14 for their children. The value of the standard deviation is 15 in the total population. Evidence now available shows a constant gradient of high to low IQ for the occupational distribution of IQs from one generation to the next. Thus it must follow that if the children of Table 1.3 are to have the same distribution of IQs when they grow up as the adults of Table 1.2, a large number will have to change to a social class different from their fathers'. It should be noted in passing that the intelligent offspring of the dull parents and the dull children of the bright parents are phenomena difficult to account for on an en-

TABLE 1.3

Distribution of Intelligence According to Father's
Occupational Class: Children (from Burt, 1961)

	Professional						
	Higher	*Lower*	*Clerical*	*Skilled*	*Semiskilled*	*Unskilled*	
IQ	*I*	*II*	*III*	*IV*	*V*	*VI*	*Total*
50–60					1	1	2
60–70				1	6	15	22
70–80			3	12	23	32	70
80–90		1	8	33	55	62	159
90–100		2	21	53	99	75	250
100–110	1	6	31	70	85	54	247
110–120		12	35	59	38	16	160
120–130	1	8	18	22	13	6	68
130–140	1	2	6	7	5		21
140+				1			1
Total	3	31	122	258	325	261	1000
Mean IQ	120.8	114.7	107.8	104.6	98.9	92.6	100

TABLE 1.4

Adults: Percentage in Each Group Whose Intelligence Is
Below, Above, or Equivalent to That of Their
Occupational Class (from Burt, 1961)

	Below	*Equivalent*	*Above*	*Number*
Class I–III	46.2	45.5	8.3	156
Class IV–V	26.6	50.1	23.3	583
Class VI		73.2	26.8	261
Total population	22.7	55.4	21.9	1000

vironmental hypothesis of the origin of individual differences in intelligence. Such findings are, however, completely predictable from the polygenic theory of intelligence (Gottesman, 1963b).

If, for purposes of illustration, we may assume that vocational adaptation depends exclusively on intelligence as measured by tests, many adults in Table 1.2 have too much or too little intelligence for their roles. In terms of IQ, the borderlines between the occupational classes could be set at 141, 127, 115, 103, and 90. Burt calculated that only 55 percent of the adults were "correctly" placed; 23 percent were above their level and 22 percent were too low. Be that as it may, the great variation among the children of a social-class stratum would make for even greater mismatching if there were no mobility. Tables 1.4 and 1.5 regroup the adults and children in terms of this "matching." In order to estimate the extent of social mobility for this British population, the task becomes one of estimating the compensating change to bring the frequency distributions for the children of Table 1.5 in line with that of the adults in Table 1.4. Burt (1961, p. 17) carried out the task.

> Let us look first at the lowest occupational class of all—the unskilled workers (class VI). Among the children, it will be remembered, as many as 57 per cent have an intelligence above what is required for work of this type as against 27 per cent of the adults. . . . Hence (57 − 27) = 30 per cent of the children will presumably move up to a higher occupational class as they grow up. Similarly (75 − 46) = 29 per cent of the upper group—that comprising classes I, II, and III—will move down. In the intermediate group—classes IV and V—the changes both upward and downward will be smaller. Thus, as a comparison of the last lines of the two tables [our Tables 1.4 and 1.5] suggests, the over-all mobility will be at least (55 − 33) = 22 per cent. This figure I regard as indicating the minimum amount of mobility—the amount that is required to maintain what (if I may borrow a phrase from the astronomers) might be called a "steady state." It constitutes what may be termed "basic mobility."

Allowing for currently greater permeability of class boundaries through greater availability of higher education, Burt goes on to estimate that the amount of intergenerational mobility must be nearer 30 percent than the derived one of 22 percent.

In comparison to the social structure of Great Britain, the "open class" aspects of democratic society are much more pronounced in the United States. In the mid-1960's more than 40 percent of secondary-school graduates are enrolling in college. It seems logical to expect that intergenerational mobility in our country is greater than 30 percent and is moving toward the thoretical maximum of 66.5 percent suggested by the bottom line of Table 1.5, at least for our white population.

It is possible to approach this topic from a slightly different point of view, one closer to home. In a society which provides for social mobility, the varieties of genotypes migrate to different strata or social ecological niches by social selection. In this schema the strata are ordered by the single major variable—money-reward. Tryon (1957), a pioneer in American behavior genetics research, outlined the workings of the model:

> Individuals receiving the same money-reward but for different kinds of ability tend to gravitate to the same social area. The hierarchy of social strata is determined by the hierarchy of money-reward characteristic of all occupations. The abilities requisite for performance in the different occupations depend upon different sensory-motor components, which are in turn determined by different independent polygenic combinations. Most matings occur within strata so that a correlation among abilities is developed not [only] because there is one general factor underlying achievement in all fields, but because of the selective influence of the common denominator, money-reward, which collects comparable levels of various abilities within the same social strata. [Assortative mating for intelligence averages about an r of 0.50 in many studies. Tryon has found an r of about 0.60 between the social area ratings i.e., neighborhood status, of

TABLE 1.5

Children: Percentage in Each Group Whose Intelligence Is
Below, Above, or Equivalent to That of Their Father's
Occupational Class (from Burt, 1961)

	Below	*Equivalent*	*Above*	*Number*
Class I–III	75.5	16.8	7.7	156
Class IV–V	34.8	34.3	30.9	583
Class VI		42.9	57.1	261
Total population	32.1	33.5	34.4	1000

spouses even when reared in different cities.] . . . The picture being drawn is a statistical one. It does not assert that *all* of the genetically controlled constitutional factors responsible for high achievement are confined to the highest social stratum or that *all* of the factors responsible for low achievement are to be found in the lowest stratum. All factors are to be found in all strata. The strata are believed to differ, however, with respect to the relative frequency with which the factors occur (Hirsch, 1958, pp. 2–3).

We have come full circle from our earlier discussion of the formation of Drosophila and human races. The reader will recall Dobzhansky's experiment showing the genetic differentiation of fruit-fly populations as a function of elevation along the Sierra Nevada mountains. It would appear that social classes too can be profitably construed as Mendelian populations that have diverged genetically and are continuing to do so. The existence of class barriers, however permeable, fosters relative reproductive isolation; yet social mobility permits a constant winnowing for achievement and learning ability. Migration to an appropriate social ecological niche follows. The net result of an open class system with equality of opportunity and assortative mating is to make genetic factors no less important for an understanding of human society than they are for other mammalian species. "Organic diversity is the adaptive response of living matter to the challenge of the diversity of environments" (Dobzhansky, 1962, p. 221).

SIMULTANEOUS CONSIDERATION OF RACE AND CLASS DIFFERENCES

Is it inconsistent to attribute race differences in intelligence to environmental differences but social-class differences to genetic factors? It must be remembered that we are dealing with differences between populations, not between individuals, and that the differences are quantitative, not qualitative. From what has already been discussed, the reader is familiar with the ongoing processes by which natural selection leads to both divergences and convergences in trait frequencies when man moves into different ecological niches.

If we estimate that our species *Homo sapiens* has been on the face of the earth for the past 500,000 years, detailed knowledge about our existence covers a period of little more than 1 percent of the total time. It was only after the introduction of agriculture and domestic animals in the Neolithic era some 10,000 years ago that two distinctive niches became available. It requires two or more niches, each with its own rate of selection pressure, for a trait such as intelligence to show eventually a divergence in trait frequencies. Only a little more than three hundred generations have passed since the introduction of agriculture. I would posit that the essential ingredients of what we call general intelligence are learning ability and problem solving, and that the two niches, or habitats, did not exert differential selection pressure for intelligence. Some evolutionists (for example, Mayr, 1963) maintain that man has not improved biologically for the past 30,000 years.

For some traits three hundred generations have been sufficient to lead to significant differences. Post (1962*a, b;* 1964) has examined the literature for population differences in color and acuity deficiencies in vision and for hearing acuity. He found evidence to support the hypothesis that contemporary hunting and gathering cultures have a much lower prevalence of vision and hearing deficiencies than populations removed in time and habitat. In support of the ideas advanced in this chapter, the observed differences were not accounted for by race per se, but by adaptation to a habitat followed by selection. For example, the Chinese, long removed from hunting and gathering, had poor color vision but the American Indian did not, and the Brahmin caste had a higher prevalence of defect than other tested castes.

For general intelligence, then, the selection pressures from one geographical race to another have either not been sufficiently different or have not yet been in effect long enough to lead to significant differences in the genetic basis for this character. However, intelligence can be partitioned into many components. Guilford (1959), a psychological authority on the character of intelligence, suggested that there may be as many as 120 factors or relatively independent components to general intelligence. It is not possible to rule out the possibility that races may differ in the trait (and gene) frequencies for any number of the *factors* of general intelligence. The possibility has yet to be explored and the appropriate tests have yet to be developed.

Within a race or other Mendelian population that has occupational diversity and provides for social mobility, large differences in general intelligence between noncontiguous strata (such as I and III, or II and VI in Table 1.2) may have an appreciable genetic component. The continuous gene migration together with fairly high degrees of assortative mating yield results somewhat analogous to the high *artificial* selection pressures seen in the improvement of crops and domestic animals. Perhaps the reader will agree that these speculations about the structure of human society arc based on a not unreasonable interpretation of the available data.

In summary, it is again relevant to invoke the concept of the reaction range. Given uniformity of trait-relevant environment, almost all the observed phenotypical variance in general intelligence is associated with genotypic differences. Given equivalent genotypes for a particular trait, almost all the observed phenotypical variance must be attributed to environmental differences. Given both genetic and environmental heterogeneity as is most frequent for human populations, trait variability must be attributed to some combination of genetic and environmental differences.

FERTILITY, FITNESS, AND THE FUTURE

Concern over the quality of human populations has been expressed by most scientists who are aware of differential reproduction. By this is meant the observation that all individuals do not contribute the same number of offspring to the next generation. Differential reproduction is the heart of the modern concept of natural selection and hence evolution (Simpson, 1958). Fitness is actually a technical term and is defined completely by the number of offspring left by an individual (or specified group) who survive to the age of reproduction. The value is expressed as a proportion of the population average. Natural selection favors reproductive success without necessarily a regard for general adaptedness (Mayr, 1963). It is for this reason that many scientists have suggested that man take a more active role in controlling his own evolution. Of the many topics that might be discussed in this section, only the relationship between intelligence and family size will be treated, and that only in an introductory fashion. More complete coverage can be found in Anastasi (1956; 1959), Burt (1952), and Spuhler (1963).

Differential fertility was recorded in Europe for urban versus rural and rich versus poor strata of society as early as the 1600s. With the advent of intelligence testing and the construction of valid instruments, surveys relating a child's IQ to the number of his siblings became feasible. It was not until the second Scottish survey of 1947 that such research was done on a truly large scale (see Maxwell, 1954, for references). The results from testing almost every eleven-year-old child in all of Scotland confirmed earlier findings. The more brothers and sisters a child had, the lower was his IQ. The correlation between family size and IQ in various studies clusters around a value of -0.30. From these kinds of evidence, many scientists predicted a gradual decline in the intellectual level of the population of from 2 to 4 IQ points per generation. If true, it meant that the total forces of selection were favoring lower intelligence.

From a comparison of the 1932 Scottish survey with the one done in 1947, it was apparent that not only had the mean IQ not declined, it had undergone a small improvement (for the group test only, not on the Stanford-Binet). Similar findings were reported by Cattell (1951) for English children. A paradox existed and efforts towards its solution finally paid off in the work of Higgins *et al.* (1962).

Direct studies of the relationship between IQ and fertility had been impossible because early IQ tests were designed for children, and no tested children had been followed to the completion of their reproductive lives. Other commentators had objected to the conclusions about the decline in IQ because a survey of children excludes the unmarried and infertile adults from the data. Other objections were reviewed by Anastasi (1959) but they turn out not to be crucial to the solution of the paradox. Penrose (1948) and Willoughby and Goodrie (1927) entertained models which may have anticipated the data provided by Higgins *et al.*

The Minnesota geneticists in their monumental study of mental retardation (Reed and Reed, 1965) covering six generations of 289 index families (82,217 persons) directed their attention to fertility and intelligence. They reasoned that if the average intelligence of those who failed to reproduce in each generation was appreciably lower than those who did reproduce, the negative *r* between family size and IQ could not be valid. Among their total population they had IQ values recorded for 1016 families in which both parents and at least one child had been tested. The parents had been tested when *they* were schoolchildren. In addition, the investigators had IQ-test data for 884 married siblings of the parents as well as for 66 unmarried and childless siblings of the parental generation.

It should be noted that most of the individuals in this large sub-sample were unrelated to the original 289 retarded subjects except by marriage. The IQ distribution for the 2032 parents was essentially normal with the mothers' mean equal to 103, and the fathers', equal to 101. The relationship between the IQs and size of family for the 2039 children of the parental sample is shown in Table 1.6. The results are quite in line with the earlier Scottish and English surveys. Up to a sibship of five, no marked difference exists in the mean IQs of the children. For the entire sample of children, the *r* between family size and IQ was —0.30.

A direct test of the relationship between IQ of parents and children was then made. The usual correlation of about +0.5 was obtained. The larger families with the lower IQ children were being produced by the lower IQ parents. It is easy to see the relationship between the IQ of parents and the average number of their children (that is, their fertility) in Table 1.7. Each of the 2032 parents is taken individually and grouped according to IQ ranges that correspond to standard deviations in the normal distribution. The mentally retarded parents, as defined by IQ 70 and below, had an average of 3.81 children. The latter average was by far the highest of any of the parent groups. Does this mean that the

TABLE 1.6

Intelligence of Children and Family Size

(after Reed and Reed, 1965)

Family Size	Mean IQ of Children	S.D.[a]	Number of Children
1	106	16	141
2	110	13	583
3	107	14	606
4	109	13	320
5	106	16	191
6	99	20	82
7	93	21	39
8	84	20	25
9	90	18	37
10	62	28	15

[a] S.D., standard deviation.

dire predictions about the decline of intelligence are indeed coming true? Not quite. At this point the geneticists proceeded to use their unique data on the other siblings in the parental generation.

First the spouses who married into the sibships under study were removed from the analysis. To the remaining parents were added *their* married brothers and sisters to form a sample of 1900 married siblings. Again the form of distribution of Table 1.7 was found. Persons under IQ 55 averaged 3.64 children; those from 56 to 70 averaged 2.84; and parents with IQs above 130 averaged 2.96. The key to the mystery must then be associated with the 66 unmarried siblings in the parental generation. When they are added to the 1900 married siblings the distribution of fertility as a function of intelligence changes markedly. Table 1.8 shows that when *all* the siblings are followed up, the lowest IQ range produced the fewest children and the highest, the most. The average number of children ranged from 1.38 to 2.96. Previously obtained negative correlations of −0.30 between the size of the family and the intelligence of the children disappear when the single siblings are included.

It would thus appear that the net direction of selective forces for intelligence is in a favorable direction for the species. One of the means by which this comes about is for the persons with low IQ to remain unmarried. Reed and Reed (1965) found that only 38 percent of their total sibling group with IQs 55 and below married. Between IQs 56 and 70 the proportion married jumped to 86 percent, still below the

TABLE 1.7

Intelligence of Parents and Reproductive Rate

(from Reed and Reed, 1965)

IQ of Parent	Number of Parents	Average Number of Children
70 and below	73	3.81 ± 0.32
71–85	180	2.98 ± 0.14
86–100	597	2.65 ± 0.05
101–115	860	2.68 ± 0.04
116–130	287	2.70 ± 0.08
131 and up	35	2.94 ± 0.25
Totals	2032	2.75

remainder of the sample which ranged from 97 percent to 100 percent married. The latter figure of 100 percent married was for the brightest group with IQs 131 and above. The mean IQ for the unmarried siblings was 80, although it was 100 for the total sample of married siblings.

Other recent work supports the suggestion that the direction of selection for intelligence is not dysgenic. Carter (1962) reports a study by Quensel in Sweden of the fertility and marriage of a large sample of IQ-tested recruits born in 1924. Although none of the men had completed their reproduction at age 29 (when the data were collected), trends were already evident. The dullest group had the highest fertility within marriage, but the lowest proportion married, that is, 57 percent.

TABLE 1.8

Intelligence of all Siblings and Reproductive Rate

(from Reed and Reed, 1965)

IQ of Siblings	Number of Siblings	Average Number of Children
55 and below	29	1.38 ± 0.54
56–70	74	2.46 ± 0.31
71–85	208	2.39 ± 0.13
86–100	583	2.16 ± 0.06
101–115	778	2.26 ± 0.05
116–130	269	2.45 ± 0.09
131 and above	25	2.96 ± 0.34
Totals	1966	2.27

In a study by Bajema (1963) in a Michigan city, the completed fertility of all native white subjects (*Ss*) born in 1916 and 1917 who had reached the beginning of the seventh year of schooling was examined. The adults had been tested at an average age of 11.6 years. Although the Bajema sample was smaller than that of Higgins *et al.*, the results are quite close. For IQ-range greater than 130 the average number of children was 3.00; it dropped to 2.05 for the range 71 to 85 (the 3 subjects under IQ 70 did not reproduce). *Relative fitness* is defined as the ratio of population growth rate per individual of a specific IQ group to the same rate for the optimum phenotype (IQ 120 and above) in the Bajema study. Thus the relative fitness value for the IQ 120 and above group was 1.0; for the IQ-range 69 to 79 it was only 0.58. An intriguing bimodal distribution for IQ and fertility was found by both the Reeds and Bajema. It should serve as a challenge to other researchers.

While this brief review of some recent findings on the direction of selection for intelligence may quiet the fears that society is headed for a chaos in which the dull would inherit the earth, it should not lull us into complacency about the quality of the species. Five million of the six million retarded persons in the United States are the offspring of a retarded parent or a normal parent who has a retarded sibling (Reed and Reed, 1965).

A SUMMING UP

The reader has been exposed to a point of view that embodies some of the principles found useful by biological scientists studying evolution and human genetics. A thesis has been advanced to the effect that data about the behavior of races and social classes become more meaningful when these groups are viewed as Mendelian populations. Human behavior is no less dependent on a biological substrate than physical characteristics. Man is continuing to evolve both culturally and biologically. At the present time Negro and white differences in general intelligence in the United States appear to be primarily associated with differences in environmental advantages. Social-class differences in general intelligence in stratified, open-class societies appear to be moving in a direction where such differences will have an appreciable genetic component. Fears about a decline in the population potential for intelligent behavior as a result of differential fertility are not warranted in the light of recent research. So long as persons at the lower end of the IQ distribution are at a reproductive disadvantage, that is, less fit, there will be positive selection for this prized human trait. Evolution should continue in an adaptive direction.

References

Allen, G. Intellectual potential and heredity. *Science,* 1961, **133,** 378–379.

Allison, A. C. Protection afforded by sickle-cell trait against subterian malarial infection. *British Medical Journal,* 1954, **1,** 290–292.

Anastasi, Anne. Intelligence and family size. *Psychological Bulletin,* 1956, **53,** 187–209.

———. *Differential psychology.* Ed. 3. New York: Macmillan, 1958*a.*

———. Heredity, environment and the question "how"? *Psychological Review,* 1958*b,* **65,** 197–208.

———. Differentiating effects of intelligence and social status. *Eugenics Quarterly,* 1959, **6,** 84–91.

Bajema, C. Estimation of the direction and intensity of natural selection in relation to human intelligence by means of the intrinsic rate of natural increase. *Eugenics Quarterly,* 1963, **10,** 175–187.

Baker, P. T. Racial differences in heat tolerance. *American Journal of Physical Anthropolgy,* 1958, **16,** 287–305.

Barnicot, N. A. Climatic factors in the evolution of human populations. *Cold Spring Harbor Symposia on Quantitative Biology,* 1959, **24,** 115–129.

Boyd, W. *Genetics and the races of man.* Boston: Little, Brown, 1950.

Brackbill, Yvonne (ed.). *Research in infant behavior: A cross indexed bibliography.* Baltimore: Williams & Wilkins, 1964.

Burt, C. *Intelligence and fertility: The effect of the differential birth rate on inborn mental characteristics.* London: The Eugenics Society and Cassell & Company, Ltd., 1952.

———. Class differences in general intelligence: III. *British Journal of Statistical Psychology,* 1959, **12,** 15–33.

———. Intelligence and social mobility. *British Journal of Statistical Psychology,* 1961,**14,** 3–24.

Carter, C. O. *Human heredity.* Baltimore: Penguin, 1962.

Casler, L. Maternal deprivation: A critical review of the literature. *Monographs of the Society for Research in Child Development,* 1961, **26,** No. 2.

Cattell, R. B. The fate of national intelligence: Test of a thirteen-year prediction. *Eugenics Review,* 1951, **42,** 136–148.

Conway, J. Class differences in general intelligence: II. A reply to Dr. Halsey. *British Journal of Statistical Psychology,* 1959, **12,** 5–14.

Coon, C. S., S. M. Garn, and J. B. Birdsell. *Races.* Springfield, Ill.: C. C. Thomas, 1950.

Cooper, R., and J. Zubek. Effects of enriched and restricted early environments on the learning ability of bright and dull rats. *Canadian Journal of Psychology,* 1958, **12,** 159–164.

Darlington, C. D. "The genetics of society." In A. V. Gregor (ed.). *A symposium on race: An interdisciplinary approach.* Honolulu: Hawaii University Press, 1963.

Dobzhansky, T. *Evolution, genetics, and man.* New York: Wiley, 1955.

———. *Mankind evolving.* New Haven, Conn.: Yale University Press, 1962.

——— and O. Pavlovsky. An experimental study of interaction between genetic drift and natural selection. *Evolution,* 1957, **11,** 311–319.

Donnan, E. Documents illustrative of the history of the slave trade to America. Carnegie Institute Publications, No. 409, Vol. IV, 1935.

Freedman, D. Constitutional and environmental interactions in rearing of four breeds of dogs. *Science,* 1958, **127,** 585–586.

Fuller, J. L. *Nature and nurture: A modern synthesis.* New York: Doubleday, 1954.

———. Comparative studies in behavioral genetics. *Acta Genetica Statistica Medica,* 1957, **7,** 403–407.

———and W. R. Thompson. *Behavior genetics.* New York: Wiley, 1960.

Garn, S. M. (ed.). *Readings on race.* Springfield, Ill.: C. C. Thomas, 1960.

———. *Human races.* Springfield, Ill.: C. C. Thomas, 1961.

Glass, B. On the unlikelihood of significant admixture of genes from the North American Indians in the present composition of the Negroes of the United States. *American Journal of Human Genetics,* 1955, **7,** 368–385.

——— and C. C. Li. The dynamics of racial intermixture—An analysis based on the American Negro. *American Journal of Human Genetics,* 1953, **5,** 1–20.

Gottesman, I. I. Science or propaganda. *Contemporary Psychology,* 1963a, **8,** 381–382.

———. "Genetic aspects of intelligent behavior." In N. Ellis (ed.), *Handbook of mental deficiency: Psychological theory and research.* New York: McGraw-Hill, 1963b, 253–296.

———. "Personality and natural selection." In S. G. Vandenberg (ed.), *Methods and goals in human behavior genetics.* New York: Academic Press, 1965, 63–80.

Guilford, J. P. Three faces of intellect. *American Psychologist,* 1959, **14,** 469–479.

Hebb, D. *The organization of behavior.* New York: Wiley, 1949.

Herskovits, M. J. *The anthropometry of the American Negro.* New York: Columbia University Press, 1930.

———. *The myth of the Negro past.* New York: Harper & Row, 1941.

Higgins, C., and C. H. Sivers. A comparison of Stanford-Binet and Colored Ravens Progressive Matrices IQs for children with low socio-economic status. *Journal of Consulting Psychology,* 1958, **20,** 465–468.

Higgins, J., Elizabeth W. Reed, and S. Reed. Intelligence and family size: A paradox resolved. *Eugenics Quarterly,* 1962, **9,** 84–90.

Hirsch, J. Recent developments in behavior genetics and differential psychology. *Diseases of the Nervous System,* 1958, **19,** No. 7 (Monograph supplement).

———. Individual differences in behavior and their genetic basis. In E. Bliss (ed.), *Roots of behavior.* New York: Harper & Row, 1962, 3–23.

Hunt, E. E. Anthropometry, genetics, and racial history. *American Anthropologist,* 1959, **61,** 64–87.

Hunt, J. M. *Intelligence and experience.* New York: Ronald Press, 1961.

Johnson, D. M. Applications of the standard-score IQ to social statistics. *Journal of Social Psychology,* 1948, **27,** 217–227.

Kennedy, W., V. Van Deriet, and J. White. A normative sample of intelligence and achievement of Negro elementary school children in the southeastern United States. *Monographs of the Society for Research in Child Development,* 1963, **28,** No. 6 (Whole No. 90).

Lerner, M. *America as a civilization.* New York: Simon & Schuster, 1957.

Liverant, S. Intelligence: A concept in need of re-examination. *Journal of Consulting Psychology,* 1960, **24,** 101–110.

Louttit, C. M. *Clinical psychology of exceptional children.* Ed. 3. New York: Harper & Row, 1957.

Maher, B. A. "Intelligence and brain damage." In N. Ellis (ed.), *Handbook of mental deficiency: Psychological theory and research.* New York: Mc-Graw-Hill, 1963, 224–252.

Maxwell, J. Intelligence, fertility and the future. *Eugenics Quarterly,* 1954, **1,** 244–274.

Mayr, E. *Animal species and evolution.* Cambridge, Mass.: Harvard University Press, 1963.

McClearn, G. E. "Genetics and behavior development." In M. L. and Lois W. Hoffman (eds.), *Review of child development research.* New York: Russell Sage, 1964, I, 433–480.

McNemar, Q. Note on Wellman's reanalysis of IQ changes of orphanage pre-school children. *Journal of Genetic Psychology,* 1945, **67,** 215–219.

Meehl, P. and A. Rosen. Antecedent probability and the efficiency of psychometric signs, patterns, or cutting scores. *Psychological Bulletin,* 1955, **52,** 194–216.

Mourant, A. R. *The distribution of the human blood groups.* Oxford, Eng.: Blackwell, 1954.

———, and I. M. Watkin. Blood groups, anthropology, and language in Wales and the western counties. *Heredity,* 1952, **6,** 13–36.

Neel, J. V. The inheritance of sickle-cell anemia. *Science,* 1949, **110,** 64.

Newman, H., F. Freeman, and K. Holzinger. *Twins: A study of heredity and environment.* Chicago: University of Chicago Press, 1937.

Newman, M. T. Adaptation of man to cold climates. *Evolution,* 1956, **10,** 101–105.

Penrose, L. J. The supposed threat of declining intelligence. *American Journal of Mental Deficiency,* 1948, **53,** 114–118.

———. *The biology of mental defect.* Ed. 3. New York: Grune & Stratton, 1963.

Pettigrew, T. *A profile of the Negro American.* Princeton, N. J.: Van Nostrand, 1964.

Pollitzer, W. S. The Negroes of Charleston (S. C.): A study of hemoglobin types, serology, and morphology. *American Journal of Physical Anthropology,* 1958, **16,** 241–263.

———, R. C. Hartmann, H. Moore, R. E. Rosenfield, H. Smith, S. Hakim, P. J. Schmidt, and W. C. Leyshon. Blood types of the Cherokee Indians. *American Journal of Physical Anthropology,* 1962, **20,** 33–43.

Post, R. H. Population differences in red and green color vision deficiency: A review and a query on selection relaxation. *Eugenics Quarterly,* 1962a, **9,** 131–146.

———. Population differences in vision acuity. *Eugenics Quarterly,* 1962b, **9,** 189–212.

———. Hearing acuity variation among Negroes and whites, *Eugenics Quarterly,* 1964, **11,** 65–81.

Reed, Elizabeth W., and S. C. Reed. *Mental retardation: A family study.* Philadelphia: Saunders, 1965.

Riesen, A. H. "Stimulation as a requirement for growth and function in behavioral development." In D. W. Fiske and S. R. Maddi (eds.), *Functions of Varied Experience.* Homewood, Ill.: Dorsey, 1961, 57–80.

Roberts, D. F. The dynamics of racial intermixture in the American Negro—

Some anthropological considerations. *American Journal of Human Genetics,* 1955, **7**, 361–367.

Roberts, J. A. F. The genetics of mental deficiency. *Eugenics Review,* 1952, **44**, 71–83.

Shields, J. *Monozygotic twins brought up apart and brought up together.* London: Oxford University Press, 1962.

———, and I. I. Gottesman. Age at separation and IQ differences in identical twins reared apart. Unpublished manuscript, 1965.

Simpson, G. G. "The study of evolution: Methods and present status of theory." In Anne Roe and G. G. Simpson (eds.), *Behavior and evolution.* New Haven: Yale University Press, 1958, 7–26.

Sinnott, E. W., L. C. Dunn, and T. Dobzhansky. *Principles of genetics.* Ed. 5. New York: McGraw-Hill, 1958.

Spuhler, J. N. "The scope for natural selection in man." In W. J. Schull (ed.), *Genetic selection in man.* Ann Arbor: University of Michigan Press, 1963, 1–111.

Thompson, W. R. Traits, factors, and genes. *Eugenics Quarterly,* 1957, **4**, 8–16.

———, and T. Schaefer. "Early environmental stimulation." In D. W. Fiske and S. R. Maddi (eds.), *Functions of varied experience.* Homewood, Ill.: Dorsey, 1961, 81–105.

Tryon, R. Behavior genetics in social psychology. *American Psychologist,* 1957, **12**, 453. (Abstract.)

Tyler, Leona E. *The psychology of human differences.* Ed. 3. New York: Appleton-Century-Crofts, 1965.

Waddington, C. H. *The strategy of the genes.* New York: Macmillan, 1957.

Willoughby, R. R., and Mirandi Goodrie. Neglected factors in the differential birth rate problem. *Journal of Genetic Psychology,* 1927, **34**, 373–393.

Workman, P. L., B. S. Blumberg, and A. J. Cooper. Selection, gene migration and polymorphic stability in a U. S. white and Negro population. *American Journal of Human Genetics,* 1963, **15**, 429–437.

Glossary

ADMIXTURE—see GENE FLOW.

ALLELE—one of two or more alternative forms of a gene, occupying the same locus of paired chromosomes.

ASSORTATIVE MATING—the tendency for like to marry like evidenced by a correlation between mates for some traits, for example, IQ and skin color.

AUTOSOME—chromosomes other than sex-chromosomes; humans have 44 autosomes.

BALANCED POLYMORPHISM—two or more distinct types of individuals co-existing in the same breeding population. The balance is maintained by the selective advantage of the heterozygote over either homozygote.

DIFFERENTIAL REPRODUCTION—see also FITNESS, DARWINIAN or BIOLOGICAL. Reproduction in which different genotypes do not contribute to the next generation in proportion to their numbers.

DOMINANCE—the expression of a gene even when present in single dose.

DYSGENIC—term applied to a trend which may be harmful in the genetic make-up of a population.

ECOLOGICAL NICHE—the configuration of environmental factors into which a species or subgroup of humans fits.

FITNESS, DARWINIAN or BIOLOGICAL—the number of offspring, left by an individual, who reach the age of reproduction.

GENE FLOW—also called (gene) migration. The spread of genes from one population to the next as a result of the migration of people; it can lead to rapid changes in gene frequency.

GENE FREQUENCY—in a population in which two or more alleles of a particular gene occur, the relative proportion of each in the gene pool.

GENE POOL—the sum total of genes of a given breeding population at a given time.

GENETIC DRIFT—the occurrence of changes in gene frequency not due to selection, mutation, or immigration but to chance; especially noticeable in small isolates.

GENOTYPE—The genetic make-up of an individual; this may refer to one, several, or all loci.

HETEROZYGOTE—an individual with different alleles at one or more corresponding loci of the two parental chromosomes.

HOMOZYGOTE—an individual with identical alleles at one or more loci.

ISOLATING MECHANISMS—properties of individuals or niches that prevent or reduce successful interbreeding between members of different populations.

LOCUS (*pl.* LOCI)—the position of a particular gene on a chromosome.

PHENOTYPE—the sum total of all observable characteristics of an individual (biochemical, anatomical, physiological, psychological, and so on). It is the result of the interaction of the genotype with the effective environment. Also used to refer to a trait associated with one or many genes.

POLYGENIC INHERITANCE—inheritance of a trait measured phenotypically in quantitative, as opposed to qualitative, fashion. Many genes (three or more) act independently to produce their effect in a cumulative manner.

POLYMORPHISM—the coexistence of several discontinuous phenotypes or alleles in a breeding population; even the rarest type is more frequent than can be accounted for by mutation.

POLYTYPIC—generally, a species composed of several geographic races or subspecies.

RECESSIVENESS—the failure of a gene to express itself phenotypically when present in single dose; only homozygous individuals show the trait.

SICKLE-CELL ANEMIA—an anemia due to a hemoglobin mutation and usually lethal to homozygotes. Heterozygotes for the recessive allele have the "sickling trait."

TRANSIENT POLYMORPHISM—temporary polymorphism observed when one adaptive type is in the process of being replaced by a more adaptive one.

PART TWO

Basic Processes in Intellectual Development

INTRODUCTION—*Arthur R. Jensen*

Animals low in the phylogenetic scale come into the world with highly detailed programs already built into their nervous systems for coping with the typical exigencies of their existence. In general, the higher the organism in the phylogenetic scale, the less specific is its built-in program and the greater is the need for the individual to acquire adaptive programs through encounters with the environment, both physical and social. Thus, the developmental period in humans extends over more time than is needed for other animals to attain behavioral maturity, and the human's interaction with his social environment is a crucial factor in his psychological development.

It is instructive to note those rare cases of children who, through unfortunate circumstances, have been forced to grow up under conditions of great isolation from the experiences which are essential for the normal development of human potentialities. A now classic case is that of Isabel, who was studied by sociologist Kingsley Davis (1947). Isabel was an illegitimate child whose "disgraced" grandparents wanted to hide her and her deaf-mute mother from the world. Isabel lived with her mother in an attic until she was discovered by the authorities at age $6\frac{1}{2}$. She had lived practically all this time isolated from the rest of the family; she communicated with her mother largely through gestures. She was totally without speech and made only "strange croaking sounds." At first there was a question whether she was deaf, but her hearing was later found to be normal. Her behavior was generally strange; on the Vineland Social Maturity Scale she had a social age of 2 years 6 months, and on the Stanford-Binet she obtained a mental age of 1 year 7 months, putting her IQ at about 25. What is especially interesting, however, is that after some two to three years of intensive, individual, educational treatment, Isabel was behaviorally indistinguishable from the average run of her classmates of the same age; she was in the average range of IQ and educational achievement. She had accomplished in two years what normally would have taken six. We can never know, of course, what her level of intelligence might have been if she had grown up in a good environment during the first six years of her life. But there remain two facts of striking importance: extreme environmental deprivation resulted, by the age of six, in a level of development that was commensurate with the lowest level of human ability to be found in institutions for the severely defective, and through intensive educational "therapy" it was possible to ameliorate this condition, by the age of eight or nine, to a level of normal functioning.

The three chapters in this part deal with some of the elements of the "programs" that humans generally acquire in the course of their development and how these are specifically affected by environmental variables. Lacks in these environmental inputs create the varieties of psychological syndrome now generally referred to as "cultural deprivation" or "cultural retardation," as distinguished from retardation due to more fundamental biological factors which limit the individual's ability to learn.

It was only as recently as the 1950's that the full extent to which the child's mental development is dependent upon the specific nature of experience in both the physical and interpersonal world began to be generally appreciated with any degree of subtlety. Prior to this time there was little attempt to analyze the precise mechanisms by which experience affects perceptual and cognitive development. It was easily noted that there were social-class differences in intelligence-test scores and in school performance, and this common observation initiated a period of seeking correlations between various indices of socioeconomic status (*SES*) and such global psychological characteristics as general intelligence and academic achievement. Most of the specific variables that entered into indices of *SES,* such as cost of the home, neighborhood characteristics, family income, father's occupation, and so on, were essentially of a nonpsychological nature and thus did little to elucidate the causal factors involved in the well-established correlations (mostly in the region of 0.20 to 0.40) between a child's *SES* background and his intellectual performance.

The first attempts to answer the question of how the development of mental ability is differentially affected by growing up in a low-*SES* as compared with a middle-*SES* environment were in terms of specific items of experience or knowledge picked up in different environments, as well as differences in general attitudes and values concerning test-taking, schooling, books, teachers, and the like. This line of thinking gave rise to the vain pursuit of culture-free and culture-fair tests of intelligence (for example, Eells *et al.,* 1949). The basic rationale of these attempts was that standard tests were biased in favor of middle- and upper-*SES* groups because of their specific content, and that if the content of the items was made appropriate to the typical experiences of culturally less advantaged children, the typical *SES* differences found with culturally biased tests would be eliminated. It was easy to point out many culturally biased items in tests, such as questions requiring knowledge of the names of musical instruments, exotic animals, or the ability to interpret the meaning of bookish proverbs, and the like.

When tests were devised to exclude such culturally biased content, however, *SES* differences still appeared to about the same degree as on standard tests (for example, Ludlow, 1956). It soon became apparent that the important environmental factors in intellectual development involved much more than the specific contents of experience. Thus the focus of research was turned to differences in the perception and processing of experience, with special emphasis on how the environment specifically influences the development of cognitive structures for coping with the peculiar experiences to which nearly all children in our society are exposed at about five or six years of age, namely, classroom instruction.

The chapter by Cynthia Deutsch analyzes recent theory and research on the developmental aspects of perceptual functions and the role of experience in their formation. Jensen's chapter gives a theoretical account, from a behavioristic standpoint, of the important role of verbal behavior in intellectual development. The chapter by Whiteman and Deutsch reports an empirical study of specific environmental correlates of mental ability. The viewpoint and methodology of this study are typical of the recent trend in this field, that is, to no longer regard the environment as a unidimensional continuum, or to deal with it solely in terms of gross indices of *SES,* but to examine those aspects of the environment which are most likely to be the actual links in the causal chain that contributes to the correlation between *SES* and intelligence. The really active ingredients of the environment involve qualities of the parent-child interaction and the family constellation. Deutsch's

Deprivation Index predicts more of the variance in educationally relevant traits than do the usual indices of *SES*.

Whiteman and Deutsch point out the essential limitations of a correlational study such as theirs. Correlational studies have always been more feasible than experimental studies in this field, largely because of the great difficulty of performing controlled experiments involving the participation of human beings over prolonged periods of time. The difficulty in a correlational study, of course, is the inability, often the impossibility, of inferring the direction of causality among the intercorrelated variables. Dependent and independent variables usually remain hopelessly confounded. Inferences concerning direction of causality must, therefore, be regarded as hypotheses, the proof of which must await other investigations. Analysis of the network of correlations among environmental variables, abilities, and school attainment is, however, an important step in mapping the territory for more detailed experimental investigation and can serve the function of pointing out which environmental or subject variables contribute only negligible amounts to the total variance in ability and achievement.

It has become clear that the more fine-grained the environmental and interpersonal analysis, the greater is the amount of the variance of children's abilities that can be accounted for. A good example is the study by Wolf, cited by Whiteman and Deutsch. Wolf obtained measures of thirteen environmental factors largely involving cognitive aspects of the parent-child interaction. A multiple correlation between these factors and the IQs of fifth-graders was 0.76. That is, 58 percent (the multiple correlation squared) of the variance in IQ was "accounted for" by Wolf's environmental variables. But "accounted for" does not always mean the same thing as "caused by"—an important distinction which is sometimes forgotten in interpreting correlations between environmental and behavioral traits. Wolf's method of environmental assessment would have produced less ambiguous results concerning the effects of environment on intellectual development if it had been applied to adopted children who were assigned to different homes at random; in other words, genotypes and environments would be uncorrelated. This would constitute a true experiment. Under the natural family conditions in Wolf's study, he could just as well have accounted for at least 50 percent of the variance in the children's IQs from only one predictor, the IQ of one of the parents. The multiple correlation could be boosted enormously by adding the IQs of other relatives, without ever measuring any environmental variables. Since no major study of the heritability of intelligence has attributed more than 25 percent of the total variance to environmental differences, some 33 percent of the variance in IQs that Wolf "accounted for" by environmental variables must actually have a genetic basis. This observation leads to interesting questions:

To what degree does the parental genotype create the deprivation or enrichment of the environment in which the offspring are reared? And to what degree does the child's genotype shape its own environment?

References

Davis, K. Final note on a case of extreme isolation. *American Journal of Sociology,* 1947, **57,** 432–457.

Eells, K., A. Davis, R. J. Havighurst, V. E. Herrick, and R. W. Tyler. *Intelligence and cultural differences.* Chicago: University of Chicago Press, 1951.

Ludlow, H. G. Some recent research on the Davis-Eells games. *School & Society,* 1956, **84,** 146–148.

CHAPTER TWO

Environment
and Perception

CYNTHIA P. DEUTSCH[1]

The field of environment and perception involves half a dozen un-resolved controversies, for each of which experimental evidence is either abundant and contradictory, or almost totally lacking. In addition, the title of the present volume demands concern with a set of variables as yet only peripherally related to perception in the research literature. Certainly, then, this paper cannot attempt to derive any universally applicable theory of the relationship between environment and perception, nor really order the untidiness which exists in this area. What this chapter will attempt to do is consider some of the viewpoints, theories, experiments, and continuing controversies in the light of the potential importance of the over-all conditions of an individual's life to the development and functioning of his perceptual processes.

The perceptual literature is altogether too voluminous for this chapter to present a full review. What has been attempted here, therefore, is a selective mention of the literature and theories most pertinent to the general points raised. This sampling approach has been followed with respect to exposition of theories as well as research.

---

[1] Institute for Developmental Studies, School of Education, New York University.

Briefly, the conclusions reached are that life conditions—including current situation, past experience, cultural and socioeconomic factors, to name only a few—influence perceptual processes through their influence on the amount and variety of stimuli to which an individual is exposed, and through influencing the nature and amount of practice an individual gets in learning to discriminate stimuli from each other. These ideas are advanced as hypotheses in the context of historical discussion of the heredity-environment dichotomy and consideration of the nativism-empiricism controversy in perception. Reference is made to the role of the stimulus in theories of perception, and the modifiability of perception through the modifying of presentation of stimuli. Another way in which perception is modified is through modification of the immediate state of the individual, and some theories and experiments related to this area are also presented. Experiments showing some effects of deprivation and of enrichment are discussed, and the questions surrounding the area of perceptual learning are briefly considered. Finally, the last part of the chapter considers the conclusions reached about the influence of environment on perception, and advances some practical suggestions as to how to use what is known about perception in enhancing children's classroom learning experiences.

Literature relating to one of the focal points of the chapter—the influence of social class on perception—is exceedingly sparse. However, programs such as the Head Start preschools and other attempts to deal with the so-called socially disadvantaged children are exposing psychologists to large numbers of nonclinic-patient children from populations not extensively included in the classical child development literature. As a result, a literature on social class and the development of basic psychological processes is beginning to grow. It is a fair prediction that by the time the present volume is ready to be revised, a chapter on "Environment and Perception" will be able to lean heavily on directly relevant research and will include only in passing the literature on severe sensory deprivation, from which today one must draw analogy for hypotheses and reasoning.

HEREDITY–ENVIRONMENT DICHOTOMY

A brief consideration of the history and progressive transformation of the heredity-environment dichotomy is relevant to an understanding of the experimental questions posed later. In modern intellectual thought, the first statement of the dichotomy was simply, "Which contributes the most to an individual's adult status and attainments— heredity or environment?" Casting the question in those terms indicated that both were considered as unitary and homogeneous causative agents, and that one would have to be considered as more important than the other. Further, in the absence of concern with the operations by which either set of variables influenced a given trait or traits, such a question would be likely to stimulate only descriptive studies. In fact, Galton (1875, 1914) in England and Goddard (1912) in the United States undertook descriptive studies, and each concluded that heredity was more important than environment. From his examination of such families as the Huxleys and the Darwins, Galton concluded that genius was inherited, since the same families produced so many men of eminence and outstanding attainment. Goddard studied two sets of progeny fathered by a revolutionary war officer whom he dubbed Martin Kallikak. One set of children was the illegitimate offspring of the soldier and a barmaid, while the other set was the progeny of a marriage to a respectable New England woman. From the fact that the descendants of the illegitimate branch of the family, as compared with the legitimate branch, included many more individuals who were feeble-minded, who were subject to social ills of various types, and who ended up in institutions, Goddard concluded that heredity was a more potent influence than environment. It remained for later interpreters to point out that the environment in which the illegitimate children of a barmaid were raised would be likely to differ substantially from that in which the legitimate children were brought up; and that the children of Galton's eminent families were exposed to unusual educational and social opportunities. The tautological reasoning in the Goddard study is also apparent in the assumption that the hereditary contribution of the barmaid would be a negative factor for her children: her occupation was seen as a direct reflection of inferior endowment.

A change in the description of the dichotomy from "heredity versus environment" to "nature versus nurture" reflected a concern with hierarchizing effects in both dimensions and made possible a greater specification of particular influences. Referring to "nature," as opposed to "heredity," allowed for the inclusion of the effects of the prenatal environment by focusing on the presumably "basic" or intrinsic attributes of an individual. Since these would be observable only after birth, the hereditary effects would be inseparable from the effects of the intrauterine environment, and therefore "nature" would refer to both. In specifying "nurture" instead of "environment" for the other term of the dichotomy, the emphasis was placed on those portions of the environment whose action on the individual is relevant to his development. While "nurture" is still a global term, it can be considered to imply some point of contact and therefore some hierarchization of influence. These restatements, then, opened the way to asking more specific questions about the amount and type of influence of each of the dichotomous variables. What followed from this greater specificity was an interactionist view: nurture acted upon or interacted with nature to produce particular individual traits. The typical statement of this view was that nature set the limits of a particular trait, and nurture determined how close to the limits an individual would come. In this way, factors of nutrition, illness, and the like, would influence how tall a person would become, within the limits set by his heredity. The implication of this statement is that nature is unmodifiable, being considered intrinsic to the individual.

Kawi and Pasamanick (1959) and Pasamanick and Knobloch (1961) studied the relationship between the socioeconomic level of the mother and the incidence of brain damage and of paranatal difficulty in the child. They found a positive relationship between low socioeconomic level and both disorders of pregnancy, including spontaneous abortion, and infant disability. In seeking the mediating variables, they gathered evidence of differential nutritional state, favoring mothers in higher socioeconomic categories. The implication here is that the environment, or "nurture," can influence the "nature" (and the survival) of the individual: a hypothesis of what the present writer prefers to call *interpenetration* of the variables rather than simply their interaction in the production of a particular trait. As indicated before, it would seem that a tenet of the interactionist point of view is that nature is not modifiable: that only its effects on particular traits can be altered. Using the term "interpenetration" would emphasize the modifiability of nature as well as nurture. A dramatic example of such interpenetration is to be found in the effects of a drug such as thalidomide on the developing fetus.

The interpenetration discussed involves the operation of environmental influences on the product of genic influences. However, modern genetics teaches that genic operation itself is responsive to environmental variation. Experiments show that incubating Drosophila larvae at one temperature will produce one color of adult fruit fly, while incubating larvae from the same genetic strain at a different temperature will result in adult individuals of a different color. The environment, then, affects the biological attributes of the organism by influencing the operation of the gene.[2]

This current end product of the old heredity-versus-environment controversy leads to consideration of the process by which both the hereditary and the environmental influences are mediated. The concepts of global influences and global effects have given way to the specifics of how particular influences produce particular effects. In genetics this can mean the investigation of the differential sensitivity of different genes to different environmental influences. In psychology

---

[2] This does not mean that relatively minor environmental factors change the genic *structure,* but simply that such factors influence the effects of genic determination.

this can mean the study of differential environmental and experiential effects on various psychological processes at various times or developmental stages.

PERCEPTION IN PSYCHOLOGY

Corresponding to the heredity-environment controversy in the field of intelligence has been the "nativism-empiricism" issue in the study of perception; that is, how much of perception is learned and how much is innate.

As with the resolution of the heredity-environment controversy into a concept of interpenetration of influences and the resulting focus on delineation of the processes involved in the mediation of influences, so with the nativism-empiricism controversy in perception; the potentially fruitful question to ask is "How do different influences modify different aspects of perception, and under what conditions and for what subjects?"

Let us, therefore, get down to the question of perception. Sensation and perception have to do with the individual's apprehension of his world, and thus have been central concerns throughout the history of psychology. Historically, this concern was inherited from both the philosophical and the physiological parents of psychology. In philosophy, the area of epistemology had to do with how the individual came to know and understand his world, and some of the emphasis had to do with the nature of the "stuff" of the universe. There was concern with the correspondence between the dimensions and attributes of the physical world and the individual's apprehension of it through his sensory apparatus. In this sense, the questions of sensation and perception, as posed in philosophy, were those of the relationship between the individual and the physical world around him. Gibson, in fact, defined perception as a "process by which an individual maintains contact with his environment (1959)."

In physiology, the concern with sensation and perception had to do in the main with the operations of the sensory apparatus and mechanisms. While the details in the philosophical emphasis dealt with the nature of the physical world, the details in the physiological approach had to do with the more minute aspects of the sensory process. Though the nature of the stimulus was an important element in physiology (the doctrine of the specific energy of nerves, for example, established an invariant relationship between the nature of the stimulus and the structures which were activated), the greatest amount of effort went into the tracing of the neural pathways and projection areas which responded to a given stimulus. The attention given to the properties of the stimulus for the most part had to do with its more minute characteristics, such as the exact wavelengths of light, or the exact frequencies of sound, and it was via this route that physics also entered into the history of psychology.

In the early days of psychology as a separate scientific pursuit, the emphasis on the relationship between the individual and his environment via his sensorium was maintained. Many of the questions investigated had to do with the minute attributes, or elements, of sensation, and the preferred method for such investigation was introspection by trained subjects. The training was undertaken to minimize the possibility of random error (and the operation of the "human equation") and to enable the subject to fractionate his sensations in such a way as to report on the dimensions of warmth, or light, and the like subjectively. There was no implication that all individuals, if sufficiently trained, would not identify the same elements on introspection. In other words, individual differences were not an issue in these investigations.

That a great part of the problem of perception was still conceived of philosophically can be seen in Fechner's psychophysical work (Boring, 1942, pp. 33–37). While his investigation concerned the effects of preceding stimuli on the perception of subsequent ones, his motivation in undertaking the work had to do with the solution of the "mind-body" problem.

In American psychology, the philosophical orientation to problems for the most part got buried under the weight of behaviorism and never reemerged in its previous form. Behaviorism also discarded introspection as a method, and the previous "elemental" approach to sensation and perception can be said to have died with Titchener in the United States.

The Nativism-Empiricism Dichotomy in Perception

The question of the "nativism-empiricism" controversy in perception cannot be avoided at this point, despite Boring's characterization of it as one of the " 'dreary' topics in the history of experimental psychology" (1942, p. 28), and Bruner's labeling of it as having ". . . some of the scent of a wrongly formulated dichotomy" (1961). Bruner may be right in saying that "If the controversy had any real meaning in the study of space perception, where it originated, it certainly has none in the study of perception generally" (pp. 198–199). The fact remains, however, that the nativism-empiricism argument has provided the basis for many of the hypotheses of perceptual studies and has stimulated the design of many experiments. Further, some of the most modern questions in perceptual theory were tackled earlier under one or another rubric stemming from that dichotomy and some of the history of current issues can be understood in that light.

Boring (1942) defines two lines of development on each side of the dichotomy: nativism and phenomenology on the one side, and empiricism and operational behaviorism on the other. His view is that the nativism of Johannes Müller (who believed that the mind perceived only the states of the nerves and therefore perceived external objects only as those objects acted on the nerves) became the phenomenology of the Gestaltists. The empiricism of Lotze and the associationists (who believed that space perception originated in the muscular sensations arising from movement through space) later became operational behaviorism. In Boring's words, ". . . empiricism disappeared because it was absorbed by behaviorism and its later sophisticated substitutes, just as nativism disappeared because Gestalt psychology kept it by swallowing it" (p. 34).

In the 25 years since Boring's historical analysis appeared, the development of neurophysiology, with its techniques for studying the process of learning in terms of neural patterns and processes, the evolution of the old heredity versus environment notions into those of interpenetration of the two influences, and the emphasis on process and mediating variables have helped to focus questions in perception on mediating influences as well. With the exception of a very few theorists, it is currently generally accepted that a certain number of perceptual reactions are innate, but that the perceptual processes are modifiable through experience. Even Pastore (1960), who labels himself a nativist by his statement that "All of the significant aspects of perceiving are unlearned," admits to a belief that perception is modified by experience. He states: "The bulk of experiments purporting to demonstrate the role of empirical factors actually deal with the question of modification and not of origin. . . . Environmental modification of a trait does not preclude its genetic determination" (p. 94). However, he does not indicate how, in describing or measuring perception, one can distinguish between the "original" trait and its subsequent modification by experience. The point is that historically there is strong precedent for considering perception in the light of environment-individual relationships, and that even the nativist theorists accept that there is at least modification of perception by environmental and experiential influences.

INFLUENCES ON PERCEPTION

The Stimulus

Two words—"environmental" and "experiential"—in the last sentence deserve some differentiation and explication. Basically, "environmental" refers to the organization or nature of the stimulus while "experiential" emphasizes the past experiences of the perceiver. To clarify the issue, let us first identify the loci at which modification of perception can occur. There is a stimulus which activates an end organ or receptor. The resulting stimulation travels up the sensory pathways and is received and interpreted in the central projection areas. Overt behavior may or may not result. Some stimuli can be internal (for example, kinesthetic, proprioceptive), but let us confine this discussion to the external ones: noise, light, and the like. If the stimulus is external, it originates in the environment of the individual: no environmental stimulus, no perception. If the stimulus is noise, one gets an auditory sensation; if light, a visual. Therefore, on this elementary level, the environment determines the presence or absence of the percept.

Let us move to the next level of complexity in considering the stimulus field. The Gestalt experiments have shown that the nature of the organization of the stimulus has a great deal to do with what is perceived. Without going deeply into Gestalt theory, we can point out that some organizations, or *Gestalten,* were found to be more easily recognized or more consistently perceived than others. Thus, a circle would be more quickly recognized than an octagon; and, in fact, when presented very briefly by means of a tachistoscope, an octagon would frequently be seen as a circle. Grouping phenomena would account for the fact that a series of asterisks like * * * * * * * * * would be seen as a line of asterisks, while a series like ** ** ** ** ** would be most likely seen as a series of pairs of asterisks. Further manipulation of the stimulus field could result in further manipulation of the perception of the stimuli. Thus, connecting the asterisks previously seen as a line of them could result in a pairing perception: *-* *-* *-* *-* *-*.

The Gestaltists maintained that stimulus organization was basic to perception. Their theory was nativistic and ahistorical, however; they accorded little influence to an individual's past experience in the determination of his perception. They believed that an isomorphic relationship existed between the stimulus field and the brain field: the organization of what was *out there* determined the organization of the percept *in here.* Köhler (1940) posited a theory of "satiation" which included the assumption that the electrochemical process of transmission of stimuli in brain tissue alters the tissue and in this way obstructs the brain's recording of immediately succeeding stimuli.

According to Koffka (1935), behavior occurred in the behavioral environment—that is, in the terms in which the individual saw his world —as opposed to the geographical environment, which was the physical world. The assumption would be that the two environments correspond quite closely. The consequences when they did not were expected to be severe, as Koffka illustrated with the story of the rider who thought he was riding across open, snow-covered fields; when informed that he had actually ridden across the frozen and treacherous Lake of Constance, the rider dropped dead.

Lewin formulated his theory of topological and vector psychology in terms also of the present forces operating on an individual (1936). However, when one is postulating, as Lewin did, that a given behavior is the result of the varying strengths of the valences of particular stimuli for a given individual, it is hard to exclude the individual's previous experience as a factor influencing the valence strengths. That is, it seems hard to maintain that a particular stimulus has a particular valence independent of the individual's previous experience with that stimulus. This would seem to open the door to some historical or experiential considerations.

The Gestalt theories have been emphasized here first because the work of the Gestaltists has contributed the most to the basic study of perception. A second reason for stressing them is the writer's conviction that the eminence in the field of this ahistorical theory has been a major—if not *the* major—factor in the previous underplaying, if not ignoring, of the potential role of an individual's conditions of life in determining or influencing his perceptual development. As long as this nativistic—or phenomenological—theory was the major one in perception, specific questions were not posed in terms of examination of specific experiential effects on perception.

Attributes and Experience of the Individual

The other locus at which influences on or modification of perception can occur is in the individual. First, let us consider the receptors and the afferent pathways. It is obvious that injury to or disease of these pathways would influence the sensation and the perception of particular stimuli. In addition, the sensitivity of the structures would determine the quantity of stimulus necessary to be perceived. One determinant of this sensitivity would be the recency of previous stimulation. For example, there are absolute and relative refractory periods of nerves. During the absolute refractory period, the pathway will not conduct further stimulation; during the relative refractory period, the stimulus must be much stronger than the usually adequate stimulus in order to activate the receptors. In this sense, then, immediate past experience must play a role in perception.

The current work on the reticular activating system seems to indicate that over-all vigilance, or being "turned on" or "tuned in," plays a role in determining whether a given stimulus is perceived or not. The presence of competing stimuli, too, influences what is perceived. In an experiment reported by Hernández-Peón (1961), clicks presented to a cat were recorded from the animal's brain stem. However, when a mouse was released within the cat's visual field, the clicks were no longer recorded from the reticular system, even though they were still presented. The highly charged visual stimulus suppressed the perception of the auditory stimulus, even though the end organ was intact. In that instance, there was not an isomorphic relationship between the cat's stimulus field and its brain field: the click stimuli never reached the central projection areas.

This experiment can be interpreted to indicate that competing stimuli can suppress the *actual reception* of a given stimulus. It does not seem at all farfetched to hypothesize that a given competing stimulus can have its effective strength influenced—if not determined—by an individual's past experience with it. Some neurophysiologists, in fact, believe that events within the brain, including the effects of past experience, are more influential in determining the brain's response to sensory stimulation than the specific characteristics of the stimulus (Brazier *et al.,* 1961, p. 714).

In considering the environmental influences on perception which act through receptors, specific afferent pathways, and the reticular activating system, what have been stressed so far are discrete and competing stimuli. However, the work of Moruzzi and Magoun (1949) on the reticular activating system has supported the notion that a constant and constantly varying sensory input is necessary in order to arouse the organism: a constant and unchanging stimulus is soon adapted to and loses its capacity to arouse the organism.

Hebb's experiments in sensory deprivation tend to support this assumption (1958). He subjected volunteer college students to from one to three days of deprivation. While the conditions of deprivation varied somewhat from one experiment to another, typically each subject was placed alone in a dimly lighted soundproof room. His hands were encased in cuffs which extended past the finger tips, and translucent, but nontransparent, lenses were placed over his eyes. Having food either constantly available or presented at irregular intervals served to disrupt temporal cues. Under these conditions many subjects experienced hallucinations; some became so uncomfortable in this isolated situation that they resigned from the experiment. The phenomenon of greatest relevance to our preceding discussion, however, is that for a period of time after the conclusion of the experiment—usually two or three days —subjects reported feelings of apathy, low energy, low motivation, and difficulty in concentrating. The implication is that the absence of a constantly varying stimulus environment impaired the arousal functions of the reticular system, resulting in later resistance to sensory input and perceptual activity. This finding could be seen as a general environmental-experiential effect on perceptual processes, acting by affecting the functioning of the neural structures of the individual.

The nature of potential experiential influences not primarily neurophysiological can best be seen against the background of certain of the aspects of the perceptual process. First, it must be recognized that the individual at any given moment is assailed by many more stimuli than he can possibly respond to. Some are perceived, others are not. The individual has applied a process of selectivity, based on some hierarchization. To a degree, the organization of the stimulus field controls the selection of stimuli to which to respond: other factors being equal, a stronger stimulus is more likely to be noticed, as is a novel one. Also, the Gestalt perceptual principles apply here. However, it seems highly reasonable to suppose that at least some of the hierarchization is established through training and experience. One learns to attend to and respond to those stimuli which are most relevant to immediate needs or to the current situation. Thus, immediately after boarding a train one might be (apparently) oblivious to the calling out of the stations by the conductor, or to the flashing by of the names of the stations. But as one nears his destination, these stimuli are attended to. The kind of "tuning out" referred to would not take place at the level of the reticular system, as that described earlier, but would imply the stimuli's reaching the central projection area but simply not being attended to. Often, on reflection, one can remember receiving a particular stimulus, even though there was no response at the time: the stimulus was minimally represented in consciousness, but overshadowed by one or more which were at the time more relevant.

The possibility of individual hierarchies of sense modalities has been hypothesized and discussed for many years, but as yet has not been firmly established. Whether or not some people tend to be "visual" (that is, more responsive to visual stimuli) while others are "auditory" is extremely difficult to test, and as a result has not been subjected to definitive research. Similarly, whether young children begin by being more "tactile" and later progress to one of the distal senses has not been established.

Just as perception can be manipulated by manipulating the stimulus field, so can it be manipulated by manipulating the attention or the set of the perceiver. Levine, Chein, and Murphy (1942) presented the same ambigious figures to two groups of subjects: one group which had been deprived of food, and one group which had not. The deprived group produced many more food labels for the pictures than did the nondeprived group.

This experiment, which has been repeated in various forms with various groups and with similar results, illustrates the fact that short-term experience, influencing the current state of the individual, can influence perception. This is what Zubin, Eron, and Schumer (1965) refer to as the "New Look" in perceptual theory. Social experience can also influence perception on a short-term basis, as illustrated in a series of experiments using a phenomenon known as the "autokinetic effect" —a tendency for a subject in a pitch-dark room to see a small light, which is actually stationary, move. A particularly cogent series of experiments was done by Sherif using this technique (1935). Asch (1952, 1955) used judgments of length of lines for the same purpose. The basic form of these experiments was to ask a subject for a judgment, either of the excursion of the light, or of the length of a particular line. Then one or more "stooges" were introduced into the experimental situation. These were subjects whose task it was to report only certain judgments and to stick to their own reports: they had been coached for that purpose by the experimenter. When the stooge reported, aloud in the presence of the original subject, a judgment greatly at variance with the subject's own, the typical finding was that the first subject modified his own report to be more in line with the stooge's. The amount of modification had to do with the number of stooges introduced, their status relationship to the original subject, and the length of time the experiment proceeded with the stooge being apparently very certain of his judgment. However, some individual variables were also found in judgment modification: some subjects were more likely than others to modify their judgments, and for some, more stooges were necessary than for others. With the introduction of individual differences into the area came an attempt to specify more accurately the conditions which influenced judgment change, and the attributes of the subjects who were more and less likely to change their judgments. One problem with these experiments, however, was their reliance on the stated judgments of the subjects. It was not possible to differentiate the subject who changed his judgmental *report* from one who modified his *judgment*.

The experimental paradigm devised by Witkin and used by him and his colleagues (1954) avoided this problem by using an objective, rather than a subjective, measure. The paradigmatic Witkin experiment seated the subject in a dark room and gave him the task of adjusting a luminous rod to be exactly vertical within a luminous rectangular frame. There were no visual spatial cues. The task was varied by tilting the frame or by tilting the chair on which the subject sat. The exact adjustment of the rod was an objective measurement, and by comparing it with the tilt of the frame and/or the tilt of the chair, it was possible to determine what cues were primary for the subject. On the basis of a series of such experiments, Witkin and his colleagues defined personality descriptions of their subjects; some they found to be "field-dependent" (judgments primarily related to the position of the frame, independent of the spatial orientation cues coming from the position of one's own body in space) and others "field-independent" (judgments related most closely to the position of one's body in space). Witkin found these two qualities to be correlated with a whole host of personality and other perceptual variables.

These experiments provide examples of the influence of recent experience, of immediate social situations, and of personality variables on perception and perceptual judgment. They are only illustrative of a substantial body of work in these areas, the findings of which substantiate the premise that experience strongly influences perception.

The personality-perception relationship is further illustrated by some of the theoretical underpinnings of the projective tests used in clinical work. The assumption is made that each individual perceives the world in terms of his own personality and the experiences which molded it. When presented with an ambiguous stimulus, therefore, the individual will interpret it in terms of his own experience, and will ascribe meaning which is consistent with his personality organization and orientation.

The way is clear to assume a personality influence on perception, and, indirectly, an influence of long-term experience on perception through the experiential influence on personality. In terms of existing experimentation and accepted theory, it is thus easy to derive a notion of experiential effects on perception *via* their influence on other qualities or attributes of the individual. However, besides the necessity for studying experiential influences as once-removed, a weakness of this approach for understanding perception is that the more ambiguous the stimuli, the more the personalistic factors are thought to play a role. The perception of (usually) relatively unambiguous stimuli, then, would be least related to personality factors and therefore presumably least related to past experience. But, it should be emphasized that a link has been established between perceptual processes and experiences of the individual: whatever influences help to mold his personality will play a role in his perception.

On this base, let us examine the possibility that experience influences perception directly, not only through the mediation of personality.

Deprivation Effects

A line of research bearing on the topic of the effects of deprivation originated in the search for the answer to the nativism-empiricism question, in terms of the issues surrounding the setting of optimal and critical times for the influence of experience on particular traits.

For the most part, these studies involved the deprivation of particular experiences, and then the evaluation of the behavior thought to be affected. When the deprivation was experimentally induced, the research was done with animals (except for the short-term adult deprivation studies previously described). The human studies were those which took advantage of accidents of nature or of cultural patterns which resulted in deprivation.

An example of the animal studies is to be found in Riesen's work (1958). He reported studies of chimps reared in the dark from birth, and then placed in a normally lighted environment. At the time the animal was exposed to the lighted environment, it was unable to learn visual tasks, and apparently could not differentiate patterns. Riesen reported also that the length of time the animals were deprived of light influenced the speed with which they were able to learn visual tasks. While it was impossible to test definitively, since subjective verbal reports are not possible with chimps, there is a question as to whether those reared in the dark for the longer periods of time ever attained fully normal pattern vision. The interpretation of this series of studies was that the visual apparatus must have light stimulation early in life in order for normal function to develop. There is also some evidence that for pattern vision to develop, there must be early pattern stimulation: simply nonpatterned light (as, for example, light received through a homogeneous translucent but not transparent shield) is not sufficient.

Von Senden (1932) reported on humans of various ages who had had cataracts from birth or who developed them very shortly thereafter. These were people whose visual sensory pathways were presumed intact. All the subjects studied underwent successful operations for the removal of their cataracts. In effect, the sample for the research was a group of individuals of varying ages who had been subject to deprivation in one sense modality, and who had been completely deprived of experience in spatial and pattern vision. After the operation, pattern discrimination was very difficult for the subjects, and typically they resorted to ancillary aids for recognition, for example, determining whether a figure presented was a square or a triangle by counting the corners. The quality known as "thing constancy" was also very difficult for them to acquire: an automobile would look like an automobile when seen from the ground, but be unrecognizable when viewed from above, as when looking out of an upper-story window. While pattern vision improved over time, for some of the subjects it never became fully normal. The Von Senden reports have been criticized severely from time to time (see Epstein, 1964) on the basis of the questioning procedure for the subjects, the kinds of conclusions which Von Senden reached, and the like. However, these criticisms appear to be related most closely to the fine points of interpretation of the results: for example, whether *any* visual development occurs in the absence of light stimulation, the role of patterned light stimulation as compared with homogeneous light, and the like. None of the criticisms, in the writer's opinion, nullifies the essential finding: that deprivation of early experience resulted in diminution of later functioning. The argument here concerns the nature of the potential influences of experience on perception, and the Von Senden data support the general proposition that experience is important to the development of adequate visual perception. The exact specifics of Von Senden's conclusions and the criticisms of them are not primary for this argument. Further, more recently Gregory and Wallace (1963) in England reported a carefully followed case of a previously blind person who through surgery was enabled to see. Their report substantiates the basic conclusions of Von Senden, as does London's report of recent Russian studies (London, 1960).

In terms of the prior discussion of personality as a mediating agent between experience and perception, it is to be noted that personality traits played no role at all in either the human studies or the chimp studies: what relationship was found to obtain between experience and perception was a direct one.

Another area of criticism of the experiential deprivation studies cannot be ignored. That is, because restriction in experience is found to relate to restriction in function, it does not follow that sheer restriction of stimulation is the sole cause of the functional lacks. Being raised in the dark, for example, creates many other lacks in addition to the lack of visual stimulation. The same is true for the humans who were functionally blind from birth or shortly thereafter. Therefore, the deprivation experiments, while pointing to the importance of experience in perception, cannot be considered as definitive.

Enrichment Effects

More recently, White (1966) has initiated a series of studies on enriching sensory experience and then evaluating the behavioral effects. Such experiments offer very real advantage over the deprivation ones, since, among other aspects, they allow for a more stringent control group. White and his colleagues did a normative study of *"fisted swiping"* (striking out at an object with the fist) and *"top-level reaching"* (reaching over an object and attempting to hit it with the open palm) of infants being reared in Tewksbury State Hospital (White, Castle, and Held, 1964). The visual conditions under which the infants were being reared were quite featureless: the infants were left supine in white-sheeted cribs whose "bumpers" were white crib pads. There were no mobiles or stabiles attached to the cribs, and except for the periods during which the babies were changed or fed, or during which they received their daily handling, their visual field was a quite unrelieved, featureless white. Under these conditions, fisted swiping appeared at an average of 65 days of age, and top-level reaching on the average of 145 days. However, when the visual field was changed by the addition of figured sheets and a complex stabile (a visually complicated object attached to the side of the crib), the onset of the behaviors was changed. When the very complex stabile was used throughout the period of stimulation (day 37 through day 124) the median age of fisted swiping was delayed to day 70, but top-level reaching was accelerated to day 95. When simpler stabiles were used at days 37 to 68, and then the complex one was introduced from day 68 to day 124, the median age for fisted swiping was reduced to day 55, and the onset of top-level reaching was reduced to an average of day 80.

It is hard to overestimate the potential importance of this work. These institutional infants provide a group of subjects whose environment can be highly controlled. They can be divided into experimental and control groups, and a given experiment can be repeated on a sufficient number of subjects to minimize the effects of individual differences. Further, because the experiment involves the addition of non-noxious stimulation, and the featureless environment is the "normal" one for the babies, no ethical questions arise.

The work shows that the *addition* of visual stimulation can affect the timing of the acquisition of visual-motor responses. Whether or not it is important to future development to speed up this responsiveness cannot be considered the issue. Rather, the fact that noninstitutional infants, and presumably especially those from more privileged environments, are raised in a visual environment more closely approximating the enriched than the nonenriched institutional one, would argue for the probability that children from such environments would show the fisted swiping and the top-level reaching behavior at ages closer to those reported for the enriched institutional infants. If it is true that further visual-motor development is built on these prior skills, then it follows that a stimulating visual environment will promote earlier and more rapid development of these functions. In this connection, it seems most important to note that the visual enrichment, even when it was presumably "too much" (that is, when it delayed the onset of fisted swiping), decreased the time between fisted swiping and top-level reaching. While it could be argued simply that the complex stabile was "right" for the time period between fisted swiping and top-level reaching, the implication could also be drawn that enrichment will speed up development, and that even a presumably too complex stimulus is preferable to no stimulus. It should be noted that the stimuli being referred to are purely sensory ones; no demand is made on the infant, and the implications drawn from this work do not lead to the placing of pressure on the baby to do something.

Again, it should be noted that these findings concern only the behaviors measured, and that properly no conclusions can be drawn with regard to their influence on later perceptual and perceptual-motor development. However, the method and the sample offer the possibility of follow-up studies to explore potential relationships between the observed behaviors and later development, and it is to be hoped that such studies will be undertaken by the investigators.

These findings also put into perspective some earlier work of Dennis and Dennis (1940), and support Hunt's reinterpretation of it (1961). Dennis, in studying cradleboarded Hopi Indian children, found that these motorically restricted youngsters were not retarded or inadequate in their walking behavior. (At the time the study was done, it related to the controversy about maturation versus the learning of activities such as walking. It was interpreted to emphasize the importance of maturation, inasmuch as the children lacked crawling experience.) Hunt reinterpreted these findings and pointed out that the children who were bound to a cradleboard were not subject to *sensory* restriction, and suggested that perhaps the sensory experiences of seeing people walk and of being upright and feeling the movements of walking (they were carried on their mothers' backs) were sufficient for the children to develop walking at the normal time. These interpretations, and White's findings as well, find further support in another investigation of Dennis (1960). In a study of children in an orphanage in Teheran, Dennis reported that the children spent most of their days in dim light on their beds, in a situation of homogeneous stimulation. The children were found to be severely retarded in their motor development, with 60 percent not sitting alone in their second year, and 85 percent not walking in their fourth year. The children were not physically restricted from motor activity—though such activity was not encouraged—but they had little sensory stimulation.

PERCEPTUAL LEARNING

In addition to providing evidence for the direct action of experience on development, the studies mentioned contribute to an area of investigation known as perceptual learning. Epstein (1967) describes this as ". . . the broad range of modifications of perception which have been attributed to learning" (p. 1). The measured variable in the experiments just discussed was a motor reaction. For White's subjects, visual-motor coordination was necessary; for Dennis', it was only motor responses. In the area of perceptual learning, the dependent variable would be a perceptual response—though this response is often inferred from a motor response.

A series of animal experiments by Gibson and her associates (1956, 1958) showed that rats exposed to geometric forms from birth learned to discriminate them faster than a nonexposed control group. This superiority held in another experiment, in which the task was to discriminate between two forms which were similar but not identical to those which had been present in the rats' environment. Since the exposure to the forms was achieved simply by pasting them to the walls of the cage in which the rats lived, the implication of the experiments is that simple exposure to particular sensory stimuli facilitates their later discrimination, and that this facilitation generalizes to the discrimination of similar forms. Forgus (1956) used a technique similar to that of Gibson, but varied the timing of the stimulus exposure as well. He used two experimental groups, one of which had earlier and the other later exposure to the forms on the cage walls. In a discrimination learning problem which used the same geometric forms as those to which the animals had been exposed, the early exposure group performed better than did the later exposure group, though both groups were superior to the control groups.

Another approach to the influence of stimulus exposure on perceptual discrimination is to be found in an experiment by Gibson and Gibson (1955). For stimulus material, they used one standard "scribble" and seventeen variations on it, plus twelve other items, easily distinguishable. All the stimuli were printed on cards. Each subject was first presented with the standard item and instructed to observe it carefully so that he could later identify it. Then a pack of stimulus cards was presented to the subject, one by one. The pack included seventeen variations, twelve additional items, and four cards depicting a scribble identical to the standard. The subject was asked only to indicate for each item whether it was the same or different from the standard. The examiner never indicated if the subject's response was correct or incorrect. After each card had been presented, the subject was shown the standard again, after which each of the stimulus cards was exposed again. A group of adult subjects and a group of children 8½ to 11 years of age achieved the criterion of an errorless run. Some of a group of younger children (6 to 8 years of age) achieved criterion, but most were not able to. In this experiment, as in the animal studies previously referred to, the subjects learned to discriminate simply as a result of the perceptual experience, independent of either motor acts or, in the case of the Gibson and Gibson experiment, reinforcement.

In combining the implications of the deprivation experiments and those from the enrichment studies, one can hypothesize that absence of stimulation will result in absence of perceptual discrimination, while presence of stimuli relevant to a later test task will result in enhanced discrimination learning over what would be found in simply a "usual" perceptual environment. These results in perceptual learning are consistent with those reported earlier for enhancement of motor development. It follows, then, that a perceptually richer environment would result in superior discrimination skill. This point should be kept in mind for the later consideration of the relationship of socioeconomic class to perceptual development.

The Gibsons' hypothesis about what is learned in perceptual learning is relevant here. They propose that what is learned is the detection of the distinctive feature of a stimulus: its relevant dimensions (that is, relevant for the learning task posed). Exposure to the stimulus, and particularly exposure to it in conjunction with similar but discriminable stimuli, gives the subject the opportunity to define the distinctive features of a stimulus and thus to differentiate it from other stimuli. This view is consistent with Zeaman's and House's "attention theory" of discrimination learning (1962). They believe that before discrimination learning can occur, the subject must attend to the relevant dimension of the stimulus. Their training of subjects was oriented to emphasizing the relevant features of stimuli. While their experiments have been done on retarded subjects, the theory is generalizable to the learning of nonretarded individuals as well.

If perceptual discrimination proceeds as a result of the definition of the distinctive features of stimuli, then it follows that any activity which emphasizes such distinctive features would enhance a subject's discrimination learning. From the Gibsons' and Forgus' experiments discussed above, it would appear that mere prior experience with a given stimulus has this effect. Another activity which enhances the learning of discrimination is labeling of the stimuli. Ellis and Muller (1964) and Ranken (1963) used labels chosen on the basis of their appropriateness to the nonsense shapes that constituted the discrimination stimuli. In both experiments, it was found that the verbal labels improved the subjects' later recognition of the forms more than the improvement in recognition provided by simple prior observation of the forms. This improvement with labels varied with the complexity of the forms, being least for the simplest forms.

There are certain seemingly consistent changes in perception as children get older, and a brief examination of these is relevant to the cue differentiation discussed above, and to some hypotheses which follow. No attempt can be made here to be thorough in examining developmental factors in perception. Rather, let us consider only the perception of visual illusions, and the measurement of constant errors. Young children are less susceptible to the vertical-horizontal illusion, for example, and there are a few experiments which show a similar departure from veridicality with increasing age.[3] Wapner and Werner (1957), for instance, report that the younger the child, the smaller is the constant error in adjusting a line to the vertical under conditions of body tilt. Similar decrease with age in veridicality of judgments of the locus of a click sound under conditions of body tilt was reported by Liebert and Rudel (1959). One explanation for these findings is that as the child grows older, he relies more and more on his own past experience in making perceptual judgments, and as a result becomes less "field dependent." Accordingly, stated Wohlwill (1960), while the young child is dependent on redundancy in stimulation (repetition of the same stimuli) in order to perceive stimuli correctly and to perform accurate discriminations between stimuli, he becomes less so as a function of age and accumulated experience.

Gibson (1963) rejects the emphasis on redundancy in explaining the acquisition of perceptual discrimination, preferring to hypothesize a "need for the education of attention to distinctive features of the world and of things" (p. 189).

The present writer would like to suggest a compromise of sorts which would allow for the potential validity of both hypotheses by subsuming one in the other. Perhaps repetition of stimuli (redundancy), both within the same stimulus modality and between modalities, is one way by which stimuli acquire their distinctiveness for the individual. For example, it might be that less repetition would be necessary for learning a particular discrimination if a direct method for conveying the relevant stimulus dimensions were employed. In this way, redundancy and some other method could complement one another in a given circumstance. (A complicating factor here would be length of stimulus exposure, and the confounding, especially in the auditory modality, of repetition of the same stimulus with the time span within which it is presented. But time could be controlled experimentally.) Or perhaps redundancy would be unnecessary if a direct method of "educating the perception" were potent enough. Conversely, with little attempt at such "education" more redundancy would be necessary.

SOCIAL ENVIRONMENT AND PERCEPTION

The initial questions posed in this paper had to do with the influence of the conditions of life of the individual on his perception. In the context of the foregoing discussion of the importance of experience to per-

---

[3] The cross-cultural studies reported by Segall, Campbell, and Herskovits (1966) indicate that the visual environment of individuals (that is, their past perceptual experiences) influences their susceptibility to these illusions.

ception, we assume that different life conditions will provide different kinds and amounts of perceptual stimuli, and therefore of perceptual experience, for the individual. This is substantiated by the findings of Segall, Campbell, and Herskovits (1966)[4] with respect to the susceptibility to visual illusions of different cultural groups. They conclude:

> Perception is an aspect of human behavior, and as such it is subject to many of the same influences that shape other aspects of behavior . . . (ours and others) findings point to the conclusion that to a substantial extent we learn to perceive; that in spite of the phenomenally absolute character of our perceptions, they are determined by perceptual inference habits; and that various inference habits are differentially likely in different societies (pp. 213–214).

To categorize "conditions of life" within our own culture we can use the shorthand of socioeconomic status (*SES*) designations. In essence, relating *SES* to amount of stimuli available to the child means that we are hypothesizing that children who come from homes having a higher income and higher educational attainment on the part of parents will, on the average, be exposed to a different and richer stimulus environment from those who come from less privileged homes. The phrase "on the average" must be considered to have substantial importance, inasmuch as *SES* is a rough indicator at best, and no group defined by it can be considered homogeneous.

There is very little work on the effects of environment defined in this way on any element of development or on any set of traits. The most work which exists is in the field of intelligence, and conclusions reached there are patently inadequate because of the culture-boundedness of the test measures used. Given the intelligence tests in use, the lower *SES* group obtains lower scores than does the middle-class group. Since the current intelligence tests correlate very highly with school success, it should be no surprise to find that children from the slums do more poorly in school, and that this fact can be seen in the differential reading retardation rates between middle-class and lower-class school children. These findings cannot be considered explanatory, but simply descriptive. The task remains of defining the mediating variables between lower-class status and inferior scholastic and intelligence test performance.

It would follow from the foregoing discussion of perceptual performance that one set of mediating variables might be found in the nature of the stimuli to which the lower-class child is exposed, and in his oppor-

---

[4] This is a monumental study of cross-cultural comparisons which is mentioned only briefly here because the area as a whole is outside the scope of this chapter. There have, however, been few such comparisons of perceptual processes, and most of those reported at all have been by-products of anthropological field studies which had other main foci.

tunity to learn the relevant dimensions of those which are most closely related to the demands of schoolwork.

The slum child is more likely than the middle-class child to live in a crowded, cluttered home—but not cluttered with objects which can be playthings for him. There is likely to be less variety of stimuli in the home, and less continuity between home and school objects. Where money for food and basic clothing is a problem, there is little for children's playthings, for furniture in which to store the family possessions, and for decorative objects in the home. Where parents are poorly educated, there is likely to be less verbal interaction with the child, and less labeling of objects (or of the distinctive properties of stimuli) for the child. There is less stress on encouraging the production of labels by the child, and on teaching him the more subtle differentiations between stimuli (for example, knowing color names and identifying them). Thus, in the terms used earlier, the slum child has, in his stimulus field, both less redundancy and less education of his attention to the relevant properties of stimuli. As a result, he could be expected to come to school with poorer discrimination performance than his middle-class counterpart.

How true this assumption is must be determined by further research; the attempt to define perceptual differences on the basis of social class factors is a very recent one. Covington's data (1967) are especially important here, therefore. In a thirty-item task requiring discrimination between abstract visual stimuli, he found that the lower-SES sample of children had initial scores substantially lower than the middle-SES group. Control and experimental groups were established within each status group. The control groups had a daily period of exposure to pictures of animals, while the experimental groups had the same amount of exposure to the abstract test forms. For both groups, the instructions for the daily presentation were simply to look at the pictures. On post-testing with the discrimination test, it was found that both experimental groups profited from the exposure to the test forms, but for the lower-status experimental group the gain was almost double that of the upper-status experimental group. In terms of level of final score, the upper-status and lower-status experimental groups obtained average scores very similar to each other, while the difference between control groups was maintained.

This experiment illustrates two major points: (1) the lower-status child was at an initial disadvantage in the perceptual discrimination task, and (2) relevant stimulation (experience with the test forms) can mean more to the performance of the lower-status child than to the performance of the child with an initially superior score.

We will return later to a consideration of the second point. First, let us consider the auditory modality. At the Institute for Developmental

Studies we have been conducting a series of auditory studies which are relevant to the argument advanced. We have reported that children who are retarded in reading have poorer auditory discrimination, as measured by the Wepman auditory discrimination test, than do children who are reading at or beyond grade level (Deutsch, 1964). With the fact that disadvantaged children have a higher rate of reading retardation, interest centers on the possibility that disadvantaged children also might have poorer auditory discrimination. A study of auditory perceptual performance of lower-class and middle-class first-, third-, and fifth-grade children is currently underway and therefore data cannot yet be reported on a large (180 children) sample. However, using small samples, McArdle found young middle-class children to be significantly superior to lower-class children of the same age on a modification of the Boston University Speech Sounds Test (1965). Clark and Richards (1966) report similar findings with the Wepman on samples of nursery-age children enrolled in Head Start and in private nursery school classes. In seeking to differentiate findings further, the performance of our own samples of retarded and nonretarded readers were analyzed in terms of the errors made when the phonemic difference occurred at the beginning of words, as compared with the errors made on end-phoneme comparisons. It was found that the major differences between the two groups occurred on the word-end comparisons, though some of the group differences on initial phoneme comparisons were also significant. This finding supports the assumption of social-class differences in auditory discrimination based on differential stimulus exposure, inasmuch as in the dialects most prevalent in slum areas, the endings of words tend to be slurred. Further, in beginning reading instruction in school, it is the initial phonemes of words which are stressed—and this experience may be one of the factors in our findings, since children were tested after they had had some reading training.

EDUCATIONAL APPLICATIONS AND

IMPLICATIONS

While it would appear that there is good theoretical justification for assuming a social-class-perceptual process relationship, and that the data in existence are consistent with this hypothesis, nevertheless scientific parsimony demands skepticism until more data are available. However, human considerations equally demand that the implications of such theories and hypotheses be taken seriously and acted upon before the data are in. A program designed to enhance perceptual skills by placing stimuli in the environment and by training the children to attend to the distinctive features of the stimuli can hardly be detrimental, even if ultimately some or all of the hypotheses and theoretical formulations are disconfirmed. On the other hand, doing nothing could mean allowing children to grow up with subtle handicaps, should these formulations be correct. The implication of the Covington findings, mentioned earlier, that relevant stimulation can mean more to the performance of the lower-status, lower-scoring child than to the performance of the middle-class child with an initially higher score, makes it all the more impera-tive that we institute programs based on the currently fragmentary data. The child who has the most to gain is the one for whom the stimuli are most apt to be lacking at home.

New programs should focus on providing appropriate stimulus expo-sure, and on training children to attend to the aspects of stimuli that are relevant for discrimination. Several methods can be used, involving the engineering of attention by proper organization of the stimulus field and/or by appropriate explanation to the child. The latter type of atten-tion engineering is practiced by good teachers generally; the researcher might contribute data on which stimulus aspects are most salient for what kinds of discriminations, but the verbal and demonstration methods are familiar and are typically taught as part of the education of teachers.

The engineering of attention by organization of the stimulus field is another matter. The typical classroom for young children contains so many visual and auditory stimuli, organized and arranged with so little regard for one another, that it is often a model for how to bury the relevant cues for each stimulus. The same perceptual principles used so effectively by advertisers can, however, be applied to classroom organization and to the design of books and equipment. Visual stimuli can be spaced and organized so that the relevant dimensions are empha-sized. For example, a display intending to illustrate color differences can be composed of elements of the same material and size and shape, differing only on the color dimension. In this way, the child's attention would be directed to the relevant parameter, and he would not be confused by differences in irrelevant dimensions such as size and shape. Materials which exemplify this principle are those developed by Montes-sori and her followers. In the Montessori materials, only one stimulus attribute varies at a time. Thus, when materials are oriented to size concepts, they are all the same shape and color; when they are oriented to weight, they are all the same size, shape, and color, and so on. Con-trast the Montessori wooden circles of decreasing diameter which fit on a stick with those commercially available: the Montessori materials are all of polished natural wood, while the kind most often seen in stores— and in kindergartens—are painted so that each is a different color. If it is hoped that the child will gain a concept of size differentials by manipulating these materials, the different colors can only offer distrac-tions, in addition to making it almost impossible for the teacher or observer to determine the basis for a child's incorrect performance: when he produces a haphazard size sequence, he might actually be responding to aspects of the colors of the circles. It is quite possible to engineer the child's attention to what is planned as the relevant aspect of the stimulus by holding the other parameters constant.

Placement of visual stimuli can also help to heighten their value. Stimuli on the blackboard behind the teacher can only distract from what she is saying, and suffer by the distraction of her voice when the child is observing them, unless they are directly relevant to the lesson being presented. Visual displays at the back of the room, on the other hand, will not suffer from auditory lesson competition. Spacing of visual displays can lessen the "noise" of their impingement on each other.

In the auditory modality the same principles hold. Whatever can be done to minimize the intrusion of traffic and other external noises in the classroom should be done: the quieter the classroom, the more the planned auditory stimulus becomes a compelling signal. Here, too, the use of earphones and taped stories and listening centers can be very effective in presenting stimuli with a minimum of ambient noise intrusion. Extrapolating from the finding that exposure helps the child to attend to the relevant cues, one could hypothesize that using a listening center will help a child later attend to the relevant auditory stimuli coming from the teacher in a group lesson; that is, his listening can be trained under conditions of greater figure-ground contrast, and this training will transfer to conditions of lesser contrast.

In addition to engineering the presentation of information and materials so as to enhance the attention-getting power of the most relevant aspects, more practice in discrimination can be provided as a by-product of everyday classroom activities. Blocks of the same diameter but of different lengths can be stacked on shelves so that they are viewed from the side, and the child is exposed to the differences, rather than the similarities, among them. Beads can be stored in color groups in clear plastic boxes, so that the color differences can be clearly seen, and when they are replaced after use, the child can help to sort them into the correct boxes. A thoughtful teacher can think of a hundred similar methods to provide discrimination practice.

This paper has attempted to examine in historical perspective some of the important current issues in the study of environment-perception relationships, and to relate them to educational concerns. The latter application arises not so much from perceptual theories themselves as from the understanding that perceptual processes underlie and relate to many of the skills taught in school. Reading, of course, is a prime example. Explication of experience-perception relationships on the one hand, and perception-school performance relationships on the other, should yield information of great importance to an understanding of the role of social background factors in school performance. Therefore, it should contribute both to theoretical understanding and to the solving of practical problems connected with the attempt to provide a quality education for all children.

References

Asch, S. E. *Social psychology*. New York: Prentice-Hall, 1952.

————. *Studies of independence and submission to group pressure. I. A minority of one against a unanimous majority*. Swarthmore, Pa.: Swarthmore College. Author, 1955 (mimeo).

Boring, E. G. *Sensation and perception in the history of experimental psychology*. New York and London: Appleton-Century-Crofts, 1942.

Brazier, Mary A. B., K. F. Killam, and A. J. Hance. "The reactivity of the nervous system in the light of the past: a story of the organism." In W. Rosenblith (ed.), *Sensory communication*. Cambridge, Mass.: MIT Press, and New York: Wiley, 1961.

Bruner, J. S. "The cognitive consequences of early sensory deprivation." In Philip Solomon *et al.* (ed.), *Sensory deprivation*. Cambridge, Mass.: Harvard University Press, 1961, pp. 195–207.

Clark, Ann D., and Charlotte J. Richards. Auditory discrimination among economically disadvantaged and non-disadvantaged pre-school children. *Exceptional Children*, Dec. 1966, 259–262.

Covington, M. V. Stimulus deprivation as a function of social class membership. *Child Development*, 1967, **38**, 2, 607.

Dennis, W. Causes of retardation among institutional children. *Journal of Genetic Psychology*, 1960, **96**, 47–59.

————, and Marsena G. Dennis. The effect of cradling practice upon the onset of walking in Hopi children. *Journal of Genetic Psychology*, 1940, **56** (77), 86.

Deutsch, Cynthia P. Auditory discrimination and learning: Social factors. *Merrill-Palmer Quarterly*, 1964, **10** (3), 277–296.

Ellis, H. C., and D. G. Muller. Transfer in perceptual learning following stimulus predifferentiation. *Journal of Experimental Psychology*, 1964, **68**, 388–395.

Epstein, W. Experimental investigations of the genesis of visual space perception. *Psychological Bulletin*, 1964, **61**, 115–128.

————. *Varieties of perceptual learning*. New York: McGraw-Hill, 1967.

Forgus, R. H. Advantage of early over late perceptual experience in improving form discrimination. *Canadian Journal of Psychology*, 1956, **10**, 147–155.

Fuller, J. L., and W. R. Thompson. *Behavior genetics*. New York: Wiley, 1960.

Galton, F. *English men of science*. New York: Appleton-Century-Crofts, 1875.

————. *Hereditary genius: An inquiry into its laws and consequences*. London: Macmillan, 1914.

Gibson, Eleanor J. "Perceptual development." In H. W. Stevenson with the assistance of J. Kagan and C. Spiker (ed.), *Child psychology, the 62nd yearbook of the National Society for the Study of Education, Part I*. Chicago: National Society for the Study of Education, 1963.

————, and R. D. Walk. The effect of prolonged exposures to visually presented patterns on learning to discriminate them. *Journal of Comparative and Physiological Psychology,* 1956, **49**, 239–242.

————, R. D. Walk, H. L. Pick, and T. J. Tighe. The effect of prolonged exposure to visual patterns on learning to discriminate similar and different patterns. *Journal of Comparative and Physiological Psychology,* 1958, **51**, 584–587.

Gibson, J. J. "Perception as a function of stimulation." In S. Koch (ed.), *Psychology: A study of science.* Study I, Vol. I. New York: McGraw-Hill, 1959, 456–501.

————, and Eleanor J. Gibson. Perceptual learning: Differentiation or enrichment? *Psychological Review,* 1955, **62**, 32–41.

Goddard, H. H. *The Kallikak Family: A study in the heredity of feeblemindedness.* New York: Macmillan, 1912.

Gregory, R. L., and J. G. Wallace. Recovery from early blindness. *Experimental Psychology Monograph,* 1963, Whole No. 2. Cambridge, England.

Hebb, D. O. The motivating effects of exteroceptive stimulation. *American Psychologist,* 1958, **13**, 109.

Hernández-Peón, R. "Reticular mechanisms of sensory control." In W. Rosenblith (ed.), *Sensory communication.* Cambridge, Mass.: MIT Press, and New York: Wiley, 1961.

Heron, W. "Cognitive and physiological effects of perceptual isolation." In Philip Solomon *et al.* (ed.), *Sensory deprivation.* Cambridge, Mass.: Harvard University Press, 1961, 6–33.

Hunt, J. McV. *Intelligence and experience.* New York: Ronald Press, 1961.

Kawi, A. A., and B. Pasamanick. Prenatal and paranatal factors in the development of childhood reading disorder. *Society for Research in Child Development Monograph,* 1959, **24** (4), Whole No. 73.

Knobloch, Hilda, and B. Pasamanick. Mental subnormality. *New England Journal of Medicine,* 1962, **266** (20).

Koffka, K. *Principles of Gestalt psychology.* New York: Harcourt, Brace & World, 1935.

Köhler, W. *Dynamics in psychology.* New York: Liveright, 1940.

Krech, D., S. Crutchfield, and L. B. Egerton. *Individual in society: A textbook of social psychology.* New York: McGraw-Hill, 1962.

Levine, R., I. Chein, and G. Murphy. The relation of the intensity of a need to the amount of perceptual distortion. *Journal of Psychology,* 1942, **13**, 283–293.

Lewin, K., *Principles of topological psychology.* Translated by F. Heider and Grace M. Heider. New York and London: McGraw-Hill, 1936.

Liebert, R. S., and Rita G. Rudel. Auditory localization and adaptation to body tilt: A developmental study. *Child Development,* 1959, **30**, 81–90.

London, I. A Russian report on the post-operative newly seeing. *American Journal of Psychology,* 1960, **73**, 478–482.

McArdle, Maureen T. *Auditory discrimination in preschool children.* Unpublished master's thesis, University of Tennessee, 1965.

Morruzzi, G., and H. W. Magoun. Brain stem reticular formation and activation of the EEG. *EEG and Clinical Neurophysiology,* 1949, **1**, 455–473.

Pasamanick, B., and Hilda Knobloch. "Epidemiologic studies on the complications of pregnancy and the birth process." In G. Caplan (ed.), *Prevention of mental disorders in children.* New York: Basic Books, 1961.

Pastore, N. Perceiving as innately determined. *Journal of Genetic Psychology,* 1960, **96**, 93–99.

Ranken, H. B. Effects of name learning on serial learning, position learning, and recognition learning with random shapes. *Psychological Reports,* 1963, **13,** 663–678.

Riesen, A. H. The development of visual perception in man and chimpanzee. *Science,* 1947, **106,** 107–108.

————, K. L. Chow, J. Semmes, and H. W. Nissen. Chimpanzee vision after four conditions of light deprivation. *American Psychologist,* 1951, **6,** 282 (Abstract).

————. "Plasticity of behavior: Psychological aspects." In H. F. Harlow and C. N. Woolsey (ed.), *Biological and biochemical bases of behavior.* Madison, Wis.: University of Wisconsin Press, 1958.

Segall, M. H., D. T. Campbell, and M. J. Herskovits. *The influence of culture on visual perception.* Indianapolis: Bobbs-Merrill, 1966.

Sherif, M. A study of some social factors in perception. *Archives of Psychology,* 1935, No. 187.

Titchener, E. B. *Experimental psychology of the thought process.* New York: Macmillan, 1909.

Von Senden, M. *Raum und Gestaltauffassung bei operierten Blindgeborener von und nach der Operation.* Leipzig: Barth, 1932. Cited by D. O. Hebb, *The organization of behavior.* New York: Wiley, 1949, 28–31.

Wapner, S., and H. Werner. *Perceptual development: An investigation within the framework of sensory-tonic field theory.* Worcester, Mass.: Clark University Press, 1957.

White, B. L., Informal education during the first months of life. Paper presented at the Social Science Research Council Conference on Pre-School Education, February 8, 1966.

————, P. Castle, and R. Held. Observations on the development of visually-directed reaching. *Child Development,* 1964, **35** (2), 349–364.

Witkin, H. A., *et al. Personality through perception: An experimental and clinical study.* New York: Harper & Row, 1954.

Wohlwill, J. F. Developmental studies of perception. *Psychological Bulletin,* 1960, **57,** 249–288.

Zeaman, D., and B. J. House. An attention theory of retardate discrimination learning. *Progress Report No. 3* (Research Grant M-1099), National Institute of Mental Health, Bethesda, Md., November 1962.

Zubin, J., L. D. Eron, and Florence Schumer. *An experimental approach to projective techniques.* New York: Wiley, 1965.

CHAPTER THREE

Social Disadvantage as Related to Intellective and Language Development[1]

MARTIN WHITEMAN[2]
and MARTIN DEUTSCH[3]

One of the writers often drives through East Harlem on his way to work. There is a school on 111th Street, and as he stopped for a light one morning he noticed two Negro children, about ten years old, having a bit of friendly horseplay before going to class. One was banging the other over the head playfully with a notebook. But the notebook slipped out of his hand and fell into a puddle of water. The two children stared at the notebook and then suddenly turned toward each other with gales of laughter and walked off toward school arm in arm and without the notebook. A policeman who had been standing nearby walked over to the puddle and stared at the notebook with some degree of disbelief.

[1] The research on which this report is based was sponsored by grants from the Taconic Foundation and the National Institute of Mental Health (Grant No. MH1098–03). In addition, we wish to acknowledge the support of the United States Office of Education and the Office of Economic Opportunity. A preliminary report of these data was presented at the Conference on Cultural Deprivation and Enrichment Programs held at Yeshiva University, April 1965. Estelle Peisach, Barbara Cohen, and Norman Wein helped in the statistical analyses.

[2] Columbia University School of Social Work; Consultant, Institute for Developmental Studies, School of Education, New York University.

[3] Institute for Developmental Studies, School of Education, New York University.

This event can be understood in terms of a discontinuity between school requirements and the child's prior preparation and experiences. The child from a disadvantaged environment may have missed some of the experiences necessary for developing verbal, conceptual, attentional, and learning skills requisite to school success. These skills play a vital role for the child in his understanding of the language of the school and the teacher, in his adapting to school routines, and in his mastery of such a fundamental tool subject as reading. In this absence of the development of these skills by the child, there is a progressive alienation of teacher from child and child from teacher. In the school, the child may suffer from feelings of inferiority because he is failing; he withdraws or becomes hostile, finding gratifications elsewhere, such as in his peer group. Notebooks may be left in puddles while the camaraderie develops.

The teacher often feels inferior because she is failing too—but she can blame the child's family, or she can assign her difficulties to what she considers the child's essential unteachability. This progressive alienation contributes to the cumulative deficit observed in experientially deprived children, that is, the decline, over time, in their scholastic achievements and in measures of "intellectual abilities."

This developmental conception has both research and action implications. From a research point of view, it would be important to examine very closely, on the one hand, the relation between family background and cognitive and learning skills, and, on the other hand, how these underlying abilities influence the performance of the child in the school situation. From an action point of view, it would seem reasonable to conclude that if learning sets or the level of underlying abilities are influential in a decline in performance, an improvement of these skills through an early enrichment program at the preschool and kindergarten levels may be helpful in arresting or reversing the cumulative deficit.

The Institute for Developmental Studies is engaged in both research and enrichment programs focused on the cognitive learnings and abilities of so-called disadvantaged children. The work to be discussed here is based on a conception of linguistic and cognitive factors as crucial intervening variables between environmental impact on the one hand and scholastic achievement on the other.

One of the major aims of a study of the verbal performance of first- and fifth-grade children (referred to as the "Verbal Survey") has been to identify some of the specific background variables which are related to the development of linguistic and cognitive skills. Accordingly, we have tried to obtain information about the child's social background which would go beyond the basic facts of the parent's occupation, education, and race.

The sample comprised 165 fifth- and 127 first-grade children. These were drawn from twelve schools in New York City, which were selected to provide a population varying in socioeconomic status (*SES*) and race, as well as one from which a sample could be drawn with comparable *SES* variation within each.

In order to check on this a priori selection of the schools, the census characteristics of the tracts in which the schools were located were analyzed. The median education and income level of these census tracts were calculated. In these computations, each census tract was weighted in proportion to its contribution (in size and population) to the area actually serviced by the school. The schools designated as more lower-class recruited from populations with lesser schooling (median of 8.7 years completed as compared to 10.7 for the more middle-class areas). This education difference was similar in both the Negro and white tracts.

The income differences between the "more middle"- and "more lower"-class groups were less apparent. This is attributable to the fact that income differences between these two groups among the predominantly white tracts were less than the comparable differences among those in the tracts which were mainly Negro. The educational and income medians for the twelve schools is fairly close to the over-all New York City figures.

On the basis of a screening interview, information was obtained from the children relating to the employment of persons living in the home. Children were tentatively assigned to *SES* levels to determine if the desired cell sizes were being attained. A mail questionnaire was sent to the guardians of all children provisionally selected. This questionnaire elicited information on the education and occupational status of the parents and/or the main support of the family. Twenty percent of the families did not return the mail questionnaire. In these cases, staff members interviewed the families in the home to secure the information on parental educational and occupational background.

The *SES* categorization was derived from the main support's education, and his occupation as assessed by the Empey Scale of Occupational Prestige (Empey, 1956). The correlation between the two variables in our sample was 0.60. The *SES* index correlated over 0.90 with the Hollingshead Two Factor Index of Social Position (Hollingshead and Redlich, 1958). A centroid factor analysis of the background data revealed a first factor which was loaded 0.88, 0.75, and 0.92 on education, occupation, and the *SES* index respectively. In addition, the *SES* index was found to be significantly related in this sample with such conditions as greater crowdedness in the household; greater dilapidation in the neighborhood surrounding the household; lower parental aspirations for the child's first job; lower educational level desired by the parent for the child; lower occupational aspiration reported by the child; absence of father in the home; parental perception of lower status in society (see Bloom *et al.,* 1965).

The lower trichotomy (*SES I*) of the index contained individuals mainly in the unskilled or semiskilled category with an average education at the seventh grade. The middle trichotomy (*SES II*) contained, in the main, those at a skilled worker or clerical level with between two and three years of high school. For the *SES III* group, the average education was two years of college with employment centered on the more professional, managerial, and technically trained statuses. The correlation between race and *SES* was 0.00 in the first grade and 0.08 in the fifth grade. This attests to the success of one of our sampling intentions, namely the elimination of a significant association between *SES* and race.

Some checks were made upon the adequacy of the sampling. Practically all the children in the first and fifth grades in the twelve schools had received the Lorge-Thorndike Intelligence Test (nonverbal form). From the 3212 children who had received this form, a random sample of 285 children was selected. The children were chosen according to the same criteria that had been used to select the original 292 children: native birth, no foreign language spoken in the home, attendance in northern schools, no repetition of the first grade, no school record of physical or emotional handicap. However, the information relevant to social-class assignment (education and occupation of head of the household) was not available for this group. Therefore social-class standing was estimated by means of a regression equation. The latter was derived from the Verbal Survey sample and yielded a multiple r of 0.49 between the *SES* index and a number of predictor variables of a demographic nature. This regression equation was then applied to the "synthetic sample" to estimate each child's *SES* standing. Table 3.1 reveals that in spite of the relatively low multiple r used in the estimation of social class in the synthetic sample, there is a rather close fit between the mean of the two samples when stratified by race, *SES,* and sex. None of the twenty-four comparisons yielded significant mean differences and only one of the obtained differences in standard deviations was significant (*SES I,* first grade). Though the comparisons are not independent, it is reassuring that only one of the forty-eight comparisons reached significance, and this significant comparison may be attributable to chance rather than real differences between the populations represented by the samples.

A second test of the sampling procedure involved a comparison between the first- and fifth-grade Verbal Survey samples with respect to significant background conditions. It was felt that any strong differences between older and younger children in the selection procedure would be reflected in such a comparison. Such a comparison would also be of additional value insofar as it would indicate whether cumulative deficits in special subgroups were specific or part of a generally worsening environmental picture associated either with the actual back-

TABLE 3.1

*N*s, IQ Means, and Sigmas for *SES*, Race, and Sex

Categories, Actual and Synthetic Samples and *t* Values

for Comparisons of the Two Samples

	Actual Sample			Synthetic Sample			
	N	*Mean*	S.D.[a]	*N*	*Mean*	S.D.[a]	*t*
			FIRST GRADE				
SES I	46	94.61	12.86	11	96.00	6.88	−0.49
II	45	102.69	13.52	122	101.52	15.99	0.44
III	36	108.00	14.11	18	110.39	9.76	−0.66
Negro	68	99.01	13.87	69	97.03	14.32	0.04
White	59	103.86	14.72	82	106.51	14.55	−1.05
Male	71	102.87	15.13	70	102.54	15.35	0.13
Female	56	99.23	13.33	81	101.86	15.08	−1.05
Total	127	101.27	14.42	151	102.18	15.16	0.52
			FIFTH GRADE				
SES I	64	94.09	16.29	16	91.31	17.73	0.17
II	54	102.65	15.97	86	101.52	15.66	0.38
III	47	110.04	15.21	32	106.69	16.45	0.95
Negro	84	95.39	14.52	65	96.22	15.78	0.23
White	81	107.70	17.37	69	106.55	15.79	0.40
Male	83	101.02	18.53	75	101.47	16.83	−0.16
Female	82	101.35	15.59	59	101.63	16.34	−0.10
Total	165	101.44	17.09	134	101.54	16.56	−0.08
			FIRST AND FIFTH GRADES COMBINED				
SES I	110	94.31	14.89	27	93.22	14.32	0.34
II	99	102.67	14.83	208	101.52	15.78	0.61
III	83	109.16	14.69	50	108.02	14.40	0.44
Negro	152	97.01	14.30	134	96.63	14.99	0.22
White	140	106.08	16.36	151	106.53	15.08	−0.25
Male	154	101.88	17.02	145	101.99	16.06	−0.06
Female	138	100.79	14.72	140	101.76	15.57	−0.53
Total	292	101.36	15.96	285	101.88	15.80	−0.39

[a] S.D., standard deviation.

grounds of the older children or with selective sampling among the older children.

Table 3.2 presents a comparison of the first- and fifth-grade samples with respect to a number of demographic and background conditions— sex, race, parental education and occupation, presence of father in home, family size, person-room ratio, kindergarten or day care experience. It can be seen that there is a close correspondence between the first- and fifth-graders relative to these factors. Of particular interest are the almost identical distributions of the two grades with respect to the *SES* variable.

SOCIAL DEPRIVATION: SOME CONCEPTUAL AND
METHODOLOGICAL CONSIDERATIONS

At this point, the relation between the concept of social deprivation and environmental background factors needs clarification. Specific environmental factors can be viewed as reflecting social deprivations when at least two conditions are fulfilled:

(a) when such factors are associated with certain social groupings, such as those of *SES* or race, *and*
(b) when they are associated with impaired performance, such as lowered academic achievement.

An environmental condition may be associated with a particular psychological deficit, but it would not be considered a social deprivation if the condition were not socially patterned. For example, a particular mode of child-rearing may be associated with cognitive deficits, but we would not consider this mode of child-rearing a social deprivation unless it were significantly located in a certain segment of the culture. Conversely, an environmental variable may be socially determined; it may be distributed rather heavily within a particular social group. But it would not be considered a deprivation unless it was also related to a functional or behavioral deficit.

The term "association" was used above in specifying the conditions under which environmental factors might be considered deprivational. From a broader conceptual viewpoint, the connotation of association changes, depending on whether the reference is to

(a) association between social grouping and environmental factor, *or*
(b) association between environmental factor and performance decrement.

Social deprivation implies that the association between social grouping and specific environmental factor is not directly causal, but is mediated by more basic societal conditions such as unemployment, poverty, and inequality of opportunity in various areas. With the removal of such conditions, the association between social grouping and disadvantaging factors may vanish. Social deprivation also implies that the association between environmental condition and performance decrement *is* directly causal, at least insofar as the disadvantaging factor hampers the learning of the performance in question.

TABLE 3.2

Comparison of First- and Fifth-Grade Samples on

Demographic and Background Characteristics

		First Grade (N = 127)	Fifth Grade (N = 165)	Total (N = 292)
1. Sex	Male	56%	50%	53%
	Female	44	50	47
2. Race	Negro	54	51	52
	White	46	49	48
3. Kindergarten	Yes	20	24	22
experience	No	80	74	76
	No response	0	2	1
4. Day care	Yes	17	24	21
experience	No	83	74	28
	No response	0	2	1
5. Education of	0–4 Years	0	0	0
father	5–6	4	4	4
	7–8	11	16	14
	Some high school	28	24	26
	HS grad.	26	27	27
	Some college	13	10	12
	College grad.	6	3	4
	Post grad.	8	8	8
	No response	5	7	6
6. Education of	0–4 Years	2	1	1
mother	5–6	2	3	2
	7–8	10	11	11
	Some high school	25	22	24
	HS grad.	37	38	38
	Some college	14	18	16
	College grad.	8	4	6
	Post grad.	1	2	2
	No response	1	1	1
7. Occupational	1	9	6	8
rating of main	2	17	16	16
support (Empey	3	22	19	21
Scale)	4	17	16	17
	5	16	14	15
	6	9	16	13
	7	5	5	5
	8	2	4	3
	9	3	2	3
	10	1	1	1
8. Socioeconomic	Lowest range	37	38	37
status	Medium "	35	35	35
	Highest "	28	27	28
9. Main support's	Unemployed	2	5	4
time on present	1 year	7	10	9
job	1–2	16	11	13
	3–4	10	10	10
	5–9	25	21	23

TABLE 3.2 *(Continued)*

		First Grade (N = 127)	Fifth Grade (N = 165)	Total (N = 292)
	10+	36%	41%	39%
	No response	4	3	4
10. Relation of present job(s) to other jobs held within past 10 years (as rated by Empey Scale)	Lower	13	11	12
	Same	61	60	60
	Higher	13	15	14
	No response	13	15	14
11. Parent's estimate of present mobility	Going down	1	2	2
	Stay same	30	33	32
	Going up	66	61	63
	No response	3	3	3
12. Presence of father in home	No	13	15	14
	Yes	84	80	82
	No response	2	5	4
13. Number in home 18 years old or over	1 person	6	7	7
	2	77	73	74
	3	7	12	10
	4	3	2	3
	5	2	1	1
	6+	0	1	1
	No response	5	4	4
14. Number in home under 18 years old	1	7	16	12
	2	36	43	40
	3	29	18	23
	4	9	10	10
	5	5	3	4
	6	6	3	4
	7	2	2	2
	8	0	1	1
	9	1	1	1
	No response	5	3	4
15. Number of rooms in home	1	0	1	1
	2	6	10	8
	3	43	39	41
	4	31	28	30
	5	13	13	13
	6	6	4	5
	7	0	2	1
	8	1	1	1
	9	1	1	1
16. Person-to-room ratio	1.0 or Less	9	6	8
	1.1–1.2	16	16	16
	1.3–1.4	22	19	20
	1.5–1.6	17	16	17
	1.7–1.8	16	14	15
	1.9–2.0	9	16	13
	2.1–2.2	5	5	5
	2.3–2.4	2	4	3
	2.5–2.6	3	2	3
	2.7–2.8	1	1	1

From this discussion it follows that *social deprivation* is a relative term. It is relative in two senses. First, a given environmental factor may be deprivational relative to one social group, for example, low *SES,* but not deprivational relative to another social group, for example, Negro. Second, the environmental factor may be deprivational with respect to one ability or performance, but neutral, or even advantageous, with respect to other behaviors or functions.

In our study of social deprivations, both conceptual and empirical steps are involved. The conceptual step is to delineate environmental conditions that, on an a priori basis, might qualify as social deprivations. In our study we have selected fifteen such conditions from a broader array of over thirty background variables on which data were available. These fifteen factors include motivational variables, such as the amount of school the parent desires for the child; factors related to family structure, such as whether or not there is a father in the home; variables related to parental interaction; to activities with adults; and to school experiences. The empirical step stems directly from our two-point concept of social deprivation: each of these fifteen variables is studied from the two vantage points of

(a) whether it is related to an important psychological function such as reading, *and*
(b) whether it is related to an important social grouping such as *SES.*

The environmental conditions which meet these dual criteria are then viewed as social deprivations. There are six such variables which have been combined into a composite score, a "Deprivation Index." The particular items and the mode of combination will be described later. First it is appropriate to summarize some of the functions which such an index can serve. The Index can play the role of *specifier:* it contains specific environmental features meeting criteria of social deprivation that we have designated above. It can play the role of *mediator:* it can help account, at least partially, for the relation between *SES* and scores on ability tests. The Deprivation Index can also play the role of *independent contributor:* it is a set of environmental conditions which accounts for aspects of performance not accounted for by *SES* or race. Finally it can serve as an *interactive variable.* Thus it may, in combination with other background factors, serve to account for performance over and beyond the contribution of the background variables taken singly.

INTERCORRELATIONS AMONG MEASURES OF BACKGROUND, ABILITY, AND ACHIEVEMENT

Table 3.3 lists the background variables under several headings— social background, economic and motivational aspects, familial setting, and educational experiences—both with the parents, and in more formal settings. The relation between the specific background factors and reading score is also shown. It can be seen that at the fifth-grade level, the kinds of background factors which correlate significantly with reading achievement are of a varied order. There are aspects dealing with the child's physical surroundings, as housing dilapidation is associated with lowered reading scores (Item 4 in Table 3.3). Of course, motivational aspects are significant, as the parent's educational aspiration for the child is related to a higher reading score. The familial composition (Item 9) plays a role—the larger the family size the lower the reading score.

TABLE 3.3

Correlations between Environmental Conditions and

Gates Reading Test and *SES* Index

(Grade 5, $N = 167$)

	Correlations with:	
	Gates Reading Test	SES Index
Social background		
1. *SES* index	0.44[a]	
2. Education, main support	0.45[a]	
3. Occupation, main support	0.35[a]	
Economic aspects		
4. Housing condition	0.28[a]	0.27[a]
Motivational aspects		
5. Parental schooling desired for child	0.32[a]	0.31[a]
6. Parent's first choice for child's job	0.16	0.23[a]
7. Parent's estimate of child's probable job	0.05	0.22[a]
Familial setting		
8. Father in home	0.12	0.28[a]
9. Number of children under 18	−0.29[a]	−0.20[a]
Educational experiences		
Parental interaction		
10. Presence of mother with child at breakfast	0.11	0.09
11. Presence of mother with child at dinner	0.04	0.09
12. Presence of father with child at dinner	−0.06	0.09
13. Conversation during dinner	0.22[a]	0.28[a]
Activities with adults		
14. Number of anticipated activities with relatives	−0.05	0.09
15. Number of anticipated cultural activities	0.25[a]	0.28[a]
School experiences		
16. Kindergarten attendance	0.20[a]	0.20[a]
17. Day-care attendance	0.03	0.03
18. School utility rating	0.11	−0.11

[a] Significant at 0.01 level.

Interaction and activities with parents and relatives are important. Thus higher reading levels are found among those children reporting conversations with parents during dinner (Item 13) or those who have the opportunity to broaden their experiences by visits with parents to such cultural sites as zoos and museums (Item 15). Finally those children score higher in reading who have had the benefit of a kindergarten experience (Item 16).

It can also be seen from Table 3.3 that each of these six variables is significantly related to the gross measure of socioeconomic status which is derived from parental education and occupation.

By contrast, there are nine background variables which are not significantly related to reading. Of these, only three are related to the *SES* measure. Thus there are six background variables which have an interesting dual relationship. On the one hand they show statistically significant associations with socioeconomic status, and on the other hand they are significantly associated with a scholastic achievement— reading. It is plausible to assume that the six items form a set of an interactive sort, a set which affords a specification of how the socioeconomic status of the home affects the scholastic achievement of the child. A comparison of those items which do and do not relate to reading points up the importance of the quality of the child's interaction with parents and other adults. Thus the sheer presence of mother or father at mealtimes (Items 10, 11, and 12 in Table 3.3) is not significantly related to reading. However, conversation with parents during dinner is related to reading. The sheer number of activities with parents or relatives (Item 14) is not associated with reading, but the number of *cultural* activities (Item 15) is. A reduced family size (Item 9) and kindergarten attendance (Item 16) allow more opportunity for stimulating interaction between adults and children, a factor which is in all probability reflected in the efficacy of increased parental scholastic aspiration for the child (Item 5).

Thus far we have been inspecting both ends of a hypothesized causal sequence comprising environmental background, ability patterns, and scholastic achievement. With the data, we can now explore some of the abilities underlying reading and the relation of these abilities to the background conditions.

Three tests are most highly correlated with the Gates Reading Score. These are the Lorge-Thorndike IQ, the WISC Vocabulary, and the Orientation Scale, which is a verbal test tapping the child's fund of general information and conceptual understanding.

The cognitive skills underlying reading at the fifth-grade level then involve a grasp of the relationships among ideas (as tapped by the Lorge-Thorndike IQ), verbal facility and knowledge (as assessed by the WISC), and a fund of basic factual and conceptual information (as measured by the Orientation Scale).

Table 3.4 brings together the variables related to environmental background, underlying abilities, and the reading achievement score with a view toward exploring their interrelation. If we work through the hypothesized causal sequence, we see, under Bracket A of Table 3.4, that the *SES* Index is significantly related to each of the specific environmental conditions, as noted above. Under Bracket B are listed the correlations between environmental conditions and the three underlying abilities. Of the eighteen correlations, sixteen are significant at the 0.01 level. Under Bracket C, the final section of the causal sequence is shown, that is, the correlations, all ranging above the 0.60 mark, between the abilities, as manifested in the three tests, and reading achievement. Several points might be noted. First, the correlations between the abilities and the achievement variable, reading, are higher than those between environmental conditions and reading (compare Brackets C and F). The median correlation between abilities and reading is 0.64 as compared to a median correlation of 0.27 between environmental conditions and reading. This suggests that these abilities may be exerting a more direct influence on reading than the more "distant" background variables. There is consistency here with the notion that environmental conditions exert their influence on underlying skills which in turn more directly affect the development of reading skills. Second, the interrelationships among the six environmental conditions and among the three tests deserve separate attention. With respect to the former, it can be seen from the coefficients under Bracket D that the interrelationships among the environmental conditions tend to be low. Thus the median of the fifteen coefficients is only 0.17. The suggestion here is that these conditions tend to show a fair degree of independence from one another. This implies that these conditions may exert their maximum effect on abilities and on achievement by means of their cumulative interaction rather than as separate representatives of some one underlying deprivational condition. The multiple correlation coefficient expressing the relation between the cumulative effect of the six environmental conditions on reading score is 0.49.[4] This may be compared to 0.32, which is the highest correlation between any specific environmental condition and reading, or to 0.27, the median coefficient between environmental conditions and reading level. If one adds the *SES* Index and the underlying abilities as independent variables, that is, brings in environmental background *and* underlying abilities as independent variables, the multiple *r* increases to 0.74.

By way of contrast to the relatively low intercorrelation among the

---

[4] The multiple *r* of 0.49 is below the zero order *r* of 0.62, which is the lowest *r* between abilities and reading reported in Table 3.4. Since the multiple *r* represents the cumulative effect of the environmental variables as well as an inflationary capitalization on sampling error, the impression is reinforced that the abilities are exerting a more direct effect on reading than the background variables.

environmental conditions are the correlations among the underlying abilities (listed under Bracket E). These coefficients hover about the 0.70 mark. This suggests the possibility of a common factor underlying these reading-related abilities. Indeed a factor analysis of a number of language measures at the fifth-grade level reveals that a factor can be extracted which correlates 0.80, 0.76, and 0.68 with the Lorge-Thorndike IQ, WISC Vocabulary, and Orientation Scale respectively. It is interesting too that this is a factor separate from one with loads 0.88, 0.85, and 0.71 with the Cloze Popular Score, Cloze Grammatical Test, and Gates Reading Test respectively. The two factors, one identifiable as intelligence and the other as a reading or contextual understanding factor, are separable. However, the three variables cited above, which define the intelligence factor, are related moderately to the reading or contextual understanding factor. This would be consistent with the notion that the intellective abilities underlie, and are related to, reading achievement, but that the two areas—ability and achievement—represent separate functional unities.

One then has a sense of a developmental progression. A child is born into a family with a particular social background. He has the kinds of experiences which allow him to develop certain cognitive and verbal skills and these in turn contribute to the subsequent learnings (in this case, reading) expected of him in school.

It should be pointed out that there is a real problem in the interpretation of causal direction from these data. Thus a child's report of expected cultural activities might be attributable to his verbal responsiveness in the test situation rather than to environmental stimulation. Against this interpretation, however, is the lack of significant correlation between cultural activities and independent measures of the child's total verbal output and verbal fluency in the test situation. Also the sheer *number of activities* with adults as contrasted with the *number of cultural activities* does not correlate with reading achievement, contrary to the verbal fluency hypothesis. Similarly, it may well be that some unknown portion of the assocation between (a) environmental conditions, such as the educational aspiration of the parents, and (b) reading achievement is due to the influence of child on parent rather than vice versa. Thus the better achieving child may stimulate higher parental aspiration. However, one would predict from the reverse causality hypothesis that the child would also stimulate higher occupational aspiration in the parent. The evidence does not support this view. Thus Items 6 and 7 in Table 3.3 reveal that the child's reading level is not significantly related to the parents' occupational aspiration for the child. However, it could be suggested that even this finding is in accord with the reverse causality hypothesis. One might assume that the child's scholastic achievement might affect the parents' scholastic aspiration more than

TABLE 3.4

Intercorrelations among Environmental Variables Related to Reading, SES, and Test Scores

(Fifth Grade, N = 167)

		SES	Environmental Conditions						Abilities			Reading
		1	2	3	4	5	6	7	8	9	10	11
SES	1	×	0.27[a]	0.31[a]	−0.20[a]	0.28[a]	0.28[a]	0.20[a]				0.44[a]
Environmental conditions												
Housing	2	0.27[a]	×						0.31[a]	0.34[a]	0.34[a]	
Scholastic aspiration	3	0.31[a]	0.28[a]	×					0.30[a]	0.35[a]	0.36[a]	
Number of Children under 18 years	4	−0.20[a]	−0.09	−0.19	×				−0.23[a]	−0.24[a]	−0.18[a]	
Dinner conversation	5	0.28[a]	0.17	0.10	−0.02	×			0.20[a]	0.27[a]	0.24[a]	
Cultural activities	6	0.28[a]	0.18	0.12	−0.07	0.25[a]	×		0.25[a]	0.27[a]	0.27[a]	
Kindergarten	7	0.20[a]	0.26[a]	0.18	−0.22[a]	0.09	0.05	×	0.25[a]	0.13	0.12	
Abilities												
IQ (Lorge-Thorndike)	8	0.37[a]	−0.31[a]	0.30[a]	−0.23[a]	0.20[a]	0.25[a]	0.25[a]	×	0.67	0.66[a]	0.66[a]
Vocabulary (WISC)	9	0.49[a]	0.34[a]	0.35[a]	0.24[a]	0.27[a]	0.27[a]	0.13		×	0.76[a]	0.62[a]
Orientation	10	0.51[a]	0.34[a]	0.36[a]	−0.18	0.24[a]	0.27[a]	0.12			×	0.62[a]
Achievement												
Reading	11	0.44[a]	0.28[a]	0.32[a]	−0.29[a]	0.22[a]	0.25[a]	0.20[a]	0.66[a]	0.62[a]	0.62[a]	×

(Correlation submatrices are bracketed and labeled A, B, C, D, E, F in the table.)

[a] Significant at 0.01 level

their occupational aspiration—hence the obtained significant correlation between reading (a scholastic achievement) and parents' educational aspiration, but a nonsignificant correlation between reading and the parents' occupational aspiration for the child. However, a more direct test of the reverse causality hypothesis is at hand. One would expect, according to this view, that the parents' perceptions of the child's reading level would be a crucial variable linking the child's achievement to parental expectation. Accordingly, the correlation between parental educational aspiration and the parents' estimate of the child's reading ability was examined. The correlation between the two measures (among the fifth-graders, where reading scores were obtained) failed to reach significance ($r = 0.11$).

THE DEPRIVATION INDEX

In order to pursue further the implication of the factors related to environmental disadvantage, a Deprivation Index was formed. The latter represents a composite score based upon the six background variables

TABLE 3.5

Description of Variables in Deprivation Index

Variable	Dichotomized
1. Housing dilapidation index for block on which S resides, and assigned to him, computed from census data	1 = Anything less than sound with complete plumbing (either dilapidated or deteriorating) 2 = Sound with complete plumbing
2. The educational aspirational level of the parent for the child	1 = College or less 2 = Graduate or professional training
3. The number of children under 18-years-of-age in the home	1 = 3 or more 2 = 2 or less
4. Dinner conversation	1 = Did not engage in conversation because: Not allowed to Others participated, but child did not No conversation, no indication why Ate alone 2 = Engaged in conversation
5. Total number of cultural experiences anticipated by child for coming weekend—visiting relatives, family, museums, library, zoo, travel outside NYC, school or lesson work	1 = None 2 = One or more experiences (1–4)
6. Attendance of child in kindergarten	1 = No attendance at kindergarten 2 = Attendance at kindergarten

whose integration with *SES,* abilities, and reading have been explored above. The six variables and their mode of dichotomy are shown in Table 3.5. With the exception of the housing dilapidation item, these data were obtained either from the parents or the subjects themselves. The estimate of housing condition was made for the dwelling unit of each subject from information contained in the United States Census of Housing, by block, for New York City (United States Bureau of the Census, 1962).

A larger *"deprived"* score on the Index was obtained by those children with a cumulation of the following conditions, each of which is significantly associated with lower *SES* and with lowered reading achievement at the fifth-grade level: the children tend to have missed kindergarten; their families are larger, perhaps more crowded, and located in more dilapidated neighborhoods; the parents have lower educational aspirations for the children; and the latter report relatively limited conversation at dinner and limited cultural activities (as defined in Table 3.5) with parents or relatives. The decision to use a composite index reflects the belief that cumulations of those variables are more significant (and more reliable) than each variable taken singly. The multiple correlations reported above attest to the enhanced effect of the joint action of these variables.

THE DEPRIVATION INDEX AND THE
CUMULATIVE DEFICIT

Thus far we have been studying environmental conditions as (1) specific and differentiated indices of social deprivation, and (2) as variables which intervene between the more global quality of socioeconomic status on the one hand and performance (ability or achievement) on the other. In its latter function, the specification of the environmental variables contributes to the explanation of the link between measures of familial *SES* and the child's performance. In the pursuit of such an explanatory link, we have therefore been concerned with the correlations of these special environmental conditions with *SES* and with ability and achievement measures.

However these environmental conditions may fulfill still another explanatory function. They may act as independent contributors. Thus they may explain differences among children's performance even when there is homogeneity in *SES* or race.

A related problem deals with the cumulative deficit. Thus we have been concerned with the question of whether the adverse effects of a socially-deprived background become more pronounced with time. The nature of the performance in which such environment-associated impairments appear also deserves close attention. Though by no means definitive, there is a body of evidence suggesting that language measures are particularly responsive to the effects of social disadvantage (see, for instance, Bernstein, 1961; Milner, 1951).

Accordingly we have analyzed the Deprivation Index simultaneously with two other background variables, *SES* and race, to determine whether differences on the Index appear independently of *SES* and race. The analysis has also incorporated age-group differences to see whether obtained decrements in performance are significantly greater among fifth-graders as compared to first-graders—as suggested by the cumulative deficit hypothesis. Finally, a comparison has been made between two measures varying in the language component. These are (a) a non-language test of general intellectual ability, the Lorge-Thorndike Intelligence Test, and (b) a test of vocabulary knowledge, the vocabulary subtest of Wechsler Intelligence Scale for Children. Forms of the Lorge-Thorndike test appropriate for each age level were used. Both forms, as reported by the authors, are designed to measure nonverbal aspects of intelligence. The first-grade form used pictorial items only to measure abstract thinking, pictorial classification, and picture reading ability. The items found in the first-grade form involved picture classification, pictorial analogies, and items requiring distinction between numerical relationships. Both forms are designed for group administration.

The following conclusions emerge from this analysis:[5]

1. With respect to the independent contribution of the Deprivation Index, the results indicate that the Index is significantly related to both the Lorge-Thorndike and the Vocabulary test even within groups homogeneous in race or *SES* level. This implies that over and above the decrements associated with race and *SES,* the specific environmental features embodied in the Deprivation Index are capable, by themselves, of producing such disadvantaging effects.

2. On both the Vocabulary and Lorge-Thorndike measures, the Deprivation Index yielded cumulative deficits. Thus if the sample is dichotomized into those who show greater and lesser disadvantage as assessed by the Index, the more disadvantaged group shows a decreasing IQ with age. The relatively advantaged group shows an increase with age (see Table 3.6). A similar pattern occurs with respect to a cumulative vocabulary deficit. Among the older fifth-grade children those who show greater disadvantage tend to do relatively poorer than the disadvantaged children of the first grade (see Table 3.7).

---

[5] The details of this analysis are reported by M. Whiteman, B. Brown, and M. Deutsch (1967). Essentially the analysis of variance is performed on the means of the various subgroups (see Winer, 1952, pp. 222 and 241–243) formed by combinations of Race, *DI,* and *SES,* controlling therefore for the disproportionate *N*s and the lack of orthogonality between the independent variables of *DI* and *SES.*

TABLE 3.6

Grade Differences on Lorge-Thorndike IQ (Nonverbal)

by Deprivation Index Levels (Fifth Grade)

	More Deprivation			Less Deprivation		
Grade	Mean	S.D.	N	Mean	S.D.	N
1	100.13	15.01	91	104.14	12.54	36
5	94.31	14.64	84	109.47	16.21	78

NOTE: Interaction of grade by Deprivation Index significant at 0.01 level.

The results also indicate that in the case of the Lorge-Thorndike, the cumulative deficit is most marked among those subjects who show the specific experiential disadvantages embodied in the Deprivation Index as compared to those identified more grossly as of lower socioeconomic level. Lower *SES,* however, is more associated with lower Lorge-Thorndike scores among the younger children, a deficit which is as pronounced as the deficit among the low *SES* older children.

3. Turning to the differences between the two tests, the findings reveal that the cumulative deficits of the verbal test (Vocabulary) are associated with a broader range of background conditions than those of the more nonverbal IQ measure. Thus cumulative deficits with the vocabulary test are associated with Negro status, lower *SES,* and greater disadvantage as assessed by the Deprivation Index. The deficits are less pervasive in the case of the Lorge-Thorndike. There is no significant cumulative deficit associated with lower *SES,* as noted above. There is, however, a significant cumulative deficit related to Negro status. Thus Negro children in the fifth grade score lower, relative to white

TABLE 3.7

Means for More- and Less-Deprived Groups within

Grade Levels on WISC Vocabulary Subtest Scores

Group	Mean	S.D.	N
Grade 1			
More deprivation	13.54	6.27	89
Less deprivation	15.30	4.35	36
Grade 5			
More deprivation	28.88	9.25	83
Less deprivation	36.09	9.28	78

NOTE: Interaction of Vocabulary by Deprivation Index significant at 0.05 level.

children, than Negro children in the first grade. However, this deficit tends to vanish when there is control over level of disadvantage, as measured by the Deprivation Index. Within homogeneous levels of deprivation the Negro cumulative deficit tends to be lessened; the older Negro children do not show a significant and progressive decline. However, the converse is not true. Regardless of race, the more disadvantaged older children (as assessed by the Deprivation Index) score relatively lower on the vocabulary test than the most disadvantaged younger children. The general tenor of these results points to the greater sensitivity of the language test to different patterns of disadvantage, whether these disadvantages are related to general socioeconomic level or to Negro status, or to the specific background factors implied in the Deprivation Index.

THE DEPRIVATION INDEX AND SELF-CONCEPT

The Deprivation Index is also related to self-concept. In the case of the fifth-grade children an index dealing with favorableness of self-evaluation was constructed from two sentence-completion items. A trichotomous categorization was used: (a) response with a favorable self-image to both items; (b) to one item; and (c) to neither of the two items.

Table 3.8 reveals that the more deprived children tend to have the lower self-concepts. As compared to the more advantaged children, about six times as many of the more deprived children fall into the least

TABLE 3.8

Deprivation Index as Related to Self-Concept Levels

(Fifth Grade)

	Self-Concept Level							
	Least Favorable		Medium		More Favorable		Total	
Deprivation Level	N	$\%$	N	$\%$	N	$\%$	N	$\%$
More	13	25	19	35	21	40	53	48
Less	2	4	21	44	25	52	48	52
							101	100

NOTE: $X^2 = 7.88$
$p < 0.05$

TABLE 3.9

Means and Standard Deviations of Combined Standard

Scores of Four Marker Variables Broken Down by

Self-Concept Category (Fifth Grade)

Self-Concept[a]	M	S.D.	N
I. Least favorable	459.32	85.51	15
II. Medium	500.63	86.56	41
III. Most favorable	515.61	82.28	47

Newman-Keuls Comparisons among Means

Self-concept levels	p
I *vs* II	<0.01
I *vs* III	<0.01
II *vs* III	NS

[a] NOTE: Main effect of self-concept significant at 0.01 level.

favorable self-concept category. This finding would be consistent with our formulation above regarding the interrelation among deprivation, self-concept, and cognitive achievement. If deprivation is related to lower ability and achievement levels, and the latter in turn results in feelings of inferiority, one would expect what was found—that there would be a significant relation between increased deprivation and a more negative self-concept.

A missing empirical link in this hypothetical causal chain is the relation between lowered ability level and more negative self-concept. To explore this relation the self-concept variable was related to four ability measures. The latter represented the marker variables for four factors derived from an analysis of a battery of verbal and cognitive measures administered to our fifth-grade sample. The tests are the Lorge-Thorndike, the Word-Distance (Distance Score) measure, the Cloze Popular, and the Form-Class Score of a word association test. The factors corresponding to these four marker variables were named intelligence, conceptual relatedness, conceptual understanding, and formal language. The results of a two-way analysis of variance (self-concept $\times$ type of test) are presented in Table 3.9. The main effect of self-concept is significant, and analysis of the over-all trend indicates that the more negative the self-concept the lower the test scores. The failure to find a significant interaction between self-concept and test indicates that the relation between more negative self-concept and lowered test score is fairly general and obtained over the various tests used in this analysis.

TABLE 3.10

Means and Standard Deviations of Gates Reading Test

Scores As Related to Self-Concept Levels (Fifth Grade)

Self-Concept Level[a]	M	S.D.
I. Most unfavorable	40.01	9.61
II. Medium	46.76	10.03
III. Least unfavorable	49.32	9.52

Newman-Keuls Comparisons Among Self-Concept Means

Self-concept levels	p
I vs II	<0.05
I vs III	<0.01
II vs III	NS

[a]NOTE: Main effect of self-concept significant at 0.01 level.

Comparisons among the self-concept means were made to explore the locus of the significant main effect. The Newman-Keuls comparisons among means (see Table 3.9) reveal that it is the group which is most negative in self-concept which stands out as significantly lower in test performance from the other two groups. The latter two self-concept categories defining the medium and more favorable groups, are not significantly different from one another in over-all test score.

The above analysis has related a self-concept measure to ability tests. A significant relation between self-concept and reading achievement, as measured by the Gates Reading Test, is shown by the results of an analysis of variance presented in Table 3.10. Self-concept differences are significantly related to reading scores. The more negative the self-concept the lower the reading achievement. As was seen above in connection with the relation between self-concept and ability measures, Table 3.10 reveals that the most negative self-concept group is most demarcated from the other two groups with respect to reading level. The difference in reading score between self-concept Groups II and III (the medium and more favorable self-concept groups) is not significant.

Though the above presentation has highlighted a particular causal direction (from deprivation to lowered ability and achievement to lowered self-concept), an alternative interpretation can be made. It is quite probable, though difficult to explore with correlational data, that the relation between performance, whether of the ability or the achievement variety, and self-evaluation is interactive—with the more negative self-evaluations producing as well as being produced by lower performance.

DEPRIVATION INDEX AND INTERACTIONS WITH

SOCIOECONOMIC STATUS, RACE, AND

INTELLIGENCE

In addition to relations with cumulative deficit and self-concept, there is a third point related to deprivation. A more advantaged environment seems to counteract other conditions which tend to bring achievement levels down. Three illustrations are presented.

Among children who are relatively undeprived, as measured by the Deprivation Index, low socioeconomic status per se is much less potent as a disadvantaging factor with respect to ability tests than is the case among children who show strong deprivation on the Index. Among the latter group of children, a low socioeconomic status is most strongly related to the linguistic and intellective measures. The evidence is presented in Table 3.11. This table presents an analysis of variance of the

TABLE 3.11

Analysis of Variance of Marker Tests with Socioeconomic

Status, Race, Deprivation (*DI*), and Type of Test

as Independent Variables (Fifth Grade)

Source	df	MS	F	p
Between *S*s				
SES	2	66,336.70	6.17	<0.01
Race	1	20,099.88	1.87	NS
Deprivation (*DI*)[a]	1	54,431.31	5.06	<0.05
SES × Race	2	7,112.40	<1	NS
SES × *DI*	2	34,916.32	3.25	<0.05
Race × *DI*	1	1,199.61	<1	NS
SES × Race × *DI*	2	966.25	<1	NS
Error (between)	123	10,759.05		
Within *S*s				
Tests	3	1,732.16	<1	NS
SES × Tests	6	8,040.48	1.45	NS
Race × Tests	3	22,927.21	4.14	<0.01
DI × Tests	3	10,351.75	1.87	NS
SES × Race × Tests	6	931.55	<1	NS
SES × *DI* × Tests	6	3,978.90	<1	NS
Race × *DI* × Tests	3	1,287.61	<1	NS
SES × Race × *DI* × Tests	6	7,381.00	1.33	NS
Error (within)	369	5,536.64		

[a] Deprivation Index dichotomized

TABLE 3.12

SES Differences in Over-all Test Score by Deprivation

Level (Fifth Grade)

	More Deprivation			Less Deprivation		
SES	*M*	S.D.	*N*	*M*	S.D.	*N*
I. Lower	454.22	94.00	38	513.83	69.78	13
II. Medium	490.18	81.45	23	526.23	97.23	25
III. Higher	536.08	52.55	6	533.11	72.87	30

four ability measures described above. Socioeconomic status, Deprivation Index, race, and the type of test are the independent variables. It can be seen from Table 3.11 that the interaction between deprivation and socioeconomic status is significant, implying that the pattern of *SES* differences in test score varies from one level of deprivation to another. Table 3.12 explores further these differing patterns by listing the *SES* differences in over-all test score separately for each deprivation level. These *SES* differences are more marked in the more deprived group. Table 3.13 indicates that the *SES* differences in test score are quite significant in this more deprived group, but are not significant in the group showing lesser disadvantage. The Newman-Keuls comparisons also reported in Table 3.13 explore the locus of *SES* differences in the more deprived group. These comparisons indicate that the lower *SES* levels I and II score significantly lower on over-all test score than the higher *SES* level III, but that the difference between the two lower levels of

TABLE 3.13

Significance Tests of *SES* Differences within Deprivation

Levels (Fifth Grade)

Within	*df*	*F*	*p*
More deprivation	2	9.00	<0.01
Less deprivation	2	<1	NS

Newman-Keuls Comparisons Among *SES* Levels
within Greater Deprivation Levels

SES comparisons	*p*
III *vs* I	<0.01
III *vs* II	<0.05
I *vs* II	NS

SES is not significant. We see therefore that *SES* differences in test score are affected by the deprivation level of the child, with lesser degrees of deprivation mitigating the effect of lower socioeconomic status.

A second illustration of the importance of deprivational background as an interactive variable is afforded by a study of the combined effects of deprivation level and intelligence on reading. Table 3.14 shows the results of an analysis of variance of Gates Reading Score among the fifth-graders with race, Lorge-Thorndike IQ (nonverbal), and Deprivation Index as the independent variables. The magnitude of differences in reading score between the higher- and lower-IQ groups is a function of deprivation level. It can be seen that reading differences attributable to intellectual gradations are more pronounced in the more disadvantaged group and less pronounced in the group with a lesser degree of deprivation. This implies that the effects of intellectual retardation on reading are ameliorated in the context of social advantage and exacerbated in the context of social disadvantage.

A third example of the interactive influence of deprivation is afforded by the study of the combined effects of differences in socioeconomic status, race, and deprivation upon the test scores of the first-grade children. The three test scores are the marker variables for three factors derived from an analysis of a battery of cognitive tests administered to the first-grade sample. The factors are labeled "intelligence," "concept formation," and "verbal fluency."

There is a significant interaction among the three independent variables. One interpretation of this significant interaction is that race, *SES,* and deprivation level define a category which differs from the others in terms of test scores. Despite the small *N*s in some of the finer sub-

TABLE 3.14

Differences between More and Less Deprived (as assessed

by Deprivation Index) on Gates Reading Score as

Related to IQ Levels (Fifth Grade)

		Deprivation Level				
		More			*Less*	
	M	S.D	*N*	*M*	S.D.	*N*
IQ						
Higher	5.23	0.60	24	5.33	0.59	55
Lower	3.84	0.85	59	4.46	1.14	22

NOTE: Interaction between IQ and Deprivation Index significant at 0.05 level.

TABLE 3.15

SES Differences in Over-all Test Scores as a Function of

Race and Deprivation Index (First Grade)

SES Level	Negro			White		
	M	S.D.	N	M	S.D.	N
Lower						
More deprived	475.96	86.23	18	483.00	92.28	20
Less deprived	464.47	84.20	5	533.83	78.51	2
Medium						
More deprived	485.42	94.75	16	503.36	83.85	13
Less deprived	504.97	116.09	10	535.67	92.91	3
Higher						
More deprived	493.36	115.30	11	530.07	113.24	9
Less deprived	580.11	122.31	6	523.80	86.48	10

NOTE: Interaction between race, Deprivation Index, and *SES* level significant at 0.05 level.

groupings, the statistical tests suggest that the differing category is the one defining the most advantaged grouping among the Negro children, that is, those Negro children who are least deprived and in the highest socioeconomic category.[6] In order to show this more clearly, the mean test scores of the Negro and white children for each deprivation and *SES* category are shown in Table 3.15. It can be seen that the Negro children of higher *SES* level and lesser deprivation show a relatively higher mean score. It does *not* mean that these Negro children score significantly higher than those white children comparable in *SES* and deprivation level. The statistical tests suggest rather that the combined effects of higher *SES* and lowered deprivation have a significantly ameliorative effect among the Negro children.

SOME IMPLICATIONS

This paper has been concerned with social disadvantage from three viewpoints: (a) with the delineation of specific environmental factors

---

[6] Within the less-deprived category (but not in the more-deprived category) simple effects of *SES* × race are significant ($p<0.05$). Within the less-deprived category, and within the Negro group (but not within the white group), *SES* differences are significant by "simple effects" test ($p<0.01$). Again within the less-deprived Negro group, higher *SES* level is significantly different from medium and lower *SES* levels ($p<0.01$ in both Newman-Keuls comparisons) but medium and lower *SES* groups are not significantly different from one another.

which help to explain the disadvantaging effects of such global background factors as lowered socioeconomic status or membership in an underprivileged racial group; (b) with the description of a causal sequence, a developmental process whereby early environmental factors manifest their disadvantaging effects upon later scholastic achievement and sense of competence through their adverse effects on the abilities underlying such achievements; and (c) with detailing ways in which social advantage may ameliorate the negative effects attributable to a cognitive factor such as intelligence, or to social-background factors such as socioeconomic status and race. Each of these concerns will be discussed in order:

(a) In the delineation of specific environmental conditions, we have pointed out the importance of the child's interactions with adults in cognitively and motivationally stimulating settings. This emphasis is supported by the recent work carried out at the University of Chicago and reported by Bloom in his book, *Stability and Change in Human Characteristics*. Thus, as reported by Bloom, Wolf has secured ratings of thirteen process variables descriptive of the interactions between parents and child and hypothetically related to intellectual growth. These items fall under the headings of parental press for academic achievement and for language development, as well as provision for general learning. Wolf found a multiple correlation of 0.76 between ratings of the above factors and the IQ measures of sixty fifth-grade students. A similar study by Dave, also reported by Bloom (1964), found a correlation of 0.80 between familial measures of the above type and achievement test performance of fourth-graders. In our study the multiple r relating the six deprivational variables to reading is 0.49. The differences may be attributable to differences in instruments assessing social disadvantage, to the tests measuring achievement, and most of all to the attenuated number of predictor variables used in this as compared to the Dave study (six as compared to thirteen). Besides their emphasis on interaction with adults, the deprivational variables reveal another attribute—their specificity, that is, their relatively slight degree of interrelation. This would suggest that remedial effects may best be attained by programs that direct attention to a number of specific areas and competencies rather than concentrate effort upon one. As suggested by the deprivational variables, such areas and competencies may be of a motivational, linguistic, and informational nature. The importance of parental motivation, it should be noted, emerges in our data at the first-grade level. Unfortunately, we did not measure reading readiness at the first-grade level, so that comparisons between first- and fifth-grade correlations between parental scholastic aspiration and achievement in school could not be made.

(b) Our results are consistent with a developmental sequence relating environmental conditions to the formation of certain abilities which in turn affect achievement and sense of competence. However, the results in supplying empirical correlations between (1) Deprivation Index; (2) the self-concept measure; (3) test scores reflecting abilities; and (4) reading score reflecting achievement are also consistent with a more complicated interactive model as well as one stressing a simple one-way progression of influence. Social disadvantage occasioned by the conditions associated with poverty may result in some cognitive and learning deficits relative to the demands of the early grades. With early failure or difficulty in academic tasks, the child's self-confidence may be impaired so that learning becomes more difficult and unrewarding. The lowered achievement level may even feed back on the slower development of the original abilities. In any case, lowered abilities may produce lower achievements, lowered achievements may induce diminished self-confidence, which in turn feeds back upon the achievements, and so on. If one adds the devaluations brought about by race prejudice, superimposed on poverty prejudice, these processes may be accelerated.

At a more abstract level, the above process is reminiscent of Piaget's accommodation and assimilation paradigm (Piaget, *Psychology of Intelligence,* and Flavell, *The Developmental Psychology of Jean Piaget*) and of Hunt's conceptions of intrinsic motivation (*Intelligence and Experience*). Piaget's fundamental notion is that intelligence comprises a series of hierarchically arranged cognitive structures. The sensorimotor schemata of the early years are structures derived from the actual physical interactions with environmental objects. With continued interaction and with the development of linguistic and symbolic functions, the essentially motoric schemata become internalized as concrete operations. With these concrete operations, the child from about seven to eleven years can mentally organize, integrate, and differentiate the concrete world about him. With further development, the concrete operations themselves become organized into systems of formal operations. The latter represent mental processes which allow the individual to explore possibilities, pursue hypotheses, and make systematic connections within imagined realities. Within each of these levels there is a process of accommodation and assimilation. The mental structure accommodates to the variety of stimulation and problems presented to it. But it can accommodate only when there is a "match," in Hunt's terms, between the internal schema or operation and the external task or requirement. Only then will the internal structure assimilate the environment. If the environment poses problems that are too difficult, the structure will not be able to assimilate it and accommodation or mental growth will not take place. Frustration and withdrawal will. If the problems are too easy, boredom and disinterest will prevail. From this purview, the period from six to ten is one where important schemata are being strengthened and integrated. If there is a continually poor match between the child's schemata and the subject matter which these schemata are supposed to assimilate, there will be little constructive accommodation, and little growth of those underlying thought forms. The cumulative deficit in our study of the first- and fifth-graders may be the results of such a process.

(c) Our final set of findings, dealing with ameliorative effects of the more advantageous circumstances implicit in the items making up the Deprivation Index, lends support to enrichment attempts. For these enrichment programs attempt to induce, by controlled intervention, some of the advantage accruing to certain groups "naturally." These findings specify the particular conditions under which socioeconomic, race, and intellective differences are more pronounced and when they are attenuated. One interpretation of these findings is that a background of greater advantage (low scores on the Deprivation Index) has a compensatory effect. Thus if race is associated with lowered ability test scores, such decrements are minimized or vanish under conditions where learning environments have been substantially improved. Similarly, if lowered intelligence scores are associated with lowered reading scores, this decrement is also ameliorated under conditions of stronger social advantage. Increased educational opportunities may produce the same ameliorating effect, as suggested in a recent publication of the Office of Education (*Equality of Educational Opportunity,* 1966). Though lowered socioeconomic status is associated with lowered test scores on intellective and language functions, interactional opportunities, as assessed by the Deprivation Index, provide for a counter effect. In sum, to the degree that intervention attempts are capable of supplying the compensatory experiences implicit in the Deprivation Index, such attempts may be successful in reversing or ameliorating the cumulative deficit discussed above.

Pertinent to this point is the distinction between the effects of race and *SES*. Thus these two background factors show different relationships to the Lorge-Thorndike. The *SES* deficit begins earlier and is as pronounced among the younger first-graders as among the older fifth-graders. The decrement associated with race, however, begins later, is more cumulative and more pronounced among the older Negro children. Our sample selection, as well as our mode of statistical analysis, has aimed at separating these two factors, race and *SES*. But in society, they are confounded. Negroes tend to be poorer than whites. The implication is that the Negro child may be sequentially disadvantaged. Factors associated with lower *SES* may produce early deficit. In addition, later deficit may be produced by environmental factors associated with Negro status. Some of these environmental factors which are independent of the *SES* measure seem to be tapped by the Deprivation Index. The lack of correlation in our sample between race and *SES,* the significant relation between race and Deprivation Index, the loss of the cumulative race deficit when the Deprivation Index is controlled, these afford evidence for this interpretation. However it should be pointed out that these findings related to the Deprivation Index are based upon the sample on which the Index was derived. A cross-validation on a fresh sample would be methodologically desirable.

References

Bernstein, B. Social structure, language and learning. *Educational Research,* June 1961, **III** (3), 163–176.

Bloom, B. *Stability and change in human characteristics.* New York: Wiley, 1964.

Bloom, R., M. Whiteman, and M. Deutsch. Race and social class as separate factors related to social environment. *American Journal of Sociology,* 1965, **LXX** (4), 471–476.

Empey, La Mar T. Social class and occupational aspirations. A comparison of absolute and relative measurement. *American Sociological Review,* December 1956, 703–709. Also in B. H. Stoodley (ed.), *Society and self.* New York: Free Press, 1962.

Flavell, J. H. *The developmental psychology of Jean Piaget.* Princeton, N. J.: Van Nostrand, 1963.

Hollingshead, A. B., and F. C. Redlich. *Social class and mental illness.* New York: Wiley, 1958.

Hunt, J. McV. *Intelligence and experience.* New York: Ronald Press, 1961.

Milner, Esther. A study of the relationship between reading readiness in Grade I school children and patterns of parent-child interaction. *Child Development,* 1951, **22** (2), 95–112.

Piaget, J. *The psychology of intelligence.* Translated from the French by Malcolm Piercy and D. E. Berlyne. London: Routledge & Kegan Paul, 1950.

United States Bureau of the Census. *United States census of population and housing: 1960 census tracts. Final report PHC (1) -104. Part 1.* Washington: United States Government Printing Office, 1962.

United States Office of Education. *Equality of education opportunity.* Washington: United States Government Printing Office, 1966. Superintendent of Documents catalog number FS. 5.283: 38000.

Whiteman, M., B. Brown, and M. Deutsch. Some effects of social class and race on children's language and intellectual abilities. In M. Deutsch *et al., The disadvantaged child.* New York: Basic Books, 1967. Pp. 319–335.

Winer, B. *Statistical principles in experimental design.* New York: McGraw-Hill, 1952.

CHAPTER FOUR

Social Class
and Verbal Learning

ARTHUR R. JENSEN[1]

Learning theorists and students of the experimental psychology of learning are rarely called upon in their professional capacity to deal with problems of the utmost social significance. Nor do they in their professional role often volunteer such service. The reason is surely not due to any dearth of socially significant problems involving learning, as we shall see; nor is it likely to be due to any exceptional deficiency of social conscience among experimental psychologists. The reason lies rather in the fact that psychologists aim to gain a scientific understanding of the learning process, and in order to make progress in this difficult endeavor they must try to achieve a reduction, simplification, and control of the many relevant variables to a degree that could hardly be attained outside the laboratory.

Understanding is sometimes arrived at through devious routes, and it is highly probable that some of the most fruitful insights and hypotheses concerning social-class influences on learning would never arise from a headlong attack on the central problem. Yet, from the basic

---

[1] University of California, Berkeley. The preparation of this chapter was aided by a National Science Foundation grant to the Institute of Human Learning.

research of many students of learning, occupied over the past years in their laboratories, with their mazes and white rats and memory drums and nonsense syllables, we are now provided with a body of fact, theory, and method that seems rich in implications for understanding social-class differences in learning. The purpose of this chapter is to point out some of these implications. The assessment of their success in explaining social-class differences in learning, however, must await the results of future investigations expressly designed to make direct applications of the suggested hypotheses.

SOCIAL-CLASS DETERMINANTS OF LANGUAGE DEVELOPMENT

It is advisable in the following discussion to substitute the term *verbal behavior* in place of "language," a word which in some educational circles has taken on certain value connotations that are best avoided in the present context. Discussion of social-class differences in "language" tends to arouse notions about the middle-class social advantages of "correct" pronunciation, "good" English, avoidance of slang, and so forth. Language differences along these dimensions, especially in the context in which they are usually discussed, are extremely superficial from a psychological viewpoint. If it were thought that social-class influences on verbal behavior implied no more than factors such as these, the topic of verbal learning as it relates to social class would be of very little interest to us. As the term is used in the following discussion, however, verbal behavior—not just the capacity for verbal behavior, but verbal behavior itself—is what most distinguishes the human being from the rest of the animal world.

The psychological consequences of verbal behavior are extremely profound in ways and degrees scarcely appreciated by those who are unfamiliar with the recent research. To the extent that a person is prevented, by whatever reason, from falling heir to these consequences of his human potential for verbal learning, he will fall short of his potential as a human being.

The aims of the following discussion, therefore, are twofold: first, to indicate how social factors might in general affect verbal development; and second, to delineate specifically some of the psychological consequences of various stages and processes of verbal development.

Since the most important external factor affecting the rate of verbal development is the quality of a child's early linguistic environment, we should first look at some of the contrasts between lower- and middle-class environment in this respect.

The child's vocalizations, which normally occur in the first year of life and are the forerunners of speech, must be reinforced or rewarded by certain kinds of responses from other persons if they are to persist and develop into speech. The more reinforcement, the better; and apparently the fewer the number of persons from whom reinforcement comes, the better. Brodbeck and Irwin (1946), for example, found that children reared by their parents or by foster parents vocalize more than children living in institutional settings, and this difference shows up as early as six months of age. Also, Rheingold and Bayley (1959) found that children who had a single mothering experience excelled children who had six to eight mother surrogates in the area of vocalization. Fewer lower-class children than middle-class children have a single mother-child relationship in their early years. The responsibility of caring for the child in the lower-class home tends to be assumed by a number of different persons, both adults and older children. In the typical lower-class home there is reportedly less verbal play, less verbal interaction, and less reinforcing behavior on the part of the older members of the household in response to the child's early vocalizations than is generally found in middle-class homes. The beginning of speech is therefore more likely to be delayed within a lower-class environment.

While the child can engage in other forms of learning such as the acquisition of motor skills largely through interaction with the inanimate environment, language acquisition depends largely upon interaction with another person, and the emotional quality and intensity of this interpersonal relationship is believed to play a crucial role in the process. The "shaping" of the child's speech sounds through the differential reinforcing behavior of the parent is carried on more persistently by middle-class than by lower-class parents in their efforts to have the child's speech patterns match their own. This "shaping" of speech by the parent also constitutes training in auditory discrimination, which in turn facilitates further language acquisition.

Speech cannot develop without this spontaneous vocal interplay between child and adult, or between one child and another who is sufficiently mature to make the auditory discriminations which almost automatically give rise in the middle-class parent to differential reinforcing behavior (by gesture, facial expression, and vocal utterance). Children who are at the same stage of development, in playing together, can practice what they already know verbally, but this arrangement will not add further to their verbal knowledge, for neither child is able to provide the other with standards for imitation or to shape the other's vocal behavior through differential reinforcement. Language learning takes place, as it were, by the child's continually having to reach to a higher level set by the adults and older children with whom he interacts. And if the child is forced to spend a great deal of his time in the company of other children who are not his verbal superiors, his language development will be retarded. For this reason, twins and triplets are on the average somewhat slower in language development than singletons; and this shows up even later in childhood as a difference in IQ, twins being a few points lower on the average than singletons. Koch (1954) has found that the child with the greatest proficiency in verbal skills tends to be the first-born whose next sibling arrives two to four years later. To account for this, the relatively undivided attention of the mother during these first two to four years is thought to be the prime factor. Thus, if the mother's time is more divided in the lower-class family, and if the children are more closely spaced and spend relatively more of their time in the company of their verbal peers than is the case in the middle-class family, the results are predictable along the lines already indicated.

When the child begins talking in his second year, his difficulties are increased if his vocal models must be perceived through a high "noise" background. The congested living conditions in many lower-class homes can be presumed to have a higher noise level plus a greater proportion of adult speech which does not constitute vocal interaction with the child. Again, the consequences are predictable.

Even after the child is already talking, the question-asking behavior which is so characteristic of young children, and which later becomes important for independent problem solving, will eventually be extinguished through lack of adequate reinforcement if the parents are too distracted to respond in a satisfying way to the child's questions.

The functions of language also seem to differ between the lower- and middle-class family. Most of the research on social-class differences in verbal behavior has been carried on in England by sociologist Basil Bernstein (1960), but many of his findings are probably valid among the lower and middle classes in America as well. Spoken language among the lower class is less like written language syntactically, grammatically, and in over-all sequential organization and logical progression, than is the case among the middle class. Consequently there should be relatively less positive transfer from lower-class verbal experience to formal language of books, newspapers, magazines, and so on. For the lower-class person, reading and writing are very different from speech. Also, language in the lower class is not as flexible a means of communication as in the middle class. It is not as readily adapted to the subtleties of the particular situation, but consists more of a relatively small repertoire of stereotyped phrases and expressions which are used rather loosely without much effort to achieve a subtle correspondence between perception and verbal expression. Much of lower-class language consists of a kind of incidental "emotional" accompaniment to action here and now. In contrast, middle-class language, rather than being a mere accompaniment to ongoing activity, serves more to represent things and events not immediately present. Thus middle-class language is more abstract and necessarily somewhat more flexible, detailed, and subtle in its descriptive aspects. In all social classes, conversational language serves mainly as a social lubricant, but in the lower class the expository function of language is relatively less prominent than in the middle class. These differences are important for psychological development because of the intimate relationship between language and thought. It would be a mistake to think of language as merely a *vehicle* for thought; developmentally and functionally both are completely interdependent.

One of the most thorough investigations of the relationship between reading readiness in first-grade children and patterns of parent-child interaction has been carried out by Esther Milner (1951). Milner specifically chose first-graders for her study, since home influences on verbal behavior are more manifestly prepotent at this educational stage than are school influences. All of the children in her study were Negro, ranging on an index of social status from lower-lower to lower-upper class. A composite score from a number of reading-readiness tests showed a correlation (Pearson *r*) of 0.86 with the social-class index. That is, dividing the children into high and low groups on the basis of reading readiness resulted in about the same two groups as when they were divided on the basis of social class. Through interviews with the children and their mothers a number of environmental differences between low and high scorers in reading readiness were discovered. Many of the differences seem to be directly related to verbal attainment. For example, it was found that the high-scoring children were surrounded by a richer verbal environment at home than the low-scoring children. More books were available to the high scorers, who also were read to by adults more than the low-scoring children. There also seemed to be more evidence of opportunities for emotionally positive interaction with the parents among the high scorers, and this often took place in a context favoring language development. For instance, mothers of low scorers indicated more frequently that as a rule they do not eat breakfast with their children or do not talk with the children during breakfast. The same was true for supper.

That much of the difference in reading readiness that Milner found between lower- and middle-class children was due to the kinds of environmental factors she describes has been shown experimentally by introducing certain middle-class practices into lower-class homes and later comparing these children with those from other lower-class homes in a matched control group. Irwin (reported in McCandless, 1961, p. 260), for example, had lower-class mothers read aloud to their children for at least ten minutes a day from the age of one, a practice that is common in the middle class but rare in the lower class. A control group of similar mothers was given no such instructions. Measures of language development showed significant differences between the experimental and control groups in all phases of speech by twenty months of age.

Can a child's language level be changed by the age of entering nursery school or kindergarten? A study by Dawe (1942) suggests that it can be. Orphanage children ranging in age from 3 years 7 months to 6 years 10 months were given special speech and language training only on weekends for a total of ninety-two hours over a period of about $7\frac{1}{2}$ months. Compared with a well-matched control group, the experimental group showed a gain of 14 IQ points (their mean initial IQ was about 80). The language training did not consist of mere test coaching; the transfer of training was quite general and showed up in a variety of assessment procedures.

THE DEVELOPMENT OF VERBAL BEHAVIOR

The preceding discussion of verbal behavior in relation to social -class has been conducted in quite gross and general terms. As long as we remain at this level of discussion, the significance of verbal behavior cannot be fully appreciated. A more thorough understanding of how verbal behavior develops and of how it affects other aspects of psychological development can be gained only through a more analytical approach.

This analysis can be facilitated by the use of a few simple stimulus-response $(S–R)$ paradigms. First, it should be made clear that these paradigms do not represent psychological theories or models and are not in any way intended as a description of what goes on in the brain when learning occurs. They are simply schemata for analyzing and classifying behavioral observations and types of experiments on learning.

One of the earliest forms of learning that takes place in the child is perceptual learning. The child must learn to "see," and sensory experiences must become integrated for the child to be capable of form discrimination, size constancy, distance judgment, figure-ground distinctions, and the like. This form of learning may be represented as $S–S$ learning, that is, the connection of one stimulus, or set of stimuli, with another. The formation of $S–S$ connections is probably not dependent upon reinforcement but probably takes place through repeated contiguity of various sensory elements. The formation of $S–S$ connections is not thought of as being mediated by any verbal or other symbolic responses.

Another basic form of learning, known as response integration, can be symbolized as $R–R$. Most forms of motor learning are good examples of this. Learning to walk, for instance, involves the integration of a large number of motor responses. To be sure, walking involves sensory feedback, both from external cues and from proprioceptive and other internal sensations, but when the total act of walking has become perfected through practice, it depends largely upon the "playing-off" of a centrally integrated sequence of motor responses. It is this central integration that we symbolize as *R–R*. This integration of motor responses can be easily understood by anyone who has engaged extensively in any form of athletics involving complex motor skills or who plays a musical instrument. The pianist who has memorized a piece of music later finds he cannot recall the notes unless he sits at the piano and begins to play. His "memory" of the composition seems to lie more in his motor behavior than in any symbolic representation of the music; he can play the piece at the piano even though at his desk he would be quite unable to write out the score. And if he makes a mistake while playing, he cannot easily stop and start again at just any point. He usually has to go back to some "beginning" point in the music and continue from there. The sequence of integrated responses involved in playing seems to "unfold" without much conscious direction on the part of the player. Often, if he tries too hard to think of the notes in a difficult but well-practiced passage, he will be more apt to fumble. The same sort of thing is seen in athletic performance; once a complex motor action is underway, it becomes extremely difficult, or even impossible, to stop it before the entire sequence is run off. This type of learning, like *S–S* learning, does not itself depend upon verbal or symbolic behavior. A good deal of verbal behavior, however, may involve such *R–R* connections. That is to say, vocal utterances tend to follow well-integrated sequences, which conform to the sequential aspects of our language. Thus it is utterly impossible for an adult to improvise totally nonsensical arrangements of words which do not markedly reflect the normal sequential properties of his own language.

Next, there is *S–R* learning, or the connection of stimuli with responses. A simple example would be Pavlov's dog salivating when the bell rings. The question of whether such learning takes place by sheer temporal contiguity of stimulus and response, or whether reinforcement is necessary for the formation of *S–R* connections, cannot be discussed here, and it is perhaps not a crucial issue for our present purpose. But we must introduce an elaboration of this *S–R* paradigm to represent those instances when a reinforcing stimulus $(S+)$ does, in fact, hasten and strengthen the formation of an *S–R* connection. This can be shown as follows: *S–R* $(S+)$, in the case of positive reinforcement or reward, and *S–R* $(S-)$, in the case of negative reinforcement or punishment. These forms of reward learning have been most thoroughly studied in animal psychology, which is not to say that such learning does not occur also in human subjects. Beyond an early age, however, simple *S–R* learning is rarely found in "pure" form; it is almost always accompanied by other response elements, usually verbal. These are illustrated in some of the following paradigms.

Verbal learning begins with the child's hearing words in connection with other stimuli in his environment. Words are at first just one of many kinds of auditory stimulation; through stimulus substitution the words come to evoke some of the same responses as do the objects with which they were associated; but since all of the stimulus elements in an object or situation that come to evoke a set of responses are not present when the word is heard alone, many of the response elements drop out or become very minimal in response to the word. Other response elements remain, however. These may consist of looking toward the object and of anticipatory movements involved in grasping or manipulating the object. There is also an affective side of this response; if the stimulus object is one which has been previously associated with affective arousal, such as the sight and sound of the parent, or touching a hot stove, or tasting a piece of candy, the words associated with these objects will also tend to arouse some of the same affective components.

In the first few months of life the child does not seem to distinguish vocal utterances from other auditory stimuli, and motor responses can be conditioned to both vocal and nonvocal sounds with about equal ease. By about one year of age, however, verbal stimuli (S_v) become much more potent than other forms of auditory stimulation. Responses (R) can be conditioned some four times faster to words than to other, nonvocal sounds (Ervin and Miller, 1963, p. 135). Therefore, at this age the acquisition of S_v–R connections begins to take place quite rapidly, and by two years of age the easiest kind of learning for the child is to learn to recognize the names of things. It would be interesting to speculate on the reasons for this prepotency of verbal stimuli. One explanation probably lies in the fact that verbal stimuli are more consistently associated with other affect-arousing stimuli, namely, the parents. The vocal sounds associated with parental attentions become singled out, so to speak, as the figure against a background of other sounds.

S_v–R learning is soon followed, usually during the child's second and third years, by S–V learning, in which the child makes his own verbal responses (V) to the stimuli (S) which had formerly been associated with their verbal labels as spoken by others (S_v). The child's own verbal responses (V) gradually come to approximate the corresponding auditory model, that is, the parent's speech. Between two and three years of age the child constantly points to objects (S), hears their verbal labels (S_v) from the parents, and tries to imitate these sounds in his own vocal utterances (V). It is at this stage that a child begins to learn that certain discrete sounds or words are associated with specific objects and acts. During this "labeling" period, as we shall call it, some very important social-class differences may exert their effects on verbal learning. Lower-class parents engage in relatively little of this naming or "labeling" play with their children. Two main consequences of this have been noted: First of all, there results a retardation of S_v–R learning, due to the fact that the parents' verbal labels are less frequently associated with other stimuli in the environment; and thus S–V learning is also retarded, with the effect that the child will have less tendency to make verbal responses to the stimuli in its environment. Second, it has been noticed by first-grade teachers that lower-class children have greater difficulty than middle-class children in discriminating and understanding isolated words. The lower-class child may reach school age before he begins to learn what the middle-class child has already acquired long before in his preschool years: learning how to associate single spoken words with objects, pictures of objects, or with printed words. These associations are made more difficult for the lower-class child by the fact that many of these tasks require that the spoken words be identified out of the context of continuous speech. That words are discrete labels for things seems to be better known by the middle-class child entering first grade than by the lower-class child. Much of this knowledge is gained in the parent-child interaction, as when the parent looks at a picture book with the child, points to each picture while saying its name, and reinforces the child's behavior with some show of approval when he utters similar sounds. Apparently a great amount of this kind of learning takes place in middle-class homes, while it seems to take place hardly at all among lower-class families. We shall see shortly why this labeling behavior is so important for other kinds of learning.

The next developmental stage of learning is characterized by the emergence of voluntary behavior, that is, overt behavior which is under the child's own verbal control. It is thus represented as V–R, or the connection of verbal responses (whether overt or covert) with other motor behavior. Psychologically it is a rather large step from S–V to V–R learning. The infant's motor behavior is mostly involuntary reflex action. Later the child's motor behavior shows the effects of R–R, S–R, and S_v–R learning. It is not until much later, usually between three and four years of age, that we see clear evidence of the V–R control of behavior. Once V–R patterns are developed, they constitute, in conjunction with S–V learning, what we shall call the S–V–R paradigm. It is when this stage is reached that we fully recognize human learning, and the ontogenetic psychological development from "animal" to "man" is, in all essentials, complete. Beyond the age of six or seven, in normal middle-class children, it is doubtful if we see many forms of learning in school that are not represented by the $S-V-R$ paradigm. (The training of specific perceptual or motor skills such as might be involved in music, art, or athletic performance are possible exceptions.) By this stage, the child much of the time is no longer responding directly and solely to his physical environment; the environmental stimuli (S) give rise to verbal responses (V), either overtly or covertly, which in turn govern the overt motor response (R). Psychologically, one of the big differences between a young child and an adult, or between a lower animal and a human beyond the age of six or seven, can be represented as the difference between $S-R$ and $S-V-R$.

An addition should be made to this paradigm, as follows: $S-V-R-V_c$; the V_c represents a verbal confirming response or "feedback." Overt behavior often results in certain environmental effects which, in terms of the person's needs or purposes, are desirable $(S+)$ and hence reinforcing, or they are undesirable $(S-)$ and hence negatively reinforcing or punishing. Adjusting the hot and cold faucets in the shower is a simple example of behavior with rather immediate environmental consequences. The person is able to respond verbally to these environmental consequences of his own behavior and this can be called a verbal confirmatory response (V_c). This verbal confirmation, or feedback, can have much the same effect on the speed of acquisition of $S-R$ or $S-V-R$ connections as the environmental consequent itself would have.

This capacity for self-reinforcement or symbolic reinforcement is extremely limited in lower animals, as it is in very young children. To establish an $S-R$ connection in an animal, it is usually necessary to follow the response to be learned by some form of primary reinforcement or reward, that is, reinforcement which has direct physiological consequences, such as biological need-reduction, pain-reduction, or some form of innately pleasurable stimulation. The V_c response is also more than merely a form of secondary reinforcement. A secondary reinforcer is a previously neutral stimulus which has gained reinforcing power through temporal contiguity with a primary or biologically relevant reinforcer. But secondary reinforcers are known to extinguish very rapidly, at least in animals. This is not the case, however, with the verbal confirmatory response, V_c. It has the effect of strengthening behavior which has desirable environmental consequences even though the V_c itself does not have any primary reinforcing properties in the biological sense. The V_c response is most often covert, especially in adults, and it may even be quite unconscious. It consists, in effect, of saying to oneself *Good!* or *That's right!* or *Wrong!*

The existence of the covert V_c response has been experimentally demonstrated in children by Russian psychologists (reported by Razran, 1959). In one experiment an autonomic conditioned response first was formed to the word *Right*. Then the children were given a set of arithmetic problems, and it was found that when a child solved a problem correctly, the autonomic response previously conditioned to the word *Right* would occur. In other words, each time the child performed correctly, he confirmed or reinforced his own answer with some sub-vocal, or perhaps even unconscious, equivalent of the verbal response *Right*. In another experiment a previously established conditioned response to the word *ten* occurred when the child was given arithmetic problems that resulted in the answer *ten*. Thus, it appears that beyond a certain age the child's own verbal behavior may become his most important source of immediate reinforcement. Much more, however, remains to be learned about this form of self-confirmatory behavior and its developmental aspects; this is one of the important tasks of future research.

Then, words also become linked to words, and thus: $V-V$. The word association experiment, in which the subject is presented with a stimulus word and is asked to respond as quickly as possible with the first word that comes to mind, is a good illustration of the existence of $V-V$ connections. There is a great deal of communality among subjects from similar cultural backgrounds in their first two or three associations to a word: for example, *black-white, table-chair, man-woman,* and so forth. As a result of these connections between verbal responses, the $S-V-R$ paradigm may be elaborated to $S-V-V-R$; there is ample experimental evidence that under certain conditions such chains of verbal mediators do, in fact, play a role in learning.

Since two or more words which are not directly associated with one another may be associated with a third word, one more type of paradigm may be described:

$$\begin{array}{c} V \\ \diagup \mid \diagdown \\ V-V \quad V \end{array}$$

This diagram makes it apparent that verbal associations exist in hierarchical arrangement. In this illustration there are two words associated with each other, and both are associated with a higher-order, more general, word; and there is another word which is not associated with the first two, except indirectly through its association with the higher-order, more general, word; an example would be the words *table, chair,* and *bed*. *Table* and *chair* are strong associates of one another, but neither is strongly associated with *bed*. All three, however, are associated with the word *furniture*. Here, obviously, is a concept in its most rudimentary form.

Now the reader must imagine for himself extensive hierarchical networks elaborated along these lines. It is into such "verbal networks," which exist in older children and adults, that environmental stimuli, both verbal and nonverbal, enter and ramify. In terms of verbal-learning theory, the adult psyche may be pictured as consisting, in part, of this extensive hierarchical network of verbal associations. A great deal of what we think of as intelligence, or as verbal ability, or learning ability, can be thought of in terms of the extensiveness and complexity of this verbal network and of the strength of the interconnections among its elements. All of these connections among various verbal elements are by no means of equal strength. Word association tests and other related techniques can be used to map out roughly the structure of the network and the relative strengths of the connections among its elements. The relative strengths of the various associations determine the channels along which semantic generalization occurs when stimuli enter the network via any given element or set of elements. The strength and richness of the connections among elements at different levels of the hierarchy determine to a large degree the ease and speed of concept attainment and the person's level of ability for conceptual and abstract thinking. This vast verbal network, as it exists in the normal adult, is awesome to contemplate; thorough exploration of it is still far from accomplished, although in recent years psychologists have increasingly devoted their attention to it.

Now we must look at these schemata in greater detail and in relation to experimental findings.

S_v–R

The acquisition of overt motor responses (such as pointing the finger at an object) in response to external verbal stimuli (such as the parent's naming the object) is not an exclusively human form of learning. Animals, too, can learn to respond to verbal stimuli. S_v–R learning differs in no essential aspects from simple S–R learning, except that in children beyond one year of age the verbal stimuli (S_v) are, as has already been pointed out, more potent than other forms of auditory stimulation, and they therefore enter into connection with motor responses more readily than do other auditory stimuli.

S_v–R learning is a necessary basis for other forms of verbal learning. Soviet psychologists have investigated some of the factors which govern the rate of S_v–R learning. This research has implications for understanding social-class differences in the rate of vocabulary acquisition and the development of verbal understanding in children. For example, learning verbal labels for objects is greatly facilitated if the labels occur with the objects repeatedly in different verbal contexts. One Russian experiment which illustrates this point was carried out with ten 20-

month-old children (Razran, 1961, p. 126). In the course of several months these children were shown a particular doll a total of 1500 times. For five of the children the presentation of the doll was never accompanied by more than three different verbalizations from the experimenter: *Here is a doll, Take the doll, Give me the doll*. Thus, though there might have been a good quantity of verbal stimulation, it was greatly limited in variety. The other five children, on the other hand, were presented with the doll an equal number of times but it was accompanied by *thirty* different verbalizations from the experimenter, such as *Look for the doll, Rock the doll, Feed the doll, Seat the doll*, and the like. In both groups the total amount of speech from the examiner was the same; only the variety of verbal context in which the word *doll* was heard differed for the two groups. At the end of the training period, each child was asked to *Pick a doll* from among a number of different dolls and other toys. The child's performance in this task reflected his understanding of the word *doll*. Children in the first group, who had heard *doll* in the context of only three different verbalizations, were indeed able to pick out a doll, but they often picked out other toys as well. The children in the second group, who had learned *doll* in a great variety of verbal contexts, picked out the experimental doll as well as other dolls from among the group of toys, but they never selected any other types of toys when told only to "Pick a doll." In short, the second group had apparently attained a more adequate concept of *doll* and had differentiated the stimulus characteristics both of the object and of the word from those of other objects and words.

All this is quite consistent with theories of discrimination learning. The word *doll* becomes more strongly associated with the object than do other verbalizations occurring at the same time the object is presented, for *doll* is the one constant verbal stimulus in each presentation, and this difference between the constant and varied words is greater for the verbalization group with thirty different sayings than for the group which had only three sayings.

The same sort of experiment was done by presenting a book twenty times to children 19 months of age. Three conditions were used: In the first condition, only one particular book and one particular verbalization (for example, "Look at the book") were presented a total of twenty times; in the second condition, one particular book but twenty verbalizations were used; in the third condition, there were twenty different books but only one verbalization. As in the previous experiment, at the end of training the children were asked to "Pick a book" from among a number of various books and other objects. Performance was by far the best in the second group; the first group had barely learned the meaning of *book* and showed very poor differentiation among the various objects from which they had to select a book, while the third group was intermediate between the other groups in adequacy of performance. Again, the auditory differentiation of the label was better in the varied verbalization group and this had a more facilitating effect on learning the meaning of *book* than was obtained through seeing a large variety of books accompanied by only one saying.

Another experiment illustrates the fact that S_v–R connections are established more quickly when the verbal label spoken by the adult is accompanied not only by the visual presentation of the object but also by permitting the child to obtain tactile and kinesthetic experience with the object. Small objects which were unfamiliar to the children were repeatedly shown to one group of children, along with the experimenter's naming the objects. Another group of children were not only shown the objects, but these were handed to them for manipulation while their names were spoken by the experimenter. Later, the children in the group allowed to have more than just visual knowledge of the objects were better able to point to the objects when they were named by the experimenter and these children were also better able to imitate the experimenter's spoken names for the objects. Unfortunately most of this work can only be regarded as suggestive for our purposes, because our knowledge of it is second-hand and many of the details of experimental procedure are either unclear or unknown. This happens to be true of a great deal of the Soviet research in child psychology. The published reports of the Russian psychologists also are often too sketchy to permit adequate evaluation and interpretation of their results. Much of this important work should be replicated in other laboratories if it is to be better understood and integrated into general behavior theory. This promises to be an especially fruitful area for research into the origins of social-class differences in learning and verbal ability and for understanding the so-called subcultural type of mental retardation.

S–V

At this stage the child learns to name things, but the naming response during the first year or so of the child's acquisition of this ability is little different in its psychological consequences from any other kind of motor response. That is to say, even though the child is able to respond verbally to things in his environment, these responses do not have any regulative feedback; they do not control the child's behavior. Verbalization, however, does serve a communicative function, drawing the parents' attention to the child's point of interest and thereby receiving some external reinforcement.

V–R

At this stage language first exerts its peculiarly human effects. The child's own verbal responses come to influence and control his overt behavior. This progression from $S_v–R$ (that is, responding to the speech of others) to $S–V$ (that is, making verbal responses to stimuli) to $V–R$ (that is, the control of one's overt behavior by his own verbalization) has been closely studied by the Soviet psychologist Luria and his colleagues (Luria, 1961*a*, 1961*b*). Some of the typical findings from the fascinating experiments carried out in their laboratory can be illustrated by one of Luria's procedures.

The apparatus and procedures are simple: the child holds in his hand a soft rubber bulb which is connected to a kymograph for recording the child's response of squeezing. The differential stimuli which signal the child's response are a blue and a red light. The child is instructed to press the bulb when the blue light goes on and not to press when the red light goes on. The experimenter reinforces the child's behavior with the commands *Press* and *Do not press*.

Here is the interesting developmental sequence of the child's behavior in this test: under two years of age the verbal commands of the experimenter have little or no effect on the child's behavior. Either colored light causes the child to squeeze the bulb; the child does not respond differentially, and once the child begins to squeeze the bulb, it is difficult for him to stop. Then, at some time between about two and two and a half years of age the experimenter's command becomes able to control the child's behavior. If the experimenter says *Press,* the child will do so; similarly, the command *Don't press* will effectively inhibit the child's response. And even though the child is perfectly able to imitate verbally the experimenter's commands, *Press* and *Do not press,* the child's own speech at this age does not regulate his own behavior. Even if he says *Press* when the blue light goes on and *Don't press* when the red light goes on, he will squeeze the bulb the moment *either* light goes on. In short, there is little or no connection between the child's verbalization and his motor behavior; the child is still learning at the *S–R* level. In fact, the verbal and motor behaviors seem to interfere with each other, and the child at this age is rarely able to make both responses simultaneously.

The child's ability to control his overt behavior through his own verbalization begins to develop at about three- to three-and-a-half years of age. The child now does not need the experimenter's command, but will follow the preliminary instructions to *Press* when the blue light goes on. But here is the interesting thing: though the child of this age can say *Press* and will respond properly to his own command, he cannot *inhibit* his response by his own speech. For example, if the child is told to *Press twice,* and repeats to himself *Press twice,* it does not control his behavior—the instant the light goes on he begins pressing the bulb repeatedly, even though there is no doubt that the child understands the concept of *twice.*

But the child can control his behavior verbally if first he is told to say *One! Two!* as he presses the bulb. Then, when the light goes on, the child says *One! Two!* and simultaneously presses the bulb twice, and only twice. The verbal control of his behavior is then nearly perfect. This is clearly an advance over the performance of the two- and two-and-a-half-year-old in this situation; at this earlier age, instructing the child to say *One! Two!,* even though the child is able to do this, does not have any regulative effect on his behavior and the child will go on pressing the bulb continuously until stopped by some external stimulus. Interestingly enough, even after this sort of practice, the three- to three-and-a-half-year-old, when again placed in this situation a few days later, but without instructions to say *One! Two!,* is not able to inhibit his squeezing of the bulb. Similarly, when a child of three or four is trained to say *I must press* to the blue light and *I must not press* to the red light, the verbal reaction will control only the positive reaction to the blue light; it will not inhibit his response to the red light. The only way to inhibit response to the red light is to train a verbal response only to the blue light and verbally to ignore the red light completely. If the child says *Do not press* when the red light goes on, this only acts as additional stimulation to press the bulb when the red light appears. The experimenter's command *Don't press,* on the other hand, is quite capable of inhibiting the response in the child of three to four. In other words, the development of verbal inhibition of overt behavior is a more advanced process than the verbal control of positive reactions to stimuli. It was found, for example, that the child could be prevented from squeezing the bulb in response to the red light if, instead of trying to train inhibition of the response, the child was merely told to make some other positive response which was incompatible with squeezing the bulb, such as dropping it and placing his hand on his knee.

By four and a half to five and a half years of age the child's own verbalization becomes more completely able to control his behavior; also, it is noted that much of this control becomes transferred from the child's overtly spoken words to his own internal speech. Thus, the experimenter's spoken directions to the child have the effect of evoking similar responses in the child which, in the experimental situation, will control the child's response of squeezing or not squeezing the bulb, even in the absence of any immediate verbal command from the experimenter. This is what is meant by saying that the child has understood the experimenter's instructions. This understanding consists of the child's being able to represent the experimenter's directions to himself verbally at a later time; and the child's behavior is then controlled by these self-directed verbal responses. The tendency to use speech to control one's own behavior gradually becomes a spontaneous part of the child's repertoire. Luria has noted that normal children from four to five years of age, when confronted with a problem that arouses some kind of difficulty, indulge in overt speech not directed at the experimenter. This speech seems to serve some self-purpose; it is not just a means of communication but also a means of representing aspects of the environment to oneself and of controlling one's own behavior. As the child gets older, his self-directed speech becomes increasingly covert—it becomes thinking.

This regulatory aspect of verbal behavior has been described in great detail by Luria and Yudovich (1959) in their intensive study of a pair of twins who were remarkably retarded in language development as a result of spending nearly all their time in each other's company. Without normal language, which plays a central role in children's fantasy, their total behavioral pattern was much more infantile than would be expected in normal children of their age. This immaturity was especially noticeable in their play. Apparently the fantasy that normally accompanies children's play and helps to sustain the child's attention, creating some degree of organization and planfulness, was conspicuously deficient in these verbally underdeveloped twins. When the twins were separated and given verbal stimulation and training, their behavior showed marked changes in the direction characteristic of normal children.

As a means of studying developmental differences between lower- and middle-class children it would seem highly worthwhile to perform experiments similar to those of Luria on the development of verbal control of behavior, and to make the kinds of careful observations Luria and Yudovich made of these twins. Though one might hypothesize social-class differences along these lines, we as yet have no direct knowledge bearing on this. The degree to which social-class factors might affect the development of what Luria calls *voluntary behavior,* that is, behavior which is under the person's own verbal control, will have to be determined by future investigations.

S–V–R

To summarize: the child acquires a strong "learning set" or propensity for acquiring *S–V* connections roughly between the ages of two and four; and between four and six the child begins to show signs of *V–R* learning. Now that both the external stimulus situation and the overt responding are linked with the child's verbalization (thus, *S–V–R*), the child has advanced to the typically human adult form of learning.

The first clear-cut indications of $S–V–R$ learning in the child, which, as we have already indicated, is the first stage that clearly sets the child apart from the lower animals psychologically, can be demonstrated in specially designed laboratory experiments at around the age of six. Until this stage of development is reached, the child shows little superiority to the chimpanzee of comparable age. But with the attainment of $S–V–R$ behavior, the child intellectually leaps far ahead of his anthropoid cousin. It is interesting that throughout history every society which has ever instituted formal education has decided that this is the best age to begin the child's formal schooling.

But the transition from $S–R$ to $S–V–R$ learning does not take place suddenly. While it is safe to say that the two-year-old's learning is predominantly of the $S–R$ type characteristic of the lower animals, and that normal children by nine or ten years of age show predominantly $S–V–R$ learning, there is no exact point at which this transition takes place. Rather, there is a gradual increase in the number and kinds of learning situations that will evoke verbally mediated behavior. For $S–V–R$ learning to be markedly superior to $S–R$ learning, the child must already have acquired a strong "set" for $S–V$ learning, that is, a propensity for labeling things, and the child also must already have reached the stage where his overt responses can be readily controlled by his own speech. And we know that both these types of learning are not fully evident until somewhere around the ages of five to six, when in conjunction they can emerge as $S–V–R$ behavior.

But the child at this age does not always spontaneously use his capacity for verbal mediation. Telling the child to respond verbally to the elements in the learning situation will often greatly facilitate his performance, since his tendency to verbalize spontaneously is weak, and without such outside prompting his verbal ability may not be brought to bear on the task before him. In older children, on the other hand, the degree of faciliation from the adult's verbal prompting will not be so great, presumably because the older child is already spontaneously using his own verbal mediation.

The superiority of $S–V–R$ over $S–R$ learning can be explained in a number of ways. First, we can invoke what Miller (1948, p. 174) has called "the acquired distinctiveness of cues," which merely describes the fact that learning to respond with distinctive labels to two similar stimuli increases the differences between them and thereby facilitates subsequent discrimination. For example, learning the names *horse* and *mule* for the respective animals makes it easier to notice the difference between them, because their distinctive features become conditioned to different verbal responses.

But $S–V–R$ learning is also far superior to $S–R$ learning even when the stimuli to which overt responses are to be conditioned are so highly dissimilar as hardly to need the benefit of this verbal aid to discrimination. In such cases something other than the "acquired distinctiveness of cues" must be involved in the verbal facilitation of learning. The explanation probably lies in the fact that the child has already acquired a strong learning set for $S-V$ learning, which makes the learning of labels to stimulus objects relatively easy. Or in many cases the child may already know the labels for the stimulus objects which are later to be associated with certain overt responses. Similarly, on the response side, the child already has a strong learning set to control his overt behavior by his verbal responses. Many of these $V-R$ connections may already exist when the child faces a new learning situation. Experimental learning situations, for example, often involve instructions to press pushbuttons, to pick up objects, to point at one thing or another, and so on. Since the $S-V$ and $V-R$ connections have often been acquired prior to the experimental learning task, the child merely has to bring these sets of prior learning into play simultaneously in order to master the new task. It turns out, in other words, that there is nothing really new the child has to learn.

All these points have been amply demonstrated in various studies. Perhaps the earliest, and still one of the best for illustration, was carried out by Marjorie Pyles Honzik (Pyles, 1932) at the University of California. It is interesting that when this study first appeared, over thirty years ago, it aroused little general interest. Now, with the revival of interest in cognitive processes in developmental psychology, this study takes on a significance which was not formerly appreciated. If we leave out the details of experimental design, such as the counterbalancing of groups, the use of equivalent forms of the test materials, and so on, the experiment is basically simple.

The subjects were eighty nursery-school, kindergarten, and first-grade children, ranging in age from two to seven years. The experimental task was essentially to learn by trial-and-error which of five hollow objects concealed a little toy under it. There were three conditions of learning: (i) The five small objects were all nonsense shapes of about the same size but differing clearly in shape. The child was repeatedly presented with the set of five shapes, always in a random arrangement, and was asked to pick the one he thought contained the reward. On the child's first successful choice, the experimenter would say "Yes, that one had it," thereby reinforcing the child's attention to the correct object. (ii) The second condition was the same as the first, except that when the child found the toy under one of the objects the experimenter would say "The name of that shape is Mobie," and the child was urged to repeat the name. The experimenter then gave names to each of the other shapes —*Kolo, Pito, Gamie,* and *Bokie.* (iii) In the third condition the forms were those of familiar animals (cat, dog, rabbit, bear, and monkey). The children usually named the animals spontaneously, but if they failed to do so, the experimenter would say the animal's name in the first few trials.

The number of trials required to learn to pick out the object containing the toy on four successive trials was markedly affected by the varying experimental conditions. The means of the unnamed forms, the named forms, and the animals, were 21.3, 14.2, and 5.3 respectively.

Note that even though the "naming" group had to learn to attach unfamiliar "nonsense" words to unfamiliar "nonsense" figures, as well as to learn which of the five figures contained the toy, they were able to attain the criterion of mastery on this test more readily than the group that did not name the objects. Learning was fastest for the animal figures, of course, since most of the children had already learned to discriminate among these and already knew their names. The differences between the named and unnamed conditions would have been even greater were it not that in the unnamed condition, thirteen of the children spontaneously gave names to the nonsense shapes, such as *cup, Old Mother shoe, the slide, a piece of cake, like Mt. Hamilton.* The children who thus spontaneously verbalized in the unnamed condition were superior learners. One five-year-old in the unnamed condition even seemed to realize the reasons for his difficulty, and remarked, "If they had names, that would be fine." Also, it was noted that in the named condition 64 percent of the children named the correct object of their own accord as they picked it up (for instance, "Where's Mobie?" "Mobie's going to have it.") This is a good example of $S–V–R$ learning.

Recent studies have demonstrated further implications of verbalization in the learning process. Bialer (1961) has shown that verbal labeling leads to secondary stimulus generalization to a much greater degree in children of normal intelligence than it does in retarded children of the same age. That is, with brief training in the experimental situation, the normal children can be made to change from an $S–R$ (that is, direct response to the physical stimulus, which in a transfer task results in primary stimulus generalization) to an $S–V–R$ (that is, response to a stimulus-produced verbal cue, which in a transfer task results in secondary stimulus generalization) type of performance in discrimination learning, while retarded children showed relatively little tendency to make this transition. The study indicates that the strength of the habit of $S–V–R$ as contrasted with $S–R$ learning is directly related to IQ.

Another effect of labeling was shown by Spiker (1956), who used a delayed-reaction procedure. The subject is shown the reward being placed under a particular stimulus object, but he is not allowed to pick up the object to get the reward until some time later when the stimulus object must also be discriminated from among other similar objects. Having previously learned verbal labels for the objects makes this task much easier; without labels the child quickly forgets which stimulus object contains the reward. The writer has informally observed a similar effect in preschool children in the following situation. A dozen common objects, such as a comb, a glass, a spoon, a bar of soap, a toy car, a toy airplane, a small book, and so on, are placed one at a time before the child, who is told merely to look at them for a few minutes so that he will be able to remember them. The objects are then hidden from the child's view and he is asked to name as many of them as he can recall. The objects are handed to the child one-by-one as he names them. Usually only three or four of the dozen objects will be recalled by the typical preschooler. The child is capable of naming each of the objects when it is handed to him, so his failure to remember the objects when they are removed from sight is not due to his inability to give their names. Now, if the child is asked to name each object the first time it is presented, his memory for the objects, when they are removed from sight, will be much better; he will recall eight or nine of the objects. It seems that the visual image of the object rapidly fades, and the subject who has not named the objects fails to recall them a few moments later. What the child more easily remembers of the situation are his verbal responses to the objects. In older children instructions to verbalize have no discernible effect on this task, presumably because the act of recognition of these objects by older children consists in part of implicit naming.

One of the factors determining the effectiveness of verbal labeling is the distinctiveness of the labels. This was shown in an experiment by Reese (1958), who had children first learn labels to two different-colored lights and then learn a differential motor response to the lights. Four groups of children learned labels for the two lights; the labels represented four degrees of distinctiveness, viz., *wug-wog, zim-zam, lev-mib,* and *wug-zam.* First of all, the more distinct the two labels were, the easier it was to learn the correct motor response to each light. In brief, the speed of acquisition of $S–V$ connections and the superiority of $S–V–R$ over $S–R$ learning are directly related to the distinctiveness of V, the stimulus-produced verbal cues. In more general terms, if vocabulary is limited and if stimuli do not evoke highly differentiated verbal mediating responses, learning will not be as facilitated as when there is a great variety and distinctiveness in the verbalization. If many things in the environment are just "thingamabobs" to their beholder, the learning of differential responses to these things will be harder than if each one has a distinct label.

Lastly, it should be pointed out that verbal cues do not invariably facilitate learning, but may even create an obstacle. Experimental situations have been devised (for example, Ranken, 1963) in which it was possible for verbalization to have either a facilitating or a hindering effect, depending upon the requirements of the task. This is because a verbal label usually leaves out or distorts certain details of the physical stimulus which may be important in certain kinds of learning.

$S–V–R–V_c$

Not only must a child acquire the ability to mediate associative learning by stimulus-produced verbal cues, as illustrated in the preceding section, but he must also learn to respond verbally to the environmental feedback so as to provide his own reinforcement for those actions which result in desirable effects. If all environmental effects were biologically rewarding, secondary reinforcement through a verbal confirmatory response (V_c) would be quite unnecessary. But most things that humans have to learn, at least by the age formal schooling begins, are not associated with primary reinforcement, that is, with consequences having direct biological effects. The feedback in most forms of human learning is usually some biologically neutral stimulus. These feedback stimuli are quite powerless as reinforcers unless they elicit in the subject some verbal response (this may be totally implicit) which confirms the correctness or incorrectness of the motor response. That lower-class children are probably deficient as compared with middle-class children in this type of verbal confirming response is indicated by the research of Terrell (1958) and Terrell, Durkin, and Wiesley (1959), which has shown that middle-class children can perform quite well under conditions where the only reinforcement or feedback is simple knowledge of results, while lower-class children need reinforcement consisting of tangible rewards.

The above points can be illustrated by a simple learning experiment performed with some very nonverbal junior high school children classed as mentally retarded on the basis of IQs in the range of 50 to 75 (Jensen, 1963). The task consisted of learning, by trial-and-error, to associate five different stimuli (colored geometric forms) with five different motor responses (pressing one of five pushbuttons). The nominal reinforcement, which was given whenever the subject made a correct response, was a green light directly below the stimulus display screen. Formally, the task can be presented as follows:

S (color-form)_____R (pressing
        a pushbutton) $S+$ (green light goes on) or
        $S-$ (green light doesn't go on).

As compared with children of average IQ, the retarded children were generally very slow learners on this test and several of them seemed not to learn at all. Then the experimenter prompted them in using verbal cues. After the slowest subjects were given a few minutes of practice in merely naming the stimuli (red circle, blue triangle, and so on), some of them markedly improved their learning rate, while others still failed to learn. It was discovered that the green reinforcement light originally had no reinforcing function for some of these children, even though they had been told it was the signal for a correct response. So the experimenter began saying *Right! That's it! Good!* and the like, every time the green light went on. As a result, the light acquired a reinforcing function, which held up long after the experimenter had stopped giving verbal reinforcement, and these children's learning rate improved markedly as a consequence.

These procedures would have been quite superfluous with normal children, who spontaneously verbalized about the essential elements of the situation, including the confirmatory responses "Right," or "Wrong," or some equivalent thereof. These confirmatory responses are usually implicit, however; it is as if the green light's going on said to the subject *Right!* and its failure to go on said *Wrong!* But to most of the retardates the green light was just that—a green light—and no more. Thus, what appeared nominally to be a nonverbal learning task—just looking at colored figures and pushing buttons—actually was affected to a large degree by the subject's verbal behavior. One could often observe the average and gifted children talking to themselves during the learning trials. In marked contrast, the retarded children were conspicuously lacking this kind of spontaneous verbal behavior.

The surprising result was that after the verbalization training, several of the "retarded" children learned faster than any of the average and did as well as gifted children whose IQs were above 135. Four of the thirty-six "retarded" children exceeded the mean of the gifted group. All these "retarded" children who performed exceptionally well after verbalization training were lower-class children. In a follow-up study, middle-class retardates in the same IQ range were tested, with and without verbalization instructions, and under both conditions were found to be markedly inferior in learning ability to the lower-class children of the same IQ. More will be said about this in the last section of this chapter, which deals with the use of learning tasks for diagnosing intellectual ability.

SPONTANEOUS VERBAL MEDIATION

In the preceding section we have seen that verbalization facilitates learning in children, at least beyond the age of four or five, and that there are individual differences in the tendency to verbalize spontaneously. Young children and some older children who are classed as mentally retarded, though capable of verbal facilitation of learning, do not benefit from such facilitation unless the experimenter prompts them to verbalize.

The determinants of the subject's tendency to verbalize spontaneously when he is confronted with a nominally nonverbal problem are not at all clearly understood. It is known that this tendency is related to chronological age and to measured intelligence. But the latter fact is of no help as an explanation, since successful performance on intelligence tests, *especially* so-called nonverbal tests, requires spontaneous verbalization on the part of the subject. The subject who does not verbalize spontaneously is even more severely handicapped in a nonverbal test such as Raven's Progressive Matrices than on a predominantly verbal intelligence test such as the Stanford-Binet, which explicitly calls for verbal responses from the subject. A nonverbal test item of the type found in the Progressive Matrices is shown in Figure 4.1.

The problem is to decide which of the six numbered figures properly belongs in the square above. The reader can see for himself how far he would get in such a problem without talking to himself. The verbal mediators which these figures must elicit for the correct solution to be arrived at involve such concepts as *clockwise, counterclockwise, rotation,* or some verbal equivalents of these. Obviously two things are necessary for the solution of such an item: (i) the prior acquisition of the relevant mediators, and (ii) their spontaneous (that is, not prompted by the examiner) elicitation by the stimulus elements of the problem.

In view of what has already been said about social class and verbal learning, it seems reasonable to hypothesize that children from a lower-class environment will have, as it were, a higher threshold for the elicitation of spontaneous verbalization in nominally nonverbal problem situations. Adequate evidence to test this hypothesis does not yet exist, but there are indications which suggest that this hypothesis merits further study. For example, although the nature of the items of the Stanford-Binet appears to sample largely experiences that would be gained in a white, middle-class environment, it was found that lower-class white and Negro children with very similar Stanford-Binet IQs differed significantly on the Progressive Matrices, with the Negro children obtaining lower scores (Higgens and Sivers, 1958). It would be interesting to know if the Negro children showed less spontaneous verbal behavior than did the white children while taking the Progressive Matrices test and if this characteristic could be linked to environmental influences. In normal middle-class children or adults taking this test one can observe lip movements and other overt signs of subvocal activity, but often the verbal mediation is completely covert. Thus, what we really need for the experimental investigation of the suggested hypothesis are methods

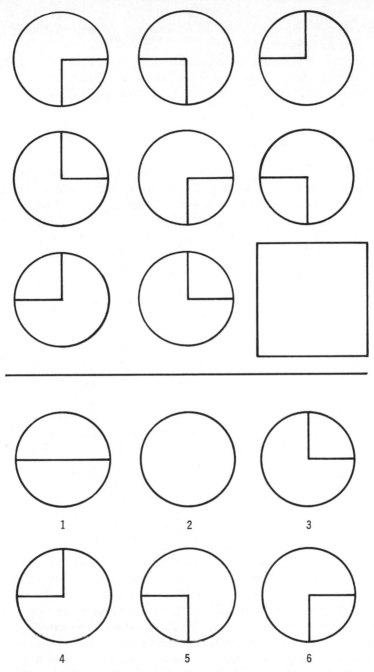

Figure 4.1. A test item of the type found in the Raven Progressive Matrices. The problem: Which of the six numbered figures belong in the empty square above?

of determining the occurrence of spontaneous verbal mediation even when it is quite implicit.

A number of experimental procedures have been used successfully to study the development of verbal mediation in children, and similar techniques could be used for the investigation of social-class differences.

Semantic Generalization

Tests of semantic generalization can be used to determine whether or not external stimuli arouse verbal mediating responses in the subject. This procedure is prominent in Soviet research (Razran, 1961), where it has been applied to the study of mental defectives. A typical experiment would consist of conditioning two different motor responses (or autonomic reflexes) to two colored lights, say blue and green. Primary stimulus generalization, which can be demonstrated in most lower animals as well as in humans, would be said to exist if colored lights of slightly different shades of blue and green were capable of eliciting the same responses conditioned to the original colors. The more the color stimuli in the transfer test differ from those in original conditioning, the less are the strength and probability of occurrence of the conditioned response. On the basis of primary generalization, stimuli in other sensory modalities will not elicit the conditioned response at all.

The test for semantic generalization consists of presenting a number of verbal stimuli, after the differential motor responses have been conditioned to the blue and green lights, and determining the degree to which the verbal stimuli elicit the conditioned response. The experimenter will say *Blue, Sky, Sea, Green, Grass,* or *Leaf,* and these stimuli which had never been directly conditioned and which certainly do not exist on the same primary stimulus dimension as the original conditioned stimuli, will elicit the conditioned response corresponding to the implied color. Thus, semantic generalization provides conclusive evidence of the existence of verbal mediators and of the fact of assocations among verbal elements. The subject's acquired network of verbal assocations determines the paths through which semantic generalization can occur.

The tendency for semantic generalization to occur, and the range of verbal stimuli to which it will occur, are strongly related to age in normal children. Mentally retarded children show correspondingly less semantic generalization, while their capacity for primary generalization is relatively strong. For example, a normal child conditioned to respond to the spoken word *Blue* will also make the conditioned response when the experimenter says *Sky* but will show no response to the phonetically similar word *Glue.* Just the opposite, however, typically occurs with a mentally retarded child.

Obviously the capacity for semantic generalization depends upon prior learning as well as upon an intact nervous system. Semantic conditioning could possibly provide means of assessing where a child stands along the developmental continuum going from *S–R* to *S–V–R* behavior.

Transposition

This phenomenon serves well to illustrate differences between performance based on *S–R* and *S–V–R* principles. In actual practice, however, the use of transposition as a laboratory technique for studying the development of cognitive functions has been fraught with methodological difficulties (White, 1963, pp. 208–211).

Transposition can be illustrated by references to Figure 4.2, which represents a series of boxes differing only in size. In the training trials we present the subject with Boxes *a, b,* and *c* (Box *d* is kept out of sight). The subject's task is to learn by trial-and-error which box contains a reward. On each trial the subject picks one box; the order of the boxes is randomly rearranged from trial to trial. Say the reward is consistently found under Box *c* and we have kept the subject at the task until he has chosen the correct box (Box *c*) on ten consecutive trials.

Then we test for transposition, as follows: Box *a* is discarded by the experimenter and Box *d* is added, so that the subject is now presented with Boxes *b, c,* and *d*. Which box will he choose?

One of two choices generally occurs. The subject either responds on an absolute basis, thereby choosing Box *c,* which had previously been associated with reward. Or the subject responds on a *relational* basis and chooses the largest of the three boxes, which now is Box *d*.

Making this relational choice is called *transposition*. What it seems to show is that the immediate stimulus for the subject's response is not

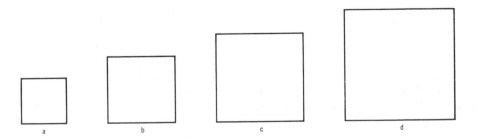

Figure 4.2.   Squares representing boxes of rated sizes used in the transposition task (see text).

the particular physical object, but the subject's own verbal response to the set of three boxes. In other words, the subject who transposes is not just learning to respond to Box *c*. He is learning to respond to some implicit verbalization, such as *the largest box*.

Transposition can occur along many different stimulus dimensions other than size, for example, hue and brightness of visual stimuli and pitch and intensity of auditory stimuli. Without going into the specific details of various experiments on transposition, the following general conclusions are possible. Lower animals differ from adult humans in not showing transposition under conditions where it usually occurs in humans. Preschool children also fail to show transposition under conditions that favor it in older children. The age of transition from absolute to relational responding in normal children is generally somewhere between five and seven years old. Transposition is highly related to the subject's ability to verbalize his reason for making the relational choice, while children who do not show transposition are generally unable to give any verbal account of their behavior in this situation (Stevenson and Iscoe, 1954). In short, it appears that the difference between absolute and relational responding in the transposition test corresponds to the difference between *S–R* and *S–V–R* learning. Thus, under certain conditions transposition might be a useful means for studying the development of verbal mediation as a function of environmental variables.

Reversal and Nonreversal Shifts

A more dependable but somewhat more complicated experimental procedure than transposition for studying the development of verbal mediating processes is a technique known as reversal shift. It has been used successfully for this purpose by Howard Kendler and Tracy Kendler in an intensive program of experimentation which has yielded many interesting findings of considerable relevance to the present discussion (see references to Kendler).

Though there are a number of minor variations in materials and techniques to be found in the large number of reversal shift experiments, performed with a diversity of subjects such as cockroaches, fish, rats, monkeys, children, and college students, we can describe the major findings in terms of just one rather typical procedure used in many experiments with human subjects.

Look at Figure 4.3. The subject is presented with a pair of figures which differ from each other in two attributes: *size* (large and small) and *brightness* (black and white). Say we begin by presenting the large black (*LB*) and small white (*SW*) figures, with the instructions to the

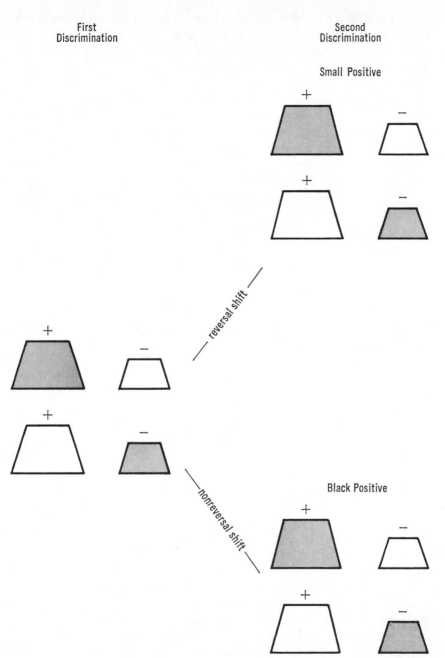

Figure 4.3. Examples of a reversal and a nonreversal shift discrimination problem (from Kendler and Kendler, 1962).

subject to find the reward (a marble) under one of the figures.[2] On the first trial the subject finds the marble under the *LB* figure; thus the marble is associated with both size and brightness. On the next trial, the large white (*LW*) and small bright (*SB*) figures are presented, and again the subject looks for the marble, to find it under the *LW* figure. Now it is clear (to us, not necessarily to the subject) that size and not brightness is the relevant cue. The reward is always under the large figure, and whether it is black or white is irrelevant.

One obvious and important difference between the reversal and non-reversal conditions should be noted. The reversal shift involves a complete change in the rewarded response, that is, for both pairs of stimuli the figure which was rewarded in the first discrimination is not rewarded in the second, and vice versa. In the nonreversal condition, on the other hand, only one of the pairs in the second discrimination is rewarded in opposite fashion to the first discrimination. Thus, one might say that the subject going from the first discrimination to the nonreversal shift problem has only half as much to unlearn and to learn anew as the subject who is transferred to the reversal shift problem.

The focus of interest in this situation is the relative amount of transfer of training from the first discrimination to the reversal or to the non-reversal problem.

In rats it has been found that nonreversal shift is easier than reversal shift. That is, nonreversal shift shows positive transfer, while reversal shift shows negative transfer. The same is true for monkeys and for most children under five years of age.

In adults just the opposite is true. Reversal shift is easier than non-reversal, although both tasks, of course, are quite easy for this age group.

What is the explanation of this interesting fact that young children in the reversal-nonreversal shift experiment produce diametrically opposite results to those produced by older children and adults?

The fact that young children produce results similar to those of lower animals is the clue that leads to a hypothesis which distinguishes between subjects who learn the first discrimination on a simple *S–R* basis and those who learn on a mediated, *S–V–R*, basis. The Kendlers' research supports this view (for example, Kendler and Kendler, 1962).

In the *S–R* learner the reinforced responses become associated with the total stimulus characteristics of each figure associated with the reward. Referring again to Figure 4.4, the subject learns that the marble is to be found under the large black figure and under the large white figure.

---

[2] The stimuli and the reinforcement are presented by a specially devised mechanical apparatus, the details of which are unessential for the present discussion (see Kendler *et al.*, 1962).

In the *S–V–R* learner, however, the presentation of the first pair of figures *(LB)* and *(SW)* gives rise to a mediational response—*size*—and when the reward is found under the *LB* figure, the response which is reinforced thereby becomes attached, not to *large-black,* but to the mediator *large.* But what if brightness rather than size were the relevant cue? Then the subject's mediational response *large* would undergo extinction as a result of no reinforcement on half of the trials and eventually another mediating response would be elicited by the stimuli, say, *brightness,* with the result that the subject would then be consistently correct in his responses. In the problem illustrated in Figure 4.4, learning is almost always much faster for subjects who mediate than for subjects who do not.

Now how do the *S–R* and *S–V–R* subjects compare when we go to the reversal shift problem? The *S–R* subject is at a disadvantage, since he has to unlearn or extinguish his response to *two* of the figures *(LB* and *LW)* and transfer his motor response to the other two figures *(SW* and *SB)*. The *S–V–R* subject is at an advantage since the reversal shift does not require a new mediating response. Size is still relevant and all the subject has to do is respond to the opposite, that is, small instead of large.

In the nonreversal shift, on the other hand, the *S–R* subject is at a relative advantage, since one of the pairs calls for the same response that was learned in the first task and only the other pair requires extinction of the old response and learning of the new. The *S–V–R* subject, however, is at a relative disadvantage, since he must extinguish his original mediator (size), which no longer results in consistent reward, and must produce a new mediating response, viz., brightness. Thus, even though *S–V–R* learning is developmentally a more advanced type of learning than *S–R* learning, it is not necessarily more efficient in every situation.

Paradoxical as it may seem at first glance, *S–V–R* learners can be slower on certain specially contrived tasks than *S–R* learners. When a problem which can be solved quite simply on a *S–R* basis elicits a great many mediational responses that are irrelevant to the solution, older and brighter children will perform less well than younger and duller children (for example, Osler and Trautman, 1961).

The reversal-nonreversal procedure can be so arranged as to permit detection of whether the subject has learned the second discrimination by an *S–R* or by a *S–V–R* process. The mediating subjects favor the reversal shift, while the nonmediators favor the nonreversal shift, for the reasons previously indicated (Kendler, *et al.,* 1962). Figure 4.4 shows the percentage of children making the reversal shift as a function of age. Approximately 50 percent responded on a *S–V–R* basis by the age that children normally begin school. The reason the curve does not

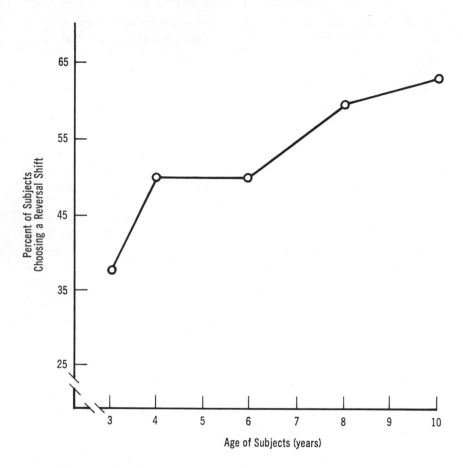

Figure 4.4.   Percentage of children responding in a reversal-shift manner as a function of age (from Kendler and Kendler, 1962).

reach a higher percentage by ten years of age is that the task becomes too simple beyond this age, such that the ease of nonreversal shift can also result from a mediational response—one involving both dimensions (size and brightness) simultaneously. When questioned about their behavior, the children at all ages who favored reversal shift were better able to verbalize the "reasons" for their choice than were the children who chose the nonreversal shift or who responded inconsistently.

Will instructions that prompt the child to verbalize influence his performance in this situation? The Kendlers have done an experiment which provides an interesting answer to this question (Kendler and Kendler, 1961).

At four years of age, learning is facilitated by relevant verbalization and is hindered by irrelevant verbalization. At seven years of age, however, relevant verbalization produced no facilitation as compared with the no verbalization control group, while irrelevant verbalization was more hindering to the seven-year-olds than to the four-year-olds. One explanation of these results is that the seven-year-olds were already spontaneously learning on a $S–V–R$ basis, so the relevant verbalization instructions did not appreciably add to their ability. But if irrelevant mediators were prompted by the experimenter these inhibited the subjects' spontaneous relevant verbalization and thereby hindered learning. Learning was relatively much less hindered in the four-year-olds presumably because their overt behavior has not yet come to be so strongly influenced by their own verbalization—the $V–R$ connections are still quite tenuous.

The reversal-nonreversal shift procedure has been used by one of my graduate students, Jacqueline Rapier, to study differences in mediational tendencies among low socioeconomic level Anglo-American and Mexican-American children (unpublished paper). A previous series of experiments had shown that Mexican-American children of low-measured IQ were superior to Anglo-American children of the same IQ on learning tasks which did not involve much verbal mediation, or in which the verbal labels were made explicit for all subjects (Jensen, 1961). From these findings it was hypothesized that Mexican-American children of low social class come from a particularly nonverbal background. Their problem in school appears to be not so much the fact that Spanish is spoken in their homes, but that they are developmentally retarded in what we have referred to as verbal mediation or $S–V–R$ behavior. Differences between Anglo-Americans and Mexican-Americans in the tendency to learn by simple $S–R$ processes or by a $S–V–R$ mediation process should be evident in their performances on reversal and nonreversal shift problems. Also, IQ should be reflected in this type of performance.

Therefore, groups of third- and fourth-grade Anglo-American and Mexican-American children were matched on the basis of IQ and social status. The groups (of twenty subjects in each) were divided into two levels of IQ: an average group with a mean IQ of 100 and a range from 90 to 109, and a low group with a mean IQ of 82 and a range from 70 to 89.

The experimental procedure was the same as that illustrated in Figure 4.4. Half the subjects in each group were transferred to the reversal condition and half to the nonreversal condition. On the first discrimination the Mexican-Americans made on the average almost twice as many errors as the Anglo-Americans. This agrees with the Kendlers' finding that slow learners on the first task are generally nonmediators.

It was also found that performance was related to IQ. Of prime interest are the results on the second discrimination. As we would expect at this age, reversal is easier than nonreversal shift. But the difference between reversal and nonreversal is smallest among the low-IQ Mexican-American children. In this respect they are like the kindergarten children in one of the Kendlers' experiments in which there was no significant difference between mean performance on reversal and nonreversal shift (Kendler and Kendler, 1959). All the other groups made fewer than half as many errors in the reversal as in the nonreversal condition. Thus the low-IQ Mexican-American group shows the least evidence of verbally mediated learning. Even the average performance of the low-IQ Anglo-Americans indicates a predominance of verbally-mediating subjects.

It is also interesting to note that in terms of scores on this type of learning, the measured IQ differentiates more clearly among the Anglo-Americans. Among Anglo-Americans the low-IQ group makes three times as many errors as the high-IQ group, while among the Mexican-Americans the low-IQ group makes only two times as many errors as the average group. But even this difference is interesting in view of the fact that on learning tasks involving little or no spontaneous verbal mediation the performance measures of the average-IQ and low-IQ groups become practically indistinguishable among Mexican-Americans but remain clearly separated among the Anglo-Americans (Jensen, 1961).

V–V

Words as external stimuli or as self-produced stimuli become associated with other verbal responses. These intraverbal associations constitute an important part of the individual's intellectual equipment. Thus, not only do single verbal units serve to mediate the learning of associations between external stimuli and overt behavior, but learning can be mediated by chains of two or more verbal responses each of which acts in turn as the stimulus for the next. The usual method of investigating these $V–V$ associations is one of the oldest techniques in experimental psychology—the word-association test. Word association is a vast and fascinating topic in itself. It would be impossible even to begin to describe all the methods and results of research in this field, so the reader must be referred elsewhere for the details that give one an appreciation of the psychological riches in this area of investigation (for example, Woodworth and Schlosberg, 1954, pp. 43–71).

The study of word association is important from our standpoint mainly for four reasons: (i) it is a method for investigating the characteristics of the person's verbal associative network, which plays a prominent role in terms of transfer and mediation in all forms of verbal learning, problem solving, and conceptual thinking; (ii) word associations closely reflect the quality and structure of the verbal environment to which the person has been exposed; (iii) word associations clearly reveal developmental trends in language behavior; and (iv) word associations reflect psychologically important social-class differences.

There is no doubt of the fact that innumerable intraverbal associations latently exist in all socialized human beings. These associations can be demonstrated by having a person say the first word that comes to mind when a stimulus word is presented. The fact that the person's response is highly predictable from word association norms—there is great communality in the responses given by many different persons brought up in the same linguistic community—along with many other kinds of lawfulness involving variables such as the frequencies of assocations in the language, the grammatical form class of the words, and the subject's speed of response (latency) to the stimulus word, indicate that we are dealing with one of the most substantial of psychological phenomena.

One of the chief determinants of the strength of association between elements of the person's associative network is the sheer frequency of exposure to verbal associations occurring in the person's linguistic environment. Siblings show greater agreement in word assocations than do unrelated children, and identical twins show even greater agreements than fraternal twins (Carter, 1938). Also, there is considerable agreement in word associations between parents and their children. The agreement is greater when same-sex comparisons are made, although children of both sexes resemble the mother more closely than the father in their word associations (Miller, 1951, pp. 176–177).

It is interesting to see how the pattern of word associations develops and changes with the age of the child (Palermo, in press). As the child gets older, the grammatical aspects of words, in addition to sheer frequency of environmental association, increasingly influence the child's word associations. Ervin (1961) has shown that with increasing age—from kindergarten to sixth grade—there is a steady increase in the proportion of word-association responses in the same grammatical form class as the stimulus word. Also, with increasing age children become more alike in their word associations. This reflects their increased exposure to a larger verbal community as they progress in school.

Though word-association techniques have been widely used in the study of personality disorders and a number of investigators have used the method in research on the mentally retarded, there are only two studies more or less directly related to race and social class. Mitchell *et al.* (1919) obtained word-association norms on three hundred Negro children and these data can be compared directly with the association norms obtained from Caucasian children (who were probably of somewhat higher social class). It was found that the Negro children were somewhat older than the Caucasian children at the same developmental level of word association.

That this difference probably reflects social-class differences between the groups is suggested by a study by Vera John (1963), which compared first- and fifth-grade Negro children from three levels of social class: lower-lower, upper-lower, and middle class. The subjects' word associations were scored according to whether or not they were in the same grammatical form class as the stimulus word, a characteristic of word association highly correlated with mental age. The three levels of social class differed in accordance with expectation—the lower-lower group showed the poorest performance. Speed of response—a sensitive measure of associative strength—was also obtained showing the lower-lower group to be the slowest. The social-class differences on both of these measures of word association were greater in the first than in the fifth grade.

A Hierarchy of Verbal Associations

Three additional tests used by John revealed further important social-class differences in the structure of verbal associations, but in order to understand these findings we must recognize the hierarchical nature of the verbal associative network. In the simplest case this would be illustrated by two words which have no direct associative connections with each other but which are both associated with a third word. For example, *chair* and *bed* have a very weak or even nonexistent direct associative connection between them, yet both are associated with *furniture*. These levels of the associative network correspond to the degree of abstraction and generality, and the strength and richness of the associative connections involved in this hierarchical structure are intimately related to the person's capacity for a host of behaviors that are recognized under such names as abstract thinking, concept formation, ability to categorize and generalize, and so on.

It is in the development of hierarchical associations, more than of direct S–V and V–V associations, that social-class differences seem to be most prominent.

One way that Vera John showed this was to administer a verbal identification test to the children in the three social classes described above. This task consisted essentially of sets of pictures of various objects. The first part of the test consisted of asking the child simply to name the various objects pictured in each set: *doll, ball, rocking-horse,* and *blocks.* This kind of picture enumeration calls only for S–V behavior. In the second part of the test, the child is asked to give a single name for each *group* of pictured objects. In the example just given, an appropriate response would be "toys." Successful performance on this task depends upon the child's possession of hierarchical verbal associations.

What was the outcome? The social-class differences in the simple *S–V* labeling task were practically nil in the first grade, but were significant in the fifth grade (although fifth-graders over-all did markedly better than the first-graders).

The important finding, however, was that social-class differences were more prominent both at the first and fifth grades on the second verbal task, which calls for higher-order associations.

John proceeded to follow up this finding with another experimental task specifically devised to elicit *classificatory* behavior. It consisted of presenting the child with a set of sixteen cards, each picturing a single familiar object, and asking the child to sort these cards into "piles of cards which belong together." The pictures actually were selected so that sets of four pictures would represent one of four concepts. Among the fifth-graders, 45 percent of the middle-class children arranged the cards into four piles according to the four concepts, while only 13 percent of the lower-lower-class children did so. The latter group tended instead to sort the pictures into pairs which represented direct, rather than hierarchical, *V–V* associations. The social-class differences were not significant on this test at the first-grade level, probably because too few of the children in any of the social-class groups performed in a hierarchical fashion. It was also noted that the lower-class children gave significantly fewer explicit verbalizations of their sorting behavior than did the middle-class children.

Associative Clustering

The associative network should not be thought of as a static structure but as a dynamic process which actively shapes and organizes learning and retention. One illustration of this dynamic aspect of the verbal network is a phenomenon known as *associative clustering* (Bousfield, 1953). A list of, say, sixty words is read aloud to a person. The list is composed of four categories of words, for example, animals, vegetables, professions, and names, with fifteen words in each category, but all sixty words are presented in a completely haphazard order so that words from the same category occur together only by chance. Soon after the list is read, the person is asked to write down as many of the words as he can recall in the order that they come to mind.

Two results stand out: (i) the person is able to recall more of the words than would be possible for a list of sixty random words, and (ii) the words are recalled in clusters corresponding to the categories. The input, in other words, becomes reorganized in accord with the superordinate verbal associations—the labels of the categories—elicited by the individual stimulus words. Recall is facilitated through the activation of the traces of the individual words in each category via their superordinate association in the verbal network.

Even when the list is composed of randomly selected words with no attempt at categorization, the order of their free recall evinces a good deal of subjective organization on the part of the learner, an organization of the items which gradually and consistently takes shape with each successive recall trial. The subjective organization in the free recall of unrelated words has been clearly demonstrated in the research of Tulving (1962), who has developed a quantitative measure of the degree to which such subjective organization occurs for an individual. Tulving's data suggest that there is a positive correlation between the degree of subjective organization and goodness of performance on a recall test. Thus, what appears at first glance to be a rather simple form of learning —free recall of a list of words in any order that they come to mind— is actually strongly influenced by the dynamic properties of the person's associative network, which in turn is largely a product of the person's verbal experience.

Another kind of experiment shows how a verbal stimulus entering the associative network can route associations to different final destinations as a function of the context established by the preceding stimuli (Howes and Osgood, 1954). For example, the most common associate to the word *night* presented alone is *day,* but if we read the series of words *devil, fearful, dark, sinister, night,* and ask for an associate to the last word in the series, there is a very low probability that it will be day. The verbal context preceding *night* diverts the train of associations into a different part of the associative network, and we are more apt to get an association such as *thief, ghost,* or *murder.*

These kinds of techniques offer possibilities for investigating the strength of the dynamic processes involved in the associative network, both with respect to their developmental aspects and to social-class differences.

$S–V–V–R$

That our hypothetical network is an active process rather than a static structure is also shown by the role it plays in the verbal mediation of learning. Mediational chains involving more than a single verbal association can be brought into play. We can symbolize this as $S–V–V–R$.

Let's look at a simple and obvious example of learning which is mediated via the person's associative network. The task consists of learning the following list of paired-associates: *A-cat, B-night, C-king, D-table,* and so on. After these associations have been mastered, we give the subject a new list, as follows: *A-dog, B-day, C-queen, D-chair,* and so on. This list turns out to be very easy for the subject to learn as compared with any other paired-associate lists we might have given him. The reason is that the subjects bring to this task the already well-learned associations *cat–dog, night–day, king–queen, table–chair.* These are a part of his associative network, and they mediate the learning of the second list, so that the only new connections the subject has to learn are those in the first list. The acquisition of the second set of paired-associates is mediated through the first, thus:

$$A\text{———}(cat)\text{———}dog$$

Verbal mediators that are never explicitly introduced into the learning situation nevertheless exist and can have the effect of facilitating learning. This phenomenon of implicit verbal chaining has been demonstrated in a now classic experiment by Russell and Storms (1955). For a comprehensive discussion of various mediation paradigms and the experimental work associated with them, the reader is referred to the review by Jenkins (1963). It is also known that the extent of verbal mediation is, as one would expect, a function of age (Reese, 1962), or more precisely, amount of verbal experience. Since the associative network is built up only through verbal stimulation, its richness, complexity, strength of connections, and hierarchical elaboration —and consequently the effectiveness of its mediating and facilitative functions—will be determined in large part by the quality of the person's verbal environment.

THE "SPEW" HYPOTHESIS

The effect of verbal input from the environment has been summarized in general terms by Underwood in what he calls the "spew" hypothesis, which states that "the frequency with which verbal units have been experienced directly determines their availability as responses in new associative connections" (Underwood and Schultz, 1960, p. 126). The term *spew* comes from the fact that the speed and the order in which words are emitted by the subject in an association test are a direct function of the frequency with which the words have been experienced by the subject, as judged from estimates of the frequency of the words in the language.

In the literature of verbal learning, one operational definition of meaningfulness (symbolized as *M*) is the number of verbal associations subjects can make to a verbal unit in a given period of time, say, one minute. By this method verbal units can be rated on *M,* and when this is done it is found that the *M*-value of a verbal unit is directly related to its frequency in the language. Thus, not only words, but nonsense syllables or trigrams (three-letter combinations) and bigrams (two-letter combinations) can be rated on *M.* Those combinations of two or three letters which occur most frequently in the language will evoke more associations than will rarer combinations.

It is also known that the ease and speed with which any verbal materials can be learned are directly related to their *M*-value. The speed of learning of lists of verbal units of low and of high *M*-values can differ as much as four to one. The fact that meaningfulness makes learning easier has long been a truism in educational psychology. Research has shown this phenomenon even when meaningless nonsense syllables are rated for meaningfulness by this operational criterion of the power of the verbal unit to elicit associations. This makes the nonsense materials, which are so frequently used in verbal learning experiments, just one part of a continuum going from verbal materials of very low to very high meaningfulness.

These points have been demonstrated in innumerable studies, which have been reviewed by Underwood and Schultz (1960). An experiment by Mandler and Huttenlocher (1956) can serve as one illustration of the effect of *M*-value on learning. These investigators presented many nonsense syllables, each for thirty seconds, to a group of subjects and asked them to give associations to each syllable. Then the subjects were required to learn a paired-associate list made up of syllables different from those used in the association test. It was found that subjects giving the largest number of associations in the first test were the fastest learners in the paired-associate list. One could, of course, argue that the superior performers on both tasks were merely the more intelligent subjects. If that is the case, this experiment further elucidates the nature of intelligence and its modus operandi.

Again, in terms of social-class implications we can say that to the extent that the amount and kind of verbal input from the environment differs as a function of social class, there should be corresponding differences in verbal-learning ability, at least the kind of verbal-learning ability called for in school learning. It should not be surprising that the largest social-class differences in school achievement are found in the area of the language arts rather than in the less linguistic subjects such as arithmetic.

SYNTACTICAL MEDIATION

As a child matures, an increasingly prominent aspect of his verbal behavior is the degree to which it corresponds to the syntactical structure of his language. The structure of the language becomes incorporated as part of the underlying processes governing the individual's verbal behavior. The degree of subtlety, diversity, and complexity of syntactical structure of the verbal environment will determine the nature of the syntactical processes incorporated by the developing child. The extent to which these structures become incorporated is a function of the frequency with which they are experienced in the environment, the degree to which the social environment reinforces their overt manifestation, and the individual's basic capacity for learning. In view of the points made earlier concerning social-class differences in spoken language, one would expect that somewhat different syntactical structures are incorporated by individuals according to their social-class background.

The key question, however, is whether the tendency for syntactical verbal behavior is of any psychological importance to learning and intellectual ability. We now have considerable evidence that it is of great importance, but the specific mechanisms through which it exerts its facilitative effect on learning are still obscure. The problem is currently under investigation in our laboratory.

Syntactical mediation is one of the most powerful of all variables affecting the speed of paired-associate learning. When pairs of items to be associated are imbedded in some syntactical structure, such as a sentence, the association is made almost at once, without the necessity of many repeated learning trials. Since subjects in paired-associate experiments are usually college students who have strong tendencies spontaneously to bring syntactical mediators to bear on the learning task, it is difficult to use them as experimental subjects when the variable we wish to control is syntactical mediation. Verbal mediational tendencies cannot be suppressed in bright college students.

Therefore, in our research on this problem we have used as subjects young children and mentally retarded adults, who show little or no spontaneous tendencies to mediate their learning verbally. A typical experiment (for example, Jensen and Rohwer, 1963*a*, 1963*b*) consisted of having retarded subjects (IQs 50–60) learn a list of eight paired-associates composed of pictures of common objects: *shoe-clock, telephone-hammer, ball-house,* and so forth. The control group of subjects was asked only to name each picture on the first trial and on subsequent trials they learned by the usual anticipation method. When the pairs were presented for the first time to the mediation groups, the experimenter stated a sentence containing each pair of items, for example, "I threw the *shoe* at the *clock*," "I smashed the *telephone* with the *hammer*," and so on. After this initial trial, the mediation group was given subsequent trials the same as the control group, without any further verbalization from the experimenter. The result was that the mediation group learned, on the average, twice as fast as the control group and made only one-fifth as many errors.

This experiment was repeated under conditions that required the re-tarded subjects to generate their own mediators, and again the great facilitative effect of such mediation was manifested. When retarded adults were compared on this task with fourth-graders of the same mental age, it was found that the retardates were about three to four times slower than the normal children in learning, under both mediated and nonmediated conditions, which indicates that this task more nearly reflects IQ than mental age. The children also benefited markedly from the mediation instructions.

To investigate the effectiveness of this form of syntactical media-tion as a function of age, Jensen and Rohwer (1965*b*) gave a paired-associate task with and without mediation instructions to groups of children from kindergarten to the twelfth grade. The children were matched for IQ and social class over all grade levels. In the mediation condition subjects were always instructed to make up their own medi-ators. The control group learned by the usual method of anticipation, without any instructions from the experimenter to form verbal medi-ators. The items to be associated were again pairs of pictures of familiar objects.

Comparing the performance of the mediation group with that of the control group, it was found that the effectiveness of the mediation in-structions was relatively slight at kindergarten age and increased steadily up to the sixth grade, after which it progressively decreased up to the twelfth grade. A reasonable interpretation of this finding is that the ability for syntactical mediation is not sufficiently developed at kinder-garten age to be of much benefit, but rapidly increases thereafter with age. But at the same time there is an increase with age in the subjects' spontaneous use of verbal mediation, so that in older subjects the medi-ation instructions add little if anything to what the subject would do on his own, and thus the difference between the mediation and control groups decreases.

Also, it was noted that the younger children made up syntactically less varied and less complex mediators. Many kindergarteners, for ex-ample, could only make up noun phrases, such as "the *hat* and the *table*." Complete, but simple, sentences are common by the second grade, with a corresponding increase in facilitation of learning. And with increasing age the mediators seem to become syntactically more sophisticated.

In order to identify more precisely the nature of these syntactical variables involved in facilitation of paired-associate learning, Rohwer (1964) controlled syntactic structure experimentally by providing 244 sixth-grade children with various mediational contexts for the eight paired-associates they were required to learn. The results showed clearly that different syntactical connectives, representing different parts of speech and different degrees of complexity, have different degrees of power in facilitating learning. The largest difference in "connective power" is that between conjunctions and prepositions.

Another feature of Rohwer's experiment was a condition which included all the same words as the previously described mediators, but presented in a nonsyntactical arrangement; that is, they did not correspond to normal English word order. Thus, the phrase "the sleeping *cow* beneath the dirty *hat*" was also presented as "dirty the beneath *cow* sleeping the *hat*." It was found that when the words were not in normal syntactical order they had no facilitating effect on paired-associate learning. The learning curve for the nonsyntactical condition did not differ appreciably from that of the control condition shown in Figure 4.5.

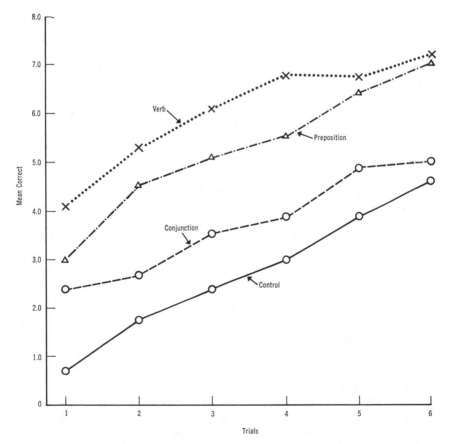

Figure 4.5.   Learning curves for paired-associate learning under various conditions of mediation (see text) (from Rohwer, 1964).

Still another variation of the experiment was to substitute nonsense paralogs, which sound like words, for the words in the mediational phrases. Thus, "The sleeping *cow* wore a dirty *hat*" was transformed in the nonsense condition to "sep shugling *cow* tofe um fenty *hat.*" As in the nonsyntactical condition, there was no facilitation of learning. The performance of the nonsense group was not significantly distinguishable from that of the control group.

A similar experiment was performed by Davidson (1964), with certain variations of additional interest. Davidson used second-graders. Twenty paired-associates, consisting of pairs of pictures of common objects, were projected on a screen at a six-second rate for the study trial. This was immediately followed by the test trial, which consisted of presenting only the stimulus member of each pair.

These subjects were divided into five groups to receive different mediation instructions. Two effects are significant statistically: (i) The type of verbalization caused large differences in learning paired-associates. Practically all of this difference is between mere naming of the items and joining them by a preposition. Additional verbalization and the imagery stimulated by presenting the objects combined in one picture added a negligible increment to the subjects' performance.

One might wonder if the more complex verbalization would be relatively more facilitating for somewhat older children, who might show a greater difference between a prepositional mediator and a complete sentence. This possibility is suggested by Rohwer's data on sixth-graders, although the conditions of his experiment were sufficiently different from Davidson's as to vitiate any such comparison.

(ii) The other significant effect in Davidson's study is the over-all difference between high- and low-pretest scorers, which indicates that the paired-associate task has a good deal of reliability, even when based on only two trials in a group-testing procedure.

Both the Rohwer and Davidson experiments leave no doubt of the powerful effects of syntactical mediation in facilitating learning. What now needs to be found out is the degree to which subjects from different social classes differ in kinds of syntactical mediators they bring to a learning situation. It is known, for example, that actual objects elicit somewhat different mediators than do pictures of the objects, and pictures elicit different responses than do the mere names of the objects (Otto, 1962). And we have found that paired-associate learning of object pairs is easier than of picture pairs (for example, Jensen and Rohwer, 1963*b*). In general, the greater the cue reduction in the stimulus terms, the fewer are the mediating associations elicited, and the more difficult is the paired-associate learning. In view of this, it is interesting that Semler and Iscoe (1963) found greater differences between lower-class Negro children and somewhat higher-status white children in paired-associate learning when the pairs consisted of pictures than when they consisted of actual objects.

For the benefit of those who might complain that paired-associate learning does not warrant so much attention because it is a laboratory method with seemingly little relevance to the tasks of education, let it be pointed out that many forms of school learning are essentially paired-associate learning: graphemes–phonemes, pictures–words, spoken words–written words, English words–foreign words, and so on. Furthermore, performance on paired-associate learning is significantly related to such important forms of school learning as reading ability, independent of IQ (Otto, 1961). In combination with other laboratory procedures (many of which, like the paired-associate technique, can be adapted to group administration) the paired-associate paradigm can be a valuable analytical method in the study of individual and group differences in learning ability.

Other psycholinguistic methods are also available for studying individual differences in the degree to which syntactical structure has been incorporated by an individual. One method, known as the "cloze" procedure consists of deleting every nth word in a passage of normal English and having the subject fill in the blanks with what he thinks are the most appropriate words. Another method consists of comparing the rates of learning nonsense syllables which do or do not correspond to the syntactical structure of the language, such as learning "the maff vlems oothly um the glax nerfs," as compared with the less syntactical "maff vlems ooth um glax nerf." Though the latter phrase has fewer syllables, it is considerably more difficult to memorize because of its lack of syntactical resemblance to English. A person for whom the learning rates of these two types of materials did not differ appreciably probably has not incorporated the syntactical structure of the English language to any strong degree. We would predict that these measures would reflect social-class differences, but tests of such hypotheses have not yet been made.

HIERARCHICAL LEARNING SETS AND TASK ANALYSIS

Learning-to-learn, or the development of learning sets, is a powerful determinant of performance in those learning situations which involve the particular learning set. A *learning set* is a set of habits which, once thoroughly established, greatly facilitates the further learning of a variety of different tasks which subsume the particular habits comprising the learning set. The research and theory concerning the formation and role of learning sets have been thoroughly reviewed by Harlow (1959) and are also treated elsewhere in the present book.

A monkey, which at first needs a great many trials to master a particular discrimination task, will, after prolonged practice on many similar tasks, eventually be able to master a new discrimination problem in just a single trial. Similarly, human subjects, in learning successive serial or paired-associate lists of verbal materials show an enormous improvement in the rate of learning from the first list to later lists (Duncan, 1960). In one experiment three bright college girls who learned a different nine-item serial list per day for twenty days learned, on the average, nearly four times as fast on the twentieth day as on the first day (Jensen and Roden, 1963). Probably no one would say that these girls had gained in intelligence as a result of this experience, and yet they became much faster learners, at least in this kind of learning.

Further, we have found in our research (as did Duncan, 1960) that the initially slowest subjects (among college students) show the greatest gain in learning rate as a result of "learning-to-learn." This suggests that these slower subjects were not necessarily initially inferior in some basic ability, but that for some reasons they had failed to acquire some of the habits comprising the relevant learning set prior to their first experience in the laboratory. In general, the range of individual differences in performance on laboratory learning tasks markedly decreases as subjects learn-to-learn through repeated experience with the same type of learning task. This decrease in intersubject variability is not always artificially imposed by a "ceiling effect" that would result if the tasks were so easy as not to leave room for further improvement by fast learners. While intersubject variability decreases with the development of a learning set, however, we have observed that the intersubject differences, though smaller, become much more stable and reliable. This fact has important implications for the laboratory assessment of individual differences in learning ability.

The conception of the individual's acquisition of knowledge as depending upon a hierarchy of learning sets, each level of which mediates positive transfer to the next higher level, offers greater possibilities for understanding social-class differences in "educability" and, what is more, for improving educational procedures, than does the less analytical approach based on the conception of an innate general capacity for acquiring education.

This theory of knowledge acquisition as learning which is mediated by positive transfer from a hierarchy of subordinate learning sets has been elaborated by Gagné (1962), largely in connection with his thinking and research on programmed instruction.

Failure in coping with a new problem or "inability" to learn some new material can usually be traced to a deficiency in one or more of the prerequisite subordinate learning sets.

This brings us directly to the important problem of task analysis, the educational implications of which are still far from being fully realized. The child is confronted in school with a new task, problem, or body of "knowledge" to be learned with "understanding." The first question of task analysis is, "What would the individual have to be able to do in order to perform successfully in this task?" Thereupon we discover a number of subordinate classes of tasks which must have been mastered as prerequisite to the task in question. The same question can then be asked about each of these prerequisite subtasks, and it will be found that they have their subordinate prerequisites. And so on, down through the hierarchy of learning sets. If there are deficiencies at the lower level, there will be learning difficulties and failures at the higher level.

This hierarchy of prerequisite learning is most obvious in the case of mathematics, but the same principle applies to practically all kinds of skills and subject matter. From a practical educational standpoint, the application of these principles of task analysis is of crucial importance in the primary grades, especially with regard to social-class factors, which can make for differences in the adequacy of the subordinate learning sets which are prerequisite to the tasks of primary education. Educational failure must be nipped in the bud, as it were. It is usually disastrous to allow the child to go on being confronted with increasingly baffling tasks under the mistaken notion that he might eventually catch up through some autonomous process of maturation. The cumulative effect of waiting for maturation to bring the child up to par, or of indiscriminately attributing the child's failure to his being a so-called slow learner and thereby channelling him into a low-geared educational program, is such that by the sixth or eighth or tenth grade the conclusion is easily reached that the child is incapable of benefiting from further education and that more advanced subject matter is simply beyond his level of learning ability. And indeed it is, in direct proportion to the deficiencies in the child's hierarchy of subordinate learning sets.

Deficiencies in these learning sets are not an all-or-none matter. Difficulty at higher levels of knowledge acquisition can result from earlier failure to *over*learn certain subordinate skills. This can happen even to bright or gifted children if they are too easily bored by the amount of practice necessary for certain subordinate skills to become "second nature." If the subskills are not fully mastered, much of the learner's time is later spent in consciously and effortfully going through many steps of the learning process which he should be able to do practically unconsciously and automatically. For example, the pianist who has not practiced his Czerny exercises to the point where they are as easy as walking will have inordinate difficulty trying to learn a Beethoven sonata. And since it is usually much too laborious and tedious for the amateur pianist to practice Czerny exercises ten hours a day (as Paderewski did at one stage in his career), the amateur's skill reaches a plateau well below the level of proficiency needed to tackle the masterpieces of the piano repertory. To a less obvious degree, the overlearning of many subskills underlies success at the higher levels of education in practically every field of learning.

The hierarchical learning-set conception of the educational process has implications for the diagnostic and remedial procedures to be applied when educational difficulties become apparent. The emphasis would seem to be best directed at early childhood education and in general at the earliest possible detection of learning difficulties. It is very difficult to take teenage high school students back to the subject matter of the primary grades in order to work through the acquisition of many of the subordinate skills that underlie the subject matter the individual is expected to acquire in high school. All through the years of a child's schooling, a lower-class environment probably affords much less opportunity, during the time the child spends out of school, for the rehearsal and overlearning of the learning sets which the school attempts to inculcate.

Now, lest someone should misinterpret what I have said about learning sets and conclude that I have thrown out the fact of individual differences in learning ability, let me add a word of clarification on this point. Certainly there are basic individual differences in the rates at which the learning sets themselves can be acquired, regardless of the adequacy of the subordinate skills involved. At the base of all learning there are probably some fundamental neurochemical determinants of learning rate which would govern the speed of acquisition of learning sets. If the process of acquisition is too slow and laborious, motivation and persistence will not be great enough to push the learning of complex behaviors to the point of such mastery that they will provide a solid foundation of positive transfer to subsequent learning. Consequently the slow learner in this fundamental sense will have a low ceiling on his intellectual attainment. My argument is that we must distinguish this fundamental type of slow learning from slowness or failure which results only from the lack of the prerequisite subskills. Public education must see to it that children who are neurologically sound and are capable of a normal rate of learning (when learning does not depend heavily upon transfer from prior learning) are in possession of the prerequisites for learning at every step of the way, from kindergarten through college. If such children have a low educational ceiling for essentially the same reason that a person will fail calculus if he hasn't first learned algebra, the fault is with the conduct of the educational process and not with the child's basic equipment for learning.

Before leaving the subject of task analysis, a word of caution is in order. Task analysis is not an armchair exercise in the logical analysis of a given subject matter. The subabilities involved in a particular learning task may be hypothesized on the basis of an a priori analysis of the task, but the job of task analysis is not complete until transfer from the hypothesized subabilities has been empirically verified. The logical structure of a task does not always correspond to its psychological structure. One can waste much time and effort on the mastery of skills assumed to be prerequisite to the goal task but which, in fact, provide no positive transfer to the learning of the goal task.

A simple example of this is the learning of a number of responses in a particular serial order—the responses may consist of a list of nonsense syllables, words, the sequence of responses involved in assembling a piece of machinery, and the like. The proper sequence of responses to be learned can be symbolized as A-B-C-D-E, and so on. The hyphens between the letters indicate the associations that are presumed to be learned when the task is mastered. Logically, it might seem that mastery of this serial learning task might be achieved more easily if we break the series down into "simpler" components, have the subject learn each of these to the point of mastery, and then combine them into the final task. Thus, the subject would first learn the simple associations A-B, B-C, C-D, D-E, and so on. And when he learns all of these connections perfectly, there should be practically 100 percent transfer to the total series, which is logically composed of these paired-associates chained together. In actual fact, the amount of transfer from the paired-associate to the serial list is practically nil (Jensen, 1962). The reverse is also true; learning the series A-B-C-D-E, and so on, does not imply that the subject has also learned the paired-associates A-B, B-C, C-D, and so on (Jensen and Rohwer, 1965a). In these cases a strictly logical approach to task analysis would lead to the wrong conclusions concerning the psychological structure of what is actually learned in serial and paired-associate tasks. The very low correlation between individual differences in ability in serial and paired-associate learning (among college students) further suggests that one of these skills is not a subskill or prerequisite of the other (Jensen, 1962).

Psychological science has not developed to the point where facts such as these can be predicted from theory. They must be determined empirically. One of the major jobs of educational psychology is the experimental task analysis of school subjects. From the standpoint of developing an educational program which can help to overcome the learning handicaps associated with a lower-class background, some form of task analysis must be intensively applied to the earliest stages of schooling, for it is very likely that the educational goals of even kinder-garten and first grade depend upon prerequisite abilities which lower-class children have not acquired by the time they enter school. When it is known more definitely what these abilities are, they can possibly be inculcated through some combination of nursery education and parental education.

RESEARCH IMPLICATIONS

If we were to attempt to elaborate critically upon each of the points in all of the foregoing discussion, it would be immediately apparent that a great many of these points could hardly be regarded as definitive knowledge. Few points could escape being called controversial and many would have to be regarded as only suggestive of the truth of the matter. Often a fine-grained analysis of the research on any given point reveals contradictions, missing links, and unsupported assumptions in the interpretation of the results, which leave us with ambiguity and doubt.

But if at this stage of research on social-class factors in learning, one insisted strictly upon maintaining a microscopic, critical approach at every point, rejecting all but that evidence which is already proved to be directly relevant, which is safely unassailable from every theoreti-cal viewpoint, and which unquestionably satisfies every canon of sci-entific and logical rigor, one would be left with a skimpy and barren distillation indeed. Therefore, I have not attempted rigorously to prove any particular point or to highlight the methodological shortcomings, the factual ambiguities, or the occasional contradictions that exist in the literature at the expense of overshadowing the positive values for research suggested by the approaches I have reviewed. Other approaches are possible, but I have indicated the ones that seem to me most closely related to the psychology of learning. I believe these approaches are worth pursuing much further.

What are some of the general directions for research suggested by the viewpoint presented here?

Experimental Description

One of the first things needed is an adequate description of the psy-chological characteristics of children from different social classes in terms of all the factors that are conceivably involved in learning. The systematic investigation of differences between lower-class and middle-class children in perceptual and learning abilities is needed along the entire developmental continuum. The $S-S$, $R-R$, $S-R$, S_v-R, $V-R$, $S-V-R$, $V-V$, and other paradigms I have described, in addition to the ideas of the verbal associative network and the hierarchy of learning sets, can provide a conceptual framework for some of this investigation.

At each stage in the development of learning abilities, in accord with these paradigms, the specific environmental determinants of social-class differences should be discovered. Some of these environmental factors may be fairly readily manipulated through parental education; others may require intervention through special nursery education or special remedial treatment at the kindergarten level. And more basic research is needed on the relationship between the learning abilities hypothesized in these paradigms and the child's general educability.

This descriptive endeavor would seem to be best pursued directly through the techniques from the experimental psychology of learning, and various adaptations thereof, as already indicated in the preceding discussions. The specific basic questions that need to be answered at this stage call for carefully designed experiments rather than massive testing programs, the gathering of enormous descriptive statistics, or large-scale field demonstrations. It is not going to be very helpful to get further evidence that lower-class children on the average obtain inferior IQs and show poorer school achievement than middle-class children, as measured by just about any test one can devise, or that children seem to like school better when they can get out of school to go on field trips, or that teachers possessing warmth and understanding seem to have fewer troublesome discipline problems than do less fortunate teachers. A much more fine-grained experimental analysis of social-class differences in abilities is needed if we are to discover the specific environmental variables controlling the development of learning abilities. Then we can institute those procedures that will most effectively raise the educational potential of lower-class children, without the wasteful inefficiency of the well-meaning, but haphazard, shotgun approach that has characterized so much of the educational effort in the field so far.

Educational Application

The main practical goal of this research would be the improvement of the educational potential of lower-class children. The educational, social, and economic implications of such a boost in educational potential among a substantial proportion of the population would be tremendous.

To accomplish this, it would be important to discover, for example, the kinds of training procedures that would most effectively remedy deficiencies found in each stage of the child's development. Quite different methods might be needed to establish certain verbal habits, learning sets, and the like, in a twelve-year-old than to establish the same habits in a six-year-old. The kinds of learning deficiencies that are later irremediable and which must be prevented from occurring in the first place—if indeed there are such kinds of learning deficiencies—must be determined.

For much the same sort of reason that fishes would be the very last creatures ever to discover water, middle-class persons easily remain unaware of the great prerequisite demands of primary education. One of the important problems for research is the task-analysis of school activities with respect to the psychological functions on which children from various cultural backgrounds are found to differ. If the necessary subskills for any particular school activity are deficient for a particular class of children, the educational system must devise means for inculcating these prerequisite skills. Furthermore, it is likely that many of the skills the school tries to teach really cannot be learned through ordinary classroom teaching, but must be learned in a one-to-one tutorial situation. This is most likely to be true in the early stages of acquisition of any new subject matter—reading, arithmetic, and other school subjects involving complex discriminations and mediational processes. This is perhaps most obvious in learning to play a musical instrument. The middle-class child has the advantage that he can bring these new tasks home to his private tutors—his parents. The lower-class parent less often serves the functions of a private tutor. If the acquisition of a particular skill depends upon minute, step-by-step observation of the child's performance with immediate differential reinforcement at each step of the way, the learning will be extremely slow, inefficient, or even altogether impossible, if it is taught by some gross classroom procedure.

Automated teaching may be a partial answer. A one-to-one tutorial relationship between older and younger pupils is another possibility. But in terms of what we believe about the intimate relationship between parent-child interaction and the development of learning abilities, it is highly doubtful that a single teacher can possibly fulfill all the relevant functions of a "good" parent for all the twenty- or thirty-odd children in her classroom. Casual questioning of the lower- and middle-class children who have served in our experiments has revealed enormous differences in their reports of the extent to which their parents tutor them in their school work. Children in special classes for the "gifted" (IQs above 135) report more of this kind of parental attention than do children of lesser ability. Lower-class children in special classes for "slow-learners" or for the "mentally retarded" report less parental attention with respect to their school work than do any other group of children.

DIAGNOSTIC IMPLICATIONS

The group of children identified by intelligence tests and by various criteria of school achievement as "slow-learners" or "mentally retarded" actually constitutes a psychologically very heterogeneous group. A necessary adjunct to research on the role of cultural factors in the development of learning abilities is some means of diagnostically differentiating retardation due to environmental factors from retardation due to more basic biological factors.

The standard tests of intelligence are not suitable for this purpose unless we know quite precisely what opportunities for learning the child's past environment has afforded. What we need is some means of independently assessing what might be called basic learning ability— the rate at which new learning can take place, new learning sets can be developed, and so on, as distinct from the amount of learning that has already occurred in the subject's past.

Take the concept of the IQ as the ratio of mental age (MA) to chronological age (CA). If MA is thought of as the product of rate of learning times the amount of time or opportunity for learning, and if CA is our estimate of this time factor, then the IQ can be interpreted as an index of the subject's rate of learning. The trouble with this is, of course, that different environments do not afford the same amount of opportunity for learning per unit of time—at least not for learning what our tests measure. Therefore, two so-called "retarded" individuals with exactly the same IQ can actually be retarded for quite different reasons—one because of a basically slow learning rate despite opportunities for learning, the other because of poor opportunities for learning even though the basic learning rate is completely up to par. This distinction is important both in terms of the kinds of educational remediation each type of low IQ calls for and in terms of the level of our educational expectations for the two types of individual. Unfortunately, there is, in effect, little difference between the one type of slow-learner and the other type in an educational setting which does not take account of their fundamental psychological differences. But when appropriate educational methods are applied to each of these two types of retarded children, the differences in their subsequent achievement and occupational level can be very great.

The question is, how are we to distinguish between children who stand at different points on these two dimensions? Some of our recent research suggests that the use of a variety of direct learning tests may provide a possible solution. We know that various laboratory learning tasks are facilitated in differing degrees by transfer from previously established verbal habits and by different levels of verbal mediation. The higher we go in this transfer hierarchy, the more the learning task reflects the degree to which the subject draws upon verbal or symbolic mediational processes. Near the bottom of the hierarchy are tasks on which speed of learning is little affected by verbal mediation. Tasks near the top of the hierarchy are highly dependent upon verbal or symbolic mediation. For example, a test of free recall of familiar nouns is less dependent upon mediational processes than is a concept attainment task.

A method we are using in our laboratory for determining the degree to which a subject is spontaneously using mediational processes in learning a particular task is to observe the subject's performance on equivalent forms of the task, first learning under conditions that involve no mediational instructions and then under conditions in which the experimenter induces the subject to use some mediational process. In some cases these mediational processes are taught to the subject in the experimental situation. If the subject's performance is not appreciably changed under the mediation conditions, it is presumptive evidence that the subject was spontaneously using some form of mediation in the first task. We have found, for example, that we can greatly facilitate paired-associate learning in young children and in mentally retarded adults by giving them instructions to use verbal mediators or by actually providing them with mediators as part of the learning task, while very little facilitation of the performance of high school seniors and college students is obtained by means of such mediation instructions. The verbally more developed subjects report making up their own mediators without any prompting from the experimenter, and thus the experimenter's providing mediators has little or no facilitating effect for these subjects.

We have also been comparing serial and paired-associate learning by the same subjects (Jensen, 1962; Jensen and Rohwer, 1963a, 1963b, 1965a, 1965b). We have found that paired-associate learning is greatly facilitated by some form of verbal mediational process, whereas serial learning is not significantly influenced by similar verbal mediation.

Thus, the ratio of a subject's scaled score in paired-associate learning to his scaled score in serial learning (PA/Sr) should provide an index of the degree of development of the subject's mediational tendency in relation to his basic learning ability. For example, a child with normal basic learning ability, but who comes from a verbally impoverished environment, should have a low PA/Sr ratio. In contrast, an organically retarded child, even though his verbal environment has been quite good, would be slow in both paired-associate and serial learning, and thus would not produce a score indicative of verbal underdevelopment in relation to his basic learning equipment.

We have not yet made any large-scale investigation of the *PA/Sr* ratio as a function of social class. One study, however, has shown that lower-class Mexican-American children of low measured IQ learn serial tasks significantly faster than Anglo-American children of the same IQ, while in paired-associate learning the Anglo-American children do better than the Mexican-American children. Again, we interpret this as reflecting the fact that paired-associate learning depends more upon past verbal experience while serial learning tends to reflect a more basic learning ability.

Here, then, are two types of laboratory learning tasks which seem to provide one means for differentiating (i) learning ability which depends relatively little on transfer from previously acquired verbal habits from (ii) learning ability which reflects the degree of development of spontaneous verbal mediation. But a great deal more needs to be known about social-class differences in these two forms of learning before they can be generally used as diagnostic or research tools.

One of the problems with using direct learning tasks as a means of individual assessment is the achievement of satisfactory reliability of measurement. We have been working on this problem in our laboratory and so far it appears that there is no very simple solution to the reliability problem.

Free-recall tests, we have found, show little of the practice effect that reduces the reliability of serial learning and paired-associate tasks. They have an equivalent-forms reliability between first and second tests of 0.70 to 0.80. Once the materials (we have used familiar objects) of a free-recall test are familiar to the subjects, as indicated by the subject's ability to name the objects immediately on sight, ability in free-recall seems not to be highly dependent on verbal-mediational processes and is therefore a relatively "culture-free" test of ability. In one experiment, matched groups of low-IQ Mexican-American and Anglo-American children showed large differences in free-recall ability, with the Mexican-American children showing the superior performance (Jensen, 1961). For children with IQs above 110, however, this free-recall test revealed no differences between Mexican-American and Anglo-American children, suggesting that the Mexican-Americans in the above-average IQ range are probably no more underdeveloped verbally in relation to their basic ability than are the Anglo-American children of comparable IQ. The low-IQ Mexican-American children, however, seem to be especially underdeveloped verbally in relation to their basic learning ability.

Another potential measure of basic ability, which may be quite culture-free as compared with most other tests, is memory span. The digit-span test has long been a part of tests of general intelligence such as the Stanford-Binet and the Wechsler tests, but its full potential as a psychological assessment technique has probably never been realized. The reliability of the digit-span test is among the lowest of the various Wechsler subtests. This is not surprising, considering the small sample of behavior on which the memory span score is based in the Wechsler test. Under controlled and refined conditions, we can obtain a reliability of measurement on memory span that compares favorably with the reliability of measurement of the subject's height and weight.

When corrected for unreliability of measurement, the Wechsler digit-span score correlates 0.75 with the total IQ (minus digit span). Though this is a very substantial correlation, we may still ask why it is not higher than this. There are two main possibilities: (i) the memory-span test may indeed represent only a rather limited aspect of general ability, or (ii) the memory-span test may be less cuturally loaded than the other Wechsler subtests which account for most of the variance in total IQ, and therefore the low correlation between total IQ and digit span is a *good* indication, if what we want is a relatively culture-free measure of ability. If the second alternative is true, we would predict a greater discrepancy between the scaled scores on digit span and total IQ among lower-class or culturally deprived children than among middle-class children. This hypothesis has not been checked; someone with access to a large number of Wechsler protocols obtained on lower-class and middle-class children should look into it.

There is reason to believe that memory span is intimately related to basic learning ability. The extent of this relationship is presently under investigation in our laboratory.

We have elaborated these memory-span tasks to enable them to yield a number of highly reliable differential scores. For example, we obtain memory-span scores for immediate recall and for recall after a delay period of ten seconds. There are reliable individual differences in the amount of decrement in memory span during this brief delay period. There is also evidence, at least among college students, that visually presented materials are translated into an auditory image system for short-term storage, and therefore auditory distraction during the delayed recall interval has a much more detrimental effect than operationally equivalent visual distraction during this period.

Another modification of the digit-span test yields measures of the subject's susceptibility to the effects of proactive and retroactive inhibition. Still another kind of score is obtained by presenting the same digit series twice in immediate succession in order to determine the increment in the subject's memory span resulting from a single repetition; by definition this can be regarded as a learning score.

When all of these different scores obtained from various elaborations of the digit-span test are combined in some weighted fashion, it is not unlikely that the composite score will account for practically all the variance in intelligence as measured by standard tests. Of course, this will be true only if the population sample is relatively homogeneous with respect to cultural background. In a college sample a battery of such tests predicted grade-point average with a multiple-R of $+0.68$ (Jensen, 1965).

If these measures do indeed get at basic learning ability, the next step will be to perfect them for wide-scale use. Fortunately, these methods lend themselves to group-testing procedures. In addition to these measures of basic learning factors, means of assessing the degree of development of verbal and other symbolic mediational processes resulting from different environmental influences will have to be developed, along with the investigation of means for inculcating these processes when the child's home environment has failed to do so.

In this chapter I have described only a few of what seem to me the most promising approaches to the problem of social-class differences in learning ability. Many other aspects of psychological development are, of course, involved in this problem. Though I have not focused on these aspects, they should not—and I am sure they will not—be ignored by other psychological researchers. It would be a mistake to view the development of learning abilities of human beings as taking place in an emotional and social vacuum. The development of learning ability is indeed intimately related to personal interaction. But many persons who are predisposed, either by temperament or as a result of some personal experience, to feeling especially concerned about the problems of culturally deprived children are overly drawn to the emotional and interpersonal aspects of the problem, almost to the complete exclusion of understanding the cognitive processes actually necessary for learning. Therefore, I have emphasized this latter side of the picture. Theory and research in verbal learning provide an analytical means for understanding the cognitive aspects of the problem and for taking constructive action. The approach outlined here seems to be replete with implications for further research and its applications to practical problems.

References

Bernstein, B. Language and social class. *British Journal of Sociology,* 1960, **11,** 271–276.

Bialer, I. Primary and secondary stimulus generalization as related to intelligence level. *Journal of Experimental Psychology,* 1961, **62,** 395–402.

Bousfield, W. A. The occurrence of clustering in this recall of randomly arranged associates. *Journal of Genetic Psychology,* 1953, **49,** 229–240.

Brodbeck, A. J., and O. C. Irwin. The speech behavior of infants without families. *Child Development,* 1946, **17,** 145–156.

Carter, H. D. A preliminary study of free association. I. Twin similarities and the technique of measurement. *Journal of Psychology,* 1938, **6,** 201–215.

Davidson, R. E. Mediation and ability in paired-associate learning. *Journal of Educational Psychology*, 1964, **55**, 352–356.

Dawe, Helen C. A study of the effect of an educational program upon language development and related mental functions in young children. *Journal of Experimental Education*, 1942, **11**, 200–209.

Duncan, C. P. Description of learning to learn in human subjects. *American Journal of Psychology*, 1960, **73**, 108–114.

Ervin, Susan M. Changes with age in the verbal determinants of word association. *American Journal of Psychology*, 1961, **74**, 361–372.

————, and W. R. Miller. "Language development." In H. W. Stevenson (ed.), *Child psychology*. Chicago: National Society for the Study of Education, 1963, 108–143.

Gagné, R. M. The acquisition of knowledge. *Psychological Review*, 1962, **69**, 355–365.

Girardeau, F. L., and N. R. Ellis. Rote verbal learning by normal and mentally retarded children. *American Journal of Mental Deficiency*, 1964, **68**, 525–532.

Harlow, H. F. "Learning set and error factor theory." In S. Koch (ed.), *Psychology: A study of a science*. New York: McGraw-Hill, 1959. II, 492–537.

Higgins, C., and C. H. Sivers. A comparison of Stanford-Binet and colored Raven Progressive Matrices IQs for children with low socio-economic status. *Journal of Consulting Psychology*, 1958, **22**, 465–468.

Howes, D., and E. E. Osgood. On the combination of associative probabilities in linguistic contexts. *American Journal of Psychology*, 1954, **67**, 241–258.

Jenkins, J. J. "Mediated associations: Paradigms and situations." In C. N. Cofer and Barbara S. Musgrave (eds.), *Verbal behavior and learning: Problems and processes*. New York: McGraw-Hill, 1963, 210–245.

Jensen, A. R. Learning abilities in Mexican-American and Anglo-American children. *California Journal of Educational Research*, 1961, **12**, 147–159.

————. Transfer between paired-associate and serial learning. *Journal of Verbal Learning and Verbal Behavior*, 1962, **1**, 269–280.

————. Learning ability in retarded, average, and gifted children. *Merrill-Palmer Quarterly*, 1963, **9**, 123–140.

————. Individual differences in learning: Interference factor. Cooperative Research Project No. 1867, United States Office of Education, 1965.

————, C. C. Collins, and R. W. Vreeland. A multiple S–R apparatus for human learning. *American Journal of Psychology*, 1962, **75**, 470–476.

————, and A. Roden. Memory span and the skewness of the serial-position curve. *British Journal of Psychology*, 1963, **54**, 337–349.

————, and W. D. Rohwer, Jr. Verbal mediation in paired-associate serial learning. *Journal of Verbal Learning and Verbal Behavior*, 1963a, **1**, 346–352.

————, and W. D. Rohwer, Jr. The effect of verbal mediation on the learning and retention of paired-associates by retarded adults. *American Journal of Mental Deficiency*, 1963b, **68**, 80–84.

————, and W. D. Rohwer, Jr. What is learned in serial learning? *Journal of Verbal Learning and Verbal Behavior*, 1965a, **4**, 62–72.

————, and W. D. Rohwer, Jr. Syntactical mediation of serial and paired-associate learning as a function of age. *Child Development*, 1965b, **36**, 601–608.

John, Vera P. The intellectual development of slum children. *American Journal of Orthopsychiatry*, 1963, **33**, 813–822.

Kendler, H. H., and May F. D'Amato. A comparison of reversal shifts and nonreversal shifts in human concept formation behavior. *Journal of Experimental Psychology*, 1955, **49**, 165–174.

Kendler, H. H., and Tracy S. Kendler. Effect of verbalization on reversal shifts in children. *Science*, 1961, **134**, 1619–1620.

—— and ——. Vertical and horizontal processes in problem solving. *Psychological Review*, 1962, **69**, 1–16.

Kendler, H. H., and M. S. Mayzner, Jr. Reversal and nonreversal shifts in card-sorting tests with two or four sorting categories. *Journal of Experimental Psychology*, 1956, **51**, 244–248.

Kendler, Tracy S. Learning, development, and thinking. *Annals of New York Academy of Science*, 1960, **91**, 52–65.

——. "Development of mediating responses in children." In J. C. Wright and J. Kagan (ed.), *Basic cognitive processes in children, Monograph of Society for Research and Child Development*, 1963, **28**, (2). Serial No. 86.

——, and H. H. Kendler. Reversal and nonreversal shifts in kindergarten children. *Journal of Experimental Psychology*, 1959, **58**, 56–60.

——, ——, and Doris Wells. Reversal and nonreversal shifts in nursery school children. *Journal of Comparative Physiological Psychology*, 1960, **53**, 83–88.

——, ——, and Beulah Learnard. Mediated responses to size and brightness as a function of age. *American Journal of Psychology*, 1962, **75**, 571–586.

Koch, Helen. The relation of primary mental abilities in five and six year olds to sex and characteristics of siblings. *Child Development*, 1954, **25**, 209–223.

Luria, A. R. *The role of speech in the regulation of normal and abnormal behavior*. New York: Liveright, 1961a.

——. "The genesis of voluntary movements." In N. O'Connor (ed.), *Recent Soviet psychology*. New York: Liveright, 1961b.

——, and R. Yudovich. Ia. *Speech and the development of mental processes in the child*. London: Staples Press, 1959.

Mandler, G., and J. Huttenlocker. The relationship between associative frequency, associative ability and paired-associate learning. *American Journal of Psychology*, 1956, **69**, 424–428.

McCandless, B. R. *Children and adolescents*. New York: Holt, Rinehart and Winston, 1962.

Miller, G. A. *Language and communication*. New York: McGraw-Hill, 1951.

Miller, N. E. Theory and experiment relating psychoanalytic displacement to stimulus response generalization. *Journal of Abnormal and Social Psychology*, 1948, **43**, 155–178.

Milner, Esther. A study of the relationship betwen reading readiness in grade one school children and patterns of parent-child interaction. *Child Development*, 1951, **22**, 95–112.

Mitchell, I., Isabel R. Rosanoff, and A. J. Rosanoff. A study of association in Negro children. *Psychological Review*, 1919, **26**, 354–359.

Osler, J. F., and G. E. Trautman. Concept attainment: II. Effect of stimulus complexity upon concept attainment at two levels of intelligence. *Journal of Experimental Psychology*, 1961, **62**, 9–13.

Otto, W. The acquisition and retention of paired associates by good, average, and poor readers. *Journal of Educational Psychology*, 1961, **52**, 241–248.

——. The differential effects of verbal and pictorial representations of stimuli upon responses evolved. *Journal of Verbal Learning and Verbal Behavior*, 1962, **1**, 192–196.

Palermo, D. S. Word associations and children's verbal behavior. *Child Development and Behavior,* **1,** in press.

Peterson, Margaret J., and K. C. Blattner. Development of a verbal mediator. *Journal of Experimental Psychology,* 1963, **66,** 72–77.

Pribram, K. H. "Neurological notes on the art of educating." In E. R. Hilgard (ed.), *Theories of learning and instruction, Sixty-third yearbook of the National Society for the Study of Education,* Part I. Chicago: Distributed by the University of Chicago Press, 1964. 78–110.

Pyles, Marjorie K. Verbalization as in learning. *Child Development,* 1932, **3,** 108–113.

Ranken, H. B. Language and thinking: Positive and negative effects of naming. *Science,* 1963, **141,** 48–50.

Razran, G. Soviet psychology and psychophysiology. *Behavioral Science,* 1959, **4,** 35–48.

———. The observable unconscious and the inferable conscious in current Soviet psychophysiology: Interoceptive conditioning, semantic conditioning, and the orienting reflex. *Psychological Review,* 1961, **68,** 81–147.

Reese, H. W. Transfer to a discrimination task as a function of amount of stimulus pretraining and similarity of stimulus names. Unpublished doctoral dissertation, State University of Iowa, 1958.

———. Verbal mediation as a function of age level. *Psychological Bulletin,* 1962, **59,** 502–509.

Rheingold, Harriet, and Nancy Bayley. The later effects of an experimental modification of mothering. *Child Development,* 1959, **30,** 363–372.

Rohwer, W. D., Jr. The verbal facilitation of paired-associate learning. Unpublished doctoral dissertation, University of California, 1964.

Russell, W. A., and L. H. Storms. Implicit verbal chaining in paired-associate learning. *Journal of Experimental Psychology,* 1955, **49,** 287–293.

Schwebel, M. Individual differences in learning abilities: Observations and research at home and abroad. *American Journal of Orthopsychiatry,* 1963, **33,** 60–71.

Semler, I. J., and I. Iscoe. Comparative and developmental study of the learning abilities of Negro and white children under four conditions. *Journal of Educational Psychology,* 1963, **54,** 38–44.

Spiker, C. C. Stimulus pretraining and subsequent performance in the delayed reaction experiment. *Journal of Experimental Psychology,* 1956, **52,** 107–111.

Stevenson, H. W., and I. Iscoe. Overtraining and transposition in children. *Journal of Experimental Psychology,* 1954, **47,** 251–255.

Terrell, G. The role of incentive in discrimination learning in children. *Child Development,* 1958, **29,** 231–236.

———, K. Durkin, and M. Wiesley. Social class and the nature of the incentive in discrimination learning. *Journal of Abnormal and Social Psychology,* 1959, **59,** 270–272.

Tulving, E. Subjective organization in free recall of "unrelated" words. *Psychology Review,* 1962, **69,** 344–354.

Underwood, B. J., and R. W. Schultz. *Meaningfulness and verbal learning.* Chicago: Lippincott, 1960.

White, S. H. "Learning." In H. W. Stevenson (ed.), *Child psychology.* Chicago: National Society for the Study of Education, 1963, 196–235.

Woodworth, R. S., and H. Schlosberg. *Experimental psychology.* New York: Holt, Rinehart and Winston, 1954, 43–71.

PART
THREE

Social
and Psychological
Perspectives

INTRODUCTION—*Irwin Katz*

Though long concerned with the study of racial prejudice and its causes, American social science generally has been content merely to speculate about the effect of prejudice on target groups. It is a matter of common observation that prejudice, when combined with discrimination, tends to create in the victim those very traits of "inferiority" that it ascribes to him. What is not so apparent is that even in the absence of the more blatant, objective forms of discrimination—poor schools, menial jobs, and substandard housing—traditional stereotypes about the low ability and apathy of Negroes and other nonwhite minorities can operate as "self-fulfilling prophecies." Thus the belief that Negroes are intellectually incompetent can cause both whites and Negroes to behave toward one another in such a manner as to yield confirmatory evidence. The underlying psychological process whereby expectancies determine behavior is most subtle and covert. Indeed, until quite recently the

175

hidden power of expectancies over behavior was hardly seen as relevant to the understanding of group differences in achievement.

Each of the chapters in this part represents a different approach to the problem of the impact of prejudice and discrimination upon object groups.

Proshansky and Newton review an extensive literature on Negro self-identity. At the heart of their discussion of the Negro's self-concept is the reality of the American racial caste system. They see this system as imposing a double burden on the Negro through severe inequalities of life opportunities and through the heavy psychological consequences suffered by the Negro who is forced to play an inferior role. Several interrelated questions concerning the self-concept of Negroes are considered, questions having to do with the early development of racial identity, the sources and consequences of emotional conflict over Negro identity, and finally, the individual and group resources for developing positive self-concepts.

One of the important values of Proshansky and Newton's chapter lies in its careful exposure of the limitations of present research and theory on Negro identity. The research findings, as they show, can only be described as incomplete, fragmentary, and at times contradictory. Their analysis should provide a useful inventory of the kinds of systematic research that are needed in this area.

The next two chapters further develop the topic of prejudice and its effects. But now the focus is shifted from Negro personality to intellectual and academic performance. Rosenthal and Jacobson report a series of intriguing studies on human and animal subjects which support the hypothesis that the expectations of power figures regarding the behavior of those whom they control, importantly influence the latter's behavior. The main part of their discussion is devoted to an account of an experiment which utilized an entire elementary school as a laboratory for a full academic year. Their findings suggest that children from whom teachers were arbitrarily led to expect strong intellectual growth (the teachers were given fictitious intelligence test scores) actually showed such growth during the ensuing year.

Unfortunately, the experiment conveys little information about the processes that mediated between the teacher's expectations and the enhanced development of intellectual skills in children earmarked for mental growth. Only direct observations of teacher-pupil interactions will provide definite answers to questions of mediation. Further, the data are not as strong as one would wish. Yet their implications for educational practice are so fundamental that further research is clearly in order. Two implications may be mentioned: that when teachers have rigid expectations of poor achievement from lower-class children, or from pupils in low-ability tracks, the expectations may function as self-fulfilling prophecies. A few studies (for example, Gottlieb, 1966; and HARYOU, 1964) do indicate that white middle-class teachers tend to underestimate the ability and misinterpret the goals of minority group children, and to express a preference for teaching white students.

In the final chapter of this section, Katz first reviews evidence relating to the effect of school desegregation on the academic achievement of Negroes. He finds that a national study of public schools conducted by James Coleman and others for the United States Office of Education provides reasonably acceptable evidence of increments in Negro performance in racially mixed classrooms. None of the studies cited suggest negative consequences of desegregation for children of either race. The main thrust of Katz's discussion is toward psychological factors that favorably or adversely influence the behavior of minority group children in biracial settings. Drawing upon evidence from a wide range of studies on the effects of stress and isolation, as well as from several experiments on Negro youth, he suggests some elements for a theory of Negro performance in the desegregated school. The reactions of white peers and teachers, both real and anticipated, and the Negro child's expectancies of success or failure on particular scholastic tasks, figure prominently in the conceptual model that is outlined.

An important proposition for which some evidence is offered is that the desegregated environment has greater potentiality both for academic success and failure than does the all-Negro environment. Whether the outcome for the individual child will be favorable or detrimental depends upon the specific social conditions that prevail in the classroom.

Thus the three contributions in this section provide complementary components of an over-all strategy in studying the psychological effects of class and race distinctions in the United States. They point the way for systematic, experimentally oriented research on the situational determinants of minority group achievement.

References

Gottlieb, D. "Teaching and students: The views of Negro and white teachers." In S. W. Webster (ed.), *The disadvantaged learner*. San Francisco: Chandler, 1966.

Harlem Youth Opportunities Unlimited, Inc. *Youth in the ghetto*. New York, 1964.

CHAPTER FIVE

The Nature
and Meaning of
Negro Self-Identity

HAROLD PROSHANSKY[1]

PEGGY NEWTON[2]

How does a Negro child learn about race? When does he learn that he is "different"—that he is in a minority in a prejudiced white society? What does he feel about himself: who he is—what he can do?

In exploring these questions we find that there are no simple or definitive answers. The child learns about race both directly and indirectly: at home, at school, in the streets. Similarly, his feelings about himself grow out of a wide variety of personal experiences. In an absolute sense, each child's answers to the questions of race and identity are unique, yet we find certain attitudes, responses, and feelings which are shared by many Negroes. In some way, each Negro-American is forced to confront the question of "who he is" in the prevailing white society.

Underlying our discussion of the Negro's self-concept is the reality of the discriminatory social caste-class system in America with its historic origins in the institution of slavery. We see this system as imposing a double burden on the Negro through severe social and economic in-

[1] Graduate Center, City University of New York.
[2] Institute for Developmental Studies, New York University.

178

equalities and through the heavy psychological consequences suffered by the Negro who is forced to play an inferior role. There are obvious differences in schools, housing, employment, and income; less visible, but equally serious, are the heavy psychological costs of low self-esteem, feelings of helplessness, and basic identity conflict.

To understand some of the issues and problems of Negro identity— its unique features, as well as its white normative aspects—we must examine Negro identity in relation to the norms and values of the dominant white society. The special properties of Negro identity reflect the idiosyncrasies of Negro institutional life as seen in family, school, church, recreational, and employment settings. In turn, we see these distinctive features of institutions as arising in direct response to the discriminatory system imposed by a white society. These characteristics of institutions which are uniquely Negro serve to protect and preserve the Negro community—but not without cost to its members. The price for the adaptive nature of Negro institutional life is the maintenance and perpetuation of existing patterns of inequality.

In the present chapter we shall consider several interrelated and significant questions concerning the self-concept of the Negro. First, we shall look at his self-identity from a developmental vantage point, examining research findings which describe the ways in which the young Negro child's beliefs and feelings about himself grow and change. These studies are primarily concerned with the early development of self-identity; unfortunately there is very little research on the development of Negro identity in adolescence and young adulthood. After having considered some of the developmental aspects of Negro identity, we shall explore the consequences and the sources of conflict over Negro identity. In looking at the consequences of this conflict, we shall be primarily concerned with how conflict over racial identity directly or indirectly influences the behavior of the Negro in culturally prescribed settings which demand specific motivation and particular motor and verbal skills. In a world that measures men not just in terms of what they want and can do, but more significantly in terms of what they actually *do,* the "performance" of the Negro in school, at home, and on the job becomes a critical social issue.

Our discussion of the sources of conflict over Negro identity will emphasize the family, as we seek to understand *how* the young child learns about himself and his unique status as a Negro. Although we have described lower-class urban Negro family patterns, it is important to realize that not all Negro families are lower-class, nor do they fit the somewhat archetypal description presented. Our purpose is to show how the young child's negative feelings about himself may be reinforced and intensified in the home setting, particularly when the problems of poverty are added to the burden of being Negro. We shall also look at some of the characteristics of the school which often provide additional conflict for the Negro child.

In the final section of the chapter, we shall examine some positive aspects of Negro identity and group resources for developing positive identification. We shall also consider very briefly the influence of the Civil Rights Movement and black nationalism on the young Negro's self-image and expectations.

Our discussion of the nature and meaning of Negro self-identity is necessarily limited by the state of research and theory in the field. While there has been considerable genuine concern about Negro identity, there has been little actual research on Negro identity. The research findings can only be described as incomplete, fragmentary, and at times contradictory. Hopefully, the present analysis should provide an inventory of the form and aspects of systematic research needed for understanding the development of the Negro's self-image.

In looking at the "quality" or value of the existing research on Negro self-concept, we find that social scientists have been severely hampered by methodological problems. Techniques for measuring self-concept have often seemed artificial; reports have frequently been highly subjective, and the number of subjects have typically been small. Researchers interested in Negro identity have also tended to think only in "black-white terms," ignoring important social-class variables. Simpson and Yinger (1965) point out the great pitfalls in drawing general conclusions from simple comparisons of Negro and white subjects, emphasizing the tremendous variability both in prejudice and its effects on minority group members. They suggest that the amount and type of prejudice and the form of reactions to prejudice depend on individual variables, such as age, education, occupation, temperament, and family training about the dominant group. Significant group factors include group cohesiveness, intergroup contact, color variations within the group, surrounding group attitudes toward prejudice, and experience with other intergroup patterns (p. 133).

Still another major problem in studies of Negro-white self-concepts, as well as in many other investigations making Negro-white comparisons, is the patent middle-class bias involved in most of the standard instruments used for measuring intelligence, achievement, and personality. Investigations of family structure, motivation, and occupational choices in Negroes have usually employed white middle-class standards as a basis for judgment. While to some extent such comparisons are inevitable, it is important to recognize their limitations and the form of inherent value judgment they impose on the Negro. In a discussion of personality differences, Georgene Seward (1956) cautions against judging the Negro by white norms. Not only is such a practice "unfair" to the Negro, it also tends to obscure important dynamic factors, which have meaning only with reference to his subculture.

> Unless an individual is viewed within his own frame of reference, his behavior cannot be accurately assessed with regard to its normality or abnormality. . . . In the case of the Negro, to follow white norms may mean indicting an entire subculture for deviations forced upon it by exclusion from the main currents of the dominant culture (p. 144f.).

When there are variations and difficulties in method and technique in studying the individual, we can expect to find corresponding differences and difficulties in concept and theory. This phenomenon is highly apparent in the field of self-concept research. The relevant literature contains a confusing assortment of terms which refer to the individual's beliefs and feelings about himself: "self-concept," "self-image," "self-identity," "self," and so on. While these differences in terminology reflect differences in theory and method, the differences are far from clear-cut. Furthermore, even when theorists or investigators actually employ the same term, they are by no means always in agreement as to its meaning.

In the present discussion, it is not our purpose to codify or integrate these various concepts to denote the individual's perception of himself as an object. We shall use the terms "self," "self-concept," and "self-identity" interchangeably. As we have already indicated, the distinctions among the terms are difficult to maintain, and in the light of the methodological limitations imposed on existing data on the development of self, little is to be gained from attempting to maintain these distinctions in this discussion. Therefore, all of these concepts will be used to refer to that constellation of interrelated, conscious and unconscious beliefs and feelings which the individual has about himself.

Like any other attitudinal object or referent, the individual both "identifies" and evaluates himself. Thus, he learns "who he is" on dimensions such as appearance, group membership, achievement, and aspirations. This learning is never a neutral process, for the process of learning "who one is" invariably carries with it value judgments, for example, "good" or "bad," "desirable" or "undesirable," "worth much" or "worth little." In addition to the limited views of self, the individual also acquires a more general evaluative view of self which is usually called self-esteem or self-acceptance. In learning that he is "black," "dark," "colored," or "Negro," the Negro child soon, if not simultaneously, learns the negative-value connotation placed on membership in his racial group. He learns that it is bad to be Negro, because he is not white.

The individual's existence is defined by many social groups or categories, so that he "identifies" and evaluates himself along many basic dimensions. These dimensions differ in their importance to the individual and in their role in determining over-all feelings of self-esteem. The weight or importance of a dimension is determined by the dimension's normative value and the number of situations to which it applies, as well as by individual needs. For example, the concept "Negro" has implications for a variety of personal characteristics, social settings, and institutional practices, while the concept "Easterner" has far less significance in influencing the individual's self-identity.

When we consider the person's self-esteem, asking whether he generally sees himself positively or negatively, the importance of a preponderance of favorable judgments covering many dimensions of self for healthy personality development is almost axiomatic. Newcomb, Turner, and Converse (1965) note, ". . . it seems quite clear that one of the individual's most basic and continuing needs is for a self-image that is essentially positive" (p. 141).

While Negro identity is the focus of the present description and analysis, many of the general findings and concepts to be presented clearly have relevance for other minority group members, for example, Puerto Ricans, Jews, Mexican-Americans, and lower-class whites. Our specific knowledge about development of self and its manifestations in individuals in particular social groups is limited. However, there is considerable evidence to support the assumption that there is a direct relationship between problems in emergence of *self* and the extent to which the child's ethnic or racial membership group is socially unacceptable and subject to conspicuous deprivation. This viewpoint is summarized eloquently by Negro psychiatrist and polemicist, Frantz Fanon:

> . . . I begin to suffer from not being a white man to the degree that the white man imposes discrimination on me, makes me a colonized native, robs me of all worth, all individuality, tells me that I am a parasite on the world, that I must bring myself as quickly as possible into step with the white world . . . (1967, p. 98).

THE DEVELOPMENT OF SELF-IDENTITY

IN THE NEGRO

Color is an undeniable fact of the Negro's existence in America. The inescapable reality of color shades and shadows the Negro child's emerging sense of self, making the development of racial identification an integral part of his total development of self. As Seward suggests: ". . . color is inherent in the concept of 'self.' As awareness of self emerges, it emerges in a race-conscious social context which assigns values to the perception of color" (1956, p. 129).

The preschool and early elementary school years (approximately ages three to seven) are generally recognized as a crucial period in the growth and differentiation of the child's feelings about himself and his feelings toward others who are ethnically different (Allport, 1954; Proshansky, 1966). During this period the child becomes increasingly aware of racial differences and learns labels and affective responses associated with various ethnic groups including his own. The research indicates that the Negro child and his white counterpart become aware of color or racial differences as early as age three or four and that within this awareness lies an inchoate understanding of the valuations placed on this color by the larger society.

Using the same basic experimental design, several investigators have documented the development of racial identification in young children. Most frequently these studies have been conducted in preschool settings, and the experimenters have employed Negro and white dolls or pictures of Negro and white children to determine their subjects' racial identification. While these studies have shown some variations in measurement techniques and in the age and geographical locus of the subjects sampled, their findings provide a relatively consistent picture of the development of racial identity in the Negro child.

In considering these investigations, we shall emphasize two basic processes involved in the development of racial identity. The first, *racial conception,* is concerned with when and how the child learns to make racial distinctions at a conceptual level. The second process, *racial evaluation,* deals with when and how the child evaluates his own racial group membership. For analytical purposes it is important to maintain this distinction between the two processes. However, in the actual development of the child, the processes by which he learns "who he is" and the *value* of "who he is" are inextricably tied to each other. The Negro child learns the meaning of the term "Negro" in a continuing context of social interactions in which others both distinguish and evaluate him by means of his racial category and label him in affectively-laden terms which refer to his race.

Racial Conceptions

The racial world for the Negro child is not only empirical but also conceptual. To be "a Negro" establishes "who he is" by relating him to all other individuals, known and unknown, who have the same defining features. In time, he must realize the *general* nature of his racial category because others label and identify him in these terms, making his racial group membership the nexus of his emerging self-identity. To achieve such understanding, the child must first learn to make racial distinctions: to recognize and be aware of the differences in skin color and related characteristics between himself and others.

Many investigators have reported that the ability to make such racial distinctions first appears at roughly age three in both Negro and white children (Clark and Clark, 1947; Stevenson and Stewart, 1958; Morland, 1958; Stevenson and Stevenson, 1960). This ability increases steadily with age until approximately age six or seven, when all children are able to make these identifications accurately. (Clark and Clark, 1947; Morland, 1958). Studies by Goodman (1952) and Morland (1958) reveal that it is during the fourth year that the greatest increase in racial awareness occurs; 77 to 85 percent of the Negro and white children exhibit a medium to high level of such awareness. In her study of 57 Negro and 46 white nursery school children between the ages of three and five and one half, Goodman reports that high awareness did not occur before the age of four years and three months, while low awareness did not occur in the sample after four years, eleven months. A more extensive study of 253 Negro children between the ages of three and seven by Clark and Clark (1947) suggests that this period— around four to five years—may be the crucial period in the formation and patterning of racial attitudes toward *onseself* and others. These investigators observe: "At these ages these subjects appear to be reacting more uncritically in a definite structuring of attitudes which conforms with the accepted racial values and mores of the larger environment" (p. 177).

It is important to note that the development of racial awareness in very young children is undoubtedly aided by the visibility factor inherent in skin color distinctions. Although little research has been done on awareness of other types of ethnic distinctions among children of these ages, there is evidence that the development of such awareness roughly parallels that found for racial distinctions. Awareness of religious and national groups also emerges relatively early in the life of the child—although probably later than racial awareness—and also shows an increase with age (Hartley, Rosenbaum, and Schwartz, 1948; Radke, Trager, and Davis, 1949).

In the studies by Hartley *et al.* (1948) and Radke *et al.* (1949), there is evidence that membership in an ethnic minority may be a predisposing factor in the *early* development of ethnic awareness. In the latter investigation it was found that Jewish children between the ages of five and nine were more aware of their group membership (and more strongly identified with their own ethnic group) than were Catholic or Protestant children. However, the comparisons between

Negro and white children in the studies previously cited have been inconclusive in determining which group first becomes aware of racial differences.

Goodman (1952) found that among the preschool children she studied in a large northeastern city those who were Negro became aware of racial differences at an earlier age than did her white subjects. In contrast, Morland (1958) and Stevenson and Stewart (1958) found that white nursery school children in Lynchburg, Virginia, and Austin, Texas, achieved racial awareness earlier than their Negro counterparts.

Several explanations have been offered for these contradictory findings. It is suggested that white children in the South, as compared with those in the North, are more sensitive to racial differences by virtue of the explicitly normative character of Negro-white relationships. Another possibility may be that Negro children in the South are less willing than Northern Negro children to verbalize their knowledge of racial differences. Goodman (1964) proposes that the difference in results might be attributed to the techniques used for measuring racial awareness. In her own study, Goodman (1952) used intensive case studies of her preschool subjects over time, while both Stevenson and Stewart (1958) and Morland (1958) relied on their subjects' ability to identify correctly pictures of Negro and white children. It is possible that the techniques used by Morland and by Stevenson and Stewart did not measure the child's level of racial awareness, but rather the Negro child's tendency to deny his own racial identification by "refusing" (rather than being unable) to discriminate between Negro and white persons.

Racial awareness is a stage in the Negro child's achievement of a "racial conception." To attain a racial conception, the child must not only have the ability to make racial distinctions, but he must also be able to elevate these distinctions to the level of a general conception of the meaning of the terms, "Negro" and "white." He must understand and be able to use terms to relate as well as distinguish among people regardless of time and place.

Not only is the Negro child racially aware by the age of four or five, but he has already learned the relevant words, concepts, and phrases, used to describe members of his own and other racial (and ethnic) groups. He uses these terms to describe himself and others; however, there is evidence that until age eight or nine his racial conception is somewhat more apparent than real—that is, the child seems to have a "verbal fluency" rather than a conceptual understanding of racial categories. In Goodman's (1952) low and medium "awareness" groups, both Negro and white children used racial terms to describe and label others, but their use of these terms was not always accurate. Even with

Goodman's older, high-awareness subjects (four to five years), who were apparently able to generalize racial distinctions, it was not clear if these children fully grasped the class nature of the racial concepts in the sense of extending these concepts beyond the nursery school. In a study of the development of racial concepts in white New Zealand children, Vaughan (1963) found that the actual attainment of racial concepts (categorization) first appears at seven years of age and only after the child has learned first to identify and then to discriminate among members of different racial groups.

As we have noted, at ages four to six the child has the ability to make racial distinctions and use racial terms in describing members of other racial groups. However, the child is still confronted with the critical task of matching the level of his understanding with his verbal fluency. While he fails to grasp the *full* meaning of racial terms and, therefore, is unable to use them consistently and correctly, his real problem is in recognizing the conceptual nature of the racial labels he uses. The child's understanding of racial concepts and his ability to generalize them appropriately is not an all-or-none situation; it is instead a gradual learning process in which the child, as he grows older, achieves increasing levels of generalization.

Racial Evaluations

In considering the questions of racial awareness and racial preference and rejection, Kenneth Clark (1955) points out

> The child . . . cannot learn what racial group he belongs to without being involved in a larger pattern of emotions, conflicts, and desires which are part of his growing knowledge of what society thinks about his race (p. 23).

The Negro child does not learn about racial distinctions in an emotional vacuum. As we have previously noted, the young child acquires value-laden racial labels and fragments of popular stereotypes to describe his own and other racial and ethnic groups. Both Negro and white children learn to associate Negro with "dirty," "bad," and "ugly," and white with "clean," "nice," and "good." For the Negro child, these emotionally charged descriptions and judgments operate to establish the white group as vastly superior to his own racial group.

The early presence of the emotional and evaluative aspects of racial learning is clearly demonstrated in a series of studies of young Negro and white children. Although different techniques have been used to measure racial evaluation—for example, playmate selection, drawings, doll play, and picture tests—the results of these studies have been consistent.

Does the Negro child like being a Negro? The empirical evidence suggests that for many children the answer to this question ranges from a qualified to an emphatic "no." Given a choice, a majority of both Negro and white children tend to choose a white doll in preference to a Negro one (Clark and Clark, 1947; Stevenson and Stewart, 1958; Radke and Trager, 1950; Goodman, 1952; Morland, 1962; Landreth and Johnson, 1953). In a more recent study of 407 young children, Morland (1962) found that 60 percent of the Negro children, but only 10 percent of the white children, preferred to play with children of the *other* race; in comparison, 18 percent of the Negro children and 72 percent of the white children preferred playmates of their *own* race.

The young Negro child does more than simply identify with the white society which surrounds him. His choices of dolls or playmates may be viewed not only as preferences for whites, but also as rejection of or hostility toward his own racial group. In her study of racial awareness, Goodman (1952) found that only 9 percent of the Negro children in the sample expressed hostility toward whites, while 24 percent of these Negro children directed hostility toward their own race. In contrast, 33 percent of the white children expressed hostility toward Negroes, but none was antagonistic toward his own racial group.

More direct evidence of the young Negro child's tendency to deprecate or reject his own racial group is provided in a study reported by Clark and Clark (1947). Employing 253 two- to seven-year-old Negro children, the Clarks showed their subjects Negro and white dolls and posed these questions: "Which doll looks nice?" "Which doll looks bad?" "Which doll is a 'nice' color?" A majority of the children picked the white doll as the one which "looked nice" and was a "nice color" and selected the Negro doll as the one which "looked bad." While there was a decrease with age in choices of the white doll as "looking nice" and being a "nice color," a majority of subjects at all ages said that the Negro doll "looked bad."

The Negro child's rejection of his own racial group is well-founded. Quite early in life the child absorbs the cultural norms and judgments about his race, learning in a rudimentary way about his limited opportunities and the prejudice against him. In a study of Negro children between the ages of three and seven, Stevenson and Stewart (1958) found that Negro children perceived children of their *own* race as aggressive, bad, and those "whom other children fear," significantly more times than white subjects saw white children with these characteristics. In addition, both Negro and white subjects most frequently picked white children as "winners in a game."

The persistence and pervasiveness of these racial stereotypes have been clearly revealed in a study (Johnson, 1941) of Negro youth, between the ages of twelve and twenty, who lived in the rural South. Given a list of six possible racial categories or colors of people, these teenagers were asked to choose adjectives from the list, to describe people in thirty value-judgment situations. Johnson found that there was "a decided tendency to classify as black a disproportionately large number of negative judgments." For example, in the choice of the color of the "ugliest girl you know," approximately 40 percent of 837 boys selected black, as compared with 11 percent who chose yellow and 7 percent who chose light brown. The results obtained for value judgments of behavior were similar to those describing physical characteristics. Approximately 43 percent of the boys and 23 percent of the girls checked black as the color of the "meanest boy (girl) you know."

It may be argued that Johnson's results are distorted because rural Southern Negro children are likely to have social contacts only with other Negro children. Therefore, the "ugliest" or "meanest" child the subjects had known may well be black. However, comments made during interviews with these subjects clearly suggest that their judgments were rooted in existing stereotypes and normative evaluations of Negroes and not in actual experience. This phenomenon is illustrated by some of the subjects' following remarks: "Black is ugly"; "Black people are mean"; "Black people are evil"; and "You can't get along with black people."

The young child's learning is not confined to behavioral stereotypes of Negroes. He also learns about the reality of the Negro's existence in America: his inferior housing, his limited opportunities for achievement, his low status, and his treatment from the larger society. When Radke and Trager (1950) asked five- to eight-year-old Negro and white children to choose either a "good" or "poor" house for white and Negro dolls, the researchers found that 82 percent of the white children and 67 percent of the Negro children gave the "poor" house to the Negro doll. Conversely, 77 percent of the white children and 60 percent of the Negro children gave the "good" house to the white doll. This finding has significance extending beyond the obvious conclusion that Negro and white children have learned that the two racial groups differ in their standards of living. Perceived differences in housing are associated with differences in economic dependence and in style of life; these differences are, in turn, linked with differences in social status, special privilege, and the ability to bring change. As Radke and Trager (1950) note,

For many of the children, concepts and feelings about race extend into adult world distinctions of status, ability, character, occupations, and economic circumstances. Social distinctions made by whites which put Negroes in an inferior status tend to be accepted as "natural" or inevitable (p. 33).

Further support for the child's early awareness of social inequalities and social distinctions is revealed in the now classic study of social class and friendship by Neugarten (1946). Using 174 fifth- and sixth-graders from five social-class levels as subjects in a survey of social perceptions and friendship, Neugarten concludes that social-class differences in friendship and reputation are well established by the fifth grade. Although the subjects were white, Neugarten's findings have implications for the Negro child who often bears the double burden of being both lower class and Negro. In the study, lower-class children were rated by their classmates as poorly dressed, not good looking, unpopular, aggressive, not liking school, being dirty and bad-mannered, never having a good time, and not playing fair (p. 310). Drawing from his observations of and interviews with Negro children in the South, Coles (1967) describes how completely these children absorb the social system and comprehend how it affects them:

> I have been continually astonished to discover just how intricately children come to examine the social system, the political and economic facts of our society . . . children . . . quickly learn to estimate who can vote, or who has money to frequent this kind of restaurant or that kind of theater, or what groups of people contribute to our police force —and why. . . . I have been struck by how specifically aware they become of those forces in our society, which, reciprocally, are specifically sensitive to *them*. They remark on the scarcity of colored faces on television, and I have heard them cheer the sight of a Negro on that screen (p. 338).

In the light of the grim "facts" the young Negro child learns about his race, his rejection of his own group and his preference for whites are readily understandable. This tendency to prefer whites and reject Negroes, as noted in previously cited studies by Goodman (1952) and Morland (1962), is revealed in sharper detail when Negro children are confronted directly with the task of "identifying" themselves. In their 1947 study, the Clarks asked their three- to seven-year-old Negro subjects [to] "Give me the doll that looks like you." Of the 253 Negro children studied, 66 percent picked the doll of their own race, but 33 percent "identified" with the white doll. Except for age three (when it might be argued that some of the children were having difficulty in making racial distinctions), the low point in identifying with Negroes was at age five, when only 48 percent of the subjects picked the Negro doll. At ages six and seven there were substantial increases in the proportion of Negro children who identified with their own racial group. Employing a comparable doll technique, Stevenson and Stewart (1958) report very similar findings.

In an even more direct approach to the question of racial self-identity, Morland (1958) asked Negro and white subjects, all of whom had been previously classified as having a high degree of race awareness, "Are you white or are you colored?" All of the white children said that they were white, but only 52 percent of the Negro subjects identified themselves as colored. Of the remaining Negro children, 32 percent claimed that they were white and 16 percent maintained they did not know or simply refused to answer the question.

In looking at Morland's (1958) results, it is important to stress that the Negro children who said they were white (32 percent) had a high degree of racial awareness and, therefore, were able to distinguish skin color differences. Their response of "white" to the question, "Are you white or colored?" seems to reflect their wish to be white rather than their actual knowledge of their own racial group membership.

The distinction between the Negro child's wish to be white and his knowledge of racial differences is clearly revealed in a study by the Clarks (1950). The investigators gave 160 Negro five-, six-, and seven-year-olds a coloring task in which the child was told, "Color this little boy (or girl) the color you are." In contrast with other measures of racial identity used in the studies previously described, the Clarks found far less evidence of identification with the white majority when using the coloring-task procedure. Even at age five, 80 percent of the children correctly identified themselves on the basis of their own skin color; at age six, 85 percent of the children made the correct response, while at age seven, 97 percent of the sample gave the appropriate identification. These results suggest that when given the highly concrete task of selecting a crayon and committing himself on paper, the child was forced to contend with the reality of "who he was."

The child's conflicts over his racial identification are highlighted when the results of the coloring task, discussed above, are compared with a second part of the same experiment in which the same subjects were asked to color the little boy (girl) "the color you like little boys (girls) to be." In this situation only 48 percent of the children colored the child brown or black, whereas 36 percent colored him white or yellow, and the remaining subjects made irrelevant responses.

Numerous studies have shown that the tendency of the Negro child to identify with the white majority and reject his own group decreases with age (Clark and Clark, 1947; Radke and Trager, 1950; Morland, 1962). This finding is to be expected, for as he grows older, the child is forced to contend with the social reality of his color and his consequent designation by society. He must face the fact that he is a Negro and that he will be treated as a Negro by members of his own group and, more significantly, he will be treated as a Negro by the very persons he wishes to be: the members of the white majority.

The Negro child is eventually forced to acknowledge and accept his Negro identity; this acceptance of his race may decrease but it does not eliminate the fundamental conflict involved in the development of his self-identity. What he is and can ever hope to be, as a Negro, is somewhat less than what he would be, or could ever hope to be, if he were white. The child's awareness of this conflict may be conscious or unconscious; however, the conflict itself tends to nourish feelings of self-doubt and a sense of inadequacy, if not actual self-hatred. Given these circumstances, we would expect the Negro child not only to be "sensitive" to the question of "who he is," but also to characterize himself in unfavorable terms, that is, to reveal a negative self-image.

Considering the importance and centrality of this basic conflict over identity, it is not surprising that some of the Negro children in the studies by the Clarks (1947) and Goodman (1952) were disturbed by the investigation, especially when they were required to make self-identifications. Morland (1958) noted similar responses among some of his subjects, observing that they made identifications "reluctantly and with emotional strain." He suggests that even among the subjects who said that they were colored, when asked if they were colored or white, there may have been some unconscious identification with whites.

The ambivalence, self-doubt, and lowered self-esteem of many Negro children, resulting from their being Negro and not white, is seen in Coles' descriptions of the drawings of Southern children involved in school desegregation. Coles (1965) suggests that the drawings often indicated a fear of white people and a feeling of "lacking something" because they were not white. Significant differences frequently appeared in the relative size of the Negroes and whites drawn. In a number of instances Negroes appeared as much smaller than whites and were drawn with missing or mutilated body parts. Coles also noted an inconsistent use of color. Some children did not want to draw themselves as Negroes, while others "compensated" by drawing whites a light shade of brown.

Where self-rejection occurs we are likely to find other psychological consequences in terms of the behavior, feelings, and sense of well-being of the individual. In the next section, we shall consider these and other consequences that follow from the racial identity conflict experienced by the Negro child. Where there is available data we shall also consider some of the more immediate factors in the life of the Negro child that reflect the plight of Negroes as a minority group and thereby have specific consequences for the kind of self-identity that emerges in the child. In the process of considering both the causes and consequences of this identity, we shall gain some insight into the nature and meaning of Negro identity.

SOURCES AND CONSEQUENCES OF CONFLICT
IN NEGRO SELF-IDENTITY

In the previous section we had begun to consider the substantive nature of the Negro's self-identity, that is, what he thinks and feels about himself as a person. To expand and elaborate on this topic in this section, we shall consider both the conditions that foster a Negro self-identity and the consequences of this identity for the behavior and experience of the individual. In undertaking such a discussion, it is necessary to specify its limitations, which are imposed by the type of available research on Negro self-identity.

The research on Negro self-identity has tended to be sporadic rather than systematic. Much has been written about the self-image of the Negro. Those writing in the field have generally agreed on the nature of the Negro's identity conflicts; however, the basis of their statements has usually been anecdotal evidence and general descriptions of the "plight of the Negro" instead of carefully collected empirical data. To complicate the picture further, we find that most of the existing data focuses on the lower-class Negro; therefore, these findings cannot be generalized to apply to Negroes in other social class categories. In addition, most studies of the self-identity characteristics of lower-class Negroes have made comparisons with middle-class whites, thus making it virtually impossible to separate the race and social class factors.

The urban slum dweller, whether white or Negro, faces problems with self-image in a society which values individual initiative, success, and status. However, some properties of the self-identity of the lower-class Negro reflect his unique place in the social hierarchy.

We may ask about the self-image of Negroes who have achieved middle-class and upper-class status. There are undoubtedly significant class-associated differences in family structure and in attitudes toward the dominant white society, which influence the child's self-image and identification, his school achievement, and his eventual occupational status. Unfortunately the empirical research on these social class differences is extremely limited. On the basis of a comparison of intelligence test scores of Negro and white subjects from three social class levels, Deutsch and Brown (1964) suggest, " . . . the influence of racial membership tends to become increasingly manifest and crucial as the social class level increases" (p. 27). They propose that lower-class status has a similar effect on Negroes and whites, but while higher status tends to bring the white increased "participation in the cultural mainstream," the Negro of similar status is often denied such participation because of his race.

The concentration of research and theory on the lower-class urban Negro has perpetuated a narrow and limited view of Negro identity. Although research has usually been confined to the urban slum dweller, there has been a tendency to generalize these findings, applying them to all Negroes, regardless of social class or geographical location. We would expect that Negroes who had achieved occupational and economic success would be confronted by a different order of identity conflicts than the lower-class Negro. It would seem likely that the accomplishments and status of middle-class Negroes would merely redefine rather than eradicate the stigma of their racial group membership. Research on middle-class and upper-class Negroes is needed both to clarify these questions and to suggest the scope and complexity of the issue of Negro identity.

A further shortcoming of the existing research has been in its problem-centered approach. In dealing with a lower-class urban population, researchers have tended to look for "problems," emphasizing negative elements of identity and seeing differences from white middle-class norms as "problems." As we shall point out in the final section of this chapter, there *are* positive and compensatory aspects of Negro identity. These positive elements of identity need to be given a larger place in research and theoretical formulations. In our concluding section, we shall consider those aspects and conditions of the Negro dilemma that strengthen rather than weaken his tie with his own racial group; we shall look at the potentially integrative rather than divisive forces in the development of Negro self-identity.

THE NEGRO SELF-IMAGE: ITS EFFECTS ON
BEHAVIOR AND EXPERIENCE

The Negro who feels disdain or hatred for his own racial group is expressing—at some level of awareness—disdain or hatred for himself. Where the self-image is rooted in and structured by this kind of self-rejection, we can expect negative effects on the behavior and experience of the individual. In the discussion that follows, we shall look at some of the research which deals with the consequences of self-hatred and rejection. For the purpose of convenience, we shall consider the studies under two categories: "personality adjustment" and "achievement orientation." By the term, "personality adjustment," we mean how the Negro reacts to and copes with his underlying sense of inferiority or lack of self-esteem. Although the Negro's achievement orientation may also be seen as a mode of adjustment in response to a negative identity, we shall consider these topics separately.

PERSONALITY ADJUSTMENT. Perhaps the "real tragedy" for the American Negro lies less in the inferior, passive, and servile role he is forced to play, and more in the fact that he comes to believe in this role. His self-image not only reflects this role structure but also confirms and supports it. As Pettigrew (1964b) points out, by judging himself the way others do, " . . . the Negro may grow into the servile role; in time the person and the role become indistinguishable" (p. 25).

Many theorists have noted that the Negro does not find satisfaction in passive compliance with the demands of a white society. The Negro who conforms to these demands and consequently rejects himself pays a high price. A report by the "Group for the Advancement of Psychiatry" suggests that beneath the Negro's mask of compliance lie anger, resentment, and fear (1957). In hiding his feelings, the Negro may suffer serious psychological consequences, such as distorting his capacity for expressing his feelings or actually lowering his "potential for affectivity" (Kardiner and Ovesey, 1962).

Kardiner and Ovesey (1962) hypothesize that the Negro bears an inescapable "mark of oppression," which reflects his strong identification with whites, who are simultaneously hated. This conflict leads to aggression which is channeled into compensatory defensive maneuvers. In a study of the responses of 100 nine- to fourteen-year-old Negro and white boys on the Thematic Apperception Test (TAT), Mussen (1953) found that the Negro boys tended to perceive the world as hostile and threatening, while the white boys were more likely to view the world as a friendly place. Palermo (1959) found greater anxiety among Negro children in the fourth to sixth grade than he did among a corresponding group of white children. In their study of the Rorshach and TAT protocols of 25 adult Negroes, Kardiner and Ovesey (1962) reported that their respondents showed a strong need to avoid "meeting reality head on" by denying, distorting, or simplifying provocative tension-producing situations.

The thread of consistency running through the studies cited above is sustained by Deutsch's extensive study of Negro and white lower-class children in grades four through six (1960). Deutsch found that the Negro children generally had more negative self-concepts, and were more passive, more morose, and more fearful than their white schoolmates. When the Negro child was aggressive, it was usually in some covert manner.

In the face of adversity, the Negro feels more than the frustration engendered by the caste system. His anger is intensified—particularly in the Negro male—by his sense of powerlessness (Drake, 1965). When hostility is expressed, it is often through indirect means. Among lower-class Negroes aggression is frequent, the chain of victimization is perpetuated, and the lower-class Negro is exploited by both whites and fellow Negroes. Other outlets for aggression are juvenile delinquency and crime, both of which provide means of "striking back" at the white society.

Covert or indirect expressions of hostility are only one form of response to the frustration and sense of powerlessness experienced by the Negro. The need to escape is frequently manifested in the form of excessive use of alcohol, drugs, and gambling (Drake, 1965). A far more subtle form of escape embodies the old adage, "If you can't beat them, join them." Some Negroes, in effect, escape by "turning white."

In the case of the very light-skinned Negro, this desire may actually by accomplished by "passing." Other Negroes may attempt to "look white" by using hair straighteners and skin bleaches. Drake (1965) suggests that this rejection of Negroid features reflects a reaction to the stereotype of the primitive and savage African. The preference for light skin also has traditional foundations in this country. Since plantation days the light-skinned Negro has been favored and granted special privileges, particularly in middle-class and upper-class society. We also find that parents tend to favor a light-skinned child (Coles, 1967; Grambs, 1964), and that dark-skinned men often try to marry wives of a lighter skin color (Kardiner and Ovesey, 1962).

Psychologists have shown great interest in the defensive strategy of "turning white" and in its implications for mental health and personality adjustment. Perhaps this interest stems in part from the fact that "passing" represents a blatant expression of self-rejection and a denial of reality. Parker and Kleiner (1965) note a large body of research documenting the unhealthiness in aspiring to be white: "Almost every clinical study of psychopathology among Negroes indicates that the Negro who is not identified with other members of his group, or who aspires to 'be white,' is relatively more prone to manifest various forms of mental ill health" (p. 157).

In spite of some serious methodological problems, Parker and Kleiner's own research raises some important speculative questions about the dynamics of racial identification. As a measure of racial identification, Parker and Kleiner asked their Negro subjects how they would feel about a friend who tried to "pass." They found that Negroes in psychiatric hospitals tended to be strongly identified with Negroes or not identified with Negroes, while Negroes in the community tended to be ambivalent about their racial identification. On the basis of this finding, Parker and Kleiner suggest that ambivalence may be "realistic and adaptive" for the Negro, but that extreme reactions or "polarization of racial identification" are likely to be psychopathogenic. In their opinion ". . . the psychiatrically healthy Negro is an individual with conflicts about his racial identification. It is the mentally ill person who tends to remove this constant conflict from conscious awareness" (p. 160). The logic implicit in this statement is that if the conflict about his racial identification becomes unbearable, the individual may deny the conflict entirely (either strongly identifying with or rejecting his racial group) and become mentally ill.

While it seems apparent that a denial of the conflict over identification is unhealthy, it cannot be assumed that conflict and ambivalence are healthy. Certainly, in light of the conditions that the Negro faces in America, such ambivalence is understandable. The crucial questions become: "How severe is the conflict?" and "How does the individual deal with this conflict?"

It seems obvious that individual Negroes will find various means of dealing with this conflict. When faced with a severe form of this conflict, not all individuals will become psychotic; some will resort to drugs, alcohol, violence, or other forms of escape. Many of these individuals, who certainly cannot be considered psychiatrically healthy, will remain in the community. Therefore, a judgment of mental health, based solely on whether or not an individual is in a psychiatric hospital, is open to serious question. We may also predict that some of the individuals in the community who are ambivalent about their racial identification may not be able to continue to function with this conflict and may later become psychotic or adopt another "unhealthy" way of dealing with the conflict.

After examining the evidence available on the Negro and his conflicts over identification and also on the possibilities for positive identification, we would hypothesize that the psychiatrically healthy Negro is one who basically identifies with Negroes, but who is aware of and realistic about the problems facing him in a "white man's" society. This form of identification with Negroes is to be distinguished from the extreme "defensive" or reactive form of identification in which the indivdual denies that there are problems in being Negro. Unfortunately the Parker and Kleiner study does not distinguish between these two forms of identification with the Negro group and does not describe individuals in the community sample who have "identified" with Negroes. It would be interesting to know if some of these individuals fit our description of a Negro who is positively identified with his race and yet realistic about his opportunities, as a Negro.

ACHIEVEMENT ORIENTATIONS. Human motivation involves a complex set of processes. Conceptually, an analysis of motivation includes analyses of the individual's end or goal, the strength of his desire, the value placed on the end, and his expectancy of achieving the end. In his consideration of achievement motivation in a modern industrial society, Rosen (1959) has suggested that achievement is dependent on three factors, which he labels collectively, the "achievement syndrome." The first factor is McClelland's "achievement motive," which Rosen (1956) has defined as involving "a personality characteristic . . . which provides an internal impetus to excel" (p. 204). The second dimension, "achievement-value orientations" involves a concern with social mobility and a development of patterns of behavior, such as "deferred gratification," which aid in the pursuit of long-term goals. The third dimension, "educational and vocational aspirations" are the levels of academic and occupational achievements *desired* by parents for their children and desired by the children themselves. According to Rosen, high achievement depends on appropriate levels on all three of these dimensions.

Employing variations of Murray's TAT measure of *n* Achievement, investigators have found that Negro children are lower in achievement motivation than white children. Mussen (1953) found that Negro boys, aged nine to fourteen, scored significantly below their white counterparts on *n* Achievement and also on *n* Understanding, a category which is intended to tap activities such as thinking, reflecting, and speculating. In measuring the achievement motivation of boys from six ethnic groups, Rosen (1959) reported that Negro boys were significantly lower in *n* Achievement than boys from four other ethnic groups: Jewish, white Protestant, Greek, and Italian.

Evidence suggests that *n* Achievement is related to social class as well as to ethnicity. In his study Rosen (1959) found that there were significant social-class differences among his subjects; he also discovered that social class was more strongly related to achievement motivation than was ethnicity. In addition, he found that Negro subjects in the top two social classes (I–II, according to a modified version of Hollingshead's Index of Social Position) were significantly higher in *n* Achievement than Class IV–V white Protestants. Rosen suggests that this relatively high Negro score may be indicative of the "strong motivation necessary for a Negro to achieve middle class status in a hostile environment" (1959, p. 53).

Rosen (1959) has explored "achievement-value orientations" through the use of personal interviews with mothers who were asked to agree or disagree with items which reflected various orientations in child rearing: active versus passive, individual versus collective, and present versus future. It seems that the active, individual, and future orientations in child rearing are most conducive to the achievement of long-term goals. Rosen found that among the six ethnic groups that he studied, Negro mothers ranked fourth in "achievement-value orientations." This score was significantly lower than that of the Jewish mothers, who ranked highest in achievement values; however, the score of Jews was not significantly higher than the scores of Greeks and of Protestants, who were in the next two ranks.

Social class is also significantly related to achievement-value orientations. As might be expected, members of higher social classes tend to have high achievement-value orientations, and conversely, those in lower-class levels have relatively low scores on achievement-value orientation (Rosen, 1959).

Many investigators have explored the third dimension of Rosen's "achievement syndrome": occupational and educational levels of aspiration. However, studies of the aspiration levels in Negro and white children and their parents have been inconsistent in their findings. In comparison with whites, Negroes have been shown to have high or low, and realistic or unrealistic, levels of aspiration.

For example, in a study of junior high school students in a small industrial town in Pennsylvania, Wylie (1963) found that Negro children generally had lower self-estimates or levels of aspiration for their schoolwork ability than did white children. However, when Negro and white subjects from lower socioeconomic levels were compared, there were no race differences. In contrast, in a somewhat similar study, Boyd (1952) reported very different results when he compared the aspiration levels of Negro and white students, matched for age, IQ, and socioeconomic status. He discovered that Negro children predicted relatively higher performances on arithmetic and target tests than did white children. Furthermore, in comparison with the white children, the Negro children had higher occupational ambitions, desired more foreign trips, and more frequently stated that they expected to be "above average" students in high school. In discussing his results, Boyd suggests that Negro children may have higher aspiration levels because of insecure feelings or because they have developed better defense mechanisms than white children and are, therefore, able to tolerate a greater discrepancy between predicted and actual performance.

To confuse the literature further, Rosen found that Negro mothers had low occupational, but high educational, aspirations for their sons. When Rosen asked the mothers, "How far do you *intend* your son to go in school?" 83 percent of these mothers mentioned college. This percentage was not significantly different from those of the Jews, Greeks, or white Protestants, but it was significantly higher than those of the Italians and French Canadians. However, when Negro mothers were given a list of occupations and were asked if they would "be satisfied" if their sons were in these occupations, they expressed satisfaction with more low-status occupations than did any other group of mothers.

In some ways Rosen's measure of vocational aspiration is a negative one, since it seems to elicit the lower limit rather than the upper limit of aspiration. Because of the Negro's traditional lack of vocational opportunity, Negro mothers may be more accepting of low-status occupations than mothers from other ethnic groups. There may be a wide *range* between the vocation a Negro mother would most like her son to follow and a vocation with which she would be satisfied if her son actually did follow it. This possibility has been suggested by other studies, showing that Negro mothers and their sons have high vocational aspirations, although many researchers have labeled such aspirations as "unrealistically high."

In part, the contradictions in findings on the Negro's level of aspiration can be explained by differences in such factors as the samples studied, the indices used for measuring the level of aspiration, and the geographical setting. However, the studies are somewhat clarified, if we consider, whenever possible, the distinction between *desired* and *expected* occupational or educational attainment. The importance of these distinctions is illustrated in a study by Weiner and Murray (1963), who compared the educational aspiration levels of middle- and lower-class parents. Weiner and Murray point out that both middle-class and lower-class parents have high levels of aspiration for their children's education. However, the concept of education has a different meaning for each social class. The key difference in meaning lies in the realistic expectations of achieving the goal. Weiner and Murray note that if middle-class and lower-class parents are asked if they want their child to attend college, both groups of parents will answer "yes." However, the middle-class parent will answer "yes" with the full expectation that his child will attend college, while the lower-class parent may hope that his child will go to college, but he will not actually expect it.

It is possible that in studies which have reported a high aspiration level for Negroes, researchers have been measuring what their subjects desire rather than what they expect. Perhaps measures of aspiration level which reflect what the subjects expect may yield lower levels of aspiration and may be more realistic. However, it is important to stress that even when a Negro's aspirations are based on his expectations, they may be distorted in light of his actual abilities and, more importantly, the opportunities available to him.

This situation is seen clearly in C. S. Johnson's (1941) study of rural Negro youth in the South. Johnson found that 58.8 percent of the boys and 65.3 percent of the girls preferred professional occupations. Of these youth, 26.4 percent of the boys and 48.8 percent of the girls actually *expected* to follow such occupations. In this case the subjects' expectations were not much more realistic than their desires. Johnson concluded: "The gap between occupational expectation and reality is at present so great as to suggest that the expectation itself borders on fantasy" (p. 223). Johnson also suggested that the desires and expectations for these occupations represented an attempt at escaping an unpleasant environment.

Ausubel and Ausubel (1958) have drawn similar conclusions about the aspiration levels of Negro children, basing their ideas on implications drawn from studies comparing lower- and middle-class children. They suggest that the lower-class child's expressed levels of vocational and academic aspiration do not necessarily reflect his "real or functional levels of striving." His aspirations seem to show a lack of realistic judgment because of continued failure and low social status; therefore, a high level of aspiration is likely to represent an attempt to bolster self-esteem by presenting an image of "aiming high" rather than actually striving for high educational or occupational goals. In the Ausubels' view, the conditions experienced by the lower-class child are intensified for the segregated Negro child. These interpretations are generally supported by Deutsch's (1960) study of the occupational aspirations of lower-class Negro and white fourth-, fifth-, and sixth-graders.

Deutsch (1960) found that *both* Negro and white boys tended to have unrealistic aspirations for high prestige occupations. Although it might be expected that Negro boys would be less realistic than white boys in these choices, only 26 percent of the Negro boys, in contrast with 38 percent of the white boys, expressed interest in high prestige professions. In comparison with the boys, the aspirations of the girls were much more realistic and the occupational desires of the Negro girls were significantly higher than those of the white girls. While 25 percent of the Negro girls indicated a preference for white-collar jobs, such as secretary or bookkeeper, only 4 percent of the white girls showed an interest in this type of job. However, the Negro girls were less interested than the white girls in the housewife-mother role and in the movie star-actress category.

In a study whose findings stand somewhat apart from those previously cited, Lott and Lott (1963) reported that Negro students had high but realistic levels of occupational aspiration. A comparison of Negro and white high school seniors in Kentucky showed significant differences in both occupational desires and expectations. The major differences between the occupational desires of the Negro and white boys were in "glamour" jobs, such as pilot or politician, and in the clerical-sales-skilled-trade field of jobs. While 27 percent of the white boys expressed interest in a "glamour" job, only 12 percent of the Negro boys did. While 18 percent of the white students desired work in the clerical-sales-skilled-trade area, 39 percent of the Negro students wanted a position in this field. An even sharper contrast was seen in the fact that 15 percent of the whites versus 40 percent of the Negroes expected to be in the clerical-sales-skilled-trade field ten years later.

The Negro boys showed somewhat exaggerated or unrealistic aspirations in their desires to enter professional or business fields; 41 percent of the Negro boys and 46 percent of the white boys wanted a professional or business career. However, only 30 percent of the Negroes, in contrast with 41 percent of the whites, actually expected to attain this type of job.

The occupational aspirations of the Negro girls described by Lott and Lott (1963) were consistent with those reported by Deutsch (1960) despite the age differences in the two samples. These findings suggest that the aspirations of these girls reflect their perceptions of their role as women—a role which places economic independence above the role of housewife and mother. In the Lott and Lott study (1963), 17 percent of the white girls and none of the Negro girls wanted to assume the roles of wife and mother. Furthermore, 54 percent of the Negro girls, but only 31 percent of the white girls, wanted a professional job, such as teaching or social work.

Although Deutsch (1960) and Lott and Lott (1963) have reported similar findings about the aspirations of Negro girls, their results differ sharply from most of the other research in this field. Lott and Lott conclude that their Negro subjects' plans for the future were realistic in terms of available opportunities. They suggest that the difference in their findings may lie either in changing social conditions or in particular factors operating in the environment of a border community.

Another relevant factor in explaining differences in the "realism" of the Negro's aspirations may be a "knowledge of the means of achievement." To understand how this factor might operate, we need to distinguish between dreams or desires and expectations. Dreams or desires, by definition, function to transcend reality; they are a source of hope and a salve against pain. In contrast, expectations are grounded in reality; they reflect the world "as it is," not the world "as it might be." A problem arises when expectations become identified with dreams and a person expects what he has little or no possibility of achieving. We would hypothesize that this situation is likely to occur when a person has little "knowledge of the means of achievement," that is, when he does not know how to achieve his goal, or when he does not recognize that his dream is unattainable. When the dream and expectation are not separated, the aspiration level is likely to be unrealistically high. The orientation toward the future would seem to reflect an emphasis on the goal, rather than on the "means of achieving the goal." Following this line of reasoning, we could infer that the Negro youth studied by Lott and Lott (1963) had a "knowledge of means," which enabled them to have realistic expectations about their occupational futures.

The significance of a "knowledge of means" is illustrated in a study of parents and their children in a suburb of New York City. The researchers Weiner and Graves (1960) found that parents and children from the lower socioeconomic status (*SES*) had occupational aspirations similar to those of parents and children from a middle socioeconomic level. In both *SES* groups most parents and children were interested in one of the professions. However, when the children from the lower *SES* group were asked how far they expected to go in school, 52 percent expected to go through college and 33 percent expected to finish only high school. Even more revealing was the fact that only 37 percent of the lower *SES* subjects were enrolled in college preparatory courses. In contrast, 95 percent of the middle *SES* students intended to go through college and 100 percent of these students were taking the college preparatory curriculum.

In line with Weiner and Murray, Drake (1965) cites evidence suggesting that lower-class and lower-middle-class Negro parents often have high aspirations for their children but no clear idea of how to implement these plans. He proposes that Negro students in segregated high schools and colleges are often unaware of the opportunities and techniques for advancement.

Preliminary evidence indicates that many of these "techniques for advancement" can be taught effectively in short periods of time. "Cram" courses in how to pass qualifying exams and how to meet job requirements—for example, filling out applications, being interviewed, and so on—have succeeded in increasing the numbers of Negroes in several fields (National Urban League, 1966; Davis, 1967). The often dramatic success of short-term educational programs supports the contention that many Negroes have high motivation for achievement but lack the more pragmatic, but also necessary, "knowledge of the means of achievement."

Sources of Conflict

Our own discussion of the sources of Negro identity conflicts will consist primarily of a description of the family setting and some specific conditions within the home which seem to be related to problems with identification and self-esteem. While we recognize the family as a crucial source of self-attitudes and values, our emphasis on the family also reflects the focus of most of the existing research and theory. We also have included in our discussion a few suggestive findings about the Negro child in the school setting. Unfortunately, because of the previously mentioned limitations and inherent difficulties of research in these settings, most of our interpretations and hypotheses about the sources and transmission of identity conflicts will be highly speculative.

FAMILY SETTING. Many of the child's earliest and most important feelings about himself are learned and nurtured in the family. Here the child receives his first impression about the world and about people and their worth. Often the teaching is indirect; feelings and attitudes are communicated through basic relationships and through the numerous interchanges and incidents which create the tone and texture of family life. Several investigators have suggested that ethnic prejudice seems to be learned in the home. Trager and Yarrow (1952) comment on this process of learning: "Parents' teaching of intergroup attitudes is frequently unconscious and is rarely direct or planned" (p. 349).

For the Negro child the home is usually the first place in which he learns about race and social discrimination, although his parents may avoid direct discussion of these topics. Georgene Seward (1956) observes, "Before the child is conscious of being a Negro himself, he is affected by the tensions in his parents over *their* being Negro" (p. 130). Elaborating on this point, Ausubel and Ausubel (1958) suggest that the parents' reaction to racial discrimination determines in part their basic attitude toward the child, whether they accept or reject him and if they use him for purposes of their own ego enhancement. In many cases the child's parents have suffered serious deprivations, both in their own emotional experiences and in their dealings with white society. Their feelings of anger, resentment, and hopelessness surround the child, making it very difficult for him to develop positive feelings about himself and his chances in the world. However, in spite of their own difficulties, some parents are able to provide a strong supportive atmosphere for their children, accepting them and fostering attitudes of self-worth. The Ausubels (1958) state ". . . the consequences of membership in a stigmatized minority group can be cushioned in part by a foundation of intrinsic self-esteem established in the home" (p. 368). Pettigrew (1964*b*) comes to a similar conclusion, emphasizing the value of a warm, supportive, and stable home.

Until this point we have been discussing the family as a source of conflict in general terms. However, as we have noted previously, there are undoubtedly significant social-class-associated differences in family life and in attitudes toward the dominant white society which have differential consequences for the self-image of the Negro child. Rainwater (1966) labels the lower-class Negro family, the "crucible of identity," focusing on the family's central role in transmitting values and attitudes toward society. The life patterns of the lower-class urban Negro form a distinctive subculture, which has arisen in response to the discriminatory system in America (Rainwater, 1966; Pettigrew, 1964). The subculture is highly adaptive, fostering "toughness" and self-sufficiency among its members, but ironically making it very difficult for its members ever to escape, to function in working- or middle-class worlds (Rainwater, 1966; Drake, 1965).

Frequently the parents of the lower-class child have been defeated and imprisoned by the dominant system. They are embittered and disillusioned and these attitudes are communicated to the child. Rainwater (1966) suggests that for most children growing up involves developing feelings of competency and mastery over the environment, but that for the slum child the process is reversed; he learns about what he cannot do, about blocks and barriers, about the futility of trying.

The most salient feature of the lower-class Negro family life is its characteristic matriarchal pattern (Frazier, 1962; Drake and Cayton, 1962; Rainwater, 1966). With its origins in the plantation system and its perpetuation in unequal opportunities for employment, maternal dominance is encouraged and maintained. The problem is especially severe in Northern urban areas where Rainwater (1966) estimates that as many as two thirds of lower-class urban Negro children will not live in a family headed by a man and a woman during the first 18 years of their lives (p. 181). The impact of this situation is heightened and intensified by the depressing effects of poverty. Not only may the father be absent, but the mother may be overburdened by many children, substandard living conditions, and her own need to work, so that she is unable to give adequate care to her children.

The attitude of the lower-class Negro mother toward her child may be one of ambivalence or indifference. Rainwater notes that there is ". . . little of the sense of the awesome responsibility of caring for children that is characteristic of the working and middle class" (1966, p. 195). In the female-headed household the responsibility for child care is often turned over to the grandmother, female relatives, or older siblings. In general, there is less parent-child interaction than in working- and middle-class families. Discipline tends to be inconsistent, but the child is expected to meet high standards of behavior and is severely punished when he fails to meet them (Kardiner and Ovesey, 1962). The emphasis is on obedience and responsibility, often encouraging the child to develop a "precocious independence" (Ausubel and Ausubel, 1958).

In lower-class families, children are usually given more freedom outside the home and are likely to form important peer group contacts earlier than middle-class children (Ausubel and Ausubel, 1958). This situation has two specific related implications: first, it decreases the influence and significance of the parents; and second, it enhances the importance of the peer group. This transfer of the role of socialization from parents to peer group may be seen in part as a search for status and self-esteem.

Children from middle-class families derive status and a sense of importance from their parents' place and achievements in society.

However, for the lower-class minority group child, the situation is reversed; his parents symbolize degradation and deprivation in the larger society. His relation to them is more likely a source of shame than one of pride.

The matriarchal character of the lower-class Negro family and its associated disorganized home life have important implications for the child's learning of sex attitudes and his attitudes toward marriage and child rearing. Parents who have had few experiences with family stability and adequacy are unlikely to be able to provide these experiences for their children. Similarly, because of their own feelings of self-doubt and self-hatred, parents may be unable to give their children needed affection and attention (Grambs, 1964, p. 18).

These findings suggest that the lower-class Negro family pattern is likely to be perpetuated. A study by Pettigrew (1964a) lends weight to this idea. Studying 21 Negro working-class individuals who had grown up with a father during childhood, Pettigrew compared them with a matched group whose fathers had been absent during early childhood. The most dramatic difference between the groups was in the subjects' marital status. In the "father-absent" group, 33 percent of the subjects were single or divorced, while only 4 percent of the "father-present" subjects were in this category. The "father-absent" individuals also felt more victimized, "less in control of the environment," and "more distrustful of others" than men in the "father-present" group (Pettigrew, 1964, p. 19f.). While the differences between the two groups were not statistically significant, the findings suggest the possible influence of father-absence in early childhood on personality development and marital adjustment.

The reversal of traditional sex roles has severe implications in a dominant culture which stresses male achievement. In spite of the distinctive Negro subculture and the reality of male-female differences in employment opportunities, the Negro male is still expected to be a responsible family provider. His failure in this role results in a serious loss of self-esteem and severe derision from the female members of the community. These factors serve to discourage him both from staying at home and from seeking and holding a job. His predicament may take the form of a "self-fulfilling prophecy." He is told that he is "no good" and "irresponsible" and to some extent he internalizes these judgments, which in turn influence his actions. When he fails, no one is surprised.

The issue of Negro male identity may be conceptualized as a twofold problem. The first is the Negro male's lack of status and economic and occupational achievement in the larger society. The second is the female's assumption of the dominant role and her critical, derogatory attitude toward males. While there has been an emphasis on the lack of adequate male models as an explanation for the Negro male's identity conflicts, we shall suggest that the female's attitudes serve to intensify the problem. We see these two factors as intimately related, feeding on each other to keep the Negro male in an inferior position. Erik Erikson (1966) has explored the consequences of the exploitation of the Negro male and the fact that the male is denied the status of "responsible fatherhood." He attaches particular significance to the imbalance in male and female roles and emphasizes that in a complex industrial setting, ". . . it may, indeed, become the gravest factor in personality disorganization" (p. 167).

Surveying studies of the effects of father-absence, Pettigrew (1964b) suggests far-reaching implications for both personality and behavior. He notes that boys raised without a father during early childhood were more immature, submissive, dependent, and effeminate than boys who had grown up with a father in the home. Father-absent children have also shown difficulty in differentiating masculine and feminine roles in comparison with father-present children. In the same line of evidence, Negro male and female high school students have reported a greater similarity of interests than their white counterparts; significantly, the interests of Negro girls were more masculine than those of white girls.

In a series of studies, Martin Deutsch and his associates have shown relationships among self-concept, family background variables, and academic performance. Comparing lower-class white and Negro children, Deutsch (1960) reported that 55 percent of his Negro but only 9 percent of his white subjects came from broken homes. He found that white subjects were superior in academic performance, had more positive self-images, and reported a more positive atmosphere than Negro children. A comparison of Negro subjects on the basis of their home status showed that subjects from intact homes exhibited significantly higher levels of academic performance than subjects from broken homes.

Studying the social influences on Negro and white intelligence differences, Deutsch and Brown (1964) found that for Negro subjects in the lower two *SES* categories, father-presence was significantly related to IQ. They also reported significant differences in IQ between Negro and white subjects at all three *SES* levels. The differences in IQ widened as social class increased. Deutsch and Brown observe that the Negro group shows greater deprivation on most social variables and ". . . whatever other measures and functions are sensitive to social effects will also reflect this deprivation" (1964, p. 34).

Other evidence suggests that the influence of father-absence on intellectual functioning may be negligible. Whiteman and Deutsch (see Chapter 3 of this book) found that father-absence was not significantly related to scores on the Gates Reading Test. Coleman *et al.* (1966) reported that father-absence was one of the weakest home background factors in predicting school achievement for Negro pupils; however, father-absence was strongly related to academic achievement for the other minority groups surveyed. In a study of Negro boys, Robins, Jones, and Murphy (1966) found that father-presence (absence) appeared to be unrelated to the child's academic and behavioral problems.

Whiteman and Deutsch have shown a relationship between *SES* and various home and family factors, many of which are, in turn, related to self-concept. In the lower *SES* homes there was greater crowding in the household and greater dilapidation in the neighborhood surrounding the household than in higher *SES* homes. Lower *SES* parents tended to have both lower aspirations for their child's first job and lower educational aspirations than higher *SES* parents; in addition, lower *SES* children reported lower occupational aspirations than children from higher *SES* groups. As might be expected, *SES* was also significantly related to father-presence, with more fathers being present as *SES* increased.

In the same study, Whiteman and Deutsch showed that deprivation, as measured by six environmental factors, was closely related to self-concept. They reported, "As compared to the more advantaged children, about six times as many of the more deprived children fall into the least favorable self-concept category" (p. 104f).

The problem of male identification is not unique to members of the Negro lower class, but also seems to be characteristic of lower-class white males. In a study of high school senior boys, McKinley (1964) asked subjects from five social class levels, "Whom do you most admire in your family or among relatives?" This question was intended to provide some measure of the boys' identification. In the upper class, all boys chose their father or a male relative as "most admired," while in the working and lower classes only 58 percent picked their father or a male relative; the others chose females.

Rainwater (1966) suggests that the problem of male identity is not necessarily due to the lack of a male figure, but rather to the type of male figure available as a model. He describes the succession of males—boyfriends, boarders, and so on—who may frequent the lower-class homes, noting that these men represent an affectional expressive role, but not that of a responsible provider.

The situation of the male may be seen in contrast with the Negro girl's learning of her sex role. She is encouraged to be independent and self-sufficient. She is also taught that males are an "unworthy and unreliable lot" and not to expect much from them. In the home, the Negro girl tends to be favored over her male siblings. Deutsch (1960) found that the Negro girl excels the Negro boy in academic performance and in personal and social adjustment. She shows a greater attention span, is more popular with classmates, and has a more positive self-concept than her male counterpart. The Ausubels (1963) view girls as "less traumatized by the impact of racial discrimination," attributing this situation to the preferential treatment given to Negro females in the white community. They suggest that Negro women have more continual contact with the white community and receive better treatment from white people than do Negro males.

In a provocative argument, Grambs (1964) questions the Ausubels' interpretation of male-female differences in school performance, as resulting from differential treatment in the community or from the lack of adequate male models. She hypothesizes that the impact of the discriminatory system is passed on to male children by their mothers, who are the prime sources of the child's self-concept.

Because of the direction and emphasis of the existing research, we have been concerned almost exclusively with lower-class family life. As we have suggested, there are important social-class differences in family patterns which we would expect to be reflected in differences in the form of identity conflicts. We also would expect that there would be important variations in family patterns within each social class. Jessie Bernard (1966) suggests that these differences within social classes are highly significant and questions the validity of discussing Negro family patterns by social-class categories. She proposes a distinction between two strands or cultures, which she tentatively labels the "acculturated" and the "externally adapted." In her view, these two strands run through all social-class levels and represent a dimension of internalization and acceptance (or lack thereof) of the values of the dominant society. She sees the difference between the two strands as one based on ethos, an acceptance of conventional standards or behavior, particularly with respect to sex and work. She points out that discussions of social class family patterns obscure two important groups: low-income families with conventional family patterns and high-income families with unconventional family patterns. Of course, only a program of systematic research on family patterns among Negroes in the various social classes can determine the validity of her analysis.

SCHOOL SETTING.   The 1954 Supreme Court decision which legally desegregated the public schools, augmented by the Civil Rights Movement and increased federal spending and legislation in education and civil rights, has greatly increased both the number and variety of people involved in and concerned with education, particularly education of the minority group child. Special attention has been concentrated on the urban lower-class Negro child, and numerous articles have been written on the special problems of the "disadvantaged." However, in spite of this display of great interest and outburst of publications, there has been relatively little research on the effects of school desegregation on Negro and white children (Proshansky, 1966; Katz, Chapter 7 of this book).

Most theorists and researchers have assumed that segregation in the schools, whether *de facto* or legal, has devastating consequences for the Negro's development of a positive self-image (Clark and Clark, 1947, 1950). However, if we examine some of the possible sources of conflict for the Negro in the school, it becomes apparent that the issue is not a simple one: integration is not an automatic cure for the ills caused by segregated schools. Although the research in this area is limited, we shall attempt to specify some of the factors relevant to school desegregation.

One of the factors most frequently mentioned in studies of racially mixed schools is the attitude of white teachers toward their Negro pupils. If we assume that prejudice is a normative value, an assumption which is strongly supported by available evidence (Bettelheim and Janowitz, 1964), then we can expect the American school teacher to express this prejudice in her treatment of the child—often in a variety of subtle ways. The issue gains increasing complexity when we realize that even a teacher who is relatively free of prejudice toward Negroes may react to class-associated differences between her own and her pupils' orientations toward learning, work, and discipline. Furthermore, the middle-class or lower-middle-class teacher's reactions to his lower-class pupil's behavior are likely to be interpreted by the child as further evidence of the general prejudice and discrimination that he experiences.

Even Negro teachers may be hostile and resentful toward lower-class Negro children. Frequently Negro teachers are from the lower middle class and have struggled to rise above their own backgrounds. They perceive lower-class children as a reminder of their past and a threat to their newly won security. In some cases, Negro middle-class teachers may displace their own self-hatred by expressing hostility toward lower-class Negro children (Grambs, 1964).

In examining the issue of teacher attitudes, it is important to recognize that the Negro pupil, as well as his teacher, brings preconceived ideas about racial differences into the classroom. The Negro child often comes bearing his parents' and his own justifiable resentment toward whites. The white teacher, in turn, reacts to this hostility, thus aggravating the conflict and prejudice in the classroom.

It also seems likely that Negro pupils who have low self-esteem or a negative self-image tend to perceive their teachers' behavior as threatening, even if the teachers' actions are not discriminatory. Bearing on this issue is a recent study by Brown (1967), comparing the self-perceptions of four-year-old Negro lower-class and white middle-class children. Brown asked his young subjects to look at pictures of themselves and to describe the child in the picture by choosing words from a list of bipolar adjectives, for example, happy–sad, good–bad, and the like. The child was asked to respond to the picture from four vantage points: his own, and those of his mother, his teacher, and his peers. On this basis, Brown derived a "self as subject" and a "self as object" measure.

One of Brown's most interesting findings was in the subjects' responses to how their teachers perceived them. Brown reported that the greatest difference between Negro and white subjects was on this part of the "self as object" measure, and that a significantly greater number of Negro children than white children believed that their teachers saw them as sad (rather than happy), as frightened of a lot of things (versus not frightened of a lot of things), and as not having a nice face (versus having a nice face). Other suggestive findings, although not statistically significant, were on the items smart (versus stupid), healthy (versus sickly), liking to talk a lot (versus not liking to talk a lot), liking the way his clothes look (versus not liking the way his clothes look). On each of these characteristics the Negro children, more often than the white children, tended to believe that their teachers perceived them negatively.

Evidence of the importance of students' positive perceptions of teachers' feelings comes from a study by Davidson and Lang (1960). Using fourth-, fifth-, and sixth-graders in New York City as subjects, Davidson and Lang found that positive perceptions of teachers' feelings were significantly related to academic achievement and "more desirable classroom behavior," as rated by the teachers. The researchers also reported significant social-class differences in perceptions of teachers' feelings, with upper- and middle-class subjects feeling that their teachers perceived them more favorably than lower-class subjects felt that their teachers perceived them. As expected, social class was significantly related to school achievement. When controlling for social class, the authors found a significant correlation between favorable perception of teachers' feelings and academic achievement. They also reported that even under controlling for achievement, children's perceptions of their teachers' feelings were significantly related to social class.

The difference between the Negro and the white subjects' notions of how their teachers perceive them is a very important one. It is suggestive not only of the Negro children's insecure and uncomfortable feelings in school, but also of actual teachers' perceptions of their Negro students. Rosenthal and Jacobson (see Chapter 6 of this book) provide evidence supporting the idea that self-fulfilling prophecies may be operating in the classroom. They found that in some classrooms students whom their teachers had expected to do well academically on the basis of fallacious test scores showed significantly greater achievement than students about whom the teachers did not have such high expectations. From these results we might also expect the converse to be true: teachers with low expectations of particular students will influence their performance in the direction of low achievement.

A Negro child may not only feel threatened by his teachers, but also by the school's curriculum, which may provide an additional source of conflict over his racial identity. The pervasiveness of white middle-class values in the schools has frequently been cited but has seldom been studied. The Negro child is reminded of his alien status in a white man's school through the books he reads, the language he hears, the behaviors that are stressed, the morals that are espoused and even probably by the food he receives as part of the "hot lunch program." With the advent of the Civil Rights Movement and school desegregation, there has been increasing pressure on school boards, principals, and teachers to diversify the curriculum by teaching "Negro culture"—its history, famous figures, and concerns—in the public school.

The effects of teaching "Negro culture" on the child's self-image are largely unknown. It would seem reasonable to expect that its possible positive effects depend largely on how the subject is presented, the teachers' own attitudes, and the perceived purpose of the curriculum. It is possible that some methods of teaching Negro history may heighten competition, increase the child's sense of isolation, and intensify identity conflicts, instead of contributing to a positive self-image.

A final factor influencing and possibly threatening the Negro child in school may be termed the "school ecology." By "school ecology" we are referring to the distribution of racial and ethnic groups within the school. With the increasing emphasis on school desegregation, this factor looms as an important consideration in examining and planning for the well-being of the Negro child. While the serious consequences of segregated schools cannot be denied, the racially mixed school also has its own special set of problems.

One of the most obvious factors contributing to possible disruption in the racially mixed school is the attitudes which Negro and white children have toward each other. The children come to school, bringing the attitudes about race which they have learned from parents and other adults in the community; these attitudes, in turn, have some influence over their behavior toward children of the other racial group. In a very early study, Criswell (1939) found that Negro children in racially mixed classrooms accepted white prestige but increasingly withdrew into their own group as a response to white rejection. Many other studies support this finding (Horowitz, 1936; Radke *et al.,* 1950). In a trenchant analysis, Katz (see Chapter 7 of this book) describes some of the factors influencing performance of the Negro child who enters a racially mixed school or classroom; in some situations, social rejection and isolation may produce such effects as intellectual impairment and anxiety. It seems that the difficulties involved extend beyond simple "mutual suspicion" and resentment between the two groups. In most cases, there are "real" differences in the form of intellectual development and scholastic performance of the Negro student in comparison with his white classmate. Therefore, the Negro child in a racially mixed school is forced to cope with feelings of inferiority, which have some basis in reality, as well as those feelings induced by his status in and treatment by the dominant white society.

Positive Self-Identity: Some Resources

Research and theory have tended to emphasize the negative aspects of Negro identity, ignoring or overshadowing its positive and compensatory features. The reader is sometimes left with the image of an entire race of psychologically crippled people, reduced to a level of minimal functioning and a state of precarious mental health. Given the "Negro problem," and particularly its reflections in lower-class urban life, this emphasis on self-rejection, ambivalence, and extreme reactions to identity conflicts is understandable. However, just as the quiet child in the classroom often receives little attention from the teacher in comparison with the noisy, disruptive troublemaker, so the Negro who is positively identified with his group often escapes the notice of the researcher. As a corollary, it is also important to recognize that not all of the extreme reactions observed among Negroes, such as alcoholism, drug addiction, and psychotic withdrawal, are mechanisms for coping with identity conflicts or feelings of self-hatred. These reactions may be in the service of other needs and conflicts.

Undoubtedly many Negroes experience ambivalence about their racial identity, but its intensity, its "history," and its ultimate effects on feelings and behavior depend on a variety of conditional and individual factors. To enumerate a few of these individual variables, we find differences in innate potentials, such as intelligence and temperament, in addition to differences in experiences, such as socialization in the family, interracial contacts, and peer group reactions. These differences must necessarily create diversity among Negroes in response to their common "self-dilemma."

Researchers need to explore the full *range* of reactions to being Negro in order to understand how some Negroes feel little or no conflict about their identity while others are severely burdened and debilitated by conflict over their racial identity. They need to look at the Negro who accepts his group membership and who may frequently gain "self-support" and "self-enhancement" from it. In such studies there must be a search for both individual and group resources which aid in coping with severe privations and adversity.

It seems likely that how the Negro child reacts to discrimination and prejudice depends largely on his "family resources." As Pettigrew (1964b) points out, although the stress of the caste system may result in some self-hatred, given a stable and complete family the Negro may maintain ". . . his self-respect as a unique and worthwhile human being apart from the position of inferior being that the racists insist he assumes" (p. 22).

For every stable, complete, and supportive Negro home, there are many more that are ravaged by the economic and social effects of discrimination and prejudice. Therefore, our concern must extend beyond a simple query into the combination of unique circumstances which may lead to positive self-identity. We must look to the much larger question of the general resources available to any group—resources which strengthen group ties and feelings of group belongingness, particularly in the face of threat and frustration. The assumption implicit in our argument is that negative self-identity is frequently rooted in negative group identification. From this assumption, we would expect the converse to follow: that positive self-identity is dependent on positive group identification. Considerable evidence supports the idea that personal or self-pride is essentially the expression of group pride (Grossack, 1956; Noel, 1964; Lewin, 1948; Chein, 1948). Such group pride or belongingness is essential for individual growth and satisfaction; for, as Chein (1948) notes, adequate self-perceptions, individual security, and feelings of personal continuity are the major psychological functions of group belongingness for the person.

Group belongingness or positive group identification is not a problem for those groups that have status, power, and prestige in a society. The problems of group identification arise for those who are deprived of these benefits and who are often granted the unwelcome status of "second-class citizenship."

What are the conditions which foster positive group identification for these deprived citizens? It seems to the writers that there are at least three major resources for Negroes (and other minority groups) to establish strong group ties in the face of economic and social adversity.

The first resource we shall designate as *social insight*. By this concept, we suggest that the minority group member—child or adult—needs to understand the source of his group dilemma. If he is Negro, he needs to view the social system and the white man, not himself, as the source of his difficulties. We have previously indicated the danger that the Negro who is forced to play the "servile inferior" may come to believe in that role and accept it as a measure of his own worth. It is very easy for the Negro to become somewhat fatalistic, to "accept his lot," believing "He is what he is, because that is just the way he is."

The Negro does not need formal schooling to acquire such social insight, however desirable extended education might be for establishing his rightful place in American society. Social insight can probably best be fostered by and in the minority group itself. Grievances, problems, and injustices can be expressed and shared by group members, thus developing a "heritage of understanding" and strengthening feelings of a "common bond." Prior to the Civil Rights Movement, which gained its momentum in the early 1960's, discussions of the Negro problem were largely confined to universities and a few select groups. Only recently has a continuing dialogue on race prejudice been achieved, and evidence indicates that the dialogue is spreading, involving more and more members of the Negro community, particularly the lower-class urban slum dweller. For some Negroes, the blame has finally been shifted from themselves to the social arrangements of the white society.

Insight without hope will not sustain the Negro in the midst of poverty and despair. The Negro must see possibilities for *action*. While he need not be involved in such action, he must feel that change is possible and that others, if not himself, are "taking action." Since the beginning of the Civil Rights Movement, these opportunities for action have greatly increased. There has been a dramatic rise since World War II in the number of local and national Negro, white, and mixed racial groups that have been formed to state and fight the case of the Negro.

At the present time, these groups vary both in their goals and the means they use (or plan to use) to achieve these goals. However, these variations are of little importance in terms of the Negro's feelings of positive identity; the crucial fact is the groups' existence. These groups represent hope and action; they are sources for group identification, even if the individual is not actually personally involved in group action. The presence of the groups also signifies a reversal of the Negro's traditional role; passive acceptance has been largely replaced by active rejection.

In this context it is necessary to examine very briefly some of the implications of the Civil Rights Movement. The writers view the achievements of the Civil Rights Movement as primarily symbolic, serving to raise hopes and establish status and token gains. The lower-class Negro has felt very little change in his daily life. The gap between "what the white man says" and "what the white man does" remains. Frustration seethes in the ghetto, as symbolized by increasing outbreaks of violence. Yet some of this frustration is being harnessed by a new and articulate black leadership, bringing together many otherwise alienated individuals of the slum community. The slogan is usually "Black Power"; the emphasis is on "separatism"—on black control of black communities. While the significance of ultimate effects of this new militancy is unknown, it is important to recognize that the tenor and rhetoric of the Negro's struggle have changed. The new young Negro is no longer willing to play the "white man's game."

The Negro's perception of the significance and historic weight of his struggle provide a further resource for feelings of self-worth. Isolated from and denied participation in the mainstream of American life for over one hundred years, the Negro has seemed to have no past, as well as no future. His forebears were vaguely defined "blacks" from Africa, whose supposed primitive existence was used by whites to confirm the "inferiority" of all Negroes. Unlike the Jews, American Negroes had no *apparent* heritage or tradition to give significance to their existence or to instill hope for their future. While they maintained and developed cultural expressions in music, art, literature, and language, these distinctive contributions were largely unrecognized, and Negroes remained isolated from other Americans and from black peoples in other parts of the world.

In the last decade, the American Negro's struggle has taken on a new, dramatic, world-wide significance. Spurred by the emergence of the African nations and the pervasive influence of the mass media, there has been a rediscovery of "Black culture" and a growing bond uniting black peoples throughout the world. In his own battle, the American Negro is able to achieve a new sense of kinship and feeling of purpose—a new, larger, black identity. The struggle of black men has become symbolic of the struggle of all oppressed groups to achieve dignity and respect in the face of bigotry and discrimination.

References

Allport, G. W. *The nature of prejudice.* Reading, Mass.: Addison-Wesley, 1954.

Ausubel, D. P., and P. Ausubel. Ego development among segregated Negro children. *Mental Hygiene,* 1958, **42,** 362–369. (Republished in A. H. Passow (ed.), *Education in depressed areas.* New York Teachers College, Columbia University, Bureau of Publications, 1963, pp. 109–131.)

Bernard, J. *Marriage and family among Negroes.* Englewood Cliffs, N. J.: Prentice-Hall, 1966.

Bettelheim, B., and M. Janowitz. *Social change and prejudice.* New York: Free Press, 1964.

Boyd, G. F. The levels of aspiration of white and Negro children in a non-segregated elementary school. *Journal of Social Psychology,* 1952, **36,** 191–196.

Brown, B. The assessment of self-concept among four-year-old Negro and white children: A comparative study using the Brown-IDS Self-Concept Referents Test. New York: Institute for Developmental Studies (mimeo), 1967.

Chein, I. Group membership and group belonging. New York: American Jewish Congress (mimeo), 1948.

Clark, K. B. *Prejudice and your child.* Boston: Beacon Press, 1955.

———, and M. P. Clark. "Racial identification and preference in Negro children." In T. M. Newcomb and E. L. Hartley (eds.), *Readings in social psychology.* New York: Holt, Rinehart and Winston, 1947, 169–178.

——— and ———. Emotional factors in racial identification and preference in Negro children. *Journal of Negro Education,* 1950, **19,** 341–350.

Coleman, J. S., et al. *Equality of educational opportunity.* Washington, D.C.: U. S. Government Printing Office, 1966.

Coles, R. It's the same, but it's different. *Daedalus,* 1965, **94,** 1107–1132. (Republished in T. Parsons and K. B. Clark (eds.), *The Negro American.* Boston: Beacon Press, 1967, 254–279.)

———. *Children of crisis: A study of courage and fear.* Boston: Atlantic-Little, Brown, 1967.

Criswell, J. H. Social structure revealed in a sociometric re-test. *Sociometry,* 1939, **2,** 69–75.

Davidson, H. H., and G. Lang. Children's perceptions of teachers' feelings toward them. *Journal of Experimental Education,* 1960, **29** (2), 107–118. (Republished in J. I. Roberts (ed.), *School children in the urban slum.* New York: Free Press, 1967, 215–230.)

Davis, C. H. Personal communication. November 1967.

Deutsch, M. Minority group and class status as related to social and personality factors in scholastic achievement. Monograph No. 2. Society of Applied Anthropology, 1960.

———, and B. Brown. Social influences in Negro-white intelligence differences. *Journal of Social Issues,* 1964, **20,** 24–35.

Drake, St. C. The social and economic status of the Negro in the United States. *Daedalus,* 1965, **94,** 771–814. (Republished in T. Parsons and K. B. Clark (eds.), *The Negro American.* Boston: Beacon Press, 1967, 771–814.)

———, and H. R. Cayton. *Black Metropolis.* Rev. ed. New York: Harper & Row, 1962.

Erikson, E. H. The concept of identity in race relations: Notes and queries. *Daedalus,* 1966, **95,** 145–171. (Republished in T. Parsons and K. B. Clark (eds.), *The Negro American.* Boston: Beacon Press, 1967, 227–253.)

Fanon, Frantz. *Peau noire, masques blancs.* Paris: Editions de seuil, 1952. (Republished: *Black skins, white masks.* New York: Grove Press, 1967.)

Frazier, E. F. *Black bourgeoisie.* New York: Collier, 1962.

Goodman, M. E. *Race awareness in young children.* Reading, Mass.: Addison-Wesley, 1952; New York: Collier, 1964.

Grambs, J. D. "The self-concept: Basis for reeducation of Negro youth." In W. C. Kvaraceus, J. S. Gibson, F. Patterson, B. Seasholes, and J. D. Grambs, *Negro self-concept: Implications for school and citizenship.* New York: McGraw-Hill, 1964, 11–34.

Grossack, M. Group belongingness among Negroes. *Journal of Social Psychology,* 1956, **43,** 167–180. (Republished in M. Grossack (ed.), *Mental health and segregation.* New York: Springer, 1963, 18–29.)

Group for the Advancement of Psychiatry. Psychiatric aspects of school desegregation. New York: Group for Advancement of Psychiatry, 1957.

Hartley, E. L., M. Rosenbaum, and S. Schwartz. Children's use of ethnic frames of reference: An exploratory study of children's conceptualizations of multiple ethnic group membership. *Journal of Psychology,* 1948, **26,** 367–386.

Horowitz, E. L. The development of attitude toward the Negro. *Archives of Psychology,* New York, 1936, No. 194.

Johnson, C. S. *Growing up in the black belt.* Washington, D.C.: American Council on Education, 1941. (Republished: New York: Shocken, 1967.)

Kardiner, A., and L. Ovesey. *The mark of oppression.* Cleveland, Ohio: World, 1962.

Landreth, C., and B. C. Johnson. Young children's responses to a picture and inset test designed to reveal reactions to persons of different skin color. *Child Development,* 1953, **24,** 63–79.

Lewin, K. *Resolving social conflicts.* New York: Harper & Row, 1948.

Lott, A. J., and B. E. Lott. *Negro and white youth.* New York: Holt, Rinehart and Winston, 1963. (Republished as "Negro and white children's plans for their futures" in J. I. Roberts (ed.), *School children in the urban slum.* New York: Free Press, 1967, 347–361.)

McKinley, D. G. *Social class and family life.* New York: Free Press, 1964, 152–166. (Republished as "Status and the socialized son" in J. I. Roberts (ed.), *School children in the urban slum.* New York: Free Press, 1967, 471–483.)

Morland, J. K. Racial recognition by nursery school children in Lynchburg, Virginia. *Social Forces,* 1958, **37,** 132–137.

————. Racial acceptance and preference of nursery school children in a southern city. *Merrill Palmer Quarterly,* 1962, **8,** 271–280.

Mussen, P. H. Differences between the TAT responses of Negro and white boys. *Journal of Consulting Psychology,* 1953, **17,** 373–376.

National Urban League. *Education and race.* New York: National Urban League, 1966.

Neugarten, B. L. Social class and friendship among school children. *American Journal of Sociology,* 1946, **51,** 305–313.

Newcomb, T. M., R. H. Turner, and P. E. Converse. *Social Psychology.* New York: Holt, Rinehart and Winston, 1965.

Noel, D. L. Group identification among Negroes: An empirical analysis. *Journal of Social Issues,* 1964, **20,** 71–84.

Palermo, D. S. Racial comparisons and additional normative data on the Children's Manifest Anxiety Scale. *Child Development,* 1959, **30,** 53–57.

Parker, S., and R. J. Kleiner. *Mental illness in the urban Negro community.* New York: Free Press, 1965.

Pettigrew, T. F. Father-absence and Negro adult personality: A research note. Unpublished paper. Cited by T. F. Pettigrew in *A profile of the Negro American.* Princeton, N. J.: D. Van Nostrand, 1964a, 20.

————. *A profile of the Negro American.* Princeton, N. J.: D. Van Nostrand, 1964b.

Proshansky, H. M. "The development of inter-group attitudes." In L. W. Hoffman and M. L. Hoffman (eds.), *Review of child development research.* New York: Russell Sage Foundation, 1966, 311–371.

Radke, M., J. Sutherland, and P. Rosenberg. Racial attitudes of children. *Sociometry,* 1950, **13,** 154–171.

————, and H. G. Trager. Children's perceptions of the social roles of Negroes and whites. *Journal of Psychology,* 1950, **29,** 3–33.

————, ————, and H. Davis. Social perceptions and attitudes of children. *Genetic Psychology Monographs,* 1949, **40,** 327–447.

Rainwater, L. Crucible of identity: The Negro lower-class family. *Daedalus,* 1966, **95,** 172–217. (Republished in T. Parsons and K. B. Clark (eds.), *The Negro American.* Boston: Beacon Press, 1967, 166–204.)

Robins, L. N., R. S. Jones, and G. E. Murphy. School milieu and school problems of Negro boys. *Social Problems,* 1966, **13,** 431. As cited in U. S. Civil Rights Commission. *Racial isolation in the public schools.* Washington, D.C.: U. S. Government Printing Office, 1967, Vol. 2, p. 177.

Rosen, B. C. The achievement syndrome: A psychocultural dimension of social stratification. *American Sociological Review,* 1956, **21,** 203–211. (Republished in J. W. Atkinson (ed.), *Motives in fantasy, action, and society.* Princeton, N. J.: D. Van Nostrand, 1958, 495–508.)

————. Race, ethnicity, and the achievement syndrome. *American Sociological Review,* 1959, **24,** 47–60. (Republished in J. I. Roberts (ed.), *School children in the urban slum.* New York: Free Press, 1966, 327–346.)

Seward, G. *Psychotherapy and culture conflict.* New York: Ronald Press, 1956.

Simpson, G. E., and J. M. Yinger. *Racial and cultural minorities.* Ed. 3. New York: Harper & Row, 1965.

Stevenson, H. W., and N. G. Stevenson. Social interaction in an interracial nursery school. *Genetic Psychology Monographs,* 1960, **61,** 37–75.

————, and E. C. Stewart. A developmental study of race awareness in young children. *Child Development,* 1958, **29,** 399–410.

Trager, H. G., and M. R. Yarrow. *They learn what they live: Prejudice in young children.* New York: Harper & Row, 1952.

Vaughan, G. M. Concept formation and the development of ethnic awareness. *Journal of Genetic Psychology,* 1963, **103,** 93–103.

Weiner, M., and M. Graves. A study of educational and vocational aspirations of junior high school pupils from two socioeconomic levels (Dittoed paper). White Plains, N. Y., Board of Education, 1960. (As cited by M. Weiner and W. Murray, "Another look at the culturally deprived and their levels of aspiration," in J. I. Roberts (ed.), *School children in the urban slum.* New York: Free Press, 1967, 296.)

————, and W. Murray. Another look at the culturally deprived and their levels of aspiration. *Journal of Educational Sociology,* 1963, **36,** 319–321. (Republished in J. I. Roberts (ed.), *School children in the urban slum.* New York: Free Press, 1967, 295–310.)

Wylie, R. S. Children's estimates of their schoolwork ability as a function of sex, race, and socioeconomic level. *Journal of Personality,* 1963, **31,** 204–224.

CHAPTER SIX

Self-Fulfilling Prophecies
in the Classroom:
Teachers' Expectations as Unintended Determinants
of Pupils' Intellectual Competence

ROBERT ROSENTHAL

LENORE JACOBSON[1]

"PYGMALION IN THE CLASSROOM"

With increasing concern over what can be done to reduce the disparity of opportunity of education, of intellectual motivation, and of competence that exists between the social classes and the colors of our school children, attention has been focused more and more on the role of the classroom teacher, and the possible effects of her values, her attitudes, and, especially, her beliefs and expectations. Asbell (1963), Becker (1952), Clark (1963), Gibson (1965), Harlem Youth Opportunities Unlimited (1964), Katz (1964), Kvaraceus (1965), MacKinnon, (1962), Riessman (1962, 1965), Rose (1956), and Wilson (1963) have all expressed their belief that the teacher's expectation of pupils' performance may serve as an educational self-fulfilling prophecy. The

[1] Robert Rosenthal is at Harvard University, and Lenore Jacobson is in the South San Francisco Unified School District. Preparation of this chapter and much of the research reported was supported by the Division of Social Sciences of the National Science Foundation. An earlier draft of this chapter was the basis for a paper read at the annual meeting of the American Psychological Association, New York City, September 1966.

teacher gets less because she expects less—that is the essence of the positions cited.

The concept of the self-fulfilling prophecy has been applied in many contexts other than educational. As early as 1898, Albert Moll mentioned ". . . the prophecy (which) causes its own fulfillment" (p. 244) as the source of cures of hysterical paralyses, insomnia, nausea, impotence, and stammering. His particular interest was in the phenomenon of hypnosis. Subjects, he believed, behaved as they were expected to behave by the hypnotist. Some six decades later Orne (1959) showed that for the hypnosis situation, Moll was quite right.

In the analysis of large-scale social and economic phenomena, both Merton (1948) and Allport (1950) applied the concept of self-fulfilling prophecies. Merton used the concept to explain racial and religious prejudice and the collapse of economic systems. Allport suggested that nations that expect to go to war, do go to war. The expectation to wage war is communicated to the opponent-to-be who reacts by preparing for war, an act which confirms the first nation's expectation, strengthens it, leads to greater preparations for war, and so on, in a mutually reinforcing system of positive feedback loops. Nations expecting to remain out of wars sometimes seem to manage to avoid entering into them.

The self-fulfilling prophecy has been investigated in everyday life situations. Whyte (1943) in a study of a street-corner gang found that the group "knew how well a man should bowl." On a given evening the group "knew" that a given member would bowl well, and so he did. On another evening, the group "knew" that some member would bowl poorly, and so he did, even if he had bowled well the week before. The group, through its behavior toward the target member, fulfilled its prophecy for that member's performance.

The self-fulfilling prophecy has been observed in the world of work as well as in the world of recreation. Jastrow (1900) tells some details. The Hollerith tabulating machine had just been installed at the United States Census Bureau. The machine, something like a typewriter, required the clerks to learn a new skill which the inventor, Hollerith, regarded as quite demanding. He expected that a trained worker could punch about 550 cards per day. After two weeks the workers were adequately trained and began to produce about 550 cards per day. After a while the clerks began to exceed the expected performance, but only at great emotional cost. Workers became so tense trying to beat the expected limit that the Secretary of the Interior forbade the establishment of any minimum-performance criterion. This was seen as a step necessary to preserve the mental health of the establishment.

Then a new group of some two hundred clerks was brought in to augment the Hollerith machine work force. These clerks knew nothing of the work, had no prior training, and had never even seen the machines. No one had told these workers what the emotional cost of the work might be, nor of the upper limit of production which could be achieved. Within three days this new group was performing at the level which was reached only after seven weeks by the earlier, properly indoctrinated, group. Whereas clerks from the initial group were exhausted from producing 700 cards per day, members of the new group began turning out three times that number without ill effects.

In the behavioral sciences the expectation of the experimenter or data-collector has been shown to affect the responses he obtains from his subjects (Rosenthal, 1966). In a variety of experimental tasks the paradigm has been the same. Half the experimenters are led to expect one type of response from their subjects; half are led to expect the opposite type of response. In some way these expectations turn out to function as self-fulfilling prophecies. Subjects contacted by experimenters expecting data Type X, give Type X responses. Subjects contacted by experimenters expecting data Type Y, give Type Y responses. Some of the studies of the self-fulfilling prophecy in experimental situations are particularly relevant to the theme of this chapter and will be described below.

The literature on the self-fulfilling prophecy in survey research is a venerable one. As early as 1929, Rice found that interviewers' expectations could be related to their respondents' replies. In a study of applicants for welfare funds, Rice found that the "causes" of destitution could be predicted from a knowledge of the interviewers' expectations. Thus, a prohibitionist interviewer obtained three times as many responses implicating Demon Rum as did a socialist interviewer who, in turn, obtained 50 percent more responses implicating industrial factors than did the prohibitionist interviewer. In this study as in most of the others reviewed, we cannot be certain whether a self-fulfilling prophecy accounted for the findings. Congruence of prophecy and prophesied behavior has been demonstrated. But the prophecy may have been based on the prior behavior of the person or persons whose behavior was prophesied so that the prophecy was, in a sense, "contaminated" by reality. If a physician predicts a patient's improvement, we cannot say whether the doctor is giving a sophisticated prognosis or whether the patient's improvement is based in part on the optimism engendered by the physician's prediction. If school children who perform poorly are those expected by their teachers to perform poorly, is the teacher's expectation the "cause" of the pupils' poor performance, or is the teacher's expectation rather an accurate prognosis of performance based on knowledge of past performance? To help answer this question, experiments are required in which the expectation is clearly the independent variable, uncontaminated by the past behavior of the person whose performance is predicted.

EVIDENCE FROM ANIMAL SUBJECTS

There is a tradition in the behavioral and biomedical sciences that animal subjects be employed in experiments even though the organism in which the ultimate interest resides is man. Sometimes this choice of the animal model for man is dictated by the greater convenience of using animals and sometimes by the nature of the experimental procedure which may be too dangerous to try on man without animal pretests. Sometimes, though, there is the positive advantage that animal subjects are less likely to try to guess the purpose of the experiment and then try to "help it along" or even "foul it up" (Orne, 1962). It would, therefore, constitute a powerful source of evidence if it could be shown that even the behavior of animal subjects could be the result of the experimenter's, trainer's, or teacher's expectation or prophecy. Pavlov thought it might be.

Not all who know the name Pavlov know of his interest in the Lamarckian theory of the inheritance of acquired characteristics. He had, in fact, gathered evidence to show that the transmission of modifications occurred in the case of the learning ability of mice. In 1929, however, at the meeting of the thirteenth International Physiological Congress, Pavlov made an informal statement to the effect that a closer check on his experiments showed no increased learning ability on the part of his mice. What the check did show was an increased teaching ability on the part of the research assistant who probably expected to obtain the increased learning ability for which he seemed responsible (Gruenberg, 1929).

Much earlier than Pavlov's Lamarckian experiments, in 1904, there was a case of self-fulfilling prophecies involving the behavior of a horse known as Clever Hans (Rosenthal, 1965). By means of tapping his hoof, Hans could add, subtract, multiply, and divide. He could spell, read, solve problems of musical harmony, and answer personal questions. His owner, Mr. von Osten, a German mathematics teacher, did not profit financially from his horse's talents, and it seemed unlikely that he had any fraudulent intent. He was quite willing to let others question Hans even in his absence so that cues from the owner could be ruled out as the reason for the horse's abilities. In a brilliant series of experiments, Pfungst (1911) discovered that Hans could answer questions only if the questioner himself knew the answer and was visible to the horse during his foot-tapping of the answer. Finally, it was discovered that whenever people asked Hans a question they leaned forward very slightly the better to see Hans' hoof. That, it turned out, was the unintentional signal for Hans to begin tapping. Then, as Hans approached the number of hooftaps representing the correct answer, the questioners would typically shows a tiny head movement. That almost imperceptible cue was the signal for Hans to stop tapping, and Hans was right again. The questioner, by expecting Hans to stop at the right answer was actually "telling" Hans the right answer and thereby fulfilling his own prophecy. Pfungst did not learn all of this so easily. It took a long and elegant series of experiments to learn the secret of Hans' success. Pfungst summarized eloquently the difficulties in discovering Hans' talents. He and others had too long been misled by, and we paraphase, "looking for, in the pupil, what should have been sought in the teacher."

Learning in Mazes

The purpose of the experiment to be described now was to test the hypothesis of the self-fulfilling prophecy with a larger number of animals than one horse (Rosenthal and Fode, 1963). A class in experimental psychology had been performing experiments with human subjects for most of a semester. Now they were asked to perform one more experiment, the last in the course, and the first employing animal subjects. The experimenters were told of studies which had shown that maze-brightness and maze-dullness could be developed in strains of rats by successive inbreeding of the well- and the poorly-performing maze-runners. There were sixty perfectly ordinary laboratory rats available, and they were equitably divided among the twelve experimenters. But half the experimenters were told that their rats were maze-bright while the other half were told their rats were maze-dull. The animal's task was to learn to run to the darker of two arms of an elevated T-shaped maze. The two arms of the maze, one white and one gray, were interchangeable; and the "correct" or rewarded arm was equally often on the right as on the left. Whenever an animal ran to the correct side he obtained a bit of food. Each rat was given ten chances each day for five days to learn that the darker side of the maze was the one which led to food.

From Table 6.1 we learn that beginning with the first day and continuing on through the experiment, animals believed to be better performers became better performers ($p = 0.01$). Animals believed to be brighter showed a daily improvement in their performance while those believed to be dull improved only to the third day and then showed a worsening of performance. Sometimes an animal refused to budge from his starting position. This happened 11 percent of the time among the allegedly bright rats; but among allegedly dull rats it happened 29 percent of the time. This difference in reluctance rates was significant at

TABLE 6.1

Mean Number of Correct Responses per Animal per Day

| | | Expectation for Performance | |
Day	Dull	Bright	p
1	0.73	1.33	
2	1.10	1.60	
3	2.23	2.60	
4	1.83	2.83	
5	1.83	3.26	
Mean	1.54	2.32	0.01

the 0.001 level. When animals did respond, and correctly so, those believed to be brighter ran faster to the darker side of the maze than did even the correctly responding rats believed to be dull ($p < 0.02$).

When the experiment was over, all experimenters made ratings of their rats and of their own attitudes and behavior vis-à-vis their animals. Those experimenters who had been led to expect better performance viewed their animals as brighter, more pleasant, and more likable. These same experimenters felt more relaxed in their contacts with the animals and described their behavior toward them as more pleasant, friendly, enthusiastic, and less talkative. They also stated that they handled their rats more and also more gently than did the experimenters expecting poor performance.

Learning in Skinner-Boxes

The next experiment to be described also employed rat-subjects, using, this time, not mazes but Skinner-boxes (Rosenthal and Lawson, 1964). Because the experimenters (39) outnumbered the subjects (16), experimenters worked in teams of two or three. Once again half the experimenters were led to believe that their subjects had been specially bred for excellence of performance. The experimenters who had been assigned the remaining rats were led to believe that their animals were genetically inferior.

The learning required of the animals in this experiment was more complex than that required in the maze-learning study. This time the rats had to learn in sequence and over a period of a full academic quarter the following behaviors: to run to the food dispenser whenever a clicking sound occurred, to press a bar for a food reward, to learn that the feeder could be turned off, and that sometimes it did not pay to press the bar, to learn new responses with only the clicking sound as a rein-forcer (rather than the food), to bar-press only in the presence of a light and not in the absence of the light, and, finally, to pull on a loop which was followed by a light which informed the animal that a bar-press would be followed by a bit of food.

Each team of experimenters conducted experiments in one of five laboratories. Table 6.2 shows separately for each laboratory the mean standardized rank of performance for the allegedly bright and the allegedly dull rats. A lower rank means a superior performance. In all five laboratories animals showed superior performance if their experi-menters expected superior performance.

Just as in the maze-learning experiment, the experimenters of the present study were asked to rate their animals and their own attitudes and behaviors toward them. Once again those experimenters who had expected excellence of performance judged their animals to be brighter, more pleasant, and more likable. Once again these "teachers" of the allegedly gifted, described their own behavior as more pleasant, friendly, enthusastic, and less talkative. Compared to the "teachers" of the "genetically-deprived" subjects, those assigned the "well-endoweds" tended to watch their animals more closely, to handle them more, and to talk to them *less*. One wonders what was said to the animals by those experimenters who believed their rats to be inferior.

The absolute amount of handling of animals in this Skinner-box experiment was considerably less than the handling of animals in the maze-learning experiment. Nonetheless, those experimenters who be-lieved their animals to be Skinner-box bright handled them relatively more, or said they did, than did experimenters believing their animals to be dull. The extra handling of animals believed to be brighter may have

TABLE 6.2

Mean Ranks of Operant Learning for

each of Five Laboratories

| | Expectation for Performance | | |
Laboratory	Dull	Bright	p
A	5.3	4.3	
B	6.5	4.9	
C	5.8	5.1	
D	4.6	3.7	
E	6.0	4.1	
Mean	5.6	4.4	0.02

contributed in both experiments to the superior learning of these animals.

In addition to the differences in handling reported by the experimenters of the Skinner-box study as a function of their beliefs about their subjects, there were differences in the reported intentness of their observation of their animals. Animals believed to be brighter were watched more carefully, and more careful observation of the rat's Skinner-box behavior may very well have led to more rapid and appropriate reinforcement of the desired response. Thus, closer observation, perhaps due to the belief that there would be more promising responses to be seen, may have made more effective teachers of the experimenters expecting good performance.

At the beginning of the Skinner-box experiment, experimenters assigned allegedly dull animals were of course told that they would find retarded learning on the part of their rats. They were, however, reassured that ". . . it has been found that even the dullest rats can, in time, learn the required responses." Animals alleged to be dull, then, were described as slow but educable. It was interesting in the light of this to learn that of the experimenters who had been assigned "dull" animals, 47 percent believed their subject to be uneducable. Only 5 percent of the experimenters assigned "bright" rats were that pessimistic about their animal's future ($p = 0.007$, one tail). From this result one wonders about the beliefs created in school teachers when they are told a child is "slow but educable."

EVIDENCE FROM HUMAN SUBJECTS

There is a growing body of literature to show that in the interaction between an experimenter and his human subject the hypothesis held by the experimenter may function as a self-fulfilling prophecy (Rosenthal, 1966). In most of the studies designed to test this hypothesis, however, the behavior of the subject which was affected by the experimenter's hypothesis was not related to the subject's intellectual competence. In this section we summarize the evidence which does have a bearing on the question of whether an experimenter, a teacher, or a trainer can, by virtue of his expectation, affect the intellectual performance of his subjects, pupils or trainees.

The Interpretation of Inkblots

The ability to produce a large number of alternative interpretations of a set of inkblots is a correlate of intellectual ability as defined by standard tests of intelligence (Wysocki, 1957). A recent experiment by Marwit and Marcia (1966) was designed to test the hypothesis that the number of responses given by a subject to a series of inkblots was a function of the examiner's expectation. Thirty-six undergraduate students enrolled in a course in experimental psychology served as the examiners. Their task was to administer an inkblot test to a total of fifty-four students enrolled in an introductory psychology course. Some of the examiners expected to obtain many responses from their subjects, either on the basis of their own hypotheses or because of the principal investigators' hypothesis. The remaining examiners expected to obtain few responses from their subjects, either because that was their own hypothesis or because that was the principal investigators' hypothesis. The results showed that the source of the hypothesis made no difference. Examiners who expected greater response productivity obtained 54 percent more responses than did examiners expecting fewer responses from their subjects ($p < 0.0003$). Both in terms of the statistical significance and in terms of the magnitude of the effect it seems safe to conclude that an examiner's expectation may be a significant determinant of his subjects' productivity in responding to an inkblot stimulus.

Not only the number of responses to an inkblot but also the proportion of responses which involve human percepts have been related to scores on standard tests of intelligence (Sommer, 1958). In a recently reported experiment, Masling (1965) led half his examiners to believe that more human percepts should be obtained from their subjects. The remaining examiners were led to believe that more animal percepts should be obtained from their subjects. This latter group it turned out obtained a ratio of animal to human percepts which was 33 percent higher than that obtained by examiners expecting or desiring more human percepts in their subjects' responses ($p = 0.04$). From the two experiments described it seems that at least the interpretation of inkblots can be determined in part by the expectancy of the examiner who administers the task.

Performance of Intellectual Tasks

In the experiments described below, the subject's response was more clearly related to one type or another of intellectual competence. Wartenberg-Ekren (1962) employed eight examiners who each administered the Block Design subtest of the Wechsler Adult Intelligence Scale to four subjects. Two of the four subjects seen by each examiner were alleged to be earning higher grades in school than the other two subjects. In spite of the fact that all the examiners expected superior performance from the subjects alleged to be earning higher grades as indicated by a postexperimental questionnaire, there were no differences obtained in the performance of the two "types" of subjects. These negative findings may have been due in part to the special efforts of the examiners to remain unaffected by their expectations. Thus, one of the eight examiners, on his own initiative, instituted a "blind procedure" by not looking at the code sheet which told which "type" of subject was coming in next. A second experimenter was blind to the status of half his subjects although not intentionally so. A secondary analysis of subjects' ratings of their examiner's behavior (Rosenthal, 1964) showed that when examiners were contacting subjects alleged to be earning higher grades, they behaved in a more friendly, likable, interested, encouraging manner, showed a more expressive face, and used more hand gestures. Though we might expect these behaviors to affect the performance of the subjects, they did not appear to in the study described.

In a more recent experiment by Hurwitz and Jenkins (1966) three male experimenters administered a rote verbal-learning task and a mathematical-reasoning task to a total of twenty female subjects. From half their subjects the experimenters were led to expect superior performance; from half they were led to expect inferior performance.

In the rote learning task subjects were shown a list of pairs of nonsense syllables and were asked to remember one of the pair members from a presentation of the other pair member. Subjects were given six trials to learn the syllable pairs. Somewhat greater learning occurred on the part of the subjects contacted by the experimenters believing subjects to be brighter although the difference was not significant statistically nor large numerically (the subjects alleged to be brighter learned 11 percent more syllables). The curves of learning of the paired nonsense syllables, however, did show a difference between subjects alleged to be brighter and those alleged to be duller. Among "brighter" subjects, learning increased significantly more monotonically over the course of the six trials than was the case for "duller" subjects. (The coefficient of determination (ρ^2) between accurate recall and trial number was 0.50 for the "bright" subjects and 0.25 for the "dull" subjects, $p < 0.02$).

In the mathematical-reasoning task, subjects had to learn to use three sizes of water jars in order to obtain exactly some specified amount of water. On the critical trials the correct solution could be obtained by a longer and more routine procedure which was scored for partial credit, or by a shorter but more novel procedure which was given full credit. Those subjects whose experimenters expected superior performance earned higher scores than did those subjects whose experimenters expected inferior performance ($p = 0.08$). Among these latter subjects only 40 percent ever achieved a novel solution while among the allegedly superior subjects 88 percent achieved one or more novel solutions. From the experiments reported here, it would appear that, at least sometimes, a subject's performance of an intellectual task may be unintentionally determined by the expectation of the examiner. Perhaps it is appropriate to stress the unintentional aspect of the self-fulfilling prophecy since in both the experiments described, the examiners and experimenters tried hard to avoid having their expectations affect their subjects' performance.

Performance in School and Industry

Though much of the work of the behavioral sciences goes on in the laboratory, an implied intent of even the most carefully controlled laboratory experiment is to be able to make accurate statements about behavior outside the laboratory, behavior sometimes referred to as *real-life*. While the implication that behavior in the laboratory is some-how less than *real* seems debatable, there is no question that behavioral scientists are more confident that a relationship is understood when it can be demonstrated in a variety of social contexts. In this section some data will be reported which come not from the laboratory but from the world of work and of school.

The first of these studies was described in a personal communication from Alex Bavelas (December 6, 1965). Some fifteen years ago, in a large industrial concern, a large number of female applicants for employment underwent an evaluation procedure. Each applicant was administered tests of intelligence and of finger dexterity. The foremen who were to supervise these employees were led to believe that certain of these women had scored high on the tests and that certain of these women had scored low. What the foremen were told bore no relationship, of course, to the actual performance of the applicants. Some time later, the foremen's evaluations of their workers and the workers' actual production records were obtained. It turned out that foremen evaluated more favorably those workers who were believed to be superior on the basis of their alleged test scores. This much could be attributed to a simple halo effect in which the perception of the foremen was affected by their expectation. Not so simply interpreted was the finding that the objective production record of the workers was superior if the foremen had expected superior performance. This result could not be attributed to a simple halo effect but rather to another case of an interpersonally self-fulfilling prophecy. Interestingly, the workers' actual test scores showed no relationship to either the foremen's subsequent evaluation or to the objective production record.

In a very recent experiment, Flowers (1966) varied experimentally teachers' expectations of the intellectual performance of their students. He worked with two seventh-grade classes in each of two cities. Both schools employed a system of grouping such that each of the many seventh-grade classes carried a designation of its average relative ability. Within each of the two cities the two classes from the same school were comparable in tested achievement and intelligence. One of these two comparable classes in each city was arbitrarily designated as a considerably higher group than it merited on the basis of the objective tests of achievement and intelligence. The remaining class in each city was not given a falsely higher ability designation, and so served as the control group. Teachers, of course, were not told that the grouping had been arbitrary.

At the end of the experiment the children falsely designated as brighter at one of the schools showed a significant, though small, gain in IQ ($p < 0.03$), but showed no gain in achievement relative to the control-group children. In the other city, the group designated as brighter tended to show a greater gain in achievement test scores than did the control-group children though the effect was not very significant statistically. In this school the experimental-group children did not show a gain in IQ relative to the gain shown by the control-group children.

One problem in the interpretation of these findings was that the experimental groups might have been assigned to a set of superior teachers. Despite this problem, however, the results of this experiment at least further suggest the possibility that a teacher's expectation of a child's intellectual performance may serve as a self-fulfilling prophecy.

SOME FURTHER EVIDENCE[2]

A recent experiment was designed to test the hypothesis that, within a given classroom, those children from whom the teacher expected greater growth in intellectual competence would show such greater growth (Rosenthal and Jacobson, 1966). The Harvard Test of Inflected Acquisition was administered to all the children in an elementary school in the spring of 1964. This test was purported to predict academic "blooming" or intellectual growth. The reason for administering the test in the particular school was ostensibly to perform a final check on the validity of the test, a validity which was presented as already well established. Actually, the Harvard Test of Inflected Acquisition was a standardized relatively nonverbal test of intelligence, Flanagan's (1960) Tests of General Ability.

[2] The research to be described was supported by the Division of Social Sciences of the National Science Foundation (GS–177 and GS–714). We are grateful to Dr. Paul Nielsen, Superintendent, South San Francisco Unified School District, for making this study possible. We also thank Dr. Jerome Kagan and Dr. David Marlowe for their valuable advice, and Mae Evans, Nancy Johnson, John Laszlo, Susan Novick, and especially George Smiltens for their assistance.

Within each of the six grades of the elementary school, there were three classrooms, one each for children performing at above-average, average, and below-average levels of scholastic achievement. In each of the eighteen classrooms of the school about 20 percent of the children were designated as academic "spurters." The names of these children were reported to their new teachers in the fall of 1964 as those who, during the academic year ahead, would show unusual intellectual gains. The "fact" of their intellectual potential was established from their scores on the test for "intellectual blooming."

Teachers were cautioned not to discuss the test findings with either their pupils or the children's parents. Actually, the names of the 20 percent of the children assigned to the "spurting" condition had been selected by means of a table of random numbers. The difference, then, between these children earmarked for intellectual growth and the un-designated control children was in the mind of the teacher.

THE SCHOOL AS A WHOLE. Four months after the teachers had been given the names of the "special" children, all the children once again took the same form of the nonverbal test of intelligence. Four months after this retest, the children took the same test once again. This final retest was at the end of the school year, some eight months after the teachers had been given the expectation for intellectual growth of the special children. These retests were not, of course, explained as "re-tests" to the teachers but rather as further efforts to predict intellectual growth.

The intelligence test employed, while relatively nonverbal in the sense of requiring no speaking, reading, or writing, was not entirely nonverbal. Actually there were two subtests, one requiring a greater comprehension of English—a kind of picture vocabulary. The other subtest required less ability to understand any spoken language, but more ability to reason abstractly. For shorthand purposes we refer to the former as a *verbal* subtest and to the latter as a *reasoning* subtest. The pretest correlation between these subtests was $+0.42$.

Table 6.3 shows the means and standard deviations of gains in IQ and MA by the children of the control group and the experimental group after eight months. For the school as a whole, the children of the experimental groups did not show a significantly greater gain in verbal IQ and mental age than did the control-group children. However, in total IQ and mental age, and especially in the reasoning IQ and mental age, the experimental children gained more than did the control children. Even after the fourth-month retest this trend was already in evidence though the effects were smaller.

Toward the end of the school year of this study, all teachers were asked to rate each of their pupils on the following variables: the extent

TABLE 6.3

Means and Standard Deviations of Gains

in Intellectual Performance

		Control			Experimental		Difference between	
	N	Mean	S.D.[a]	N	Mean	S.D.	Means	p[b]
Verbal IQ	269	7.8	17.7	68	9.9	21.9	2.1	
Reasoning IQ	255	15.7	28.6	65	22.9	31.3	7.2	0.03
Total IQ	255	8.4	13.5	65	12.2	15.0	3.8	0.02
Verbal *MA*	269	1.8	1.8	68	2.0	2.2	0.2	
Reasoning *MA*	255	2.3	2.4	65	3.0	2.8	0.7	0.02
Total *MA*	255	1.8	1.3	65	2.1	1.4	0.3	0.02

[a] S.D., standard deviation.
[b] Error term for all tests of significance is mean square within treatments in classrooms.

to which they would be successful in the future, and the degree to which they could be described as interesting, curious, happy, appealing, adjusted, affectionate, hostile, and motivated by a need for social approval. A comparison of the experimental and control children on each of these variables was thought to be valuable to obtain some idea of the effect of the experimental treatment on behavior other than intellectual-test performance. In addition, it was thought that differences in teachers' perceptions of the experimental and control children might be suggestive of the mechanism whereby a teacher communicates her expectation to her pupils. There is, of course, no way to be sure that the children's behavior was accurately described by the teachers. If it were, and if the experimental- and control-group children differed in their classroom behavior, we would know at least that changes in intellectual ability were accompanied by changes in other classroom behavior. If the teachers' descriptions of the children's behavior were not accurate, any differences in the descriptions of the experimental and control children could be ascribed to a kind of halo effect. Such a halo effect might suggest the possibility that altered perceptions of children's behavior might be associated with differences in teachers' treatment of the children, such treatment differences leading to differences in intellectual performance and remaining to be discovered. In Table 6.4 are found the mean ratings of the children of each experimental condition on each of the nine characteristics described earlier.

The children from whom intellectual growth was expected were described as having a significantly better chance of becoming successful in the future, as significantly more interesting, curious, and happy.

There was a tendency, too, for these children to be seen as more appealing, adjusted, and affectionate and as lower in the need for social approval. In short, the children from whom intellectual growth was expected became more intellectually alive and autonomous, or at least were so perceived by their teachers.

We have already seen that the children of the experimental group gained more intellectually so that the possibility exists that it was the fact of such gaining that accounted for the more favorable ratings of these children's behavior and aptitude. But a great many of the control-group children also gained in IQ during the course of the year. Perhaps those who gained more intellectually among these undesignated children would also be rated more favorably by their teachers. Such was not the case, however. The more the control-group children gained in verbal IQ the more they were regarded as less well-adjusted ($r = -0.13$, $p < 0.05$). Among the experimental-group children the greater their gains in verbal IQ the more they were regarded as more likely to be successful in the future ($r = +0.22$, $p < 0.10$), as happier ($r = +0.21$, $p < 0.10$), and as less affectionate ($r = -0.22$, $p < 0.10$).

Those children of the control group who gained more in reasoning IQ came to be regarded as less interesting ($r = -0.14$, $p < 0.05$) and less affectionate ($r = -0.13$, $p < 0.05$). The children of the experimental group who gained more in reasoning IQ came to be regarded as more likely to succeed ($r = +0.22$, $p < 0.10$), better adjusted ($r = +0.36$, $p < 0.01$), more affectionate ($r = +0.25$, $p < 0.05$) and as lower in their need for social approval ($r = -0.24$, $p < 0.10$). Relative to the control-group children who gained more in reasoning IQ, the experimental-group children who gained more in reasoning IQ were seen as

TABLE 6.4

Mean Ratings by Teachers of Children in

Experimental and Control Groups

Characteristics	Control	Experimental	Difference	p
Future success	5.53	6.48	0.95	0.0006
Interesting	5.46	6.43	0.97	0.0008
Curious	5.50	6.25	0.75	0.01
Happy	5.77	6.33	0.56	0.05
Appealing	5.78	6.23	0.45	0.14
Adjusted	5.67	6.04	0.37	0.22
Affectionate	5.72	6.01	0.29	0.28
Hostile	3.84	3.97	0.13	
Needs approval	5.35	4.97	−0.38	0.20

TABLE 6.5

Means and Standard Deviations of Gains

in Total IQ for Six Grades

Grade	Control			Experimental			Difference	
	N	Mean	S.D.	N	Mean	S.D.	between means	p^a
1	48	12.0	16.6	7	27.4	12.5	15.4	0.002
2	47	7.0	10.0	12	16.5	18.6	9.5	0.02
3	40	5.0	11.9	14	5.0	9.3	0.0	
4	49	2.2	13.4	12	5.6	11.0	3.4	
5	26	17.5	13.1	9	17.4	17.8	− 0.1	
6	45	10.7	10.0	11	10.0	6.5	− 0.7	

[a] Error term for all tests of significance is mean square within treatments in classrooms.

significantly more interesting, more happy, better adjusted, and more affectionate.

From these results and from the similar results based on total-IQ gains it would seem that when children who are expected to grow intellectually do so, they are considerably benefited in other ways as well. When children who are not especially expected to develop intellectually do so, they seem either to show accompanying undesirable behavior, or at least are perceived by their teachers as showing such undesirable behavior. If a child is to show intellectual gains it seems to be better for his real or perceived intellectual vitality and for his real or perceived mental health if his teacher has been expecting him to gain intellectually. It appears that there may be hazards to unpredicted intellectual growth.

THE SIX GRADES.   So far we have examined the effects of teachers' expectations only for the school as a whole. Table 6.5 shows the mean gains in total-IQ points from the pretest to the final posttest among experimental- and control-group children for each of the six grades. As we go from the higher grades to the lower grades we find the effects of teacher expectations increasing almost monotonically ($rho = 0.94$, $p = 0.02$) and only in the first and second grades do we find the total IQ changes to be affected to a statistically significant degree. In one of the three classrooms comprising the first grade, the control-group children gained an average of 16.2 IQ points, whereas the experimentals gained an average of 41.0 points, a difference of nearly 25 points ($p < 0.006$). The largest effect of teachers' expectations to occur in the second grade was in a classroom which found the control-group children gaining 4.3 IQ points while the experimental-group children gained 22.5 points, a difference of over 18 points ($p < 0.002$).

Another useful way to show the effects of teachers' expectations on their pupils' total-IQ gains is to show the percentage of experimental and control-group children who achieve various amounts of gain. In Table 6.6 such percentages are shown for the first and second grades only. Less than half the control-group children gained 10 or more total IQ points, but about four out of five experimental-group children did. Every fifth control-group child gained 20 or more total-IQ points, but nearly every second experimental-group child did. While only one out of twenty control-group children gained thirty or more total-IQ points, one out of five experimental-group children did.

Earlier it was noted that for the school as a whole the effects of teachers' expectations on children's gains in reasoning IQ were greater than they were on children's gains in verbal IQ. The results for grades and for classrooms were consistent with the over-all finding. On the whole, verbal IQ was not much affected by teachers' expectations. In only twelve of the eighteen classrooms was there a greater gain in verbal IQ among children from whom intellectual gains were expected ($p = 0.12$) and the bulk of the verbal-IQ gain favoring the experimental-group children occurred in the first two grades.

It was in the gains in reasoning IQ that the effect of teachers' expectations showed itself more clearly. Of the seventeen classrooms in which the posttest reasoning-IQ tests had been administered (one class was inadvertently not retested for reasoning IQ) fifteen showed greater gains among the children from whom intellectual growth had been expected ($p < 0.001$). Although the advantage in terms of gain in reasoning IQ of having been predicted to "spurt" was significant statistically only in the second grade, the absolute magnitude of advantage was not trivial

TABLE 6.6

Percentages of First- and Second-Grade Children Gaining

10 or more, 20 or more, 30 or more, Total IQ Points

IQ *Gain* at *Least:*	*Control* N = 95	*Experimental* N = 19	*p of* *difference*
10 points[a]	49	79	0.02
20 points[b]	19	47	0.01
30 points	5	21	0.04

[a] Includes children gaining 20 and 30 points or more.
[b] Includes children gaining 30 points or more.

TABLE 6.7

Differences in Mean Ratings by Teachers of Children in

Experimental and Control Groups in Six Grade Levels

	Grade Level					
Characteristics	1	2	3	4	5	6
Future success	$+2.4^d$	$+1.7^c$	-0.0	$+0.4$	$+0.6$	$+1.2^a$
Interesting	$+3.0^e$	$+0.9$	$+0.2$	$+0.3$	$+0.1$	$+1.8^c$
Curious	$+2.4^c$	$+1.1^a$	-0.5	$+0.7$	-0.8	$+1.9^c$
Happy	$+1.6^a$	$+1.0$	-0.5	$+0.1$	$+0.5$	$+1.1$
Appealing	$+1.6^a$	$+0.7$	-1.3^b	-0.1	-0.2	$+2.2^d$
Adjusted	$+2.2^b$	$+0.9$	-0.7	-0.2	$+0.3$	$+0.7$
Affectionate	$+1.1$	-0.1	-0.7	$+0.8$	-0.4	$+1.2^a$
Hostile	$+0.4$	-0.2	$+1.3^a$	-0.1	-0.4	-0.4
Needs approval	-2.2^b	-1.0	-0.1	$+0.6$	-0.4	$+0.3$

$^a p < .10.$
$^b p < .05.$
$^c p < .01.$
$^d p < .005.$
$^e p < .0005.$

in any of the first five grades. In fourteen of the seventeen classrooms in which the comparison was possible, the excess of reasoning-IQ gain of the experimental- compared to the control-group children was greater than the excess of verbal-IQ gain ($p = 0.006$).

For each of the six grade levels, the mean rating made by teachers of the control-group children's classroom behavior was subtracted from the mean rating assigned the children of the experimental group. Table 6.7 shows the mean differences in ratings for each of the six grades and their statistical significance. It was in the first-grade classrooms that teachers saw the greatest differences in the classroom behavior of the experimental- and control-group children. Children who had been expected to show greater intellectual growth (and these were the children who *had* shown the greater intellectual growth) were seen as significantly more likely to succeed, more interesting, curious, happy, appealing, and better adjusted than were the children from whom no intellectual growth had been expected. First-graders were also seen as significantly lower in the need for social approval when intellectual growth had been predicted for them.

Among the children of the second grade, those who had been singled out for growth were judged more intellectually curious and more likely to succeed than the rest of the children.

Among the children of the third grade, those who had been predicted so show greater intellectual growth were perceived as less appealing and as more hostile than the rest of the children. It was in the third grade, too, that the children of the experimental group tended to show less gain in verbal IQ than did the control children.

In the fourth and fifth grades, the children of the experimental group were not judged to differ in their classroom behavior from the children of the control group. However, in the sixth grade, children who were expected to show intellectual gain were seen in much the same way as the experimental-group children in the first grade were seen, except that they did not differ from the control children in their need for social approval. It was surprising to find the sixth-graders of the experimental group as well-differentiated in their teachers' eyes from the control children as in the first grade, when in the sixth grade, unlike the first grade, there seemed to be no effect of teachers' expectations on their pupils' intellectual growth.

Within each grade separately, the correlations were computed between the gain in verbal, reasoning, and total IQ and the teachers' ratings of the children of the experimental and control groups. Since these computations resulted in 324 correlations, the tables are not shown, but the significant trends will be summarized. In the first grade none of the teachers' ratings of the control children were correlated with their gain in verbal IQ. Among the children of the experimental group, however, those first-graders who showed greater gains in verbal IQ were rated as less interesting ($r = -0.93$, $p < 0.005$), less curious ($r = -0.89$, $p < 0.01$), and less affectionate ($r = -0.90$, $p < 0.01$) than the children who gained less in verbal IQ.

Still considering only the first-grade level, there was no relationship between the amount of gain in reasoning IQ and teachers' ratings of the children of the experimental group. Among the control-group children, however, those who showed a greater gain in reasoning IQ were rated as less interesting ($r = -0.32$, $p < 0.05$), less curious ($r = -0.38$, $p < 0.01$), and less affectionate ($r = -0.43$, $p < 0.005$) than the children who gained less in reasoning IQ.

At least among first-graders, those who are expected to show intellectual growth are rated relatively more favorably when the gains they do show are in reasoning rather than in verbal intellectual performance. First-graders from whom no particular intellectual growth is expected, on the other hand, are regarded relatively more favorably by their teachers when the growth that occurs is found more in the verbal than in the reasoning areas of intellectual functioning. No such clear-cut patterns of correlations were found in the higher grades between amount of gain in verbal or reasoning IQ and teachers' ratings.

THE THREE TRACKS.   Within each of the six grades of the elementary school there were three classrooms arranged such that one was on a "fast" track, one on a "medium" track, and one on a "slow" track. (The mean pretest total IQ of the fast-track children was about 23 IQ points higher than the mean-pretest total IQ of the slow-track children.) After eight months, gains in IQ favored the experimental-group children in all tracks, with none of the tracks showing a significantly greater effect of the teachers' expectations than the other tracks except that for total IQ, verbal IQ, and for reasoning IQ, it was the children of the medium track who showed the greatest effect numerically of their teachers' expectations. That was a surprising finding, for it had seemed most likely that the slowest-track children would have shown the greatest advantage attributable to a change in their teachers' expectations. It was they who had the furthest to go, and, in general, it is the children thought to be "slowest" academically who have been most often discussed by educational theorists as most affected by the teachers' expectations. The finding that it was the educationally most-average children who gained the most intellectually when their teachers expected such gains, does not, of course, show that the "slower" children had not been affected in the past by negative expectations in the course of their having been labeled "slow."

For each of the three tracks, the mean rating made by teachers of the control-group children's classroom behavior was subtracted from the mean rating assigned the children of the experimental group. Table 6.8 shows the mean differences for each of the three tracks and the statistical significance of these mean differences. In the fast track those children who had been expected to show intellectual gains were judged as more likely to succeed in the future and as more interesting. In the medium-track group those children who had been expected to show intellectual gains were judged as more likely to succeed, as more interesting, more curious, more appealing, better adjusted and lower in the need for social approval. In the slow-track group, those children who had been expected to show intellectual gains were not judged to differ in their classroom behavior from those children for whom no intellectual gains had been expected.

Within each of the three tracks, the correlations were computed between the gain in verbal, reasoning, and total IQ and the teachers' ratings of the children of the experimental and control groups. The resulting correlations, 162 of them, are too many to present here, but some of the significant trends can be described. We shall consider first the correlations between teachers' ratings and gains in verbal IQ over the eight-month period of the experiment.

Among the children of the experimental group, those who gained more in verbal IQ were judged as significantly more likely to succeed,

TABLE 6.8

Differences in Mean Ratings by Teachers of Children in
Experimental and Control Groups in Three Tracks

| | | *Tracks* | |
Characteristics	Fast	Medium	Slow
Future success	+0.8[a]	+1.7[d]	+0.3
Interesting	+1.0[b]	+1.5[c]	+0.4
Curious	+0.4	+1.6[d]	+0.4
Happy	+0.6	+0.8	+0.2
Appealing	+0.1	+1.1[a]	+0.2
Adjusted	−0.0	+1.0[a]	+0.3
Affectionate	+0.3	+0.5	+0.2
Hostile	+0.5	−0.6	+0.3
Needs approval	+0.2	−1.4[b]	−0.2

[a] $p < .10$.
[b] $p < .05$.
[c] $p < .01$.
[d] $p < .005$.

but only if they were in the fast or medium tracks (combined $r = +0.30$, $p = 0.05$) and not if they were in the slow track ($r = +0.03$). This was the case despite the fact that the slow-track children showed as great an average gain in verbal IQ, as did the children of the fast track. There is, of course, no way to decide whether this finding was due to the slow-track children's acting less "successful" in class in spite of their intellectual growth, or whether it becomes difficult for a teacher even to see the "blooming" slow-track children as potentially successful intellectually.

Among the children of the medium track, those who gained more in verbal IQ were judged to be more appealing by their teachers, but only if they were the children who had been expected to show intellectual gains ($r = +0.48$, $p < 0.05$). The greater the gain in verbal IQ of children from whom no such growth had been expected the less appealing they tended to be judged by their teachers ($r = −0.18$, *NS, p* of difference < 0.01).

Among the children of the experimental group, those who showed greater gains in reasoning IQ were judged as more interesting by their teachers, but only if they were in the fast or medium tracks (combined $r = +0.30$, $p = 0.06$), and not if they were in the slow track ($r = −0.05$), although the slow-track children had shown as great a gain in reasoning IQ as had the children of the fast track. Again, there is no way to decide whether the children of the slow track who gained more in reasoning IQ were actually relatively less interesting in their classroom behavior, or whether it is relatively more difficult to view a child known to be "slow-track" as more interesting when he has gained in intellectual abilities, particularly when these gains may not have been reflected in his verbal behavior.

Among the children of the control group those who showed greater gains in reasoning IQ were seen as less happy ($r = -0.29$, $p < 0.01$), less appealing ($r = -0.19$, $p < 0.10$), less well-adjusted ($r = -0.20$, $p < 0.10$), and less affectionate ($r = -0.28$, $p = 0.02$) if they were in the slow track. In addition, these slow-track children were seen as less intellectually curious ($r = -0.21$, $p = 0.07$) and as less interesting ($r = -0.32$, $p < 0.01$) when they showed greater gains in reasoning IQ. Earlier, when the discussion was of results for the school as a whole, it was suggested that there may be hazards to unpredicted, unexpected intellectual growth. The data just presented suggest that this appears to be true primarily for those children placed in a slow track; none of the correlations between gains in reasoning IQ and teachers' judgments approached significance for the children of the fast or medium tracks. Again, it should be pointed out that we cannot say whether the teachers' ratings reflected the children's classroom behavior as an external paradigm observer might perceive it, or whether the teachers' ratings reflected only a more idiosyncratic halo effect. In either case the finding may have some importance because it seems relevant to a child's course in school not only how he behaves "really," but also how his behavior is viewed by his teacher.

Among the children of the experimental group, those who showed greater gains in total IQ were judged as more interesting if they were in the fast or medium tracks (combined $r = +0.38$, $p < 0.02$) but not if they were in the slow track ($r = -0.21$, NS). Similarly those children of the fast and medium tracks who gained more in total IQ were judged as more appealing ($r = +0.33$, $p < 0.05$), better adjusted ($r = +0.37$, $p < 0.02$), and more affectionate ($r = +0.30$, $p < 0.07$); whereas among children of the slow track, those who gained more in total IQ were not seen as more appealing ($r = -0.05$), or as better adjusted ($r = +0.02$), and were seen actually as *less* affectionate ($r = -0.47$, $p = 0.04$) and as lower in the need for social approval ($r = -0.59$, $p < 0.01$).

Reliabilities and Initial-IQ Values

To help in the interpretation of the results of this experiment, it was necessary to know the retest reliabilities of the verbal, reasoning, and total-IQ scores from the pretest to the posttest, one year later. These reliabilities were computed separately for the experimental and control groups, for each grade level, for each track, and for the entire school. Table 6.9 shows these reliabilities. The over-all mean reliability of the verbal and total IQs was $+0.75$, while the over-all reliability of the reasoning IQ was $+0.49$. The average reliability of the IQ scores was not different among the experimental and the control groups, suggesting that among the children of the experimental group, where intellectual gains did occur, the gains did not disturb the ranking of the children within their own experimental condition.

In spite of random allocation of pupils to the experimental condition, the children of the experimental group scored slightly higher in pretest IQ than did the children of the control group. This fact suggested that those children who were brighter to begin with might have been the ones who would in any case have shown the greater gains in intellectual performance. To check this hypothesis, the correlations were computed between children's initial pretest IQ scores and the magnitude of their gains in IQ after eight months. If those who were brighter to begin with showed greater gains in IQ the correlations would be positive. Table 6.10 shows that such was not the case. In general, the over-all correlations were negative: for total IQ, $r = -0.23$, ($p < 0.001$); for verbal IQ, $r = -0.04$, (NS); and for reasoning IQ, $r = -0.48$, ($p < 0.001$). Although for the school as a whole the correlations between

TABLE 6.9

Retest Reliabilities after One Year

Grades	Verbal IQ		Reasoning IQ		Total IQ	
	Control	Experimental	Control	Experimental	Control	Experimental
1	+0.74	+0.77	+0.46	+0.26	+0.59	+0.75
2	0.71	0.83	0.58	0.62	0.79	0.82
3	0.68	0.60	0.41	0.67	0.70	0.72
4	0.83	0.77	0.63	0.73	0.80	0.90
5	0.78	0.81	0.46	0.31	0.79	0.75
6	0.89	0.88	0.74	0.87	0.88	0.97
Tracks						
Fast	0.67	0.71	0.46	0.51	0.66	0.73
Medium	0.77	0.87	0.36	0.24	0.58	0.80
Slow	0.72	0.49	0.25	0.37	0.61	0.25
Total	0.75	0.76	0.50	0.47	0.74	0.78
N	269	68	255	65	255	65

TABLE 6.10

Intellectual Performance Gain as a Function

of Initial IQ

	Verbal IQ		Reasoning IQ		Total IQ	
Grades	Control	Experi-mental	Control	Experi-mental	Control	Experi-mental
1	-0.36^a	-0.78^a	-0.80^c	-0.93^b	-0.65^c	-0.73^a
2	-0.37^b	$+0.52^a$	-0.28^a	$+0.17$	-0.37^b	$+0.39$
3	$+0.26^a$	-0.41	-0.37^a	-0.08	-0.07	-0.09
4	-0.19	$+0.17$	$+0.04$	-0.18	-0.14	-0.01
5	-0.01	$+0.03$	-0.40^a	-0.18	-0.02	$+0.07$
6	$+0.11$	$+0.34$	$+0.01$	$+0.35$	$+0.05$	$+0.49$
Tracks						
Fast	-0.01	$+0.09$	-0.29^b	-0.10	-0.29^b	$+0.05$
Medium	-0.27^a	$+0.46^a$	-0.77^c	-0.62^a	-0.57^c	$+0.11$
Slow	-0.39^c	-0.70^c	-0.74^c	-0.06	-0.48^c	-0.76^c
Total	-0.08	$+0.04$	-0.54^c	-0.28^a	-0.30^c	-0.05
N	269	68	255	65	255	65

[a] $p < .10$, two tail
[b] $p < .01$, two tail
[c] $p < .001$, two tail

initial IQ and gain in IQ were somewhat less negative among the children of the experimental group than among the children of the control group, this seemed to be no simple effect. Instead there appeared to be an interaction effect of the experimental group's difference from the control group as a function of the type of IQ considered and the track position of the children. Thus among the children of the medium track, those who started at a higher pretest level of verbal IQ gained less in verbal IQ if they were in the control group, but gained more in verbal IQ if they were in the experimental group. No such difference was observed in the children of the medium track when the pretest level and gains in reasoning IQ were considered. Among the children of the slow track, those who started at a higher pretest level of verbal IQ gained relatively less in verbal IQ if they were in the experimental rather than the control group. In this same track, there was no relationship for the children of the experimental group between their pretest level of reasoning IQ and their subsequent gain in reasoning IQ, whereas for the children of the control group, the relationship was very large and negative ($r = -0.74$). More detailed examination of Table 6.10 shows only more such hard-to-explain interactions when individual grade levels are considered. To summarize, there appears to be no way in which the relatively greater gains of the experimental children can be accounted for on the basis of the correlations between initial level of IQ and magnitude of gain in IQ.

The Question of Mediation

How did the teachers' expectations come to serve as determinants of gains in intellectual performance? The most plausible hypothesis seemed to be that the children for whom unusual intellectual growth had been predicted would be more attended to by their teachers. If teachers were more attentive to the children earmarked for growth, we might expect that teachers might be robbing Peter to see Paul grow. With a finite amount of time to spend with each child, if a teacher gave more time to the children of the experimental group, she would have less time to spend with the children of the control group. If the teacher's spending more time with a child led to greater gains, we could test the "robbing-Peter" hypothesis by comparing the gains made by children of the experimental group with gains made by children of the control group in each class. The "robbing-Peter" hypothesis predicts a negative correlation. The greater the gains made by the children of the experimental group (with the implication of more time spent on them) the less should be the gains made by the children of the control group (with the implication of less time spent on them). In fact, however, the correlation was positive, large, and statistically significant ($rho = +0.57$, $p = 0.02$, two tail). The greater the gain made by the children of whom gain was expected, the greater the gain made in the same classroom by the children from whom no special gain was expected. The evidence presented that teachers did not take time from control-group children to spend with the experimental-group children is indirect. More direct evidence was available.

Some ten months after the posttest had been administered, each of the teachers was asked to estimate how much time, relatively, she had devoted to each of four children. All four of these children had been in her classroom the preceding academic year; two had been in the control group and two had been in the experimental group. There was one boy and one girl in each of these two subgroups. The boys of each group were matched on their pretest IQ, as were the girls. The mean difference in IQ was less than one-half point in favor of the children of the experimental group ($t < 0.71$). The specific question asked of the teacher was: Given a unit of time available to spend on these four children (100 percent), how much of that unit was spent with each child? For each matched pair of boys and girls the percentage of time allocated

TABLE 6.11

Differences in Time Spent with Children of the

Experimental and Control Groups

	Mean Difference	*Median Difference*	*N of Pairs*[a]
	%	%	
All children	−2.6	0.0	31
Boys	+0.3	+5.0	15
Girls	−5.3	0.0	16
Fast track	−2.4	0.0	12
Medium track	−5.0	0.0	8
Slow track	−1.1	0.0	11
Grade 1	+5.0	0.0	6
Grade 2	−8.8	0.0	5
Grade 3	+10.0	+10.0	4
Grade 4	−3.3	0.0	6
Grade 5	−2.5	−2.5	4
Grade 6	−12.8	0.0	6

[a] No data were available from the two teachers who had left the school.

to the control-group child was subtracted from the percentage of time allocated to the experimental-group child. A positive difference score, then, meant that the experimental-group child was given more time by the teacher according to her own assessment. Table 6.11 shows the mean and median difference scores for the entire school, for boys and girls, for each of the three tracks, and for each of the six grades. None of the obtained mean differences was significantly different from zero. In fact, there was a slight tendency for the children of the experimental group to be given less time than the children of the control group ($t < 0.66$).

That the children of the experimental group were not favored with a greater investment of time seems less surprising in view of the pattern of their greater intellectual gains. If, for example, teachers had talked to them more we might have expected greater gains in verbal IQ but, we recall, the greater gains were found not in verbal but in reasoning IQ. It may be, of course, that the teachers were inaccurate in their estimates of time spent with each of the four children. Possibly direct observation of the teacher-pupil interactions would have given different results, but that method was not possible in the present study. Even direct observation by judges who could agree with one another might not have revealed a difference in the amounts of teacher time invested in each of the two groups of children. It seems plausible to think that it was not a difference in amount of time spent with the children of the two groups which led to the difference in their rates of intellectual development. It may have been more a matter of the type of interaction which took place between the teachers and their pupils which served as the determinant of the expected intellectual development.

By what she said, by how she said it, by her facial expressions, postures, and perhaps, by her touch, the teacher may have communicated to the children of the experimental group that she expected improved intellectual performance. Such communications together with possible changes in teaching techniques may have helped the child learn by changing his self-concept, his expectations of his own behavior, his motivation, as well as his cognitive skills. It is self-evident that further research is needed to narrow the range of possible mechanisms whereby a teacher's expectations become translated into a pupil's intellectual growth. It would be valuable, for example, to have sound films of teachers interacting with their pupils. We might then look for differences in the way teachers interact with those children from whom they expect intellectual growth compared to those from whom they expect less. On the basis of films of psychological experimenters interacting with subjects from whom different responses are expected, we know that even in such highly standardized situations unintentional communications can be incredibly subtle and complex (Rosenthal, 1966). How much more subtle and complex may be the communications between children and their teachers who are not constrained by the demands of the experimental laboratory.

Before leaving the topic of the mediation of the teacher's expectation, we must raise the question of whether these effects of her expectation were gradual and cumulative over the course of the year, or whether they acted primarily on the children's test-taking behavior. Because that is the way standardized tests are administered in schools, we had the teachers themselves administer the posttests to their classes in a group administration. This posttest was administered some eight months after the teacher had been given the names of the "special" children. Perhaps during the posttest she treated these children differently from the way she treated the other children. A number of considerations weaken the plausibility of this interpretation. First, while from our point of view the retest was a posttest from which to measure differential gains in IQ, from the teachers' point of view the retest was more like a pretest from which we would again, as we had the year before, make predictions as to which children would in the future show spurts of intellectual growth. Second, postexperimental interviews with the teachers one year later suggested that they could neither accurately recall the names of the children destined for intellectual growth, nor even select their names out of a larger list of children which included the names of an equal number of experimental and control children. The worst recall occurred among teachers of the second-grade children. Of the twelve children originally alleged to be potential spurters who remained in the school for the entire year of the experiment, not a single one was recalled as a potential spurter by any second-grade teacher. Yet, it will be recalled, effects of teachers' expectations were prominent in the second grade. It was of special interest, too, to learn that most of the teachers had merely "glanced at the names" of the "special" children when these were first given them and then "forgot about them." If the ordinary laws of forgetting apply, this suggests that whatever mediated the effects of teachers' expectations operated early in the academic year.

A third consideration weakening the plausibility of the hypothesis of differential treatment of children during the retest has to do with the nature of the test itself. The verbal subtest is administered by the teacher while the reasoning subtest is self-administered. During the administration of the verbal subtest the teacher contacts children individually to see whether they are following the instructions properly. During the administration of the reasoning subtest the teacher does not contact children individually. We would expect, therefore, that differential treatment of the children might occur during the administration of the verbal, but not the reasoning, subtest. Yet it was on the reasoning subtest that we found the major effect of the teachers' expectations to occur.

Though it seemed unlikely that differential treatment of the experimental-group children during retesting could account for our results we wanted to know whether someone who did not know the children's experimental- or control-group membership would obtain similar post-test results. Therefore, three classrooms were retested by a school administrator not attached to the particular school. She did not know which of the children were in the experimental group, and the results of her retesting were no different from the results of the classroom teachers' retesting. In fact, there was a tendency for the results of her retesting to show even greater effects of teachers' expectations.

SOME IMPLICATIONS

The results of the experiment just now described provide further evidence that one person's expectations of another's behavior may serve as a self-fulfilling prophecy. When teachers expected that certain children would show greater intellectual development, those children did show greater intellectual development. The effect was in evidence, however, primarily at the lower-grade levels, and it is difficult to be certain why that was the case. A number of interpretations suggest themselves, and these are not mutually exclusive.

First, younger children are generally regarded as more malleable, less fixed, more capable of change. It may be, then, that the experimental conditions of this experiment were more effective with younger children simply because younger children are easier to change than older ones. (It should be recalled that when we speak here of change we mean it as change relative to control-group change. Table 6.5 shows that even fifth-graders can change dramatically in IQ, but there the change of the experimental-group children is not greater than the change of the control-group children.)

A second interpretation is that younger children within a given school have less well-established reputations within the school. It then becomes more credible to a teacher to be told that a younger child will show intellectual growth. A teacher may "know" an older child much better by reputation and be less inclined to believe him capable of intellectual growth simply on someone else's say-so.

A third interpretation is a combination, in a sense, of the first two. It suggests that younger children show greater gains associated with teachers' expectancies not because they necessarily *are* more malleable but rather because they are believed by teachers to be more malleable.

A fourth interpretation suggests that younger children are more sensitive to, and more affected by, the particular processes whereby teachers communicate their expectations to children. Within this interpretation, it is possible that teachers react to children of all grade levels in the same way if they believe them to be capable of intellectual gain. But perhaps it is only the younger children whose performance is affected by the special things the teacher says to them, the special ways in which she says them, the way she looks, postures, and touches the children from whom she expects greater intellectual growth.

A fifth interpretation suggests that the effects of teachers' expectations were more effective in the lower-grade levels not because of any difference associated with the children's age but rather with some correlated sampling errors. Thus it is possible that the children of the lower grades are the children of families which differ systematically from the families of the children of the higher-grade levels.

A sixth interpretation also suggests that the greater IQ gain in younger children attributable to teacher expectation is a result of sampling error, not in the sampling of children this time but in the sampling of teachers. It may be that in a variety of demographic, intellectual, and personality variables the teachers of the younger children differed from the teachers of the older children such that they may have (1) believed the communications about their "special" children more, or (2) been more effective communicators to their children of their expectations for the children's performance.

Those children from whom greater intellectual gains were expected showed advantages over their classmates other than greater gain in intellectual performance. They were also judged by their teachers to be more likely to succeed, to be more intellectually alive and to be more superior in their socioemotional functioning and mental health. These effects on teachers' perceptions of the children might have been reflective of either actual behavior differences in the children or of the operation of a halo effect. Even if these ratings reflected only halo effects, however, they may not be trivial in implications. Halo effects may determine not only teachers' perceptions of children but, as the results of this experiment suggest, the subsequent behavior of children as well.

The more the children who were expected to gain intellectually did so, the more favorably they were evaluated by their teachers. Not so, however, for the children who were not expected to show any particular growth in intellectual functioning. The trend, in fact, was for these children to be regarded less favorably the more they gained intellectually. That finding suggests the hypothesis that there may be hazards to unexpected intellectual growth. Classroom teachers may not be prepared to assimilate the unexpected classroom behavior of the intellectually upwardly mobile child.

If the hypothesis were tenable that there are hazards to unexpected intellectual development, we would expect to find that among the children of the slow track there is the greatest negative relationship between intellectual growth and favorable evaluation by the classroom teacher. It is from the slow-track children, almost by definition, that the least intellectual gain is expected. The results of this experiment support the tenability of the hypothesis. It was among the slow-track children of the control group from whom no particular intellectual growth had been expected by virtue of both their experimental condition and their slow-track status that the effects of intellectual gains were most adverse in terms of teachers' perceptions of their behavior. Even within the experimental group, the children of the slow track did not show the advantages of more favorable perceptions by their teachers which had been shown by those children of the fast and medium track from whom intellectual growth had been expected. This result was obtained despite the fact that the experimental-group children of the slow track showed as great a gain in IQ relative to the control-group children as did the experimental-group children of the fast track.

The substantive implications of the evidence presented in this chapter have been primarily short-range implications. There is also a longer-range implication which suggests that as teacher-training institutions acquaint teachers-to-be with the possibility that their expectations of their pupils' performance may serve as self-fulfilling prophecies, these teacher-trainees may be given a new expectancy—that children can learn more than they had believed possible (as Bruner (1960) has suggested, though for different reasons).

In addition to the substantive implications discussed up to now, there are methodological implications of the evidence presented in this chapter. These are best introduced by citing the results of a "total-push" educational program, which after three years led to a 10-point IQ gain by 38 percent of the children and a 20-point IQ gain by 12 percent of the children (Clark, 1963). Table 6.6 of the present chapter shows that such gains were smaller than the gains found among the first- and second-grade children of our control group and very much smaller than the gains found among the children of our experimental group.

It is not possible to be sure about the matter but it may be that the large gains shown by the children of our control group were attributable to a Hawthorne effect. The fact that university researchers, supported by federal funds, were interested in the school in which the research was conducted may have led to a general improvement of morale and teaching technique on the part of all the teachers. Such improvements may have led to the substantial gains in IQ shown by the children of the control group. (In part, of course, such gains may simply have reflected a practice effect in the taking of the specific IQ test or even a tendency for teachers to "teach the test" though the nature of the test makes that unlikely.) In any case, the possibility of a Hawthorne effect cannot be ruled out either in the present experiment or in other studies of educational practices. Any educational practice which is assessed for effectiveness must be able to show some excess of gain over what Hawthorne effects alone would yield. Some investigators have been well aware of this problem (Bruner, 1965) but others seem not to have been.

When the efficacy of an educational practice is investigated we want to know its efficacy relative to the Hawthorne effect of "something new and important" but the present chapter suggests that another baseline must be introduced. We will want to know, too, whether the efficacy of an educational practice is greater than that of the easily and inexpensively manipulatable expectation of the teacher. Most educational practices are more expensive in time and money than giving teachers names of children "who will show unusual intellectual development."

When educational innovations are introduced into ongoing educational systems, it seems very likely that the administrators whose permission is required and the teachers whose cooperation is required will expect the innovation to be effective. If they did not, they would be unlikely to give the required permission and cooperation. The experimental innovation, then, will likely be confounded with favorable expectations regarding their efficacy.

When educational innovations are introduced into newly created educational systems with specially selected and specially trained teachers and administrators, the problems are similar. Those teachers and those administrators who elect to go, and are selected to go, into newly created educational systems are likely to have expectations favorable to the efficacy of the new program. In this situation, as in that in which changes are introduced into preexisting systems, teachers' and administrators' expectations are likely to be confounded with the educational innovations. All this argues for the systematic employment of the "Expectancy-Control Group" (Rosenthal, 1966).

In expectancy-control designs applied to a simple experiment in educational innovation in which only an experimental and control group are employed, the experiment is subdivided into a total of four conditions, two of them involving the experimental treatment and two of them involving the control "treatment." In one experimental treatment subcondition, teachers are given reason to believe that the experimental innovation will be successful. In the other experimental subcondition teachers are led to believe that the treatment is "only a control condition." In one of the control group subconditions, teachers are led to believe that their condition is "only a control condition" which, in fact, it is. In the other control-group subcondition, teachers are given reason to believe that the "treatment" is actually an experimental innovation which should give good results.

The data from such an expectancy-controlled experiment can be analyzed by a simple two-way analysis of variance. Such an analysis permits us to make inferences about the magnitudes of the effects of the educational innovation, the teachers' expectations, and the interaction between these two sources of variance. There may be experiments in which the magnitude of the effects of the innovation will be large relative to the effects of the teachers' expectations. But there may also be experiments in which the effects of teachers' expectations turn out to be more important sources of variation than the educational innovation under investigation. Without the use of expectancy-control groups, however, it is impossible to tell whether the results of experiments in educational practices are due to the practices themselves or to the correlated expectations of the teachers who are to try out the educational reforms.

Perhaps the most suitable summary of the hypothesis discussed in this chapter and tested by the described experiment has already been written. The writer is G. B. Shaw, the play is *Pygmalion,* and the speaker is Eliza Doolittle:

> You see, really and truly, apart from the things anyone can pick up (the dressing and the proper way of speaking, and so on), the difference between a lady and a flower girl is not how she behaves, but how she's treated. I shall always be a flower girl to Professor Higgins, because he

always treats me as a flower girl, and always will; but I know I can be a lady to you, because you always treat me as a lady, and always will.

References

Allport, G. W. "The role of expectancy." In H. Cantril (ed.), *Tensions that cause wars.* Urbana, Ill.: University of Illinois, 1950, 43–78.

Asbell, B. Not like other children. *Redbook,* October, 1963.

Becker, H. S. Social class variations in the teacher-pupil relationship. *Journal of Educational Sociology,* 1952, **25,** 451–465.

Bruner, J. S. *The process of education.* Cambridge, Mass.: Harvard University Press, 1960.

———. The growth of mind. *American Psychologist,* 1965, **20,** 1007–1017.

Clark, K. B. "Educational stimulation of racially disadvantaged children." In A. H. Passow (ed.), *Education in depressed areas.* New York: Teachers College, Columbia University, 1963, 142–162.

Flanagan, J. C. *Tests of general ability: Technical report.* Chicago: Science Research Associates, 1960.

Flowers, C. E. Effects of an arbitrary accelerated group placement on the tested academic achievement of educationally disadvantaged students. Unpublished doctoral dissertation, Teachers College, Columbia University, 1966.

Gibson, G. Aptitude tests. *Science,* 1965, **149,** 583.

Gruenberg, B. C. *The story of evolution.* Princeton, N. J.: Van Nostrand, 1929.

Harlem Youth Opportunities Unlimited, Inc. *Youth in the ghetto.* New York: HARYOU, 1964.

Hurwitz, Susan, and Virginia Jenkins. Effects of experimenter expectancy on performance of simple learning tasks. Unpublished paper, Harvard University, 1966.

Jastrow, J. *Fact and fable in psychology.* Boston: Houghton Mifflin, 1900.

Katz, I. Review of evidence relating to effects of desegregation on the intellectual performance of Negroes. *American Psychologist,* 1964, **19,** 381–399.

Kvaraceus, W. C. Disadvantaged children and youth: Programs of promise or pretense? *Proceedings of the 17th annual state conference on educational research.* California Advisory Council on Educational Research, Burlingame: California Teachers' Association, 1965.

MacKinnon, D. W. The nature and nurture of creative talent. *American Psychologist,* 1962, **17,** 484–495.

Marwit, S., and J. Marcia. Tester-bias and response to projective instruments. Unpublished paper, State University of New York at Buffalo, 1966.

Masling, J. Differential indoctrination of examiners and Rorschach responses. *Journal of Consulting Psychology,* 1965, **29,** 198–201.

Merton, R. K. The self-fulfilling prophecy. *Antioch Review,* 1948, **8,** 193–210.

Moll, A. *Hypnotism.* Ed. 4. New York: Scribner's, 1898.

Orne, M. T. The nature of hypnosis: Artifact and essence. *Journal of Abnormal and Social Psychology,* 1959, **58,** 277–299.

———. On the social psychology of the psychological experiment: With particular reference to demand characteristics and their implications. *American Psychologist,* 1962, **17,** 776–783.

Pfungst, O. *Clever Hans (the horse of Mr. von Osten): A contribution to experimental, animal, and human psychology.* Translated by C. L. Rahn. New York: Holt, Rinehart and Winston, 1911.

Rice, S. A. Contagious bias in the interview: A methodological note. *American Journal of Sociology,* 1929, **35,** 420–423.

Riessman, F. *The culturally deprived child.* New York: Harper & Row, 1962.

————. Teachers of the poor: A five point plan. *Proceedings of the 17th annual state conference on educational research.* California Advisory Council on Educational Research. Burlingame: California Teachers' Association, 1965.

Rose, A. *The Negro in America.* Boston: Beacon Press, 1956.

Rosenthal, R. "The effect of the experimenter on the results of psychological research." In B. A. Maher (ed.), *Progress in experimental personality research.* New York: Academic Press, 1964, Vol. I, 79–114.

————. "Clever Hans: A case study of scientific method." Introduction to O. Pfungst, *Clever Hans;* New York: Holt, Rinehart and Winston, 1965, ix–xlii.

————. *Experimenter effects in behavioral research.* New York: Appleton-Century-Crofts, 1966.

————, and K. L. Fode. The effect of experimenter bias on the performance of the albino rat. *Behavioral Science,* 1963, **8,** 183–189.

————, and Lenore Jacobson. Teachers' expectancies: Determinants of pupils' IQ gains. *Psychological Reports,* 1966, **19,** 115–118.

————, and R. Lawson. A longitudinal study of the effects of experimenter bias on the operant learning of laboratory rats. *Journal of Psychiatric Research,* 1964, **2,** 61–72.

Sommer, R. Rorschach M responses and intelligence. *Journal of Clinical Psychology,* 1958, **14,** 58–61.

Wartenberg-Ekren, Ursula. The effect of experimenter knowledge of a subject's scholastic standing on the performance of a reasoning task. Unpublished master's thesis, Marquette University, 1962.

Whyte, W. F. *Street corner society.* Chicago: University of Chicago Press, 1943.

Wilson, A. B. "Social stratification and academic achievement." In A. H. Passow (ed.), *Education in depressed areas.* New York: Teachers College, Columbia University, 1963, 217–235.

Wysocki, B. A. Assessment of intelligence level by the Rorschach Test as compared with objective tests. *Journal of Educational Psychology,* 1957, **48,** 113–117.

Addendum

Some time after the preparation of this chapter a number of questions about our school experiment were raised by a helpful reader. These questions seem to be of sufficient general interest that they may be usefully discussed here, though it will be necessary to be brief. One question deals with the small number of first- and second-grade children (nineteen) of the experimental group for whom the gains in total IQ as a function of teacher expectation were large. That is not a serious statistical problem since a wise statistic always knows its own *N.* More importantly, this question should remind us that for the school as a whole, and not only for the lower grades, experimental-group children gained more than control-group children in both total IQ and in reasoning IQ. In verbal IQ, we recall, the "special" children were benefited more than "ordinary children" in only 67 percent of the classrooms ($p = 0.12$), while in reasoning IQ the "special" children benefited more in 88 percent of the classrooms ($p < 0.001$). Just exactly why expectancy advantages occurred for reasoning IQ, but not verbal IQ, is a question for which we have no answer.

Another question deals with the relative statistical unreliability of the intelligence test employed. The reasoning subtest is less reliable than the verbal subtest, which itself is less reliable than an individually-administered test of intelligence. In point of statistical fact, however, the unreliability of the instrument makes the results the more dramatic. The reason is that as test reliability decreases a more robust relationship must exist between the instrument and other variables for these relationships to become significant statistically.

Another question deals with the fact that in several places we report several correlation coefficients that have been chosen for mention because they were "significant" statistically. Such a procedure, though a great space-saver, can lead to difficulties. In an array of correlation coefficients made up of variables that are in fact unrelated to one another, one will by chance find a few significant correlations. In such an array of correlation coefficients, however, the laws of probability lead us to expect half these significant correlations to speak for any given interpretation and half to speak against that interpretation. Whether a given pattern of correlations fits a given interpretation is a matter to be judged first by the investigator, then by the reader. What should be pointed out most explicitly is the fact that *all* rs reaching a $p < 0.10$ were reported, not simply those favoring any given position or interpretation.

The final question deals with the generality and persistence of the expectancy advantages reported. No information was available on these questions at the time the chapter was prepared. Additional data, now being analyzed, will become available and will be reported in due course. A preliminary analysis suggests that gains in reading achievement were significantly greater among children from whom greater intellectual gains were expected. Preliminary data from a one-year follow-up shows very little over-all loss in the IQ advantage of children who had been expected to "bloom" by different teachers the year before.

Since preparing this chapter and its addendum, the authors have had a much fuller report of their research published in *Pygmalion in the classroom: Teacher expectation and pupils' intellectual development*, New York: Holt, Rinehart and Winston, 1968.

CHAPTER SEVEN

Factors Influencing
Negro Performance
in the Desegregated School

IRWIN KATZ[1]

This chapter focuses on the problem of identifying the important motivational determinants of Negro performance in the racially mixed classroom. Only a few studies have dealt directly with this problem, so that much of the evidence to be surveyed is only inferential. Included are the following: reports on the academic progress of Negro children attending integrated schools, evidence on aspects of the minority child's experience of desegregation that presumably affects his motivation to learn, relevant research on the behavioral effects of psychological stress, and, finally, a series of experiments on the intellectual performance and social reactions of Negro youths in biracial settings.

[1] University of Michigan.

This chapter is a revised version of a paper that appeared in the *American Psychologist,* 1964, **19,** 381–399. All the research on Negro performance by the author and his associates that is described was conducted under Contract Nonr 285(24) between the Office of Naval Research and New York University.

NEGRO AMERICANS.   In this paper the term *Negro Americans* refers to a minority segment of the national population that is more or less distinguishable on the basis of skin color, hair texture, and so on, and that occupies a subordinate position in American culture. The extent of subordination varies in different regions and localities, but usually includes some degree of restriction on educational and economic opportunities, as well as social exclusion by whites and an attribution by whites of intellectual inferiority. While the term *race* will be used for convenience, no meaning is intended other than that of distinctiveness of appearance and commonality of experience; the issue of whether there are consequential differences in the genetic endowment of Negroes and whites will not be considered. Thus the present discussion should be more or less applicable to any American minority group whose status is similar to that of Negroes (for example, people with Puerto Rican or Mexican backgrounds).

DESEGREGATION.   Educational desegregation is a politico-legal concept referring to the elimination of racial separation within school systems. As such it embraces a great variety of transitional situations having diverse effects upon the scholastic performance of Negro children. The meaning of desegregation has been broadened in recent years to include the reduction of racial clustering due to factors other than legal discrimination—that is, *de facto* segregation. A number of recent court decisions in the North have ruled that racial imbalance in a school (a preponderance of minority-group children) constitutes *de facto* segregation (The United States Commission on Civil Rights, 1962*a* and 1962*b*). Also described as *de facto* segregation by various social scientists are the racially homogeneous classes often found in schools where children are grouped according to ability (Dodson, 1962; Deutsch, 1963; Tumin, 1963).

   The present concern is mainly with instances of desegregation that are marked by a substantial increase in the proportion of white peers, or both white peers and adult authorities, in the immediate environment of the Negro student. (In the South integration with white classmates is usually also the occasion of initial contacts with white teachers, while in the North the proportion of white teachers may be high even in schools where Negro students predominate.) Almost invariably in this type of desegregation experience the minority-group child is confronted with higher educational standards than prevail in segregated Negro schools (The United States Commission on Civil Rights, 1962*a* and 1962*b*). Both aspects of the Negro's experience—change in the racial environment and exposure to relatively high academic standards—are likely to have important influences on his scholastic motivation.

POSTULATED SITUATIONAL DETERMINANTS OF
NEGRO PERFORMANCE IN DESEGREGATION

SOCIAL THREAT.   Social threat refers to a class of social-stimulus events that tend to elicit anxious expectations that others will inflict harm or pain. One may assume that novel types of contact with white strangers possess a social-threat component for members of a subordinated minority group. The degree of threat should be a direct function of (a) the amount of evidence of white hostility (or the extent to which evidence of white friendliness is lacking), and (b) the amount of power possessed by whites in the contact situation, as shown by their numerical predominance, control of authority positions, and so forth. It seems likely that Negro children would be under some degree of social threat in a newly integrated classroom. Mere indifference on the part of white peers may frustrate their needs for companionship and approval, resulting in lowered self-esteem and the arousal of impulses to escape or aggress. In more extreme instances, verbal harassment and even physical hazing may elicit strong fear responses. These external threats are likely to distract the minority child from the task at hand, to the detriment of performance.

In addition, various psychological theories suggest that the Negro's own covert reactions to social threat would constitute an important source of intellectual impairment. In discussing the effect of psychological stress on the learning of skills, Deese (1962) mentions distraction by the internal stimuli of autonomic activation, as well as disruption of task responses by neuromuscular and other components of the stress reaction. Mandler and Sarason (1952) and others call attention to the disruptive role of task-irrelevant defensive responses against anxiety. Spence (1958) and Taylor (1963) propose that anxiety, conceptualized as drive, increases intratask response competition. And according to Easterbrook (1959), emotion lowers efficiency on complex tasks by narrowing the range of cue utilization. Also relevant is Bovard's (1959) hypothesis of a specific physiological mechanism to account for the apparent lowering of the stress threshold under conditions of social isolation.

Another way in which social threat may impair performance is by causing Negro children to abandon efforts to excel in order not to arouse further resentment and hostility in white competitors. That is, the latter may possess what French and Raven (1960) refer to as "coercive power." When academic success is expected to instigate white reprisals, then any stimulus which arouses the motive to achieve should also generate anxiety, and defensive avoidance of such stimuli should be learned.

This response pattern would not be wholly nonadaptive in a situation where a small number of Negro students stood relatively powerless against a prejudiced white majority—if one assumes that evidence of Negro intellectual competence might have an ego-deflating effect on these white students. The Group for the Advancement of Psychiatry (1957, p. 10) has put the matter this way: ". . . A feeling of superior worth may be gained merely from the existence of a downgraded group. This leads to an unrealistic and unadaptive kind of self-appraisal based on invidious comparison rather than on solid personal growth and achievement. . . ."

Finally with regard to possible social threat emanating from a white teacher—given the prestige of the adult authority, any expression by a white teacher of dislike or devaluation, whether through harsh, indifferent, or patronizing behavior, should tend to have unfavorable effects on Negro performance similar to those just described, and perhaps of even greater intensity.

SOCIAL FACILITATION.   When the minority newcomer in a desegregated school is accepted socially by his white classmates, his scholastic motivation should be influenced favorably. It was noted earlier that achievement standards tend to be higher in previously all-white schools than in Negro schools. From studies based on white subjects it is apparent that individuals are responsive to the standards of those with whom they desire to associate (reviewed by French and Raven, 1960; Bass, 1961; and Thibaut and Kelley, 1959). That Negro children want friendship with white age-mates was shown by Horowitz (1936); Radke *et al.* (1950); and Yarrow (1958). Another study, by Criswell (1939), suggests that Negro children in racially mixed classrooms accept white prestige but increasingly withdraw into their own group as a response to white rejection. Thus, if their desire for acceptance is not inhibited or destroyed by sustained unfriendliness from white children, Negro pupils should tend to adopt the scholastic norms of the high-status majority group. Experimental support for this supposition comes from Dittes and Kelley (1956), who found with white college students that private as well as public adherence to the attitudinal standards of a group were highest among persons who had experienced a fairly high degree of acceptance from the group, with a possibility of gaining even fuller acceptance, while those who received a low degree of acceptance showed little genuine adherence to group norms.

Friendliness and approval on the part of white teachers should be beneficial to Negro motivation by increasing the incentive strength of scholastic success. Assuming that white teachers have more prestige for the minority child than do Negro teachers, the prospect of winning their approval should be more attractive. Hence, when such approval can be expected as a reward for good performance, motivation should be favorably influenced.

PROBABILITY OF SUCCESS.   When the minority child is placed in a school that has substantially higher scholastic standards than he knew previously, he may become discouraged and not try to succeed. This common sense proposition is derivable from Atkinson's (1958*a*) theory of the motivational determinants of risk-taking and performance. For individuals in whom the tendency to approach success is stronger than the tendency to avoid failure, task motivation is assumed to be a joint function of the subjective probability of achieving success and the incentive value of success. From a postulated inverse relationship between the latter two variables (assuming external influences on incentive strength are held constant) he derives an hypothesis that the strength of motivation is at a maximum when the probability of success is 0.50, and diminishes as this probability approaches zero or unity. The hypothesis is supported by findings on arithmetic performance of white college students (Atkinson, 1958*b*), and white elementary school children (Murstein and Collier, 1962), as well as on digit-symbol performance of white high school students (Rosen, 1961). (In these studies, the effect occurred regardless of whether subjects had scored relatively high or low on a projective personality measure of the motive to approach success.) It follows that if the Negro newcomer perceives the standards of excellence in a desegregated school as being substantially higher than those he encountered previously, so that the likelihood of his attaining them seems low, his scholastic motivation will decline.

FAILURE THREAT.   Failure threat is a class of stimulus events in an achievement situation which tend to elicit anxious expectations of harm or pain as a consequence of failure. High probability of failure does not by itself constitute failure threat—it is necessary also that the failure have a social meaning. But in Atkinson's formulation, the negative incentive strength of failure varies inversely with the subjective probability of failure, so that fear of failure is most strongly aroused when the probability of failure is at an intermediate level. This leads to the paradoxical prediction that as the probability of failure increases beyond 0.50, fear of failure declines. The paradox is resolved when one recognizes that Atkinson's model deals only with that component of incentive strength that is determined by the apparent difficulty of the task. Sarason *et al.* (1960) call attention to the important influence of anticipated disapproval by parents and teachers on the negative valence of failure. (While their primary interest is in test anxiety as a personality variable, their discussion seems applicable to the present problem of identifying situational determinants of fear of failure.) Presumably, the child's belief that his failure to meet prevailing standards of achievement will bring adult disapproval is relatively unaffected by his own perception of the difficulty of a given task. Hence, fear of disapproval should increase as it becomes more probable—that is, as the subjective probability of failure increases. Sarason and his associates suggest that a high expectancy of failure arouses strong unconscious hostility against the adults from whom negative evaluation is foreseen. The hostility is turned inward against the self in the form of self-derogatory attitudes, which strengthen the expectation of failure and the desire to escape the situation. Distraction by these and other components of emotional conflict may cause a decrement in the child's performance.

REPORTS ON ACADEMIC ACHIEVEMENT OF

NEGROES IN DESEGREGATED SCHOOLS

There is a dearth of unequivocal information about Negro performance in desegregated schools. A number of factors have contributed to this situation. (1) Many desegregated school systems have a policy of racial nonclassification, so that separate data for Negroes and whites are not available. (2) Where total elimination of legal segregation has occurred it has usually been accompanied by vigorous efforts to raise educational standards in *all* schools; hence the effects of desegregation per se are confounded with the effects of improved teaching and facilities. (3) In several southern states only small numbers of highly selected Negro pupils have been admitted to previously all-white schools, and since before–after comparisons of achievement are not usually presented, reports of "satisfactory" adjustment by these Negro children shed little light on the question of relative performance.

Taking the published information for what it is worth, we find that most of it presents a favorable picture of Negro academic adjustment in racially mixed settings. Stallings (1959) has reported on the results of achievement testing in the Louisville school system in 1955–1956, the year prior to total elimination of legal segregation, and again two years later. Gains were found in the median scores of all pupils for the grades tested, with Negroes showing greater improvement than whites. The report gave no indication of whether the gains for Negroes were related to amount of actual change in the racial composition of schools. Indeed, Stallings stated, "The gains were greater where Negro pupils remained by choice with Negro teachers." A later survey on Louisville by Knowles (1962) indicated that Negro teachers had not been assigned to classrooms having white students during the period covered by Stallings' research. This means that the best Negro gains observed by Stallings were made by children who *remained in segre-*

gated classrooms, and can only be attributed to factors *other* than desegregation, such as a general improvement in educational standards.

In both Washington, D.C., and Baltimore, where legal segregation was totally abolished in 1954, The United States Commission on Civil Rights found "some evidence that the scholastic achievement of Negroes in such schools has improved, and no evidence of a resultant reduction in the achievement of white students" (*Southern School News,* 1960). A detailed account of academic progress in the Washington schools since 1954 has been given by Hansen (1960). The results of a city-wide testing program begun in 1955 indicated year-to-year gains in achievement on every academic subject tested at every grade level where the tests were given. The data were not broken down by race. As in the case of Louisville, it seems reasonable to attribute these gains primarily to an ambitious program of educational improvement rather than to racial mixing. For several years, the Washington schools have had a steadily increasing predominance of Negro pupils (over 76 percent in 1960); this, combined with a four-track system of homogeneous ability-grouping which has the effect of concentrating Negroes in the lower tracks, has resulted in a minimal desegregation experience for the majority of Negro children.

Little relevant data have been published on other southern states where desegregation has been initiated. In 1960, twelve administrators of desegregated school systems testified at a federal hearing on whether integration had damaged academic standards (The United States Commission on Civil Rights, 1960). They unanimously replied in the negative, but only one official (from Louisville) mentioned gains in the achievement of Negro pupils. Reports of widespread academic failure on the part of desegregated Negro children are rare. Among those that have appeared recently is one by Day (1962) on Chapel Hill, N.C. Referring to a total of about forty-five Negroes in predominantly white schools, he stated that the experience of two years of desegregation has shown ". . . a disturbing portion of Negro children attending desegregated schools have failed to keep pace with their white classmates. . . . The question remains as to how to raise the achievement of Negro pupils disadvantaged by their home background and lack of motivation" (p. 78). Wyatt (1962) quoted the Superintendent of Schools in Nashville, Tenn., as stating there was substantially more difficulty with Negro students entering desegregated situations in the upper grades. The official ascribed most of the difficulties to problems of social adjustment, although the cumulative effect of the generally lower achievement in the Negro schools was credited with some responsibility for the situation.

The most adequate data on the relationship between Negro academic achievement and racial balance in northern schools are contained in the report by Coleman *et al.* (1966) on American public education. An extensive sampling of metropolitan and rural communities revealed that as the proportion of white pupils in schools increased, Negro scores on achievement tests tended to rise. The apparent impact of desegregation can be illustrated by comparing percentile scores on reading comprehension for northern Negro high school students who never had a white classmate with scores of northern Negroes who attended integrated schools from the early grades. When figures from Table 3.3.2 of the Coleman report are consolidated, it is revealed that Negro ninth-graders with the longest experience of integrated schooling had an average point score of 48.2. This is about five points below the white norm for the same region, but less than two percentiles below the national norm of 50. In contrast, ninth-grade minority-group children who never had white classmates averaged 43.8. Thus it seems that desegregation reduced the racial achievement gap by almost half. (The Coleman report also gives scores of twelfth-graders, which were excluded from the present comparisons because the high rate of Negro dropouts makes them unrepresentative. Actually, the picture would not have been changed materially by their inclusion. The possibility exists that superior performance of Negroes in desegregated schools was due at least in part to their having come from superior family or neighborhood backgrounds. However, the report does state that "cross tabulations on indicators of socioeconomic status showed that the differences [in achievement] are not accounted for by family background" (p. 331).)

When the influence of the student body's educational background and aspirations was controlled, the relationship between racial composition of schools and Negro test scores was sharply reduced. Thus much of the apparent beneficial effect of having a high proportion of white classmates comes not from racial composition per se, but from the high educational quality that is, on the average, found among white students.

Desegregation also appeared to have the effect of increasing the variability of Negro test scores. The differences in variance were small but consistent, and accorded with notions advanced earlier in this paper regarding the complex determination of Negro motivation in predominantly white settings: because of the high prestige of white teachers and age peers, rejection by them is more disturbing to the Negro pupil, and their acceptance more facilitative, than similar responses from Negro teachers and peers.

Further unpublished analyses of the Coleman data by James McPartland reveal the expected difference between truly *integrated* and merely *desegregated* schools. Those schools with more than half white-student bodies whose Negroes score well, when compared with similar schools whose Negroes score poorly, are characterized by greater cross-racial acceptance as predicted. Their students were much more likely to report close friends among members of the other race than were students in the merely desegregated schools.

The academic achievement of Negro graduates of segregated southern high schools who attended integrated colleges has been reviewed by the National Scholarship Service and Fund for Negro Students (1963). In a period of fifteen years, NSSFNS helped over 9000 Negro students to enroll in interracial colleges, situated mostly in the North. The report stated (p. 9) that "5.6 percent of these students had a scholastic average of A or A—; 50.3 percent B+, B, or B—; 32.4 percent C+, C, or C—; and 0.7 percent D or below. Not listing grades were 11 percent. Fewer than 5 percent withdrew from college for any reason. This record of college success . . . is far above the national average, which shows an over 40 percent incidence of dropouts from all causes."

It should be noted that these students were carefully selected by NSSFNS for their academic qualifications. Nonetheless, the NSSFNS experience demonstrates that qualified southern Negro youth can function effectively in predominantly white colleges of good quality. Later, there will be mention of additional material on these students which suggests that academic success was associated with social acceptance on the campus.

EVIDENCE OF DESEGREGATION CONDITIONS
THAT MAY BE DETRIMENTAL TO THE
PERFORMANCE OF NEGROES

It was proposed that the achievement motivation of Negro children in desegregation may be strongly influenced by the social behavior of their white classmates and teachers (social threat and facilitation), by their level of expectancy with regard to academic success (probability of success), and by their perception of the social consequences of failure (failure threat). In this section, evidence about conditions of desegregation that are assumed to have unfavorable effects will be considered. The focusing on negative factors is not meant to suggest that conditions favorable to Negro performance are lacking in present-day situations of desegregation, but rather that the former have received more attention from social scientists—apparently because they are more salient.

Social Rejection and Isolation

The rationale for assuming that social rejection is detrimental to the minority child's academic behavior has already been discussed. To what extent are Negroes rejected by white classmates? It is clear that this varies greatly from one community to another. The bulk of early studies on the racial attitudes of white school children in the North indicated that from an early age they expressed strong preference for their own racial group (for example, Horowitz, 1936; Criswell, 1939; Radke *et al.*, 1949; and Radke *et al.*, 1950). Two examples of desegregation that were highly stressful for Negro children have been described by a psychiatrist, Coles (1963). He writes of the first Negroes to enter white schools in Atlanta and New Orleans:

> . . . When they are in school they may experience rejection, isolation, or insult. They live under what physicians would consider to be highly stressful circumstances . . . (p. 4).
> During a school year one can see among these children all of the medical and psychiatric responses to fear and anxiety. One child may lose his appetite, another may become sarcastic and have nightmares. Lethargy may develop, or excessive studying may mark the apprehension common to both. At the same time one sees responses of earnest and effective work. . . . Each child's case history would describe a balance of defenses against emotional pain, and some exhaustion under it, as well as behavior which shows an attempt to challenge and surmount it (p. 5).

Out of thirteen original students who were studied during the first two years of integration, and forty-seven who became involved in integration one year later and were studied during the second year, "only one child has really succumbed to emotional illness." Coles does not present a systematic analysis of the various specific sources of fear and anxiety, but he suggests that worries about schoolwork were of less importance than reactions to the prejudice of white children. Nor does he present adequate information about academic success, merely noting that very few learning difficulties "were insurmountable."

Severe stress due to social rejection has been experienced also by Negro students at various newly desegregated colleges and universities in the South. For example, several months after entering the University of Mississippi as its first Negro student, during which time he was often in considerable physical danger, James Meredith emphasized that rejection and social isolation were the most difficult features of his experience. He referred to himself as "the most segregated Negro in the world," despite his enrollment at the University. "Through it all," he said, "the most intolerable thing has been the campaign of ostracizing me" (*Southern School News*, 1963).

Two Negro students who initiated integration at the University of Georgia experienced rejection and isolation during their entire two-year enrollment. Trillin wrote (1964, p. 83): "As Hamilton (Holmes) began his final ten-week quarter at Georgia, he had never eaten in a University dining hall, studied in the library, used the gymnasium, or entered the snack bar. He had no white friends outside the classroom. No white student had ever visited him and he had never visited one of them."

The other student, Charlayne Hunter, eventually entered into friendly relationships with several white classmates, and was generally in the company of other students when walking to and from classes or eating on campus. However, she remained totally ostracized in the dormitory where she occupied a room by herself. Both Negroes have since graduated, Holmes with a distinguished academic record. Miss Hunter is now married to a white southerner who was a fellow student at the university.

Desegregation under more favorable conditions has been investigated by Yarrow (1958). Comparable groups of Negro and white children of both sexes were observed in segregated and desegregated summer camps during two-week sessions. The campers were from low-income families in southern and border states. The biracial camps had integrated adult staffs that were highly motivated to "make desegregation work." It was found that the behavior of children in segregated and integrated groups was quite similar. An initial tendency for both white and Negro children to prefer white friends lessened during the two-week period studied. Satisfaction with the camp experience, as indicated by the percentage of children who expressed a desire that the camp session be extended, was somewhat higher in the desegregated camps. However, there were also indications of social conflict and emotional tension associated with the integration process. In older groups (ages twelve and thirteen) white children initially directed almost twice as much aggression toward Negro cabin mates as toward white age peers. At the beginning of contact 29 percent of all actions by white campers toward Negroes were hostile. On the other hand, Negro children of all ages aggressed more against one another than against whites. Overt manifestations of white prejudice tended to diminish during the two-week period. Nonetheless, tension symptoms appeared in almost twice as many children in desegregated as in segregated groups (71 percent compared with 38 percent). Frequencies were the same for Negroes and whites. But Negro children in desegregation were more likely to manifest covert or internalized signs of distress (enuresis, fears, nightmares, withdrawal, physical symptoms) than those that were more overt (fighting, generally disruptive behavior, obscene language, complaining). Of the Negro campers showing tension, 85 percent showed reactions of the covert type. For the white children showing tension, neither covert nor overt responses predominated. That Negroes were particularly fearful of white disapproval is suggested by their oversensitiveness in desegregation to aggressive and dominative behavior in other Negroes, and their denial of such impulses in themselves. Both reactions are further evidence of a tendency to conceal tensions in the presence of whites.

Regarding the relevance of this study to school integration, it should be noted that the total period of interracial contacts was brief, but peer interactions were probably more intimate and intense than the usual classroom contacts. A generally favorable picture of race relations in southern integrated schools was presented in an article by a journalist, Tanner (1964). He found that "younger white and Negro children attending desegregated classes seem to accept each other better than the older ones. Negro and white youngsters can be seen playing together on the slides and swings of almost any desegregated southern elementary school's playground."

One investigation has shown that experiences of social acceptance are associated with academic success. In the earlier-mentioned NSSFNS program of placing qualified Negro graduates of southern high schools in northern integrated colleges, it was found that those who participated in extracurricular activities, dated, and had a satisfactory number of friends got better marks than those who did not (National Scholarship Service and Fund for Negro Students, 1960). Though this finding is merely correlational, it is consistent with the proposition that acceptance by white peers is beneficial to the achievement motivation of Negro students.

Fear of Competition with Whites

It was suggested that low expectation of success is an important detrimental factor in the performance of minority children attending integrated schools. The evidence is strong that Negro students have feelings of intellectual inferiority which arise from an awareness of actual differences in racial achievement, or from irrational acceptance of the white group's stereotype of Negroes.

INADEQUACY OF PREVIOUS TRAINING. The low quality of segregated Negro education is well documented. Plaut (1957) has summarized the over-all situation:

> Negroes, furthermore, have long been aware that most of their schools in the South, and often the *de facto* segregated schools in the North, are rundown, poorly staffed, and shorthanded. Second- and third-rate schooling for Negroes leaves them without the ability to compete with white students and robs them of the initiative to compete. Even the 1955 Speaker of the Georgia House of Representatives admitted recently that "Negro education in Georgia is a disgrace. What the Negro child gets in the sixth grade, the white child gets in the third" (p. 5).

A few specific instances of educational disparity at the grade-school level will be cited. Findley (1957) found in testing for achievement in the Atlanta schools that from 40 percent to 60 percent of white pupils met the standards set by the top 50 percent of a national sample on the different tests; but only 2 percent to 10 percent of Negro pupils met this standard on the various tests. In Tennessee, according to Wyatt (1962), Negro students averaged one and one half to two years behind grade level when transferred to biracial schools in the upper grades. In earlier grades, transfers performed satisfactorily. The same report described the status of Negro and white teachers in a Tennessee urban area. Only 49 percent of 901 academically qualified Negro teachers passed the National Teachers Examination; among white teachers, more than 97 percent of 783 qualified teachers passed the test. The Tennessee survey showed that the academic retardation of the segregated Negro elementary school pupil is progressive.

The situation in northern Virginia was summarized by Mearns (1962) in a report written for The United States Commission on Civil Rights:

> The Negroes themselves have recognized that the achievement gap exists, but the only obvious reaction among most Negroes is reluctance to transfer to white schools. The question is raised as to whether Negroes really obtain a better education in desegregated schools where they must compete with better prepared, highly motivated white students. Frustration and failure engulf the ill-prepared Negro pupils. . . . (pp. 209–210)

Other data indicate that the racial gap in achievement continues to widen through high school and college. Roberts (1963) pointed out that less than 3 percent of Negro graduates of segregated high schools would meet the standards of nonsegregated colleges. Roberts estimated that not more than 10 to 15 percent of Negro American college youth were capable of exceeding the threshold level score on the ACE that was recommended by the President's Commission (100 on the 1947 edition).

Even in the urban North, where schools are legally integrated, the education afforded Negroes tends to be inadequate. Deutsch (1960), for example, found that in time-samples of classroom activity, from 50 to 80 percent of all classroom time in New York City elementary schools with predominantly Negro lower-class children was "devoted to disciplining and various essentially nonacademic tasks." By comparison, only 30 percent of classroom time was given over to such activities in elementary schools attended mainly by white children of roughly similar economic status.

The foregoing material indicates that when grade-a-year plans of desegregation are adopted, it is obviously desirable from an educational standpoint to begin integration at the lowest grade and work upward. However, many southern school systems are on grade-a-year plans of reverse order, with integration starting in the twelfth grade and proceeding down.

UNREALISTIC INFERIORITY FEELINGS.   Apparently, the Negro child's feeling of intellectual inferiority is based not only on reality experience, but reflects an emotional accommodation to the demeaning role in American culture that has been imposed upon his racial group by the dominant white majority. The Group for the Advancement of Psychiatry (1957) has summarized the observations of numerous investigators of Negro personality:

> Wherever segregation occurs, one group, in this instance the Negroes, always suffers from inferior social status. The damaging effects of this are reflected in unrealistic inferiority feelings, a sense of humiliation, and constriction of potentialities for self-development. This often results in a pattern of self-hatred and rejection of one's own group, sometimes expressed by antisocial behavior toward one's own group or the dominant group. These attitudes seriously affect the levels of aspiration, the capacity to learn, and the capacity to relate in interpersonal situations (p. 10).

Two experiments with Negro male college students suggest the marked extent to which loss of confidence when competing with whites can override reality. Preston and Bayton (1941) found that when students at a Negro college were told that their own scores on intellectual tasks were the same as the average scores of white students, they tended to set their goal levels lower on the next few trials than they did when told that their scores equaled those of other Negro students. The results can be interpreted on the basis of Atkinson's (1958a) theory of goal-setting behavior. Assuming that his motive to succeed tended to be stronger than his motive to avoid failure, the Negro subject should have set his goal where the probability of success was 0.50. When a given level of performance was said to represent the white norm its apparent difficulty became greater than when it was supposed to represent the Negro norm, hence the goal level at which the expectancy of success was 0.50 tended to be lower immediately following the announcement of these norms. In an investigation of small biracial workteams at a northern university, Katz and Benjamin (1960) observed that Negro students who had actually scored as well as their white teammates on various intellectual tasks, afterwards rated their own performance as inferior. Here knowledge of white performance levels apparently influenced the Negro subjects' cognitions of their own *actual* performance, rather than just their estimations of *future* performance.

In an experiment suggested by Whyte's (1943) observations of status influence in a white street-corner gang, Harvey (1953) had members of white high-school cliques take turns on a dart-throwing task. After several practice trials, the boys openly estimated their own and their companions' future performance. Guesses were directly related to social rank in the group. Only boys of lowest rank showed a tendency to *under*estimate their own performance. Moreover, they were expected by those of middle and high status to perform more poorly than they actually did. It should be noted that it is unclear from Harvey's results whether rank influenced perception of own ability or merely what one was willing to say in front of higher-ranking clique-mates who had coercive power (French and Raven, 1960) to keep those of lesser rank "in their place."

EXPERIMENTS ON STRESS AND PERFORMANCE

Earlier some situational factors were described that presumably are detrimental to Negro academic achievement: social threat, low expectancy of success, and failure threat. Also, evidence was presented (some of it inferential) of their occurrence in actual situations of racial integration. A good deal of experimentation having to do with the influence of these factors on verbal and motor performance has been stimulated by the concept of psychological stress. Applezweig and Moeller (1957) proposed a definition of stress which focuses on the condition of the individual: stress occurs when a motive or need is strongly aroused and the organism is unable to respond in such a way as to reduce its motivation. Deese (1962) finds it more useful to define stress as a class of stimulus events that elicit a set of correlated responses, among which are feelings of discomfort. He points out that the effects of stress on performance are specific to particular components of the performance under consideration—that is, responses to stress may be either compatible or incompatible with the responses required in a given task.

Early studies of stress and performance did not employ the type of analytic comparison of stress responses and dimensions of ability in specific skills that Deese suggests. The general trend of findings on verbal performance (reviewed by Lazarus *et al.,* 1952) has been that stress impairs efficiency on relatively complex and difficult tasks, while on simple tasks stress has sometimes been shown to improve performance. The types of stress that have been used in experiments include failure feedback or threat of failure, exposure to highly difficult tasks (often under time pressure), annoying or painful stimulation such as electric shock, distraction such as flashing lights or noises, disapproval or disparagement.

Many investigations have employed stress inductions that apparently aroused fear of failure. For example, using nine-year-old boys, Lantz (1945) observed an impairment of Stanford-Binet scores following a failure experience, but no such effect after a successful experience. An examination by Lantz of the differential effects of this failure experience upon the various subtests indicated that tasks requiring visual or rote memory were not affected, while those involving reasoning or thinking suffered a decrement. In other studies that were reviewed by Lazarus *et al.,* failure stress produced decrements in scores on the following verbal-symbolic tasks: learning and recall of nonsense syllables, digit-symbol substitution, arithmetic, recognition of briefly exposed sentences, sentence-formation, and digit span. Similar effects were obtained on various types of perceptual-motor performance (for example, card-sorting, reaction time).

Turning to some representative studies of stress not directly involving failure, Barker *et al.* (1941) observed regression in the mental age of nursery-school children, as measured by the constructiveness of their play, when the children were frustrated by being denied access to attractive toys. Stress associated with the blocking of hostile impulses against an instigating agent (a teacher who arbitrarily disregarded the expressed desire of students) was found by Goldman *et al.* (1954) to impair performance on three tasks: retention of learned material, digit-span, and problem solving. Laird (1923) reported loss of body steadiness in college students who were "razzed" by future fraternity brothers while working on simple motor tasks. Klein (1957) found that a strong task-irrelevant drive (thirst) caused a reduction in the accuracy of visual-size judgments; and Callaway and Thompson (1953) obtained a similar effect when their subjects were required to hold one foot in a bucket of ice water.

During the past decade much research has been done on the role of personality factors in reactions to stress, with particular focus on the role of individual differences in chronic anxiety as measured by Taylor's Manifest Anxiety Scale and Mandler and Sarason's Test Anxiety Questionnaire. A lengthy review of this work would fall outside the scope of this paper, inasmuch as the primary concern here is with *situational* factors that affect Negro performance. Yet it is of interest to note the general pattern of experimental results. Greater decrements due to stress are found in the performance of highly-anxious individuals than in the performance of subjects lower in the anxiety-score distribution. These studies have been reviewed by Sarason (1960) and Taylor (1963).

Speculating about underlying physiological processes in stress, Bovard (1959) places the organizing center of bodily-emotional responses to stress in the posterior and medial hypothalamus. Of particular interest are his hypotheses that (a) activity in the anterior hypothalamus tends to inhibit or dampen posterior activity, and (b) excitation in the anterior hypothalamus is produced by certain types of social stimuli. *Thus an organism's vulnerability to stress depends upon the nature of its social environment.* Bovard reviewed studies which suggest that the presence of companions or members of the same species has a supportive effect under stress. At the human level it has been observed that separation from the family and evacuation from London was more stressful for London children than enduring the bombings with their families (Titmuss, 1950). Mandlebaum (1952) and Marshall (1951) dealt with the importance of social contact among soldiers in resisting battle stress. Research at Boston Psychopathic Hospital (1955) has shown that lysergic acid diethylamide (*LSD*) taken in a group situation results in less anxiety and inappropriate behavior than when taken individually. Schachter (1959) reported that fear, as well as hunger, increased the affiliative tendency in college students; and Wrightsman (1960) found that being with others in a similar plight was anxiety-reducing for students who were first-born or only children.

Similar phenomena have been observed at the animal level. Liddel (1950) found that the presence or absence of the mother goat determined whether young goats would develop an experimental neurosis in a conditioning situation. In experiments with rats, animals tested together under stressful conditions gave less fear-response (Davitz and Mason, 1955) and had less resultant ulceration (Conger *et al.,* 1957) than animals tested alone. Similarly, monkeys showed fewer fear-responses in a strange situation when another monkey was present (Mason, 1960). Monkeys raised in total isolation from age peers were deficient in normal defensive responses to environmental threat (Harlow and Harlow, 1962).

If Bovard's theory is correct, the extreme social isolation that is often experienced by Negroes in predominantly white environments would weaken their resistance to other stress conditions, such as might arise from the inherent difficulty of academic work, time pressure, financial problems, and so on.

Various theories have been invoked to account for the tendency of stress to reduce efficiency on complex tasks, but to facilitate performance, or have no effect, on simple tasks. Sarason and others (Mandler and Sarason, 1952; Child, 1954; Sarason *et al.,* 1960) have dealt primarily with the effects of individual differences in vulnerability to failure stress. They emphasize the interference that occurs when expectation of failure generates anxiety which, in turn, acts as an internal stimulus for defensive, task-irrelevant responses. Similarly, Deese (1962) mentions task interference from responses to the internal stimuli of stress-induced autonomic activity.

Some writers have concerned themselves with the effect of drive on specific characteristics of task-relevant behavior. Thus Easterbrook (1959) postulates an inverse relationship between drive level and the range of cue utilization. Complex tasks require a relatively broad awareness of cues for optimal efficiency, whereas simple tasks by definition require apprehension of only a few cues for successful responding. Hence, when drive is very high (as in stress), relevant cues will be missed on hard tasks, but more closely attended to on easy tasks. Hullian theory, as developed with respect to anxiety drive and learning by Spence *et al.,* deals with the energizing effect of drive on task responses. As strength of drive increases the number of habitual response tendencies that can be elicited in a given task increases also. When activation is strong (as in stress) intratask response competition is heightened. The theory is supported by the results of experiments in which high and low scorers on Taylor's Manifest Anxiety Scale were required to learn competitional and noncompetitional paired-word lists (reviewed by Spence, 1958; and Taylor, 1963). Thus Easterbrook and the Hullians have each dealt with a particular component of a great number of tasks, and have tried to predict either favorable or detrimental effects of stress from the presence or absence of this component.

Discussing the effects of stress on perceptual motor skills, Deese (1962) points out the need for systematic analysis of (a) the characteristics of motor arousal under stress, in relation to (b) the dimensions of psychomotor abilities that are requisite for various task performances. Both Deese and Spence (1958) mention that a fundamental weakness of present thinking about the effects of stress on *verbal* learning is that not enough dimensions of verbal skills have yet been explored to know what kinds of effects to look for.

Summarizing this section, there is a considerable amount of experimental evidence that types of stress which may be present in desegregation (as varieties of social threat and failure threat) impair certain kinds of verbal and perceptual-motor learning. However, there does not exist at present any comprehensive system of variables for predicting the specific effects of different conditions of stress on the Negro child's performance of various academic tasks.

EXPERIMENTS ON NEGRO PERFORMANCE IN
BIRACIAL SITUATIONS

In recent years this author and his associates have been engaged in a series of experiments on the intellectual productivity of Negro male college students in situations involving white peers and/or white authority figures. The general aim of the research is the identification of underlying psychological factors that have either favorable or detrimental effects on Negro efficiency. In connection with the interpretation of the results that are now to be presented, there evolved the set of postulated situational determinants of performance that were discussed earlier in this chapter.

BIRACIAL TEAMS.   In two exploratory studies, conducted at a northern university (Katz *et al.,* 1958; and Katz and Benjamin, 1960), various cognitive and motor tasks were assigned to groups composed of two Negro students and two white students. Initially the men were total strangers. They worked together in several sessions for a total of 12½ hours. In general, it was found that Negroes displayed marked social inhibition and subordination to white partners. When teams were engaged in cooperative problem solving, Negro subjects made fewer proposals than did whites, and tended to accept the latter's contributions uncritically. On all tasks combined, Negroes made fewer remarks than did whites, and spoke more to whites, proportionately, than to one another. White men, on the other hand, spoke more to one another, proportionately, than to the Negro men. These behaviors occurred even when group members could expect a monetary bonus for good teamwork, and were informed that their abilities were higher than those of subjects in other teams. Moreover, in the second experiment Negro and white partners were matched on intelligence, and were even made to display equal ability on certain group tasks (by means of secret manipulation of tasks). Yet on a terminal questionnaire Negroes ranked whites higher on intellectual performance, preferred one another as future work companions, and expressed less satisfaction with the group experience than did whites.

The findings on Negro behavior may have been a result of (a) social threat (that is, Negroes were fearful of instigating white hostility through greater assertiveness); (b) low task-motivation in confrontation with white achievement standards (as derived earlier from Atkinson's model); or (c) failure threat (high expectancy of failure combined with anxious anticipation of disapproval and rejection by white peers and the white experimenter). The experimental data provide no basis on which to reject any of these factors as irrelevant.

In the next experiment, Katz and Cohen (1962) attempted to modify Negro behavior toward white partners in the direction of greater assertiveness and autonomy. It was predicted that (a) when Negroes were compelled to achieve on a task that was performed cooperatively with a white peer, they would subsequently display an increased amount of achieving behavior on another shared task of different content, and (b) Negro subjects who were not compelled to achieve on the first task would show an opposite tendency. Negro-white student dyads at a northern university engaged in cooperative solving of problems adapted from the Raven Progressive Matrices. Some of the problems were made easy, to ensure that both participants would perceive the correct answer. On other problems the subjects unknowingly received different information, so that one person had an easy version, while the other person had an insoluble version. Each subject had the easy version half the time. On every problem partners had to agree on a single team-answer, after which the experimenter announced the correct solution. Before and after the problem-solving experience a disguised measure of social influence between the two men was obtained on a task which required group estimates of certain quantitative characteristics of briefly exposed photographs (for example, the number of paratroopers in the sky).

In a control condition, the rules of the problem-solving situation did not require that each person openly propose an answer to every problem. It was found that Negroes tended to accept passively the suggestions of their white companions *even when they held the easy version and the teammate had to be in error.* With respect to intellectual efficiency, the private responses of Negroes, which they wrote down before each discussion began, showed *more errors than were made on the same problems at an earlier, individual testing session.* White subjects, on the other hand, made *fewer* private errors than they had made previously. As a consequence of the problem-solving experience in the control condition, Negroes showed increased social compliance on the picture estimations.

In an "assertion-training" condition the men were given their answer sheets from the previous session when they had worked alone. On every problem the two partners were required to read aloud their previous answers before negotiating a team reply. Thus, Negro subjects had the experience of openly announcing correct solutions in about half of all instances of disagreement (both men read off approximately the same number of correct answers). In the subsequent interactions over picture estimation there was an *increase* in the amount of influence Negroes had over the white partner. Further, Negro subjects were now inclined to accept the other person's influence only to the extent that he had displayed superior accuracy on previous pictures.

Thus, unless *forced* to express opinions at variance with those of a white peer, Negro students tended to suppress their own ideas in deference to the other person, and to show increased compliance on another task. But when they were *forced* to act independently on one task, they achieved greater autonomy in the second situation. The responses of white subjects on a postexperimental questionnaire indicate there may have been some hostility aroused against Negro partners who displayed intellectual competence. After working in the assertion-training condition whites tended to downgrade the Negro's performance and to accept him less as a future coworker. However, since there were no all-white control groups, it is not known whether these reactions of white subjects were specifically interracial.

The results suggest that Negro submissiveness with the white companion was an effect primarily of social threat, and that probability of success was a relatively unimportant factor. As already mentioned, in both the "assertion-training" and control conditions, disagreement was experimentally arranged on almost all problems, with random alternation between partners in the assignment of easy and insoluble versions (on a few items *both* men had either easy or hard versions). Also, after each team decision the experimenter announced the correct answer (fictitious when both men had hard items) so that subjects could check the accuracy of their own private response and of the solution the partner had openly proposed. While there was a stable tendency in control teams of whites to make slightly fewer private errors than Negroes (all partners had been matched on pretest scores), it is doubtful that the average race difference of about two private errors on forty-nine items could have been discriminated by the average Negro subject. Hence, the relative accuracy of own and partner's solutions was much the same for Negro subjects in the two experimental conditions, and the only difference between conditions was that in "assertion training" the Negro subject was forced to *disagree openly* with the partner. The disinhibiting effect of this experience on the Negro subject's behavior on another task seems attributable to a reduction in anxiety about instigating white hostility.

THE EFFECT OF INDUCED THREAT IN DIFFERENT RACIAL ENVIRONMENTS   In the next experiment, Katz and Greenbaum (1963) examined more directly the influence of threat on Negro verbal performance by systematically varying the level of threat in different racial environments. Individual Negro students at a predominantly Negro college in the South were given a digit-symbol substitution task in the presence of two strangers who were both either white or Negro—an adult administrator and a confederate who pretended to be another student working on the same task. In order to minimize the amount of uncontrolled threat implicit in the white condition, there was no social interaction between the Negro subject and his white peer, and the task was described as a research instrument of no evaluative significance.

In addition to the variation of racial environment, the students were exposed to a condition of either high or low threat. Since the purpose of the threat variation was to determine whether individual Negroes were more vulnerable to debilitative effects of stress when they were alone with whites than when they were with other Negroes, it seemed desirable to use a threat stimulus that would not lead to intentional suppression of responses by changing the social meaning of the task situation. The experimenters used an announcement that severe electric shock (high-threat condition) or mild electric shock (low-threat condition) would be administered to the subject and the coworker at random times during the task. No shocks were actually delivered.

The results indicated that Negro students' scores on the digit-symbol task depended upon the particular combination of stress and racial-environment conditions under which they worked. When only mild shock was threatened they performed better in the presence of whites than of other Negroes. But when told to expect strong shock their efficiency in the Negro condition improved, while in the white condition it went down. Apparently, the prospect of successful competition against a white peer, and of approval from a white authority figure, had greater incentive strength than the corresponding prospect in the all-Negro situation. This is reasonable on the assumption that the whites (particularly the experimenter) had higher prestige for the subject than their Negro counterparts. Since in all experimental conditions the instructions for the task played down its intellectual significance, Negro subjects in the white environment, low shock-threat condition would not have experienced strong failure threat. Hence, they could respond to the stronger incentive strength of success in the white condition.

There are a number of ways of looking at the effects of shock threat. First, if Negro subjects cared more about performing well in the white condition they would have been more fearful lest the strong shock disrupt their task responses (failure threat). The expected stimulus would thus become more salient and distracting. An upward spiral of debilitation could then be set in motion as distraction and fear made the task seem more difficult, and this in turn aroused further emotion. Subjects in the Negro environment, on the other hand, had a relatively relaxed attitude toward the task in the low-threat condition (*too* relaxed for good performance). Hence they would not have been fearful of possible decrements due to shock, but perhaps just enough concerned to work harder than before. Also relevant to these data is Bovard's earlier mentioned notion that the ability to withstand stress is strengthened by the presence of familiar social stimuli that have nurturant associations (in this case other Negroes).

The Hullian conception of the energizing effect of drive is also applicable: efficiency declined in the white condition because the subject's initial stimulation in this racial environment, in combination with the additional stimulation of the strong shock threat, produced a total drive strength that exceeded the optimum for the assigned task. In the Negro condition initial stimulation was relatively low, so that the increment in arousal due to strong threat brought the total drive level closer to the optimum than it had been under mild threat.

One practical implication of Katz and Greenbaum's findings is that *in desegregation the performance of Negroes may show a wider range of variation in both upward and downward directions than in segregated situations, depending upon specific features of the situation.*

EFFECTS OF IQ VERSUS NON-IQ INSTRUCTIONS.   In a follow-up on the preceding experiment, Katz *et al.* (1965) investigated the effects on Negro students' efficiency of three factors: the race of the task administrator, the difficulty of the task, and the evaluative significance of the task. All subjects were students at a southern Negro college. Half of them were tested individually by a Negro adult and the other half were tested by a white adult. In addition, one third of the total sample worked on a relatively easy digit-symbol code, one third were given a code of medium difficulty, and one third had to do a relatively hard code. In order to attach a relatively nonthreatening significance to the situation, the task was described as a research instrument for studying eye-hand coordination, a nonintellectual characteristic. Unlike the Katz and Greenbaum experiment, there was no experimental confederate who posed as a second subject. The findings were consistent with results obtained in the low-threat condition of the earlier study—Negro subjects worked more efficiently when tested by a white adult than when tested by a Negro adult. However, the favorable influence of the white administrator was apparent only on the most difficult of the three tasks. On the two easier codes there were no statistically reliable differences in achievement associated with the skin color of the experimenters. Apparently the easier tasks were too simple to reflect the differences in motivation.

Then two additional groups of Negro students were tested by the same Negro and white administrators on the most difficult task only. But instead of being told that the task measured eye-hand coordination, it was presented to these subjects as a test of intelligence. Now the subjects did not attain higher scores in the presence of a white experimenter; rather, the effect of the IQ instructions was to elevate, slightly, performance with a Negro tester, and to lower scores markedly in the white-tester group, so that the means for both testers were at about the same level. Thus, in this experiment, making the most difficult task relevant to intellectual ability had effects not unlike those of strong-shock threat in the previous study (by Katz and Greenbaum). On the assumption that intellectual instructions were more highly motivating than the motor-test instructions, one can again apply the Hullian interpretation that motivation in the IQ test with white-administrator treatment was excessive.

More directly relevant is Atkinson's (1958*a*) conception of motivation as a joint function of the subjective probability and incentive value of success, which was discussed earlier. Assuming again that a white experimenter has higher prestige for the Negro student than does a Negro experimenter, the prospect of eliciting the white person's approval would be more attractive. It follows that when the likelihood of winning approval by scoring well is equally high, whether the tester is Negro or white, the subject will work harder for the white person. Thus in this experiment Negro students performed better with a white adult than with a Negro adult when the task was supposed to assess an ability which Negroes are not stereotyped as lacking (eye-hand coordination). Presenting the task as an intelligence test ought to have raised the incentive value of achievement in both racial conditions, with perhaps an even greater increment occurring when the experimenter was white (since *intellectual* approval by a white adult might be uniquely gratifying to the Negro student's self-esteem).

But suppose that on the intellectual task the Negro subject saw very little likelihood of meeting the white experimenter's standard of excellence. Unless the incentive strength of success increased enough to counterbalance the drop in subjective probability, Atkinson's model would predict a reduction in task motivation. As an additional source of impairment in this situation, low expectancy of success could have aroused fear of earning the white tester's disapproval (failure threat).

Turning now to the situation where the tester is Negro, there is no reason to assume that the subject's expectation of success would be markedly lower when the task was described as intellectual than when it was presented as a motor test. In both instances the racial identity of the tester would tend to suggest to the subject that he was to be compared with other Negroes. Accordingly, performance with the Negro tester ought to go up under IQ instructions. The fact that it rose only slightly in our experiment may be ascribed to the subject's lack of clarity about the tester's frame of reference for evaluating his score. That is, he was not actually informed whether he would be compared with norms for Negro students only, or with norms for *all* college students. The next study deals directly with this issue.

EFFECTS OF VARIATIONS IN ANTICIPATED COMPARISON. Katz *et al.* (1964) investigated the effects on Negro students' digit-symbol performance of being told that they would be compared intellectually with other Negro students, or with white students. Hard and easy versions of the digit-symbol task were administered by a Negro to different groups of students at a southern Negro college under three different instructions: no test, scholastic aptitude test with own-college norms, and scholastic aptitude test with national-(that is, predominantly white-) college norms. Scores in all three conditions were reliably different from one another, with highest achievement occurring in the Negro-norms condition, intermediate achievement in the white-norms condition, and lowest achievement when no comparison was expected. These differences tended to be larger on the hard task than on the easy one.

Again referring to Atkinson's model, Negro performance was lowest in the no-test condition because of low incentive, while the difference between the two test conditions was due to higher subjective probability of success (closer to 0.50) when Negro subjects believed they were competing with members of their own race than when they expected to be compared with whites.

White students from a nearby state university were tested by a white person under comparable instructions on the hard task only. It was found that scores of the two norms groups—that is, own college and national—did not differ, and *both* groups were more efficient than subjects in the no-comparison condition.

Future research can determine the usefulness of this application of Atkinson's theory for understanding Negro behavior in integrated schools. For example, the present formulation predicts that if the subjective probability of success were held constant, Negro subjects would perform *better* on certain types of intellectual test when the administrator was white than when he was Negro, or when they were competing with white peers rather than with Negro peers.

AN EXPERIMENT ON THE EFFECT OF PROBABILITY-OF-SUCCESS FEEDBACK   In a recent unpublished study, the race of the tester, the race of the comparison group, and the probability of success were all manipulated independently. Freshmen at a southern Negro college were first administered, en masse, a digit-symbol task by a Negro experimenter, with neutral instructions. A few days later subjects were again tested, this time in small groups. The tester, who was now either white or Negro, introduced himself as a psychologist from the "Southern Educational Testing Service," a fictitious organization. Subjects were informed that the earlier session had really been a practice tryout for the scholastic-aptitude test which they were about to take, and that test norms were available. For the white-norms condition they were told that their scores would be compared with the average scores of students in all colleges and universities of the state, and for the Negro-norms condition the story was that they would be compared with the freshmen average at their own college. The men were also told that immediately following the testing, the administrator would see each person individually, score the test immediately, and render an evaluation to the individual of his intelligence and his aptitude for college work. This was done to create a strong expectation of face-to-face evaluation by the adult authority.

Then for the probability-of-success manipulation each subject was handed a printed form letter in an envelope bearing his name. Ostensibly from the "Testing Service," the letter explained that from the subject's score on the practice trial of the digit-symbol test, it was possible to state the statistical probability of his achieving a score on the actual test that was at least equal to the average of his age group. The typed-in probability was either 10 percent, 60 percent, or 90 percent. It had no relation to the individual's true score on the pretest. (In a control condition no letters were distributed.) Finally, the digit-symbol test was administered.

The effect on performance of the three independent variables is shown in Figure 7.1. Each square or circle represents the average digit-symbol score gain (posttest minus pretest) of about thirty Negro undergraduates. As Figure 7.1 suggests, the feedback of probabilities had a statistically significant effect on performance. The nature of the feedback effect is shown by the shape of the curves: for every combination of tester and norm the 60 percent feedback was superior to the 10 percent and 90 percent feedbacks, and also superior to no feedback. Each of these comparisons was statistically significant. Clearly the best motivation and performance occurred, regardless of racial conditions, when the subject was told he had a slightly better-than-even chance of succeeding. If his chances seemed very low or very high he apparently lost interest. This fits well with findings from a variety of other studies of achievement and risk-taking behavior.

One may speculate about possible relationships that are suggested by the shape of the curves, though they are not statistically significant. In the white-tester–white-norm treatment, scores dropped sharply from no feedback to 10 percent feedback, as though subjects were discouraged and perhaps made anxious by the feedback. With 60 percent feedback, performance improved considerably. It would seem that variations in probability of success have especially marked effect when the tester is white and the comparison group is also white. By way of contrast, in the Negro-tester–Negro-norm condition, the 10 percent feedback appears to have stimulated the subject to greater effort, as though he were determined to redeem himself.

Another finding in this experiment was a significant interaction effect of race of tester and race of norm. When the tester was white, the Negro norm occasioned better performance than did the white norm. But when the tester was Negro the relationship reversed—the white norm elicited higher scores than the Negro norm. These differences were significant. A full interpretation of the experimental findings must await analysis of subjects' replies to a postexperimental questionnaire.

The alert reader may have detected a striking discrepancy between the findings of the last experiment and those of the preceding one by Katz *et al.* In the earlier investigation a Negro tester was used and the

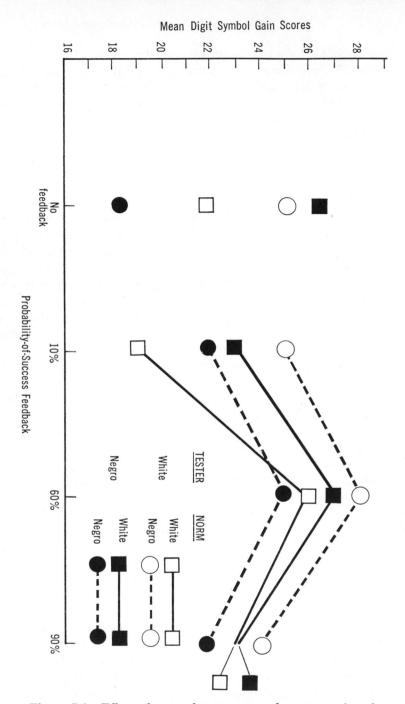

Figure 7.1   Effect of race of tester, race of norms, and probability feedback on digit-symbol scores of southern-Negro-male college students.

race of the comparison group was varied. Digit-symbol scores were higher in the Negro-norm condition than in the white-norm condition. In the last study the results when the tester was Negro were in the opposite direction, regardless of the kind of feedback used. There may be a simple regional explanation for these contradictory findings, since the earlier experiment was done in Florida, and the later one in Tennessee. Perhaps the Negro student in the Deep South is more fearful of competition with white peers than is the Negro student in the Upper South.

EMOTIONAL REACTIONS TO TEST SITUATIONS.   Another line of investigation has to do with the appraisal of Negro subjects' emotional reactions to various test situations. In connection with the earlier discussion of failure threat, reference was made to the research of Sarason and his associates (1960) on emotional factors in the test-taking behavior of white school children. In their view, the child who chronically experiences anxiety when tested is reacting with strong unconscious hostility to the adult tester, who he believes will in some way pass judgment on his adequacy. The hostility is not openly expressed, but instead is turned inward against the self in the form of self-derogatory attitudes, which strengthen the child's expectation of failure and his desire to escape the situation. Thus he is distracted from the task before him by his fear of failure and his impulse to escape.

Sarason has not as yet presented direct evidence that situations of adult evaluation arouse hostility in highly test-anxious children. However, in clinical studies by Lit (1956), Kimball (1952), and Harris (1961), difficulty in expressing aggression openly was found to be associated with scholastic underachievement. Rosenwald (1961) found that students who were relatively unwilling to give aggressive responses on a projective test showed greater impairment in solving anagrams after a hostility induction than did students who showed less inhibition of aggression on the projective test. Mention has been made of a study by Goldman *et al.* (1954), which demonstrated an association between the degree to which strong hostility against an instigator was denied expression and the amount of disruption of intellectual functioning.

These studies are pertinent to the problem of Negro children's learning efficiency in integrated classrooms, because these children often have to suppress strong hostility. It was seen that Yarrow (1958) found a much higher incidence of covert symptoms of emotional disturbance in Negro children than in white children at a desegregated summer camp. White children, it will be recalled, aggressed openly against their Negro cabinmates, but the latter did not respond in kind. Rather, they tended to deny aggressive impulses in themselves and to show heightened alertness to aggressive behavior in other Negro children. Another investigator who has reported stronger trends toward denial of hostile impulses in Negro children than in white children is Karon (1958), who examined individual personality by means of a projective technique, the Picture Arrangement Test.

It was suggested earlier that when the administrator of an intellectual test is white, or when comparison with white peers is anticipated, Negro subjects tend to become fearful of failure. Anticipation of failure would tend to generate feelings of victimization and covert hostility against the white tester. Since hostility against white authorities is dangerous, the hostile impulse would be strongly inhibited. Katz *et al.* (1964) undertook to find out whether suppression of hostile responses occurs when a white adult makes Negro students take an intelligence test. Negro male students at a segregated high school in the South were given a test of aggression disguised as a concept-formation test. It consisted of fifty-eight four-word items, with instructions to "circle the word that does not belong with the others." In half of the items one word had aggressive meaning, one word was nonaggressive, and two words were ambiguous. Hence the subject could choose either a hostile or a neutral concept. Two equivalent forms of the test were administered on successive days. On the first day it was given informally to all subjects by a Negro teacher. The following day the entire sample was divided into four groups, each of which was tested by either a white or a Negro adult stranger, with instructions that described the task as either an intelligence test or a research instrument.

The results show that when neutral instructions were used on the second day, average scores in both the white-tester and Negro-tester groups were the same as on the pretest. But in the intelligence-test condition, hostility scores *increased* over the previous day when the experimenter was a Negro, and they *decreased* when the experimenter was white. The authors' interpretation is that both administrators instigated hostile impulses in the subjects when they announced that the task would be used to evaluate intelligence; when the adult authority was a Negro person, students revealed their annoyance by responding to the aggressive connotations of ambiguous words, but when the adult was a white person the need to deny hostile feelings resulted in avoidance of aggressive word meanings. (The "denial" interpretation is, of course, inferential, since the results merely show that hostility scores in the white-adult–IQ-test condition went down; there was no *direct* evidence of increased emotional conflict in this condition.)

If we assume that these findings actually reflect variations in ability to express hostile impulses under different testing conditions, they furnish an interesting clue as to the nature of emotional processes attendant upon the disruption of Negro students' performance in the white-adult–IQ-test condition of an earlier experiment (Katz *et al.*).

SUMMARY

This chapter brings together evidence relating to the effect of school desegregation on the academic performance of young Negroes. Negro Americans are defined as a subordinated minority group, and the focus of attention is on their adjustment in schools where white age peers and teachers predominate. In situations of this type there appear to be a variety of favorable and detrimental influences on Negro performance.

Low probability of success—where there is marked discrepancy in the educational standards of Negro and white schools, or where feelings of inferiority are acquired by Negro children outside the school, minority-group newcomers in integrated classrooms are likely to have a low expectancy of academic success; consequently, their achievement motivation should be low. *Social threat*—given the prestige and power of the white-majority group, rejection of Negro students by white classmates or teachers should tend to elicit emotional responses (fear, anger, and humiliation) that are detrimental to intellectual functioning. *Failure threat*—when academic failure entails disapproval by significant others (parents, teachers, and perhaps also classmates), low expectancy of success should elicit emotional responses that are detrimental to performance.

On the other hand, *acceptance* of Negroes by white peers and adults should have a *social facilitation* effect upon their ability to learn, by motivating them to adhere to white standards of academic performance; anticipation that high performance will win white approval should endow scholastic success with *high incentive value*.

Reports on the academic progress of Negro children in desegregated schools are on the whole inadequate for drawing any conclusions about the effects of biracial environments upon Negro performance. However, other types of evidence indicate that any or all of the situational factors mentioned above may be operative in specific instances. Research on psychological stress generally supports the assumption that social threat and failure threat are detrimental to complex learning.

Experiments on Negro male college students by the author and his associates have shown that in workteams composed of Negro and white students of similar intellectual ability, Negroes are passively compliant, rate their own performance as inferior even when it is not, and express less satisfaction with the team experience than do their white companions. These results are seen as due to social threat and/or failure threat. Later studies have sought to identify specific situational determinants of Negro behavior in biracial settings.

Forcing Negro subjects into attempts to influence nonhostile white partners in problem solving had the effect of increasing their influence over the same white partner on another task, apparently mainly through reduction of their fear of instigating hostility.

Experimentally creating a verbal task situation that was low in both social threat and failure threat resulted in better performance by Negroes in the presence of whites than in the presence of other Negroes, suggesting that the incentive value of success was greater in the white environment. But when threat of strong electric shock was introduced, the white setting became less favorable to performance than the Negro one. Thus *vulnerability* to stress was greater in the white condition, even though it was not apparent until a strong explicit threat was introduced.

The evaluative significance of a verbal task (that is, whether it was described as a perceptual motor test or an intellectual test) interacted with race of the tester in determining Negro performance, in a manner consistent with the notions that (a) the incentive value of success was higher with a white tester than with a Negro tester, and (b) the probability of success was lower with a white tester than with a Negro tester only when the task was defined intellectually.

Among Florida Negro college students, anticipated intellectual comparison with Negro peers was found to produce a higher level of verbal performance than anticipated comparison with white peers, in accordance with the assumption that the subjective probability of success was lower when the expected comparison was with whites. In Tennessee, Negro undergraduates responded more favorably to white norms than to Negro norms when the tester was Negro, but showed a reverse tendency when the tester was white. Information about the probability of success had marked effect on performance in all tester-norm treatments.

Finally, suppression of hostile impulses appeared to occur in Negro boys who were tested by a white adult, but not in those who were tested by a Negro adult.

Further research is needed to clarify the effects of the various situational factors mentioned above on the cognitive functioning of Negroes in biracial settings. However, it is possible even now to point out some implications for educational practice of the findings that have been reviewed.

IMPLICATIONS FOR EDUCATIONAL PRACTICE

The experiments on Negro performance have implications for understanding the problems of adjustment that face minority children in the integrated classroom. If the Negro student comes from a background that has oriented him toward scholastic achievement, the presence of a white teacher and white age peers may have strong emotional and motivational impact. The integrated situation is likely to be double-edged in the sense that failure will be more devastating and success more rewarding than similar experiences in the segregated school. Moreover, whether the Negro child succeeds or fails will depend to a great extent not only on his actual ability but on his expectations. If he expects to fail his actual chances of failing will be greater than they would be in an all-Negro setting, because his fear of failure will be more intense. On the other hand, if he has a high expectation of success in the integrated school he should be aroused to greater effort than he would be by a similar expectation of success in the segregated school. These generalizations must remain highly tentative, pending research on a wider variety of mental tasks than have as yet been studied.

The material that has been presented in this chapter is relevant also to a number of recent suggestions by social scientists on ways to foster movement toward equal education for all children (for example, Klopf and Laster, 1963):

1. Educational standards of Negro schools should be raised to the level of white schools, so that minority group children who transfer to previously all-white schools will have a reasonable chance of succeeding academically. This means, among other things, that the quality of training received by Negro teachers and the criteria used in selecting them for jobs must be raised to white levels, and racial integration of school faculties must be carried out.

2. Programs should be instituted for contacting parents and helping them to understand what they can do to prepare children for schooling, and to foster achievement once children are in school.

3. There should be in-service training of teachers and other personnel in newly integrated schools to develop awareness of the emotional needs of children in biracial situations. The training should include the imparting of techniques for helping children get acquainted with one another.

4. The widely accepted practice of assigning children to homogeneous ability groups (the "track" system) should be modified to afford maximum opportunity for periodic reevaluations of potentiality. Ability grouping tends inevitably to freeze teachers' expectations as well as children's own self-images, hence it is particularly dangerous to intellectual development in the early grades.

5. Where grade-a-year plans of desegregation are adopted, the process should begin at the lowest grades, where Negro children have the smallest educational handicap and where unfavorable racial attitudes are least strongly learned.

References

Applezweig, M. H., and G. Moeller. The role of motivation in psychological stress. *Office of Naval Research Technical Report,* 1957, No. 3.

Atkinson, J. W. "Motivational determinants of risk taking behavior." In J. W. Atkinson (ed.), *Motives in fantasy, action, and society.* Princeton, N. J.: Van Nostrand, 1958*a*, 322–340.

————. "Towards experimental analysis of human motives in terms of motives, expectancies, and incentives." In J. W. Atkinson (ed.), *Motives in fantasy, action, and society.* Princeton, N. J.: Van Nostrand, 1958*b*, 288–305.

Barker, R., Tamara Dembo, and K. Lewin. Frustration and regression: An experiment with young children. *University of Iowa Studies of Child Welfare,* 1941, **18** (1).

Bass, B. M. "Conformity, deviation, and a general theory of interpersonal behavior." In I. A. Berg and B. M. Bass (eds.), *Conformity and deviation.* New York: Harper & Row, 1961, 38–100.

Boston Psychopathic Hospital. Experimental psychoses. *Scientific American,* 1955, **192** (6), 34–39.

Bovard, E. W. The effects of social stimuli on the response to stress. *Psychological Review,* 1959, **66,** 267–277.

Callaway, E., and S. V. Thompson. Sympathetic activity and perception. *Psychosomatic Medicine,* 1953, **15,** 443–455.

Child, I. L. "Personality." In C. P. Stone and Q. McNemar (eds.), *Annual Review of Psychology.* Stanford, Calif.: Annual Reviews, 1954, 149–170.

Coleman, J. S., and staff. *Equality of Educational Opportunity.* United States Department of Health, Education and Welfare. Washington, D. C.: United States Government Printing Office, 1966.

Coles, R. *The desegregation of southern schools: A psychiatric study.* New York: Anti-Defamation League, 1963.

Conger, J. J., W. L. Sawrey, and E. S. Turrell. An experimental investigation of the role of social experience in the production of gastric ulcers in hooded rats. *American Psychologist,* 1957, **12,** 410. (Abstract)

Criswell, Joan H. A sociometric study of race cleavage in the classroom. *Archives of Psychology, New York,* 1939 (235).

Davitz, J. R., and D. J. Mason. Socially facilitated reduction of a fear response in rats. *Journal of Comparative Physiology and Psychology,* 1955, **48,** 149–151.

Day, R. E. "Part 2, North Carolina." In the United States Commission on Civil Rights, *Civil Rights U.S.A.—public schools, Southern states.* Washington, D.C.: United States Government Printing Office, 1962, 57–104.

Deese, J. "Skilled performance and conditions of stress." In R. Glaser (ed.), *Training research and education.* Pittsburgh: University of Pittsburgh Press, 1962, 199–222.

Deutsch, M. Minority group and class status as related to social and personality factors in scholastic achievement. *Society of Applied Anthropology Monographs,* 1960 (2).

————. "Dimensions of the school's role in the problems of integration." In G. J. Klopf and I. A. Laster (eds.), *Integrating the urban school.* New York: Teachers College, Columbia University, Bureau of Publications, 1963, 29–44.

Dittes, J. E., and H. H. Kelley. Effects of different conditions of acceptance upon conformity to group norms. *Journal of Abnormal and Social Psychology.* 1956, **53**, 100–107.

Dodson, D. Statement read at *Conference before the United States Commission on Civil Rights: Fourth annual education conference on problems of segregation and desegregation of public schools.* Washington, D.C.: The United States Commission on Civil Rights, 1962, 137–141.

Easterbrook, J. A. The effect of emotion on cue utilization and the organization of behavior. *Psychological Review,* 1959, **66**, 183–201.

Findley, W. G. *Learning and teaching in Atlanta public schools.* Princeton, N.J.: Educational Testing Service, 1956.

French, J. R. P., Jr., and B. Raven. "The bases of social power." In D. Cartwright and A. Zander (eds.), *Group dynamics.* Ed. 2. Evanston, Ill.: Row, Peterson, 1960, 607–623.

Goldman, M., M. Horwitz, and F. J. Lee. Alternative classroom standards concerning management of hostility and effects on student learning. *Office of Naval Research Technical Report,* 1954.

Group for the Advancement of Psychiatry. *Psychiatric aspects of school desegregation.* New York: GAP, 1957.

Hansen, C. F. The scholastic performances of Negro and white pupils in the integrated public schools of the District of Columbia. *Harvard Educational Review,* 1960, **30**, 216–236.

Harlow, H. F., and Margaret K. Harlow. Social deprivation in monkeys. *Scientific American,* 1962, **207** (5), 136–146.

Harris, I. *Emotional blocks to learning.* New York: Free Press, 1961.

Harvey, O. J. An experimental approach to the study of status relations in informal groups. *American Sociological Review,* 1953, **18**, 357–367.

Horowitz, E. The development of attitudes toward the Negro. *Archives of Psychology, New York,* 1936 (194).

Karon, B. P. *The Negro personality: A rigorous investigation of the effects of culture.* New York: Springer, 1958.

Katz, I., and L. Benjamin. Effects of white authoritarianism in biracial work groups. *Journal of Abnormal and Social Psychology,* 1960, **61**, 448–456.

Katz, I., and M. Cohen. The effects of training Negroes upon cooperative problem solving in biracial teams. *Journal of Abnormal and Social Psychology,* 1962, **64**, 319–325.

Katz, I., E. G. Epps, and L. J. Axelson. Effect upon Negro digit-symbol performance of anticipated comparison with whites and with other Negroes. *Journal of Abnormal and Social Psychology,* 1964, **69**, 77–83.

Katz, I., Judith Goldston, and L. Benjamin. Behavior and productivity in biracial work groups. *Human Relations,* 1958, **11**, 123–141.

Katz, I., and C. Greenbaum. Effects of anxiety, threat, and racial environment on task performance of Negro college students. *Journal of Abnormal Social Psychology,* 1963, **66**, 562–567.

Katz, I., S. O. Roberts, and J. M. Robinson. Effects of difficulty, race of administrator, and instructions on Negro digit-symbol performance. *Journal of Personality and Social Psychology,* 1965, **70**, 53–59.

Katz, I., J. M. Robinson, E. G. Epps, and Patricia Waly. Effects of race of experimenter and test vs. neutral instructions on expression of hostility in Negro boys. *Journal of Social Issues,* 1964, **20**, 54–59.

Kimball, Barbara. Sentence-completion technique in a study of scholastic underachievement. *Journal of Consulting Psychology,* 1952, **16**, 353–358.

Klein, G. S. "Need and regulation." In M. R. Jones (ed.), *Nebraska sym-*

posium on motivation: 1957. Lincoln: University of Nebraska Press, 1957, 224–274.

Klopf, G. J., and I. A. Laster (eds.). *Integrating the urban school.* New York: Teachers College, Columbia University, Bureau of Publications, 1963.

Knowles, L. W. "Part 1, Kentucky." In the United States Commission on Civil Rights, *Civil Rights U.S.A.—public schools, Southern states.* Washington, D.C.: United States Government Printing Office, 1962, 19–56.

Laird, D. A. Changes in motor control and individual variations under the influence of "razzing." *Journal of Experimental Psychology,* 1923, **6,** 236–246.

Lantz, Beatrice. Some dynamic aspects of success and failure. *Psychological Monographs,* 1945, 59 (1, Whole No. 271).

Lazarus, R. S., J. Deese, and Sonia F. Osler. The effects of psychological stress upon performance. *Psychological Bulletin,* 1952, **49,** 293–317.

Liddell, H. "Some specific factors that modify tolerance for environmental stress." In H. G. Wolff, S. G. Wolf, Jr., and C. C. Hare (eds.), *Life stress and bodily disease.* Baltimore: Williams and Wilkins, 1950, 155–171.

Lit, J. Formal and content factors of projective tests in relation to academic achievement. *Dissertation Abstracts,* 1956, **16,** 1505–1506 (Order No. 16,311).

Mandlebaum, D. G. *Soldier groups and Negro soldiers.* Berkeley: University of California Press, 1952.

Mandler, G., and S. B. Sarason. A study of anxiety and learning. *Journal of Abnormal and Social Psychology,* 1952, **47,** 166–173.

Marshall, S. L. A. *Men against fire.* Washington, D. C.: Combat Forces Press, 1951.

Mason, W. A. Socially mediated reduction in emotional responses of young rhesus monkeys. *Journal of Abnormal and Social Psychology,* 1960, **60,** 100–104.

Mearns, E. A., Jr. "Part 4, Virginia." In The United States Commission on Civil Rights, *Civil Rights U.S.A.—public schools, Southern states.* Washington, D.C.: United States Government Printing Office, 1962, 155–217.

Murstein, B. I., and H. L. Collier. The role of the TAT in the measurement of achievement as a function of expectancy. *Journal of Projective Techniques,* 1962, **26,** 96–101.

National Scholarship Service and Fund for Negro Students. *Annual report 1959–1960.* New York: NSSFNS, 1960.

———. *Annual report 1962–1963.* New York: NSSFNS, 1963.

Plaut, R. L. *Blueprint for talent searching.* New York: National Scholarship Service and Fund for Negro Students, 1957.

Preston, M. G., and J. A. Bayton. Differential effect of a social variable upon three levels of aspiration. *Journal of Experimental Psychology,* 1941, **29,** 351–369.

Radke, Marian, Jean Sutherland, and Pearl Rosenberg. Racial attitudes of children. *Sociometry,* 1950, **13,** 154–171.

———, Helen G. Trager, and Hadassah Davis. Social perceptions and attitudes of children. *Genetic Psychology Monograph,* 1949, **40,** 327–447.

Roberts, S. O. Test performance in relation to ethnic group and social class. Report, 1963, Fisk University, Nashville (mimeo).

Rosen, M. Valence, expectancy, and dissonance reduction in the prediction of goal striving. *Dissertation Abstracts,* 1961, **21,** 3846 (Order No. 61–2062).

Rosenwald, G. The assessment of anxiety in psychological experiments. *Journal of Abnormal and Social Psychology,* 1961, **63,** 666–673.

Sarason, I. G. Empirical findings and theoretical problems in the use of anxiety scales. *Psychological Bulletin,* 1960, **57,** 403–415.

Sarason, S. B., K. S. Davidson, F. F. Lighthall, R. R. Waite, and B. K. Ruebush. *Anxiety in elementary school children.* New York: Wiley, 1960.

Schachter, S. *The psychology of affiliation.* Stanford: Stanford University Press, 1959.

Southern School News. Untitled. *Sth. Sch. News,* 1960 (August), **7,** 6 Cols. 1–2).

———. Untitled. *Sth. Sch. News,* 1963 (April), **9,** 11 (Col. 2).

Spence, K. W. A theory of emotionally based drive (D) and its relation to performance in simple learning situations. *American Psychologist,* 1958, **13,** 131–141.

Stallings, F. H. A study of the immediate effects of integration on scholastic achievement in the Louisville Public Schools. *Journal of Negro Education,* 1959, **28,** 439–444.

Tanner, J. C. Integration in action. *Wall Street Journal,* January 26, 1964, **64** (1).

Taylor, Janet A. "Drive theory and manifest anxiety." In Martha T. Mednick and S. A. Mednick (eds.), *Research in personality.* New York: Holt, Rinehart and Winston, 1963, 205–222.

Thibaut, J., and H. H. Kelley. *The social psychology of groups.* New York: Wiley, 1959.

Titmuss, R. M. *Problems of social policy.* London, England: His Majesty's Stationery Office and Longmans, Green, 1950.

Trillin, C. *An education in Georgia.* New York: Viking Press, 1964.

Tumin, M. "The process of integration." In G. J. Klopf and I. A. Laster (eds.), *Integrating the urban school.* New York: Teachers College, Columbia University, Bureau of Publications, 1963, 13–28.

United States Commission on Civil Rights. *Second annual conference on education, Gatlinburg, Tenn.* Washington, D.C.: United States Government Printing Office, 1960.

———. *Civil Rights U.S.A.—public schools, cities in the North and West.* Washington, D.C.: United States Government Printing Office, 1962a.

———. *Civil Rights U. S. A.—public schools, Southern states.* Washington, D.C.: United States Government Printing Office, 1962b.

Whyte, W. F. *Street corner society; the social structure of an Italian slum.* Chicago: University of Chicago Press, 1943.

Wrightsman, L. S., Jr. Effects of waiting with others on changes in level of felt anxiety. *Journal of Abnormal and Social Psychology,* 1960, **61,** 216–222.

Wyatt, E. "Part 3, Tennessee." In The United States Commission on Civil Rights, *Civil Rights U.S.A.—public schools, Southern states.* Washington, D.C.: United States Government Printing Office, 1962, 105–130.

Yarrow, Marian R. (Issue ed.) Interpersonal dynamics in a desegregation process. *Journal of Social Issues,* 1958, **14** (1, entire issue).

PART
FOUR

On the Education
of the Disadvantaged

INTRODUCTION—*Martin Deutsch*

The last few years have seen a large-scale reinvolvement of psychology with education on levels other than psychometrics and clinical concerns. This reinvolvement has been stimulated in part by the rediscovery of the importance of cognitive factors in development. Another source of the new involvement with education has been the growth of a sophisticated environmentalist approach to understanding development —an approach which emphasizes the role of specific individual experience. Given these sources, it should not be surprising that a major form of the involvement with education has been the formulation of theories about, and programs for, the education of children of the population who are thought to have the fewest educationally salient experiences.

This part reflects this concern. Most of the material relates to early childhood education, and this emphasis simply reflects the fact that most of the thinking and programming are oriented to young children.

A major impetus for the new character of the environmental emphasis came from J. McVicker Hunt's book, *Intelligence and Experience,* and his chapter in this part extends some of the thinking in that book and applies it to problems in the education of the disadvantaged. Hunt relies on the Piaget model of developmental stages and emphasizes the importance of achieving a close correspondence—a "match"—between the child's developmental level and the experiential opportunities offered if cognitive development is to be stimulated. He uses this basic schema to argue that preschool enrichment, beginning preferably at two years of age, could constitute an effective "antidote" to deprivation. In order to support his main thesis, Hunt ranges widely over the findings of both human and animal research on the influences of early experience on sensory and intellective processes. He also covers areas in motivation, brain function, and a variety of other related complex topics, including a discussion of the Montessori educational approach.

The chapter by Carl Bereiter reports a specific example of a method for early compensatory education. The program described is highly structured and emphasizes language. The training procedures represent quite a departure from those in any other early childhood program, and Bereiter emphasizes that they were developed on a pragmatic rather than a theoretical basis.

The chapters by Celia Stendler and by Edmund Gordon report and discuss specific programs of intervention. Both include substantial sections on language and development.

Stendler particularly relates her discussion to stages of cognitive development and the types and effects of intervention programs for children at different ages. She points out the initial results which various programs have achieved, but cautions that more data and more time for longitudinal studies are needed before firm conclusions can be reached. She concludes, however, that infancy and early childhood are important periods for intervention and that intervention can be effective.

Gordon, in his review of compensatory programs, uses a more cross-sectional approach, emphasizing comparisons between social-class groups and relating program purposes and results to changes in the observed differences between groups. In an epidemiological approach, he relates both organic and functional differences between groups to social-background factors. In discussing programs for the disadvantaged, he describes deficit models as being drawn from the field of special education of the handicapped, and socially oriented models as based on the supposition that the prime problem is the inadequacy of the schools because they reflect social inequality.

The Stendler and Gordon chapters complement one another in their emphases, and together give a quite comprehensive coverage to the theories, practices, and orientations of current compensatory and enrichment programs.

The four chapters taken as whole represent a fairly comprehensive overview of the field, and its relationship to contemporary psychological theory and educational practice.

CHAPTER EIGHT

Environment, Development, and Scholastic Achievement

J. McVicker Hunt[1]

It is very interesting, and very exciting for me, to encounter people who are generally considered sensible, planning to utilize preschool experiences as an antidote for what we are now calling cultural deprivation and social disadvantage. The group at the Child Welfare Research Station in Iowa, under George D. Stoddard (see Stoddard and Wellman, 1940), described effects of nursery school which they considered evidence that would justify just such a use of nursery schools. This was over twenty-five years ago. Their work, however, was picked to pieces by critics and in the process lost much of the suggestive value it was justified in having. Many of you will recall the ridicule that was heaped upon the "wandering IQ" (Simpson, 1939) and the way in which such people as Florence Goodenough (1939) derided in print the idea

[1] University of Illinois.

This is a revised version of a paper originally published in the *Merrill-Palmer Quarterly of Behavior and Development* and is published here with their permission. The paper was originally prepared for the Arden House Conference on Pre-School Enrichment of Socially Disadvantaged Children (December 1962) with the support of USPHS Grant No. MH K6–18,567. The author also wishes to acknowledge grants from the Carnegie Foundation, The Commonwealth Fund, and the Russell Sage Foundation.

of a group of thirteen "feeble-minded" infants being brought within the range of normal mentality through training by moron nurse-maids in a institution for the feeble-minded (referring to the work of Skeels and Dye, 1939, to which we shall return). The fact that just such a use of preschool experience is now being seriously planned by sensible people with widespread approval means that something has changed.

The change, of course, is not in the nature of man or in the nature of his development; it is rather in our conceptions of man's nature and of his development. Some of our most important beliefs about man and his development have changed or are in the process of changing. It is these changes in belief which have freed us to try as demonstrative experiments that only as recently as World War II would have been considered a stupid waste of effort and time. It is also these changes in theoretical belief about man and his development which provide my topic, namely, the psychological basis for using preschool enrichment as an antidote for cultural deprivation.

I number these changed or changing beliefs as six. Let me state them in their prechange form; in the form, in other words, that has so much hampered the sort of enterprise in which this group is about to engage:

1. a belief in fixed intelligence;
2. a belief in predetermined development;
3. a belief in the fixed and static, telephone-switchboard nature of brain function;
4. a belief that experience during the early years, and particularly before the development of speech, is unimportant;
5. a belief that whatever experience does affect later development is a matter of emotional reactions based on the fate of instinctual needs;
6. a belief that learning must be motivated by homeostatic need, by painful stimulation, or by acquired drives based on these.

Let me discuss the evidential and conceptual bases for the change which has been taking place since World War II in these hampering beliefs, one by one. Then I shall close by trying to justify the sort of enterprise you propose, and by indicating how the largely forgotten work of Maria Montessori may well contain practical suggestions concerning the way to go about the enterprise.

THE BELIEF IN FIXED INTELLIGENCE

Almost every idea has roots in a communicated conceptual history and in observed evidence. The notion of fixed intelligence has conceptual roots in Darwin's (1859) theory of evolution and in the intense emotional controversy that surrounded it. You will recall that Darwin believed that evolution took place, not by changes wrought through use or disuse as Lamarck (1809) had thought, but by changes resulting from variations in the progeny of every species or strain which are then selected by the conditions under which they live. Their selection is a matter of which variations survive to reproduce so that the variations are passed on into the successive generations. The change is conceived thus to be one that comes via the survival of a variation in a strain through reproduction. Implicit in this notion was the assumption that the characteristics of any organism are predetermined by the genetic constitution with which the organism comes into being as a fertilized ovum. Probably this implicit assumption would never have caught on with anywhere near the force it did, had it not been for two outstanding figures in the history of relatively recent thought. The first of these is Sir Francis Galton, Charles Darwin's younger cousin. You will remember that it was Galton who made the assumption of the hereditary determination of adult characteristics explicit. Galton reasoned, furthermore, that if his cousin were correct, it would mean that the hope of improving the lot of man does not lie in *euthenics,* or in trying to change him through education; rather, such hope lies in *eugenics,* or in the selection of those superior persons who should survive. Second, he saw that if decisions were to be made as to which human beings were to survive and reproduce, it would be necessary to have some criteria for survival. So he founded his anthropometric laboratory for the measurement of man, with the hope that by means of tests he could determine those individuals who should survive. Note that he was not deciding merely who should be selected for jobs in a given industry, but who should survive to reproduce. This was his concern. Because of the abhorrence which such a plan met, Galton talked and wrote relatively little about it. However, the combination of the context of his life's work with the few remarks he did make on the subject gives these remarks convincing significance (see Hunt, 1961).

Galton had a pupil who was very influential in bringing such conceptions into the stream of American thought. This was J. McKeen Cattell, who brought Galton's tests to America and, beginning in 1890, gave them to college students, first at the University of Pennsylvania and then at Columbia University. Because Cattell was also an influential teacher at both Penn and Columbia, his influence spread through the many students he had before World War I—when his sympathies with Germany led to a painful separation from Columbia.

A second psychologist who was almost equally influential in bringing the stream of thought supporting fixed intelligence into American thought is G. Stanley Hall. Hall did not personally know Galton; neither did he personally know Darwin, but he read about evolution while still a college student, and, as he has written in his autobiography, "it struck me like a light; this was the thing for me." Hall's importance lies in that he communicated a strong attachment to the notion of fixed intelligence to his students at Clark University, of which he was the first President, and these students became leaders of the new psychology in America (see Boring, 1929, p. 534). Among them were three of the most illustrious leaders of the testing movement. One was Henry H. Goddard, who first translated the Binet tests into English for use at the Vineland Training School and also wrote the story of the Kallikak family (1912). Another was F. Kuhlmann, who was also an early translator and reviser of the Binet tests and who, with Rose G. Anderson, adapted them for use with preschool children. The third was Lewis Terman, who is the author of the Stanford-Binet revision, the most widely known version of the Binet tests in America. These three communicated their faith in fixed intelligence to a major share of those who spread the testing movement in America.

So much for the conceptual roots of the belief in fixed intelligence that come by way of communication in the history of thought.

The assumption of fixed intelligence also had an empirical basis. Not only did test-retest reliabilities show that the positions of individuals in a group remained fairly constant, but also the tests showed some capacity to predict such criterion performances as school success, success as officers in World War I, and so on. All such evidence concerned children of school age for whom the experience to which they are exposed is at least to some degree standardized (see Hunt, 1961). When investigators began to examine the constancy of the developmental quotient (DQ) or IQ in preschool children, the degree of constancy proved to be very much lower. You will recall some of the very interesting interpretations of this lack of constancy in the preschool DQ (see Hunt, 1961, p. 311ff). Anderson argued that since the tests at successive ages involved different functions, constancy could not be expected. But an epigenesis of man's intellectual functions is inherent in the nature of his development, and the implications of this fact were apparently missed by these critics of the findings from the infant tests. While they knew that the basic structure of intelligence changes in its early phases of development just as the structures of the body change in the embryological phase of morphological development, they appear not to have noted that it is thus inevitable that the infant tests must involve differing content and functions at successive ages.

It was Woodworth (1941) who argued, after examining the evidence from the studies of twins, that there might be some difference in IQ due to the environment but that which exists among individuals in our culture is largely due to the genes. In the context of cultural deprivation, I believe Woodworth asked the wrong question. He might better have asked: What would be the difference in the IQ of a pair of identical twins at age six if one were reared as Myrtle McGraw (1935) reared the trained twin, Johnny (so that he was swimming at four months, roller-skating at eleven months, and developing various such skills at about one-half to one-fourth the age that people usually develop them), and if the other twin were reared in an orphanage, like the one described by Wayne Dennis (1960) in Teheran, where 60 percent of the infants two years of age are still not sitting up alone, and where 85 percent of those four years of age are still not walking alone? While observations of this kind come from varied sources and lack the force of controlled experimentation, they suggest strongly that lack of constancy is the rule for either IQ or DQ during the preschool years and that the IQ is not at all fixed unless the culture or the school fixes the program of environmental encounters. Cross-sectional validity may be substantial, with predictive validity being little above zero (see Hunt, 1961). In fact, trying to predict what the IQ of an individual child will be at age eighteen from a DQ obtained during his first or second year is much like trying to predict how fast a feather might fall in a hurricane. The law of falling bodies holds only under the specified and controlled conditions of a vacuum. Similarly, any laws concerning the rate of intellectual growth must take into account the series of environmental encounters which constitute the conditions of that growth.

THE BELIEF IN PREDETERMINED DEVELOPMENT

The belief in predetermined development has been no less hampering, for a serious consideration of preschool enrichment as an antidote for cultural deprivation than that in fixed intelligence. This belief also has historical roots in Darwin's theory of evolution. It got communicated into the main stream of psychological thought about development by G. Stanley Hall (see Pruette, 1926). Hall gave special emphasis to the belief in predetermined development by making central in his version of the theory of evolution the conception of recapitulation. This is the notion that the development of an individual shows in summary form the development of the species. Hall managed to communicate many valuable points about psychological development by means of his parables based on the concept of biological recapitulation. One of the most famous of these is his parable of the tadpole's tail. To Hall also goes a very large share of the responsibility for the shape of investigation in child and developmental psychology during the first half of this century. This shape was the study of normative development, or the description of what is typical or average. It was, more-over, as you all know, Arnold Gesell (see 1945, 1954), another student of G. Stanley Hall, whose life's work concerned the normative description of children's behavioral development. Gesell took over Hall's faith in predetermined development in his own notion that development is governed by what he has termed "intrinsic growth." It should be noted that once one believes in intrinsic growth, the normative picture of development is not only a description of the process but an explanation of it as well. Thus, whenever little Johnny does something "bad," the behavior can be explained by noting that it is just a stage he is going through. Moreover, following Hall's parable of the tadpole's tail—in which the hind legs fail to develop if the tail is amputated—Johnny's unwanted behavior must not be hampered else some desirable future characteristic will fail to appear.

This notion of predetermined development also has an empirical basis, for the evidence from various early studies of behavioral development in both lower animals and children was readily seen as consonant with it. Among these are Coghill's (1929) studies of behavioral development in amblystoma. These demonstrated that behavioral development, like anatomical development, starts at the head-end and proceeds tailward, starts from the inside and proceeds outward, and consists of a progressive differentiation of more specific units from general units. From such evidence Coghill and others inferred the special additional notion that behavior unfolds automatically as the anatomical basis for behavior matures. From such a background came the differentiation of the process of learning from the process of maturation.

Among the early studies of behavioral development are those of Carmichael (1926, 1927, 1928), also with amblystoma and frogs, which appeared to show that the circumstances in which development takes place are of little consequence. You will recall that Carmichael divided batches of amblystoma and frog eggs. One of these batches he chloretoned to inhibit their activity; another batch he kept in tap water on an ordinary table; and a third group he kept in tap water on a work bench, where they received extra stimulation. Those kept in tap water on an ordinary table swam as early as did those that got the extra stimulation from the work bench. Moreover, even though those that were chloretoned had been prevented from activity through five days, they appeared to be as adept at swimming within a half an hour after the chloretone was washed out as were either of the two batches reared in tap water. Although Carmichael himself was very careful in interpreting these results, they have commonly been interpreted to mean that development is almost entirely a function of maturation and that learning, as represented in practice, is of little consequence.

Such an interpretation got further support from early studies of the effects of practice. In one such study of a pair of identical twins by Gesell and Thompson (1929), the untrained twin became as adept at tower-building and stair-climbing after a week of practice as was the trained twin who had been given practice in tower-building and stair-climbing over many weeks. In another such study by Josephine Hilgard (1932), a group of ten preschool children were given practice cutting with scissors, climbing a ladder, and buttoning over a period of twelve weeks; yet they retained their superiority over the control group, which had received no special practice, for only a very short time. One week of practice in those skills by the control group brought their performance up to a level which was no longer significantly inferior to that of the experimental group from a statistical standpoint. Later work by two other investigators appeared to lend further support. Dennis and Dennis (1940) found that the children of Hopi Indians raised on cradleboards, which inhibited the movements of their legs and arms during waking hours, walked at the same age as did Hopi children reared freely, in the typical white-man's manner. Moreover, Dennis and Dennis (1935, 1938, 1941) found the usual sequence of autogenic behavior items in a pair of fraternal twins reared under conditions of "restricted practice and minimal social stimulation." Many such studies appeared to yield results which could be readily seen as consonant with the notion that practice has little effect on the rate of development, and that the amount of effect to be got from practice is a function of the level of maturation present when the practice occurs.

It was just such a notion and just such evidence that led Watson (1928) to argue in his book, *The Psychological Care of the Infant and Child,* that experience is unimportant during the preschool years because nothing useful can be learned until the child has matured sufficiently. Thus, he advised that the best thing possible is to leave the child alone to grow. Then, when the child has "lain and grown," when the response repertoire has properly matured, those in charge of his care can introduce learning. He conceived that learning could "get in its licks" tying these responses to proper stimuli, via the conditioning principle, and by linking them together in chains to produce complex skills. I suspect that the use of B. F. Skinner's baby-box, with controlled temperature, humidity, and so on, may be based upon just such assumptions of predetermined development and of an automatic unfolding of a basic behavioral repertoire with anatomical maturation.

It should be noted that the animal evidence cited here comes from amblystoma and frogs, which are well down the phylogenetic scale.

They have brains in which the ratio of those portions concerned with association or intrinsic processes to the portions concerned directly with input and output is small; that is, the A/S ratio, as formulated by Hebb (1949), is small. When organisms with higher A/S ratios were studied, in somewhat the fashion in which Coghill and Carmichael studied the behavioral development of amblystoma and frogs, the evidence yielded was highly dissonant with the implications of predetermined development. When Cruze (1935, 1938) found that the number of pecking errors per twenty-five trials decreased through the first five days, even though the chicks were kept in the dark—a result consonant with the notion of predeterminism—he also found facts pointing in a contrary direction. For instance, chicks kept in the dark for twenty consecutive days, and given an opportunity to see light and have pecking-experience only during the daily tests, *failed* to attain a high level of accuracy in pecking and exhibited almost no improvement in the striking-seizing-swallowing sequence.

Similarly, Kuo's (see Hunt, 1961) wonderful behavioral observations on the embryological development of chicks in the egg indicate that the responses comprising the pecking and locomotor patterns have been "well-practiced" long before hatching. The "practice" for pecking seems to start with head-bobbing, which is among the first embryonic movements to be observed. The practice for the locomotor patterns begins with vibratory motions of the wing-buds and leg-buds; these movements become flexion and extension as the limbs lengthen and joints appear. At about the eleventh day of incubation, the yolk sac characteristically moves over to the ventral side of the embryo. This movement of the yolk sac forces the legs to fold on the breast and to be held there. From this point on, the legs cannot be fully extended. They are forced henceforth to hatching to remain in this folded position with extensive thrusts only against the yolk sac. Kuo argues that this condition establishes a fixed resting posture for the legs, and prepares them for lifting of the chick's body in standing and locomotion. Moreover, his interpretation gets some support from "an experiment of nature." In the 7000 embryos that he observed, nearly two hundred crippled chicks appeared. These crippled chicks could neither stand nor walk after hatching. Neither could they sit in the roosting position, because their legs were deformed. Over 80 percent of those with deformed legs occurred in those instances in which the yolk sac failed for some reason, still unknown, to move over to the ventral side of the embryo.

Such observations suggest that the mammalian advent of increasingly long uterine control of embryological and fetal environment in phylogeny reflects the fact that environmental circumstances more and more become important for early development, as the central nervous system control becomes more predominant. It should be noted, moreover, that as central-nervous-system control becomes more predominant, capacity for regeneration decreases. Perhaps this implies a waning of the relative potency of the chemical predeterminers of development as one goes up the phylogenetic scale.

Perhaps even more exciting in this connection is the work of Austin Riesen (see 1958), Brattgård (1952), and others. Riesen undertook the rearing of chimpanzees in darkness in order to test some of Hebb's (1949) hypotheses of the importance of primary learning in the development of perception. What he appears to have discovered—along with Brattgård (1952); Liberman (1962); Rasch *et al.* (1961); and Weiskrantz (1958)—is that even certain anatomical structures of the retina require light stimulation for proper development. The chimpanzee babies who were kept in the dark for a year and a half have atypical retinas; and, even after they are brought into the light, the subsequent development of their retinas goes awry and they become permanently blind. The result of such prolonged stimulus deprivation during infancy appears to be an irreversible process that does not occur when the chimpanzee infant is kept in darkness for only something like seven months. Inasmuch as Weiskrantz (1958) has found a scarcity of Müller fibers in the retinas of kittens reared in the dark, and since other investigators (especially Brattgård, 1952) have found the retinal-ganglion cells of animals reared in the dark to be deficient in the production of ribonucleic acid (RNA), these studies of rearing under conditions of sensory deprivation appear to be lending support to Hydén's (1959, 1960) hypothesis that the effects of experience may be stored as RNA within the glial component of retinal tissue, of Deiter's nucleus (Hydén and Pigon, 1960) and, perhaps, of brain tissue as well.

For our present purposes, it is enough to note that such studies are bringing evidence that even the anatomical structures of the central nervous system are affected in their development by encounters with circumstances. This lends credence to Piaget's (1936) aphorism that "use is the aliment of a schema."

Consider another study of the effects of early experience. This is a study by Thompson and Heron (1954), comparing the adult problem-solving ability of Scotty pups which were reared as pets in human homes from the time of weaning until they were eight months of age with that of their litter-mates reared in isolation in laboratory cages for the same period. The adult tests were made when the animals were eighteen months old, after they had been together in the dog pasture for a period of ten months. Adult problem-solving was measured by means of the Hebb-Williams (1946) test of animal intelligence. In one of these tests, the dog is brought into a room while hungry. After being allowed to smell and see a bowl of food, the dog is permitted to watch as his food is removed and put behind a screen in one of the opposite corners of the room. Both pet-reared and cage-reared dogs go immediately to the spot where the food disappeared. After the same procedure has been repeated several times, the food is then placed, while the animal watches, behind a screen in another opposite corner of the room. In order to see this clearly, think of the first screen being in the corner to the dog's right, the second in the corner to the dog's left. Now, when the dog is released, if he is pet-reared he goes immediately to the screen in the left corner for food. But, if he was cage-reared, he is more likely to go to the screen in the right corner where he had previously found food. In his tests of object permanence, Piaget (1936) describes behavior of children about nine months old resembling that of the cage-reared pups, and of children about fourteen months old resembling that of the pet-reared pups.

It is interesting to compare the results of this study by Thompson and Heron (1954), in which dogs were the subjects, with the results of various studies of the effects of early experiences on adult problem-solving in which rats were subjects (see Hebb, 1947; Gauron and Becker, 1959; Wolf, 1943). Whereas the effects of early experience on the problem-solving of dogs appear to be both large and persistent, they appear to be both less marked and less permanent in the rat. Such a comparison lends further credence to the proposition that the importance of the effects of early experience increases as the associative or intrinsic portions of the cerebrum increase in proportion, as reflected in Hebb's notion of the A/S ratio.

But what about the fact that practice appears to have little or no effect on the development of a skill in young children? How can one square the absence of the effects of practice with the tremendous apathy and retardation commonly to be found in children reared in orphanages? In the case of the orphanage in Teheran reported on by Dennis (1960), the retardation in locomotor function is so great, as I have already noted, that 60 percent of those in their second year fail to sit up alone, even though nearly all children ordinarily sit up at ten months of age; and 85 percent of those in their fourth year still fail to walk alone even though children typically walk at about fourteen or fifteen months of age. I believe the two sets of results can be squared by taking into account the epigenesis in the structure of behavior that occurs during the earliest years. The investigators of the effects of practice neglected this epigenesis. They sought the effects of experience only in practice of the function of schema to be observed and measured. The existence of an epigenesis of intellectual function implies that the experiential roots of a given schema will lie in antecedent activities quite different in structure from the schema to be observed and measured. Thus, antecedent practice at tower-building and buttoning may be relatively unimportant for the development of skill in these activities; but an unhampered antecedent opportunity to throw objects and to manipulate them in a variety of situations, and an even earlier opportunity to have seen a variety of sights and to have heard a variety of sounds, may be of tremendous importance in determining both the age at which tower-building and buttoning will occur and the degree of skill that the child will manifest. I shall return to this topic.

BRAIN FUNCTION CONCEIVED AS A STATIC SWITCHBOARD

One can not blame Darwin for the conception of brain function as static, like that in a telephone switchboard. The origin of the ferment leading to these conceptions, however, does derive from Darwin's (1872) shift of attention from the evolution of the body to the evolution of mind. This he began in his book, *The Expressions of the Emotions in Man and Animals*. It was thus Darwin who provided the stimulus for what was later to be called *comparative psychology*. The original purpose was to show that there is a gradual transition from the lower animals to man in the various faculties of mind. It was Romanes (1882, 1883) who took up this task in an attempt to show the manner in which intelligence has evolved. Romanes' method was to show through anecdotes that animals are capable of intelligent behavior, albeit at a level of complexity inferior to man's. It was C. Lloyd Morgan (1894) who said that it was reasoning by very loose analogy to impute to dogs, cats, and the like, the same kind of conscious processes and faculties that man can report. It was Morgan who applied Ockham's "razor of parsimony" to the various mental faculties. Then, shortly, Thorndike and Woodworth (1901) knocked out such old-fashioned faculties as memory with their studies showing that such forms of practice as daily memorizing poetry does not improve a person's capacity to memorize other types of material, and that being taught mathematics and Latin does not improve performance on reasoning tests.

It was still obvious, however, that animals do learn and that they do solve problems. Morgan (1894) saw this occurring by a process of trial-and-error. According to this conception, as Hull (1943) later elaborated it, an organism comes to any given situation with a ready-made hierarchy of responses. When those at the top of the hierarchy fail to achieve satisfaction, they are supposed to be weakened (extinguished). Other responses lower in the hierarchy then take their places and become connected with stimuli from the situation. Or, as Thorndike

(1913) put it earlier, new *S–R* bonds are established. Complex behavior was explained by assuming that one response can be the stimulus for another, so that *S–R* chains could be formed. The role of the brain in such learning also needed explanation. Here the telephone was the dramatic new invention supplying a mechanical model for a conception of the brain's role. Inasmuch as the reflex arc was conceived to be both the anatomical and the functional unit of the nervous system, the role of the brain in learning could readily be conceived to be analogous to that of a telephone switchboard. Thus, the head was emptied of active functions, and the brain, which filled it, came to be viewed as the focus of a variety of static connections.

All this led to what I think is a basic confusion in psychological thought, one which has been prominent for at least the last thirty-five or forty years. This is a confusion between *S–R* methodology, on the one hand, and *S–R* theory on the other. We cannot escape *S–R* methodology. The best one can possibly do empirically is to note the situations in which organisms behave and to observe what they do there. But there is no reason why one should not relate the empirical relationships one can observe between stimulus and response to whatever the neurophysiologist can tell us about inner-brain function and to whatever the endocrinologist can tell us. The broader one makes his nomological net, the better, in that the more nearly his resulting conceptions will approach those of the imaginary, all-seeing eye of Deity.

Stimulus-Response (*S–R*) methodology appeared at first to imply the notion of the empty organism. It is interesting to recall, however, that very shortly after the mental faculties had been removed by C. Lloyd Morgan with Ockham's razor of parsimony, Walter Hunter (1912, 1918) discovered that various animals could delay their responses to stimuli and also learn double alternation. Both achievements implied that there must be some kind of representative or symbolic process intervening between stimulus and response. It was to explain just such behavior, moreover, that Hull (1931) promulgated the notion of the pure-stimulus act. This became in turn the response-produced cues and the response-produced drives of Miller and Dollard. When Miller and Dollard (1941, p. 59) began conceiving of the responses which serve as stimuli occurring within the brain, traditional *S–R* theory with its implicit peripherality of both stimulus and response began to fade. The demise of peripheral *S–R* theory became nearly complete when Osgood (1953) turned these response-produced cues and drives into central mediating processes. It is interesting to note in this connection that it is precisely observations from *S–R* methodology which have undone traditional peripheral *S–R* theory, and it is these observations which are now demanding that brain function be conceived in terms of active processes.

The theoretical need for active brain processes, however, has been stimulated by and has gotten much of its form from cybernetics (Wiener, 1948). Such investigators as Newell *et al.* (1958), in the process of programming computers to solve problems, and especially logical problems, have been clarifying the general nature of what is required for solving such problems. They have described three major kinds of requirements: (1) memories or information stored somewhere, and presumably in the brain; (2) operations of a logical sort which are of the order of actions that deal with the information in the memories; and (3) hierarchical arrangements of these operations and memories in programs. Thus, the electronic computer has been replacing the telephone switchboard as the mechanical model for brain function.

Such a notion of memories and, even more, the notion of operations of a logical sort as actions, and the notion of hierarchical arrangements of these operations—these notions differ markedly from the notion of reflexes being chained to each other. Moreover, ablation studies have been showing that it is not communication across the cortex from sensory-input regions to motor-output regions that is important for behavior. The cortex can be diced into very small parts without serious damage to behavioral function; but if the fibers, composed of white matter, under an area of the gray-matter cortex are cut, behavior is damaged seriously. Thus, the notion of transcortical association gives way to communication back-and-forth from the center to the periphery of the brain (see Pribram, 1960). With such changes in conception of brain function being dictated by their own observations, when neuropsychologists become familiar with what is required in programming computers to solve logical problems, it is not surprising that they ask themselves where one might find a locus for the various requirements of computer function—that is, for the memories, the operations, and the hierarchical arrangements of them. Carl Pribram (1960) has reviewed the clinical and experimental findings concerning the functional consequences of injuring various portions of the brain, and he has come up with a provisional answer. The brain appears to be divided into intrinsic portions and extrinsic portions. This is the terminology of Rose and Woolsey (1949), and here the term *intrinsic* is used because this portion has no direct connections with either incoming sensory fibers or outgoing motor fibers. The extrinsic portion is so called because it does have such direct peripheral connections. What Pribram suggests is that these components of what is required for the various kinds of information processing and of decision-making may well reside in these intrinsic portions of the brain.

There are two intrinsic portions: One is the frontal portion of the cortex, with its connections to the dorsal frontal nuclei of the thalamus; the other, the nonsensory portions of the parietal, occipital, and temporal lobes with their connections with the pulvenar or the posterior dorsal nucleus of the thalamus. Injury to the frontal system disrupts executive functions and thereby suggests that it is the locus of the central, neural mechanism for plans. Injury to the posterior intrinsic system results in damage to recognitive functions, which suggests that it may be the locus of central, neural mechanisms for information-processing per se. The intrinsic portions of the cerebrum appear to become relatively larger and larger as one samples organisms up the phylogenetic scale. Perhaps what Hebb (1949) has called the A/S ratio might better be called the I/E ratio—for "Intrinsic/Extrinsic."

From such studies, one can readily conceive the function of early experience to be one of "programming" these intrinsic portions of the cerebrum so that they can later function effectively in the forms of learning and problem-solving traditionally investigated.

PREVERBAL EXPERIENCE UNIMPORTANT

Early experience, particularly preverbal experience, however, has historically been considered to be relatively unimportant. It has been argued that such experience can hardly have any effect on adult behavior, because it is not remembered. There have been, of course, a few relatively isolated thinkers who have given at least lip-service to the importance of early experience in the development of the personality.[2] Plato is one who thought that the rearing and education of children was too important a function to be carried out by mere amateur parents. But when he described the rearing that children should have in his *Republic,* he described only experiences for youngsters already talking. Rousseau (1762) gave somewhat more than lip-service in *Emile* to the importance of early experience. Moreover, at least implicitly, he attributed importance to preverbal experience with his prescription that the child, Emile, should very early be exposed to pain and cold in order that he might be toughened.

An even earlier example is to me somewhat embarrassing. I thought that I had invented the notion of split-litter technique for determining the effects of infant feeding-frustration in rats—but later I found, in reading Plutarch's *Lives,* that Lycurgus, the Law-Giver of the Spartans, took puppies from the same litter and reared them in diverse ways, so that some became greedy and mischievious curs while others became

---

[2] When this was written, I was unfamiliar with Book VII of *The Laws.* There Plato concerns himself with not only preverbal experience but also prenatal experience. I am indebted to Richard Kobler, the engineer who invented the "talking typewriter" in collaboration with O. K. Moore, for calling these pages of *The Laws* to my attention.

followers of the scent and hunters. He exhibited these pups before his contemporaries, saying, "Men of Sparta, of a truth, habit and training and teaching and guidance in living are a great influence toward engendering excellence, and I will make this evident to you at once." Thereupon he produced the dogs with diverse rearing. Perhaps it is from the stories of the Spartans that Rousseau got his notion that Emile should be toughened. Such followers of Rousseau as Pestalozzi and Froebel certainly saw childhood experience as important, but as educators they were concerned with the experiences of children who had already learned to verbalize. So far as I can tell, the notion that preverbal experience is seriously important for adult personal characteristics comes from Freud (1905) and his theory of psychosexual development

Unimportance of Psychosexual Development

Freud not only attributed importance to preverbal experience; he also proposed a hypothesis concerning the nature of the kinds of experience important for later development. These were the experiences deriving from the fate of instinctive impulses arising out of homeostatic need, painful stimulation, and, especially, the pleasure-striving which he saw as sexual in nature (Freud, 1905). If one examines the objective studies of the effects of the various kinds of factors deemed to be important from the standpoint of their theory of psychosexual development, one has a very hard time finding clear evidence that they are important (see Hunt, 1945, 1956; Orlansky, 1949). For every study that appears to show an effect of some given psychosexual factor in early infancy, there is another study to be matched with it that fails to show an effect. Furthermore, the more carefully the various studies appear to be controlled, the more nearly the results tend to be consonant with the null hypothesis. The upshot of all this is that it looks very much as if the kinds of factors to which Freud attributed importance in his theory of psychosexual development are not very important.

It was commonly believed before World War II that early experience was important for emotional development and for the development of personality characteristics, but unimportant for the development of intellect or intelligence. Some of the animal studies of early experience were widely quoted to support this belief. One of these was my own study of the effects of infant feeding-frustration upon adult hoarding in rats (Hunt, 1941). Actually, the effects of the infantile feeding-frustration were exhibited in both eating rate and hoarding, and exhibited in the eating rate more regularly than in the hoarding. Rats do not always hoard as a consequence of infantile feeding-frustration, although they do regularly eat faster than litter-mates without such experience. Yet, the feeding or drinking frustration need not occur in infancy to get the effect of speeded eating or speeded drinking (Freedman, 1957). In the case of the work of my colleagues and myself, much of it still unpublished, various kinds of effects that should, theoretically, have followed did not occur. The upshot of all this, I now believe, is that our theoretical expectations were wrong. I also believe that the general notion that the emotional characteristics of persons are most influenced by early experience while the intellectual characteristics are not influenced is also quite wrong.

Importance of Preverbal Experience for Intellect

I am prompted to change my belief because the approach to the study of the effects of early experience suggested by Donald Hebb's theorizing about cerebral functioning has regularly yielded results confirming his hypothesis. According to Hebb's (1949) theory, firing systems, which he terms *cell assemblies* and *phase sequences,* must be built into the cerebrum through what he has termed *primary learning.* This may be seen as another way of expressing the idea that the intrinsic regions of the cerebrum must be properly programmed by preverbal experience if the mammalian organism is later to function effectively as a problem-solver. Most of this primary learning Hebb (1949) presumed, moreover, to be based upon early perceptual experience. It is in this presumption that he broke most radically with the traditional emphasis on the response side in learning (a point to which I shall return).

It was this conception which led Hebb (1947) early to compare the problem-solving ability in adulthood of those rats which had their perceptual experience limited by cage-rearing, with that of rats which had had their perceptual experience enriched by pet-rearing. As I have already noted in connection with my comments on the notion of predetermined development, the problem-solving ability of the cage-reared rats was inferior to that of the pet-reared rats. The theory, as encouraged by these exploratory results, led then to a series of studies in which various kinds of early perceptual experiences were provided for one sample of rats and not for an otherwise comparable sample. Thus, the difference between the groups in later problem-solving, or maze-learning provided an index of both the presence and the degree of effect. Such studies have regularly yielded substantial effects for various kinds of early perceptual experience. These studies, moreover, appear to be clearly reproducible (Hunt and Luria, 1956). Furthermore, as I have already noted in connection with my remarks on predetermined development, these effects of early perceptual experience on adult problem-solving appear to become more and more marked up the phylogenetic scale as the intrinsic portions come to constitute a higher and higher proportion of the cerebrum. It looks now as though early experience may be even more important for the perceptual, cognitive and intellective functions than it is for the emotional and temperamental functions.

Change in the Conception of Trauma

The investigations of the effects of early experience in animals appear to be calling for still further changes in our conception of the nature of the most important kinds of early experience. Freud (1900, 1915, 1926) had various theories of anxiety. But in his later theorizing about it he not only relied upon the notion of association but also conceived of painful stimulation, either through excessive homeostatic need or an overflow of excitement, as a basis for trauma. He also presumed that organisms which had experienced high levels of such traumatic excitement during infancy were made more prone to be anxious and neurotic later in life.

With the goal of demonstrating just such effects, Levine et al. (1956) undertook the experiment in which they shocked rats daily for two minutes, keeping them squealing frantically throughout this period, on each of the first twenty days of their lives. A second sample of rats were picked up and brought to the grid-box, where they were put down without being shocked. Those of a third group were left unmolested in the maternal nest. One of the adult tests (at sixty days of age) involved defecation and urination in an unfamiliar situation. This is the test of so-called emotionality invented by Hall (1934). Those animals that had been shocked during infancy did not defecate and urinate more than those handled or than those left unmolested in the nest, as would be expected from trauma theory. On the contrary, the shocked animals defecated less on the average. The difference in this experiment fell short of statistical significance; but various subsequent experiments by both Levine and Denenberg (see Denenberg, 1962) yielded results showing that rats shocked in infancy defecated and urinated significantly less than those left unmolested in the maternal nest. Levine, Chevalier, and Korchin (1956) also found that the animals shocked in infancy, and the animals handled in infancy, both learned to avoid shock, by learning to respond to a signal before the onset of shock, in fewer trials than did those animals which had remained unmolested in the maternal nest. Confirming results have been obtained by Denenberg (1962).

Other evidence has come from the work of my own students. Goldman (1963) has shown that the intensity of shock required to move a rat over a barrier, from one end of a runway to the other end, is greater for rats that have been shocked during their preweaning stage of infancy than it is for those which have been left unmolested in the warm maternal nest. Salama (Salama and Hunt, 1964) has repeated the Farber (1948) study, in which rats shocked just past the choice point in a T-maze became "rigid" about giving up the place where they had got food, even after food had ceased to appear there. Salama compared the number of trials required to bring about such a shift in goal-box by animals shocked in infancy, by animals merely picked up in infancy, by animals petted in infancy, and by animals left unmolested in the maternal nest. While animals shocked in infancy require more trials (nine, on the average) to make the shift from the "fixated" arm and goal-box to the other arm of the T-maze than do animals which have not been shocked at the choice point (an average of 2.8 trials), they require substantially fewer than do animals handled or left unmolested in the maternal nest before weaning (an average of 20.7) or than do those petted (an average of 21.4 trials). Thus, the experience of having been shocked regularly before weaning appears actually to diminish the capacity of shock either to motivate behavior or to fixate a response.

Such evidence appears to call for a revision of the trauma theory. I find this evidence from animal studies especially interesting, moreover, because there is a study of human children with results which are consonant. This is a study by Holmes (1935) in which fear scores for children of a day-care center proved to be much lower than those for children of a nursery school. These results have seldom been cited in the secondary literature, perhaps because they were troublesomely dissonant with the dominant theoretical expectations. The dominant expectation would be that the opposite should have prevailed, because the children of day-care centers came from the lower class where painful experience and hunger (that is, traumatizing experiences) were common; whereas the children of the nursery schools came from the upper class where such presumably traumatizing experiences are relatively rare. I believe this is an item of evidence from human subjects to indicate that children, as well as infant animals, who have been through a great many painful circumstances are not as fearful in strange or unfamiliar situations as are children who have not experienced such painful circumstances. This evidence lends support to the recommendations that Rousseau made for Emile, and it helps to clarify how the Spartan culture could have survived for something like five hundred years even though it practiced what has sometimes been seen as "infant torture."

It now looks as if there may be two quite different kinds of effect of early infantile experience. One is that just described, in which the effect of painful experience is one of reducing the aversiveness of later painful or strange circumstances. Although the evidence is not clear yet, that from Salama's experiment indicates that such other kinds of early experience as mere picking up or petting do not have this effect. The other kind of effect is one increasing the capacity of an organism to learn. I have already mentioned that both the shocked rats and the handled rats in the study by Levine *et al.* (1956) learned to respond to a signal to avoid shock more rapidly than did the rats that remained unmolested in the maternal nest. This is adaptive. Denenberg (see 1962) has shown that even shocking animals once on the second day of life will decrease the number of trials they require to learn an avoidance response, as compared with those left unmolested in the maternal nest. This kind of effect appears to result not only from shock during the preweaning phase of development but also from handling and petting. It looks very much as if any increase in the variation of circumstances encountered during those first three weeks of life will facilitate later learning, not only in the avoidance situation but also in such problem-solving situations as those to be found in the Hebb-Williams (1946) tests of animal intelligence.

Change in Conception of the Relative Importance of the Sensory and the Motor

Yet another belief about what is important in early experience appears to need correction. G. Stanley Hall was fond of the aphorism that "the mind of man is handmade" (Pruette, 1926). Watson (1919) and the other behaviorists have believed that it is the motor side, rather than the sensory side, that is important in learning. Dewey (1902) gave emphasis to the motor side also in his belief that the child learns chiefly by doing. Dewey went even further to emphasize that the things that the child should be encouraged to do are the things that he would later be called upon to do in taking his place in society. More recently, Osgood (1952) has conceived that the central processes which mediate meanings are the residues of past responses. I am simply trying to document my assertion that in the dominant theory of the origin of mind or of central mediating processes, these have been conceived to be based upon the residues from past responses.

Hebb's (1949) theorizing, as I have already noted, took sharp issue with this dominant theoretical position. He has conceived the basis for primary learning to be chiefly on the sensory side. Riesen (1958) began his experiments on the effects of rearing chimpanzees in darkness with what he called *S–S*, or Stimulus-Stimulus relations. Piaget (1936), although he has emphasized "activity as the aliment of a schema," has conceived of *looking* and *listening*, both of which are typically viewed as sensory input channels, as existing among the schemata ready-made at birth. Moreover, it is looking and listening to which he attributes key importance during the first phases of intellectual development. This emphasis is registered in his aphorism that "the more a child has seen and heard, the more he wants to see and hear" (Piaget, 1936, p. 276).

Evidence requiring this correction of belief comes from more than just the studies of the effects of early perceptual experience on the later problem-solving capacity of animals. It also comes from comparing the effects of the cradling practice on the age of onset of walking in Hopi children, with the effects of the homogeneous auditory and visual stimulation on the age of onset of walking in the children in a Teheran orphanage. The cradling practice inhibits actions of an infant's legs and arms during his walking hours through most of the first year of his life. Yet, the mean and standard deviation of the age of walking for those cradled proved to be the same as that for those Hopi children reared with free use of their legs and arms (Dennis and Dennis, 1940). Contrariwise, 85 percent of the children in the Teheran orphanage were still not walking alone in their fourth year—and here the factor in which the circumstances of these children most differ from those of most young infants was probably the continuous homogeneity of auditory and visual experience (Dennis, 1960). The children of the Teheran orphanage had full use of the motor function of their legs and arms. The Hopi children reared with the cradling practice did not have free use of their legs and arms—but they were exposed, by virtue of their being carried around on their mothers' backs, to a very rich variety of auditory and visual inputs.

Perhaps this emphasis on the motor side is erroneous only as another example of failure to take into account the epigenesis of behavioral and intellectual functions. While it may be true that education by doing is best for children of kindergarten and primary-school age, it appears that having a variety of things to listen to and look at may be most important for development during the first year of life (see also Fiske and Maddi, 1961).[3]

ALL BEHAVIOR AND ALL LEARNING IS

MOTIVATED BY PAINFUL STIMULATION OR

HOMEOSTATIC NEED

The fact that both apathy and retardation have been regularly noted in orphanage-reared children who typically live under conditions of

---

[3] Since this was written, various lines of evidence have led me to believe my emphasis is wrong here. Variety of changes in input is probably of great importance only during the first two or three months. Thereafter, what appears to be most important is ability to get feedback or reinforcement from self-initiated actions. The apathy and retardation observed in infants reared in orphanages is probably more a matter of failure of the latter than of the former.

homogeneous circumstances (especially marked of the children observed by Dennis in the Teheran orphanage) suggests that homogeneous stimulation somehow reduces motivation. This suggestion brings me to yet another major change of theoretical belief.

It is common to state that "all behavior is motivated." But to make this statement specific, it must be completed with the complex phrase, "by homeostatic need, painful stimulation, or by innocuous stimuli which have previously been associated with these." This has been the dominant conception of motivation for most of the last half-century—dominant because it has been held both by academic behavior theorists (for example, Dashiell, 1928; Freeman, 1934; Guthrie, 1938; Holt, 1931; Hull, 1943; Melton, 1941; Miller and Dollard, 1941; Mowrer, 1960) and by psychoanalysts (for example, Fenichel, 1945; Freud, 1915).

This notion implies that organisms should become quiescent in the absence of painful stimulation, homeostatic need, or the acquired drives based upon them. Since World War II, evidence has accumulated to indicate quite clearly that neither animals nor children actually do become quiescent in the absence of such motivating conditions (see Hunt, 1963a). Bühler (1928) noted earlier that the playful activity of children is most evident in the absence of such motivating conditions, and Beach (1945) has reviewed evidence to show that animals are most likely to show playful activity when they are well-fed, well-watered, and in comfortable circumstances. Harlow *et al.* (1950) have found that monkeys learn to disassemble puzzles with no other motivation than the privilege of disassembling them. Similarly, Harlow (1950) found that two monkeys worked repeatedly at disassembling a six-device puzzle for ten continuous hours even though they were quite free of painful stimulation and homeostatic need. Moreover, as he notes, at the tenth hour of testing they were still "showing enthusiasm for their work."

In an important series of studies beginning in 1950, Berlyne (see 1960) found that comfortable and satiated rats will explore areas new to them if only given an opportunity, and that the more varied the objects in the region to be explored, the more persistent are the rats' explorations. In a similar vein, Montgomery (1952) has found that the spontaneous tendency for rats to go alternately to the opposite goal-boxes in a T- or Y-maze is no matter of fatigue for the most recently given response, as Hull (1943) contended, but it is one of avoiding the place which the animals have most recently experienced. The choice of place is for the one of lesser familiarity (Montgomery, 1953), and rats learn merely in order to get an opportunity to explore an unfamiliar area (Montgomery, 1955; Montgomery and Segall, 1955). In this same vein, Butler (1953) has observed that monkeys will learn discriminations merely to obtain the privilege of peeking through a window in the walls of their cages, or (Butler, 1958) of listening to sounds from a tape recorder. All these activities appear to be most evident in the absence of painful stimulation, homeostatic need, and cues which have previously been associated with such motivating stimuli. It is these findings which call for a change in the traditionally dominant theoretical conception of motivation.

Some of the directions of change in belief show in the modes of theoretical significance given to such evidence. One of these ways is drive-naming. Thus, in recent years, we have been hearing of a manipulatory drive, an exploratory drive, a curiosity drive, and so on. This form of theoretical recognition, which is logically circular, appears to be revisiting McDougall's (1908) theory of instincts.

A second mode of theoretical recognition is naming what appears to be the telic significance of an activity. This is what Ives Hendrick (1943) has done in conceiving of the delight which children take in their new-found accomplishments as evidence of an "urge to mastery." This is also what White (1959) has done in his excellent review of such evidence by attributing the various activities observed to "competence motivation." Such terms of telic significance may be helpful as classificatory and mnemonic devices, but they provide few implications of antecedent-consequent relationships to be investigated.

A third mode of theoretical recognition has consisted in postulating *spontaneous activity*. I have been guilty of this (Hunt, 1960) and so also have Hebb (1949), Miller *et al.* (1960), and Taylor (1960). When my good colleague, Lawrence I. O'Kelly, pointed out that the notion of spontaneous activity may be just as malevolently circular as drive- and instinct-naming, however, I could readily see the force of his argument. But I could also see that I had begun to discern at least the outlines of a mechanism of what I have termed "intrinsic motivation" or "motivation inherent in information processing and action" (Hunt, 1963*a*).

Intrinsic Motivation

The outlines of the nature of this mechanism of intrinsic motivation are to be discerned from the evidence which has called for a change in the conception of the functional unit of the nervous system from that of the reflex arc to that of the feedback loop. The concept of the reflex was first formulated by Hall (1843). However, it was developed and popularized by Sherrington (1906), who clearly recognized, in spite of the anatomical evidence for the reflex arc, that the reflex was a logical construct rather than an obvious and palpable reality. It must be noted that the anatomical evidence for the notion of a reflex arc is based on an overgeneralization of the Bell-Magendie Law, which states that the dorsal roots of the spinal nerve are composed entirely of incoming sensory fibers and that the ventral roots are compsed entirely of outgoing motor fibers. The statement is untrue. It is clear from recent neurophysiological investigation that the dorsal roots contain motor as well as sensory fibers and that the ventral roots contain sensory as well as motor fibers (see Hunt, 1963*a*). Illustrative evidence for the first portion of this new statement comes from such observations as the cessation of the firing associated with the onset of a tone or a buzzer in the cochlear nucleus of a cat when the cat is shown a mouse in a bell jar (Hernández-Péon *et al., 1956*). Evidence for the second portion may be illustrated by the observation that eye-movements can be elicited by electrical stimulation of any portion of the visual receptive area in the occipital lobes of monkeys (Walker and Weaver, 1940). Such evidence makes way and calls for the concept of the feedback loop.

The notion of the feedback loop provides, in turn, the basis for a new answer to the motivational question concerning what starts and stops behavior. So long as the reflex served as the conception of the functional unit of neural function, any given kind of behavior was presumed to be started by the onset of a drive stimulus and to be stopped by its cessation. As the feedback loop takes the place of the reflex, the onset of behavior becomes a matter of incongruity between the input from a set of circumstances and some standard within the organism. Miller *et al.* (1960) have termed this the Test-Operate-Test-Exit (TOTE) unit (see Figure 8.1).

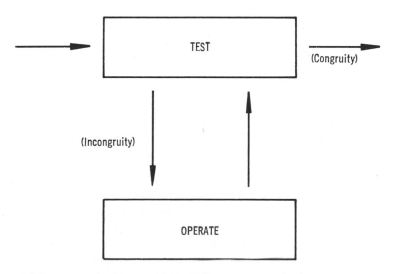

Figure 8.1 Diagram of the TOTE unit. After Miller, Galanter, and Pribram (1960, p. 26).

This TOTE unit is, in principle, not unlike the thermostat which controls the temperature of a room. In such a case, the standard is the temperature at which the thermostat is set. When the temperature falls below this standard, the "test" yields an incongruity which sets the furnace into operation (see the arrow connecting the "test" to the "operate"). The furnace continues to operate until the temperature in the room has been raised to the standard. This congruity stops the operation, and this particular motive system can be said to "exit."

One can base a taxonomy of incongruities upon the various kinds of standards existing within organisms. One class of incongruities may be based on the "comfort standard." While no one would have invented the TOTE unit to account for pain avoidance, conceiving of a "comfort standard" brings the facts of pain avoidance into a consonant relationship with the notion of the TOTE unit. A second class of incongruities may be conceived to be based on what Pribram (1960) has termed the "biased homeostats of the hypothalamus." Organisms have standards, for the most part innately established, for such things as the concentrations of blood-sugar or of sodium ions in the blood stream. When, for instance, the blood-sugar concentration falls below a certain level, the receptors along the third ventricle are activated. At one level of incongruity they serve to release glycogen from the liver; but at a higher level, they prime the receptors to respond to the signs of food, the organism follows them with avid excitement, and the hunger motive is said to be activated. It is not easy to make the sex system consonant with such a scheme.

On the other hand, a variety of standards can develop in the course of an organism's informational interaction with its circumstances. Perhaps the most primitive of such informational standards is the ongoing input of the moment. Whenever there is change from this standard, an organism exhibits what the Russians have termed the "orienting reflex" (see Berlyne, 1960; Razran, 1961). The operation elicited by such incongruity consists of an orientation toward the source of the change in input and arousal, as registered by the classical expressive indicators of emotion or by the electroencephalogram. A second kind of informational incongruity is based upon a standard of expectations, where the expectations are based on information stored in the course of previous encounters with the same object, person, or place. Such systems of expectations as the self-concept appear to take on special importance in motivation. Esthetic standards appear to be another variation of expectations.

Another category of standards appears to be comprised of ends or goals. These are what Miller *et al.* (1960) have termed *plans*. Some plans are tied to painful stimulation or to homeostatic needs, but others are quite independent of these. Piaget (1936) has described how an infant will make holding onto an interesting input, or regaining it, a goal. Typically, inputs have become interesting through repeated encounters by becoming recognizable. It would appear that emerging recognition can make objects, persons, and place attractive. Later it is novelty which is attractive. The full range of the various kinds of standards that emerge in the course of a child's informational interaction with his circumstances during the process of psychological development has never been described. At adolescence, however, an important variety of standards consists of ideals. This kind of standards appears to emerge with the development of what Piaget (1947) has termed "formal operations." With the emergence of these operations, the adolescent can imagine a world more desirable than the one he encounters, and the incongruity between the world observed and the imagined ideal can instigate plans for social reforms. These same formal operations enable the adolescent to formulate "theories" of how various aspects of the world operate, and incongruities between observed realities and these theoretical creations instigate inquiry. Thus, one may view scientific work as but a professionalization of a form of cognitive motivation inherent in the human organism's informational interaction with circumstances.

Incongruity and the Direction-Hedonic Question

The concept of incongruity also provides a tentative, hypothetical answer to the puzzling direction-hedonic question—the question of what it is that determines whether an organism will approach or withdraw from the source of incongruous or novel information (see also Schneirla, 1959). This is also an answer to the hedonic question, because approach presumably indicates a positive hedonic value in the source of stimulation, and withdrawal presumably indicates a negative hedonic value.

The evidence that incongruous or novel information will instigate approach to its source and that it has positive hedonic value derives from several sources. In an early study by Nissen (1930)—which has never got into the textbooks, apparently because it was far too dissonant with the dominant beliefs—it was shown that rats will suffer the pain of electric shocks from a Warden obstruction apparatus in order to get from empty cages into a Dashiell maze filled with novel objects. Once the animals have discovered the fact that such a maze exists at the end of the runway beyond the obstruction apparatus, they will endure the pain of the crossing in order to achieve the opportunity to explore this "interesting place" and to manipulate the "interesting objects." The behavior of the rats in this study of Nissen's resembles in many ways that of Butler's (1953) monkeys, which would undertake the learning of discriminations in order to peek through the window at students passing in the hall beyond. In fact, most of the evidence cited to show that animals and children do not become quiescent in the absence of homeostatic need and painful stimulation may be arranged to support the notion that a certain degree of incongruity is appealing, and that too little is boring and unappealing.

Perhaps even more convincing are the results from the studies of so-called stimulus deprivation in the McGill laboratory by Bexton *et al.* (1954). You will recall that the McGill students who served as subjects in these experiments were paid $20 a day to lie on a cot in a room with temperature and humidity controlled to provide an optimum of comfort, with translucent glasses on that provided for light to reach the eyes but did not permit pattern vision, with sound variation attenuated as much as possible, and with movement inhibited by the padded cardboard sleeves for arms and legs. Yet they could seldom endure such homogeneous circumstances for longer than two or three days, even for such a liberal monetary reward. The strength of the tendency to withdraw from such homogeneity of circumstances and to approach any source of stimulation that would provide some variety is dramatized by the word-of-mouth story of a student with "highbrow" musical tastes who, several times an hour, pressed a key that brought the playing of a scratchy, well-worn recording of "country music." This makes it look as if it were a case of, to paraphrase the seaman's aphorism, "any port of relative incongruity in a storm of homogeneous circumstances."

Withdrawal from the source of incongruous information also occurs, this when the degree of incongruity between the incoming information and that already stored in the memory from previous experience is too great. Here the evidence comes largely from the work of Hebb (1946). His studies of fear in chimpanzees were designed to call into question Watson's notion that emotional reactions to innocuous stimuli are based upon their having been associated with earlier painful stimulation (see Watson and Rayner, 1920). This traditional conception of fear met with sharply dissonant evidence, when Hebb and Riesen (1943) noted that fear of strangers does not appear in chimpanzee infants reared in the nursery of the Yerkes Primate Laboratory until these infants approach about four months of age. The fact that the histories of these infants were fully recorded made it possible to know with certainty that these strangers had not been associated with previous painful stimulation. Later, Hebb (1946) found that even intense panic reactions could be induced in adult chimpanzees reared in this laboratory merely by showing them the sculptured head of a chimp or human being, or by showing them an anesthetized infant chimpanzee. Such figures were clearly familiar but definitely without previous association with painful or other fearful stimuli. The fact that an infant chimpanzee, which had been a pet, withdrew in fear upon seeing its beloved experimenter-master in a Halloween mask or even in the coat of an equally familiar "keeper" suggested that the basis for the fearful withdrawal resided in seeing "a familiar figure in an unfamiliar guise." Thus, the absence of the expected remainder of the body in the case of the sculptured head of a chimpanzee or human being, and the absence of the expected motions and customary postures in the case of the anesthetized infant chimpanzee, provide "the unfamiliarity of guise"—or the discrepancy between what is expected on the basis of past experience and what is observed, that I am calling incongruity.

Puzzling emotional disturbances in children and pets become readily understandable in these terms. It was, for instance, fear of the dark and fear of solitude in the human child that puzzled Freud (1926) and made him unhappy with even his later theory of anxiety, and it was such behavior in the chimpanzee that puzzled Köhler (1925, p. 251). These can be readily seen as incongruity which results from the presence of unaccustomed receptor inputs or from the absence of accustomed receptor inputs within any given context. Still other examples are that of the child who becomes disturbed when a familiar nursery rhyme is altered in the reading; that of the pet dog that barks excitedly and whines when he observes his young master walking on his hands; and that of the cat that runs frantically to hide at the sight of his child-mistress being hoisted onto the shoulders of a familiar neighbor. Although Piaget (1936) was without special concern about the point, he noted in his observations that his children showed emotional distress in seeing altered versions of things with which they had become familiar.

The fact that incongruous information can elicit both an approach to its source and a withdrawal from its source may be puzzling until one notes that this implies that there is an optimum of incongruity (see Hunt, 1963a). Hebb (1949) first gave at least implicit recognition to the notion of an optimum of incongruity in his theory of the nature of pleasure. In this theory he noted that organisms tend to be preoccupied with "what is new but not too new" in any situation. This suggests that controlling intrinsic motivation is a matter of providing an organism with circumstances that provide a proper level of incongruity—that is, incongruity with the residues of previous encounters with such circumstances that the oganism has stored in his memory. This is what I find myself calling "the problem of the match" between the incoming information and that already stored (Hunt, 1961, p. 267ff).

Relevant experiments in this area are difficult to find; but one by Dember *et al.* (1957) is particularly interesting. Incongruity can be a matter of the discrepancy between the level of complexity encountered and the level of complexity with which an organism has become accustomed. The efforts to keep an optimum of incongruity, or discrepancy and complexity, provides a kind of explanation for the sort of "growth motivation" which Froebel (1826) postulated and which Dewey (1900) later appears to have borrowed from Froebel. What Dember *et al.* (1957) did in their experiment was to present rats placed in a figure-8 maze with a choice between two levels of complexity. In the two mazes used, the walls of one loop were painted in a solid color and those of the other loop in black-and-white horizontal stripes, or the walls of one loop had horizontal stripes and the other had vertical stripes. On the basis of theorizing similar to that presented here, these experimenters made no attempt to predict which loop would be preferred immediately by any given rat because they had no knowledge concerning the degree of incongruity to which the rats had become accustomed. They did, however, predict that any animal registering a change of choice of loop between his first and second exposures to this choice would make a change toward the more complex loop. This would mean that they would expect no changes of preference from the striped loop to the one painted a solid color, but would rather expect all changes to occur in the opposite direction. This prediction was confirmed. In a total of thirteen animals making such spontaneous changes of choice, twelve were clearly in the predicted direction. Such experiments need to be repeated and elaborated. In the light of such considerations, the problem for a parent or a teacher endeavoring to keep children interested in intellectual growth is one of providing circumstances so matched, or mismatched, to those with which the children are already familiar that an interesting and attractive challenge is continually provided.

Epigenesis of Intrinsic Motivation

In the traditionally dominant theory of motivation, the basic structure of the motivational system is essentially preformed. Learning is conceived to operate only by way of the conditioning principle, wherein previously innocuous circumstances acquire motivational significance by virtue of being associated with either painful stimuli or homeostatic needs. The fact that Piaget's observations indicate so clearly that there is an epigenesis in the structure of intelligence and in the construction of such aspects of reality as the object, causality, space, and time suggests that there may also be a hitherto unnoted epigenesis in the structure of what I am calling "intrinsic motivation." Piaget has been unconcerned with motivation; he has narrowed his field of concern largely to intelligence and to the development of knowledge about the world. Nevertheless, many of his observations and certain of his aphorisms have implications which provide at least a hypothetical picture of an epigenesis of intrinsic motivation (see Hunt, 1963*b*). Such is the case with Piaget's aphorism mentioned earlier, that "the more a child has seen and heard, the more he wants to see and hear."

Three phases appear to characterize this epigenesis of intrinsic motivation. These phases, or stages, may well characterize the organism's progressive relationships to any completely new set of circumstances (Harvey *et al.,* 1961). They may appear as phases of infantile development only because the infant is encountering various sets of completely new circumstances almost simultaneously during his first two years of life.

During the first phase, the child is, of course, motivated by homeostatic need and painful stimulation, as O. C. Irwin's (1930) classic studies have shown. Studies of the Russian investigators (see Berlyne, 1960; Razran, 1961) have shown that the orienting reaction is also ready-made at birth in all mammals including the human being. During this first phase, which lasts from birth to something like four or five or six months of age, the child is chiefly a responsive organism, responding to the short-term incongruities of change in characteristics of the ongoing input. Thus, the relatively sudden dimming of a light or the sudden disappearance of a sound which has been present for some time will instigate a young infant's orienting response or attention to bring about physiological evidences of arousal. During this first phase, the ready-made schemata of sucking, of looking, of listening, of vocalizing, or grasping, and of wiggling each change by something like the traditional conditioning process, in which various new kinds of change in stimulation acquire the capacity to evoke the schemata consistently. Thus, something heard becomes something to look at, something to look at becomes something to grasp, and something to grasp becomes something to suck. This phase terminates with a "landmark of transition" in which the child comes gradually to try actively to retain situations or circumstances or forms of input which he has encountered repeatedly (see Hunt, 1963*b;* Piaget, 1936).

The second phase begins with this landmark of transition in which the infant manifests intentional interest in what may be characterized as the newly familiar. The newly familiar is, of course, some circumstance or situation which has been encountered repeatedly. Presumably, this course of encounters has gradually constructed and stored somewhere within the intrinsic system of the cerebrum some kind of template which provides a basis of recognition for the circumstance when it recurs. One evidence for such recognition comes in the infant's smile. Rene Spitz (1946) has conceived of this smiling response as social in nature. But Piaget's (1936) observations indicate that recognition of the parental face is but a special case of a more general tendency to smile in the presence of a variety of repeatedly encountered situations—which include the toys over an infant's crib, Piaget's newspaper laid repeatedly on the hood over his son's bassinette, and the child's own hands and feet. Such behavior may properly be described as intentional, because it occurs when the situation disappears and the child's efforts clearly imply an anticipation of the circumstance or spectacle to be regained. Moreover, inability to get the newly recognized circumstance or spectacle to return commonly brings on frustrative distress. Separation anxiety and separation grief appear to be special cases of the emotional distress that follows inability to restore the recognized circumstance or spectacle. This consideration suggests that the process of repeated encounters leading to recognition may in itself be a source of emotional gratification and pleasure which may be at least one basis for the reinforcement important in the early emotional attachments or cathexes—which Freud (1905) attributed to the libido, and which Hull (1943) and Miller and Dollard (1941) have attributed to drive reduction, and which Harlow (1958) has recently attributed to the softness of the surrogate mothers of the infant chimpanzees in his experiments. This second phase in the epigenesis of motivation terminates when repeated encounters with familiar objects have led gradually to something like the boredom that comes with too little incongruity, and when this boredom provides the basis for an interest in novel variations in the familiar.

This interest in the newly familiar may well account for such autogenic activities as the repetitious babbling commonly appearing in the second, third, and fourth months, and the persistent hand-watching and foot-watching commonly beginning in the latter part of the fourth month and possibly persisting well into the sixth month. It would appear to be in the process of babbling that the infant brings his vocalizing schema under the control of his listening schema. It would appear to be in the course of hand-watching, and sometimes foot-watching, that the infant establishes his eye-hand, and eye-foot, coordinations. This second phase terminates when, with repeated encounters with various situations, boredom ensues and the infant comes to be interested in what is new and novel within the familiar situation and in what is increasingly complex (see Hunt, 1963b).

The third phase begins with the appearance of this interest in novelty. Typically, this begins at about the end of the first year of life, or perhaps somewhat earlier. Piaget (1936) describes its beginnings with the appearance of the throwing schema. In the course of this throwing, the child's attention shifts from the act of throwing to observing the trajectory of the object thrown. It shows also in an interest not only in familiar ways of achieving ends but also in the development of new means through a process of groping. It shows in the child's attempts to imitate not only those schemata, vocal and otherwise, which he has already developed, but also new schemata. This development of interest in the novel is accompanied by a marked increase in the variety of the infant's interests and actions. He learns in this way new phones within the vocalization schema, and these become symbols for the images he has already developed, and pseudo-words make their appearance (see Hunt, 1961, 1963*b;* Piaget, 1945).

With the development of interest in novelty and in what is increasingly complex, the child has achieved the basis for the "growth motivation" already illustrated in the intriguing experiment by Dember *et al.* (1956).

APPLICATIONS OF SUCH THEORIZING FOR THE DEVELOPMENT OF AN ANTIDOTE FOR CULTURAL DEPRIVATION

It remains for me to examine some applications of the theoretical fabric that I have been weaving to the development of a preschool enrichment program for the culturally deprived. First of all, cultural deprivation may be seen as a failure to provide an opportunity for infants and young children to have the experiences required for adequate development of those semiautonomous central processes demanded for acquiring skill in the use of linguistic and mathematical symbols and for the analysis of causal relationships. The difference between the culturally deprived and the culturally privileged is, for children, analogous to the difference between cage-reared and pet-reared rats and dogs. At the present time, this notion of cultural deprivation or of social disadvantage is gross and undifferentiated indeed.[4] On the basis of the evidence and conceptions I have summarized, however, I believe the concept points in a very promising direction. It should be possible to arrange institutional settings where children now culturally deprived by the accident of the social class of their parents can be supplied with a set of encounters with circumstances which will provide an antidote for what they may have missed.

---

[4] It is much less undifferentiated today than it was when this was originally written, in 1962, by virtue of the studies of Bernstein (1960, 1961) in England, of Cynthia Deutsch (1964), Hess and Shipman (1965), Vera John (1963), John and Goldstein (1964), and Suzanne Keller (1963) in the United States, of Lewis (1966) in Latin American countries, and of Smilansky (1961, 1964) in Israel. These studies and others, coming long after those pioneering investigations of Davis (1948) and Davis and Havighurst (1946), are helping greatly to clarify the nature of cultural deprivation and its psychological effects on the development of intelligence and motivation.

The important study of Skeels and Dye (1939), that met with such a derisive reception when it first appeared, is highly relevant in this context. You will recall that it was based on a "clinical surprise." Two infants, one aged thirteen months with a Kuhlman IQ of 46 and the other aged sixteen months with an IQ of 35, after residence in the relatively homogeneous circumstances of a state orphanage, were committed to a state institution for the feeble-minded. Some six months later, a psychologist visiting the wards noted with surprise that these two infants had shown a remarkable degree of development. No longer did they show either the apathy or the locomotor retardation that had characterized them when they were committed. When they were again tested with the Kuhlman scale, moreover, the younger had an IQ of 77 and the older an IQ of 87—improvements of 31 and 52 points respectively, and within half a year. You will also remember that in the experiment which followed this clinical surprise, every one of a group of thirteen children showed a substantial gain in IQ upon being transferred from the orphanage to the institution for the feeble-minded. These gains ranged between 7 points and 58 points of IQ. On the other hand, twelve other youngsters, within the same age-range but with a somewhat higher mean IQ, were left in the orphanage. When these children were retested after periods varying between twenty-one and forty-three months, all had shown a substantial decrease in IQ, ranging between 8 and 45 points of IQ, with five of these decreases exceeding 35 points.

In recent years, Harold Skeels has been engaged in a following-up study of the individuals involved in these two groups. With about three-fourths of the individuals found, he has yet to find one of the group transferred from the orphanage to the institution for the feeble-minded who is not now maintaining himself effectively in society. Contrariwise, he has not yet found any one of the group remaining in the orphanage who is not now living with institutional support (1965). Although the question of the permanence of the effects of experiential deprivation during infancy is far from answered, such evidence as I have been able to find, and as I have summarized here, would indicate that if the experiential deprivation does not persist too long, it is reversible to a substantial degree. If this be true, the idea of enriching the cognitive fare in day-care centers and in nursery schools for the culturally deprived looks very promising.

Probable Nature of the Deficit from Cultural Deprivation

The fact that cultural deprivation is such a global and undifferentiated conception at present invites at least speculative attempts to construe the nature of the deficit and to see wherein and when the infant of the poor and lower-class parents is most likely to be experientially deprived.

One of the important features of lower-class life in poverty is crowding. Many persons live in little space. Crowding, however, may be no handicap for a human infant during most of his first year of life. Although there is no certainty of this, it is conceivable that being a young infant among a large number of people living within a room may actually serve to provide such wide variations of visual and auditory inputs that it will facilitate development more than will the conditions typical of the culturally privileged during most of the first year.

During the second year, on the other hand, living under the crowded conditions of poverty must almost inevitably be highly hampering. Under these conditions, the child encounters a markedly smaller variety of objects than does the middle-class child. As he begins to throw things and as he begins to develop his own methods of locomotion, he is likely to find himself getting in the way of adults already made ill-tempered by their own discomforts and by the frustrations of getting into each other's ways. Such considerations are dramatized by Lewis' (1961) *The Children of Sanchez,* an anthropological study of life in poverty. In such a crowded atmosphere, the activities in which the child must indulge for the development of his own interests and skills must almost inevitably be sharply curbed. "Being good" comes to be defined as both doing nothing and getting nothing interesting. Moreover, adult utterances provide such poor models of the vocal side of language that it is no wonder that children of the poor lag in their language development and in the abilities which depend upon language for their development (Bernstein, 1960; Deutsch, 1964; Deutsch and Brown, 1964; John, 1963; John and Goldstein, 1964).

In the third year, moreover, when imitation of novel patterns of action and verbalization should presumably be well-established and should provide a mechanism for learning vocal language, the models of vocal patterns are wrong for standards to be encountered later in school. When the toddler has achieved the "learning sets" that "things have names" and that "things come in groups" and is prompted by these sets to ask such questions as "what's that?" or "is it a this or a that?" his questions are typically met with "shut up!" Seldom do such parents, who are preoccupied with the problems associated with their poverty or who are chronically in a state of disorganization and apathy, ask the child questions that will force him to use language to identify prepositional relationships and to organize sequences of his experience in linguistic form. With things to play with and with room to play in highly limited, with opportunities to learn standard English—or any other standard language—markedly reduced, the youngster beyond his first year who is in the typical conditions of lower-class life has little opportunity to develop at an optimal rate in the direction demanded for later adaptation in schools and in our highly technological culture (see also Beilin and Gotkin, 1964; Bernstein, 1961; Keller, 1963).

If this armchair analysis has any validity, it suggests that the infant developing in the crowded circumstances of lower-class poverty may develop well through the first year; begin to show retardation during the second year; and show even more retardation during the third, fourth, and fifth years. Presumably, that retardation which occurs during the second year, and even that during the third year, can probably be reversed to a considerable degree by supplying proper circumstances in either a nursery school or a day-care center for children of four and five—but I suspect it would be preferable to start with children at three years of age. The analysis made here, which is based largely upon what I have learned from Piaget (1936) and from my own observations of development during the preschool years, could be tested. Dr. Ina Uzgiris and I have developed an instrument for assessing infant psychological development which consists of six series of situations, arranged according to their difficulty for a sample of eighty-four infants (Uzgiris and Hunt, 1966, 1967). These are situations designed to evoke the various early sensorimotor schemata that Piaget (1936) has described for the first two years. It should provide a tool with which to determine when and how the conditions of development within the crowded circumstances of poverty begin to result in retardation and/or apathy.

Preschool Enrichment and the Problem of the Match

Our traditional emphasis in education upon arithmetic and language skills can well lead us astray in the attempt to develop a program of preschool enrichment. If Piaget's (1945) observations are correct, spoken language—that is to say the motor side of the language skill—comes only after images, or the central processes representing objects and events, have been developed out of repeated encounters with those objects and events. The fact that chimpanzees show clearly the capacity to dissemble their own purposes even though they lack language (Hebb and Thompson, 1954) lends support from phylogenetic comparisons to this notion of Piaget's. You have most likely heard that O. K. Moore, of Yale, has been teaching preschool children to read with the aid of an electric typewriter hooked up to an electronic system of storing and retrieving information. The fact that, once children have learned to recognize letters by pressing the proper keys of a typewriter, they are enabled to discover spontaneously that they can draw these letters with chalk on a blackboard, lends further support to the image-primacy thesis. Moreover, Moore has observed that the muscular control of such four-year-olds—who have presumably acquired solid imagery of the letters in the course of their experience with those letters at the electric typewriter—corresponds to that typical of seven- or eight-year-olds (personal communication).

What appears to be important for a preschool enrichment program is an opportunity to encounter circumstances which will foster the development of these semiautonomous central processes that can serve as imagery representative of objects and events and which can become the referents for the spoken symbols required in the phonemic combinations of spoken or written language. Moore's results also suggest to me that these semi-autonomous central processes, if adequately developed, can serve as the basis for motor control. Such considerations suggest that a proper pre-school enrichment program should provide children with an opportunity to encounter a wide variety of objects and circumstances. They suggest that the children should also have an opportunity to imitate a wide variety of models of action and of motor language. The danger of attempting to prescribe materials and models at this stage of knowledge, however, is that the prescriptions may well fail to provide a proper match with what the child already has in his storage. The fact that most teachers have their expectations based on experience with culturally privileged children makes this problem of the match especially dangerous and vexing in work with the culturally deprived.

Revisiting Montessori's Contribution

In view of the dangers of attempting prescriptions of enrichments for prescool children, it may be well to re-examine the educational contributions of Maria Montessori. Her contributions have been largely forgotten in America. In fact, until as late as August 1962, I could have identified Maria Montessori only by saying that she had developed some kind of kindergarten and was an educational faddist who had made quite a splash about the turn of the century. I was, thus, really introduced to her work by Dr. Jan Smedslund, a Norwegian psychologist, who remarked to me, during a conference at the University of Colorado, that Maria Montessori had provided a practical answer to what I have called "the problem of the match" (Hunt, 1961, p. 276ff).

When I examined the library for materials on Maria Montessori, I discovered that the novelist, Dorothy Canfield Fisher, had spent the winter of 1910–1911 at the Casa de Bambini in Rome and that she had returned to write a book on Montessori's work. This book, entitled *A Montessori Mother* (1912), may still be the best initial introduction to Montessori's work. Books by E. M. Standing (1957) and Nancy Rambusch (1962) have brought the record up to date, and the book by Rambusch contains a bibliography of the materials in the English language concerning Montessori's work assembled by Gilbert E. Donahue.

Montessori's contribution is especially interesting to me because she based her methods of teaching upon the spontaneous interest of children in learning, that is, upon what I am calling "intrinsic motivation." Moreover, she put great stress upon teachers observing the children under their care to discover what kinds of things foster their individual interests and growth. Furthermore, she put great stress on the training of what she called sensory processes, but what we might more appropriately call information processes today. The fact that she placed strong emphasis upon the training of sensory processes may well be one of the major reasons why her work dropped out of the main stream of educational thought and practice in America before World War I. This emphasis was too dissonant with the dominant American emphasis in learning upon the motor response, rather than upon the sensory input or information processes. It was Montessori's concern to observe carefully what interested a child that led her to discover a wide variety of materials in which she found children showing strong spontaneous interest.

Second, Montessori broke the lock step in the education of young children. Her schools made no effort to keep all the children doing the same thing at the same time. Rather, each child was free to examine and to work with whatever happened to interest him. This meant that he was free to persist in a given concern as long as he cared to, and also free to change from one concern to another whenever a change appeared appropriate to him. In this connection, one of the very interesting observations made by Dorothy Canfield Fisher concerns the prolonged duration of children's interest in given activities under such circumstances. Whereas the lore about preschoolers holds that the nature of the activity in a nursery school must be changed every ten or fifteen minutes, Mrs. Fisher described children typically remaining engrossed in such activities as the buttoning and unbottoning of a row of buttons for two or more hours at a time.

Third, Montessori's method consisted in having children from three to six years old together. As I see it, from taking into account the epigenesis of intellectual development, such a scheme has the advantage of providing the younger children with a wide variety of models for imitation. Moreover, it supplies the older children with an opportunity to help and teach the younger. Helping and teaching contain many of their own rewards.

There may well be yet another advantage, one in which those financing preschool enrichment will be heartily concerned. Montessori's first teacher was a teen-age girl, the superintendent's daughter in the apartment house in the Rome slums where the first Casa de Bambini was established in 1907. In that school, this one young woman successfully set the stage for the learning of fifty to sixty children from three to seven years old. I say "successfully" because, as Dorothy Canfield Fisher (1912) reported, some of the children had learned to read by the time they were five years old. On the other hand, current observations suggest that the Montessori approach may need supplementation to correct the linguistic deficit of children from culturally deprived backgrounds. It may be well to supplement the Montessori approach with the very recently developed approach of Bereiter *et al.* (1966). Their academically oriented preschool for culturally deprived children focuses directly on language and arithmetic; and their teaching method combines concrete experience with the modern method of teaching foreign languages. Starting with four-year-olds one and one-half to two and one-half years below chronological age on the Illinois Test of Psycholinguistic Abilities (see Kirk and McCarthy, 1961), they increased the median psycholinguistic test-age of these children by two years within six months in their program—a program consisting of merely three twenty-minute sessions for groups of five with a teacher on each of five days a week. This approach reverts to the lock step for short periods, and doctrinaire followers of Montessori may resist using such a supplement. Alternatively, one might consider adding to the Montessori apparatus something like O. K. Moore's "talking typewriter" (1963), reported effective in correcting the language deficit. Before any confident assertions can be made about such matters, however, solid evaluative investigations are necessary.

SUMMARY

I began by saying that it was very exciting for me to encounter people—generally considered sensible—in the process of planning to utilize preschool experience as an antidote for the effects of cultural deprivation. I have tried to summarize the basis in psychological theory and in the evidence from psychological research for such a use of preschool enrichment. I have tried to summarize the evidence: (1) that the belief in fixed intelligence is no longer tenable; (2) that development is far from completely predetermined; (3) that what goes on "between the ears" is much less like the static switchboard of the telephone than it is like the active information processes programmed into electronic computers to enable them to solve problems; (4) that experience is the programmer of the human brain-computer and, thus, that Freud was correct about the importance of the experience which comes before the advent of language; (5) that, nonetheless, Freud was wrong about the nature of the experience which is important, since an opportunity to see and hear a variety of things appears to be more important than the fate of instinctual needs and impulses; and, finally (6) that learning need not be motivated by painful stimulation, homeostatic need, or the acquired drives based upon these, for there is a kind of intrinsic motivation which is inherent in information processing and action.

In applying these various lines of evidence and these various changes in conception, I have viewed the effects of cultural deprivation as analogous to the experimentally found effects of experiential deprivation in infancy. I have pointed out the importance of "the problem of the match" and the dangers of using our present knowledge to prescribe programs of circumstantial encounters to enrich the experience of culturally deprived preschool children. In this connection, I have suggested that we re-examine the work of Maria Montessori for suggestions. For she successfully based her teaching method on children's spontaneous interest in learning; she found a solution to the "problem of the match" by carefully observing children's interests and then giving them individual freedom to choose which circumstances they would encounter.

References

Beach, F. A. Current concepts of play in animals. *American Naturalist,* 1945, **79,** 523–541.

Beilin, H., and L. Gotkin. Psychological issues in the development of mathematics curricula for socially disadvantaged children. Paper presented to the Invitational Conference on Mathematics Education, Chicago, April 1964.

Bereiter, C., S. Engelmann, Jean Osborn, and P. A. Redford. "An academically oriented pre-school for culturally deprived children." In F. M. Hechinger (ed.), *Pre-school education today.* New York: Doubleday, 1966, Ch. 6.

Berlyne, D. E. *Conflict, arousal, and curiosity.* New York: McGraw-Hill, 1960.

Bernstein, B. Language and social class. *British Journal of Psychology,* 1960, **11,** 271–276.

————. "Social class and linguistic development: A theory of social learning." In A. H. Halsey, Jean Floud, and C. A. Anderson (eds.), *Education, economy, and society.* New York: Free Press, 1961, 288–314.

Bexton, W. H., W. Heron, and T. H. Scott. Effects of decreased variation in the sensory environment. *Canadian Journal of Psychology,* 1954, **8,** 70–76.

Boring, E. G. *A history of experimental psychology.* New York: Appleton-Century-Crofts, 1929.

Brattgård, S. O. The importance of adequate stimulation for the chemical composition of retinal ganglion cells during early postnatal development. *Acta Radiologica,* Stockholm, 1952, Suppl. 96.

Bühler, K. "Displeasure and pleasure in relation to activity." In M. L. Reymert (ed.), *Feelings and emotions: The Wittenberg symposium.* Worcester, Mass.: Clark University Press, 1928, Ch. 14.

Butler, R. A. Discrimination learning by rhesus monkeys to visual exploration motivation. *Journal of Comparative Physiology and Psychology*, 1953, **46**, 95–98.

―――. The differential effect of visual and auditory incentives on the performance of monkeys. *American Journal of Psychology*, 1958, **71**, 591–593.

Carmichael L. The development of behavior in vertebrates experimentally removed from influence of external stimulation. *Psychological Review*, 1926, **33**, 51–58.

―――. A further study of the development of behavior in vertebrates experimentally removed from the influence of external stimulation. *Psychological Review*, 1927, **34**, 34–47.

―――. A further study of the development of behavior. *Psychological Review*, 1928, **35**, 253–260.

Cattell, J. McK. Mental tests and measurements. *Mind*, 1890, **15**, 373–381.

Coghill, G. E. *Anatomy and the problem of behavior*. Cambridge, Mass.: Cambridge University Press, 1929.

Cruze, W. W. Maturation and learning in chicks. *Journal of Comparative Psychology*, 1935, **19**, 371–409.

―――. Maturation and learning ability. *Psychological Monograph*, 1938, 50 (5).

Darwin, C. *Origin of the species*. London: Murray, 1859.

―――. *The expressions of the emotions in man and animals*. New York: Appleton-Century-Crofts, 1873 (originally published: London: Murray, 1872).

Dashiell, J. F. *Fundamentals of objective psychology*. Boston: Houghton Mifflin, 1928.

Davis, W. A. *Social-class influences upon learning*. Cambridge, Mass.: Harvard University Press, 1948.

―――, and R. J. Havighurst. Social-class and color differences in child-rearing. *American Sociological Review*, 1946, **11**, 698–710.

Dember, W. N., R. W. Earl, and N. Paradise. Response by rats to differential stimulus complexity. *Journal of Comparative Physiological Psychology*, 1957, **50**, 514–518.

Denenberg, V. H. "The effects of early experience." In E. S. E. Hafez (ed.), *The behavior of domestic animals*. London: Ballière, Tindall, Koch, 1962.

Dennis, W. Causes of retardation among institutional children. *Journal of Genetic Psychology*, 1960, **96**, 47–59.

―――, and Marsena G. Dennis. The effect of restricted practice upon the reaching, sitting and standing of two infants. *Journal of Genetic Psychology*, 1935, **47**, 21–29.

―――― and ―――. Infant development under conditions of restricted practice and minimum social stimulation: A preliminary report. *Journal of Genetic Psychology*, 1938, **53**, 151–156.

―――― and ―――. The effect of cradling practice upon the onset of walking in Hopi children. *Journal of Genetic Psychology*, 1940, **56**, 77–86.

―――― and ―――. Infant development under conditions of restricted practice and minimum social stimulation. *Genetic Psychology Monograph*, 1941, **23**, 149–155.

Deutsch, Cynthia. Auditory discrimination and learning: Social factors. *Merrill-Palmer Quarterly*, 1964, **10**, 277–296.

Deutsch, M., and B. Brown. Social influences in Negro-white intelligence differences. *Journal of Social Issues*, 1964, **20**, 24–35.

Dewey, J. *The school and society*. Chicago: University of Chicago Press, Phoenix Books, p. 3, 1960 (first published 1900).

———. *The child and the curriculum*. Chicago: University of Chicago Press, Phoenix Books, p. 3, 1960 (first published 1902).

Farber, I. E. Response fixation under anxiety and non-anxiety conditions. *Journal of Experimental Psychology*, 1948, **38**, 111–131.

Fenichel, O. *The psychoanalytic theory of neurosis*. New York: Norton, 1945.

Fisher, Dorothy Canfield. *A Montessori mother*. New York: Holt, Rinehart and Winston, 1912.

Fiske, D. W., and S. R. Maddi. *Functions of varied experience*. Homewood, Ill.: Dorsey Press, 1961.

Freedman, A. Drive conditioning in water deprivation. Unpublished doctoral dissertation, University of Illinois, 1957.

Freeman, G. L. *Introduction to physiological psychology*. New York: Ronald Press, 1934.

Freud, S. "The interpretation of dreams." In A. A. Brill (trans. & ed.), *The basic writings of Sigmund Freud*. New York: Modern Library, 1938. (*The interpretation of dreams*, originally published 1900).

———. "The psychopathology of everyday life." In A. A. Brill (trans. & ed.), *The basic writings of Sigmund Freud*. New York: Modern Library, 1938. (*Three contributions to the theory of sex*, originally published 1905.)

———. Instincts and their vicissitudes. *Collected Papers*, **4**, 60–83. London: Hogarth, 1927. (*Instincts and their vicissitudes*, originally published 1915.)

———. *The problem of anxiety*. (H. A. Bunker, trans.) New York: Norton, 1936. (*Hemmung, Sympton an Angst*, originally published 1926.)

Froebel, F. *The education of man*. (W. N. Hailmann, trans.) New York: Appleton-Century-Crofts, 1896. (*Die Menschenerziehung*, originally published 1826.)

Galton, F. *Hereditary genius: An inquiry into its laws and consequences*. London: Macmillan, 1869.

Gauron, E. F., and W. C. Becker. The effects of early sensory deprivation on adult rat behavior under competition stress: An attempt at replication of a study by Alexander Wolf. *Journal of Comparative Physiology and Psychology*, 1959, **52**, 689–693.

Gesell, A. *The embryology of human behavior: The beginnings of the human mind*. New York: Harper & Row, 1945.

———. "The ontogenesis of infant behavior." In L. Carmichael (ed.), *Manual of child psychology*. New York: Wiley, 1954, Ch. 6.

———, and Helen Thompson. Learning and growth in identical twin infants. *Genetic Psychological Monograph*, 1929, 6, 1–124.

Goddard, H. H. *The Kallikak family: A study in the heredity of feeble-mindedness*. New York: Macmillan, 1912.

Goldman, Jacquelin R. The effects of handling and shocking in infancy upon adult behavior in the albino rat. *Journal of Genetic Psychology*, 1964, **104**, 2, 301–310.

Goodenough, Florence. A critique of experiments on raising the I.Q. *Educational Methods*, 1939, **19**, 73–79.

Guthrie, E. R. *The psychology of human conflict: The clash of motives within the individual*. New York: Harper & Row, 1938.

Hall, C. S. Emotional behavior in the rat: 1. Defecation and urination as measures of individual differences in emotionality. *Journal of Comparative Psychology*, 1934, **18**, 385–403.

Hall, M. *New memoire on the nervous system.* London: Proc. Royal Academy, 1843.

Harlow, H. F. Learning and satiation of response in intrinsically motivated complex puzzle performance by monkeys. *Journal of Comparative and Physiological Psychology,* 1950, **43,** 289–294.

———. The nature of love. *American Psychologist,* 1958, **13,** 673–685.

———, M. K. Harlow, and D. R. Meyer. Learning motivated by a manipulation drive. *Journal of Experimental Psychology,* 1950, **40,** 228–234.

Harvey, O. J., D. E. Hunt, and H. M. Schroeder. *Conceptual systems and personality organization.* New York: Wiley, 1961.

Hebb, D. O. On the nature of fear. *Psychological Review,* 1946, **53,** 259–276.

———. The effects of early experience on problem-solving at maturity. *American Psychologist,* 1947, **2,** 306–307.

———. *The organization of behavior.* New York: Wiley, 1949.

———, and A. H. Riesen. The genesis of irrational fears. *Bulletin of Canadian Psychology Association,* 1943, **3,** 49–50.

———, and W. R. Thompson. "The social significance of animal studies." In G. Lindzey (ed.), *Handbook of social psychology.* Reading, Mass.: Addison-Wesley, 1954, Ch. 15.

———, and K. Williams. A method of rating animal intelligence. *Journal of Genetic Psychology,* 1946, **34,** 59–65.

Hendrick, I. The discussion of the "instinct to master." *Psychoanalytical Quarterly,* 1943, **12,** 561–565.

Hernàndez-Péon, R., H. Scherrer, and M. Jouvet. Modification of electric activity in cochlear nucleus during "attention" in unanesthetized cast. *Science,* 1956, **123,** 331–332.

Hilgard, Josephine R. Learning and maturation in pre-school children. *Journal of Genetic Psychology,* 1932, **41,** 36–56.

Holmes, Frances B. "An experimental study of children's fears." In A. T. Jersild and Frances B. Holmes (eds.), *Children's fears.* New York: Teachers College, Columbia University, *Child Development Monograph,* **20,** 1935.

Holt, E. B. *Animal drive and the learning process.* New York: Holt, Rinehart and Winston, 1931.

Hull, C. L. Goal attraction and directing ideas conceived as habit phenomena. *Psychological Review,* 1931, **38,** 487–506.

———. *Principles of behavior.* New York: Appleton-Century-Crofts, 1943.

Hunt, J. McV. The effects of infant feeding-frustration upon adult hoarding in the albino rat. *Journal of Abnormal Social Psychology,* 1941, **36,** 338–360.

———. "Experimental psychoanalysis." In P. L. Harriman (ed.), *Encyclopedia of Psychology.* New York: Philosophical Library, 1945.

———. Psychosexual development: The infant disciplines. Urbana: Psychological Development Laboratory, University of Illinois, 1956 (mimeographed paper).

———. Experience and the development of motivation: Some reinterpretations. *Child Development,* 1960, **31,** 489–504.

———. *Intelligence and experience.* New York: Ronald Press, 1961.

———. "Motivation inherent in information processing and action." In O. J. Harvey (ed.), *Motivation and social interaction.* New York: Ronald Press, 1963*a.*

———. Piaget's observations as a source of hypotheses concerning motivation. *Merrill-Palmer Quarterly,* 1963*b,* **9,** 263–275.

————, and Zella Luria. Investigations of the effects of early experience in sub-human animals. Urbana: Psychological Development Laboratory, University of Illinois, 1956 (mimeographed paper).

Hunter, W. S. The delayed reaction in animals and children. *Behavior Monographs,* 1912, **2** (1), 1–85.

————. The temporal maze and kinesthetic sensory processes in the white rat. *Psychobiology,* 1918, **2,** 339–351.

Hydén, H. Biochemical changes in glial cells and nerve cells at varying activity. In F. Brücke (ed.), *Proceedings of the 4th International Congress of Biochemistry, III. Biochemistry of the central nervous system.* London: Pergamon Press, 1959.

————. "The neuron." In J. Brachet and A. E. Mirsky (eds.), *The cell: Biochemistry, physiology, morphology, IV. Specialized cells.* New York: Acaddemic Press, 1960, pp. 215–323.

————, and A. Pigon. A cytophysiological study of the functional relationship between oligodendroglial cells and nerve cells of Deiters' nucleus. *Journal of Neurochemistry,* 1960, **6,** 57–72.

John, Vera P. The intellectual development of slum children: Some preliminary findings. *American Journal of Orthopsychiatry,* 1963, **33,** 813–822.

————, and L. S. Goldstein. The social context of language acquisition. *Merrill-Palmer Quarterly,* 1964, **10,** 266–275.

Keller, Suzanne. The social world of the urban slum child: Some early findings. *American Journal of Orthopsychiatry,* 1963, **33,** 813–822.

Köhler, W. *The mentality of apes.* New York: Harcourt, 1925.

Lamarck, J. Chevalier de. *Zoological philosophy* (trans. of *Philosophie Zoologique,* by H. Elliot). London: Macmillan, 1914. Original date of publication, 1809.

Levine, S., J. A. Chevalier, and S. J. Korchin. The effects of early shock and handling on later avoidance learning. *Journal of Personality,* 1956, **24,** 475–493.

Lewis, O. *The children of Sanchez.* New York: Random House, 1961.

Liberman, R. Retinal cholinesterase and glycolysis in rats raised in darkness. *Science,* 1962, **135,** 372–373.

McDougall, W. *An introduction to social psychology.* Boston: Luce, 1908.

McGraw, Myrtle B. *Growth: A study of Johnny and Jimmy.* New York: Appleton-Century-Crofts, 1935.

Melton, A. W. "Learning." In W. S. Munroe (ed.), *Encylopedia of educational research.* New York: Macmillan, 1941.

Miller, G. A., E. H. Galanter, and K. H. Pribram. *Plans and the structure of behavior.* New York: Holt, Rinehart and Winston, 1960.

Miller, N. E., and J. Dollard. *Social learning and imitation.* New Haven: Yale University Press, 1941.

Montgomery, K. C. A test of two explanations of spontaneous alternation. *Journal of Comparative Physiology and Psychology,* 1952, **45,** 287–293.

————. Exploratory behavior as a function of "similarity" of stimulus situations. *Journal of Comparative Physiology and Psychology,* 1953, **46,** 129–133.

————. The relation between fear induced by novel stimulation and exploratory behavior. *Journal of Comparative Physiology and Psychology,* 1955, **48,** 254–260.

————, and M. Segall. Discrimination learning based upon the exploratory drive. *Journal of Comparative Physiology and Psychology,* 1955, **48,** 225–228.

Moore, O. K. *Autotelic responsive environments and exceptional children.* Hamden, Conn.: Responsive Environments Foundation, 1963.

Morgan, C. L. *An introduction to comparative psychology.* Ed. 2. London: Scott, 1909. Original date of publication, 1894.

Mowrer, O. H. *Learning theory and behavior.* New York: Wiley, 1960.

Newell, A., J. C. Shaw, and H. A. Simon. Elements of a theory of human problem solving. *Psychological Review,* 1958, **65,** 151–166.

Nissen, H. W. A study of exploratory behavior in the white rat by means of the obstruction method. *Journal of Genetic Psychology,* 1930, **37,** 361–376.

Orlansky, H. Infant care and personality. *Psychological Bulletin,* 1949, **46,** 1–48.

Osgood, C. E. The nature and measurement of meaning. *Psychological Bulletin,* 1952, **49,** 192–237.

Piaget, J. *The origins of intelligence in children.* (Margaret Cook, trans.) New York: International Universities Press, 1952. (Originally published 1936).

———. *Play, dreams, and imitation in childhood.* (C. Gattegno and F. M. Hodgson, trans.) New York: Norton, 1951. Originally published as *La formation du symbole chez l'enfant,* 1945.

———. *The psychology of intelligence.* (M. Piercy and D. E. Berlyne, trans.) London: Routledge & Kegan Paul, 1947.

Pribram, K. H. A review of theory in physiological psychology. *Annual Review of Psychology,* 1960, **11,** 1–40.

Pruette, Lorine. *G. Stanley Hall: A biography of a mind.* New York: Appleton-Century-Crofts, 1926.

Rambusch, Nancy M. *Learning how to learn: An American approach to Montessori.* Baltimore: Helicon Press, 1962.

Rasch, E., H. Swift, A. H. Riesen, and K. L. Chos. Altered structure and composition of retinal cells in dark-reared mammals. *Experimental Cellular Research,* 1961, **25,** 348–363.

Razran, G. The observable unconscious and the inferable conscious in current Soviet psychophysiology: Interoceptive conditioning, semantic conditioning, and the orienting reflex. *Psychological Review,* 1961, **68,** 81–147.

Riesen, A. H. "Plasticity of behavior: Psychological aspects." In H. F. Harlow and C. N. Woolsey (eds.), *Biological and biochemical bases of behavior.* Madison: University of Wisconsin Press, 1958, 425–450.

Romanes, G. J. *Animal intelligence.* New York: Appleton-Century-Crofts, 1883 (1882).

———. *Mental evolution in animals.* New York: Appleton-Century-Crofts, 1884 (1883).

Rose, J. E., and C. N. Woolsey. The relations of thalamic connections, cellular structure and evocable electrical activity in the auditory region of the cat. *Journal of Comparative Neurology,* 1949, **91,** 441–466.

Rousseau, J. J. *Emile.* (Barbara Foxley, trans.) New York: Everyman's Library, 1916. Original date of publication, 1762.

Salama, A. A., and J. McV. Hunt. "Fixation" in the rat as a function of infantile shocking, handling, and gentling. *Journal of Genetic Psychology,* 1964, **105,** 1, 131–162.

Schneirla, T. C. "An evolutionary and developmental theory of biphasic processes underlying approach and withdrawal." In M. R. Jones (ed.), *Nebraska symposium on motivation.* Lincoln: University of Nebraska Press, 1959, 1–43.

Sherrington, C. S. *The integrative action of the nervous system.* New York: Scribners, 1906.

Simpson, B. R. The wandering IQ. *Journal of Psychology,* 1939, **7,** 351–367.

Skeels, H. M. Some preliminary findings of three follow-up studies on the effects of adoption on children from institutions. *Children,* 1965, **12** (1), 33–34.

————, and H. B. Dye. A study of the effects of differential stimulation on mentally retarded children. *Proceedings of the American Association of Mental Deficiency,* 1939, **44,** 114–136.

Spitz, R. A. The smiling response: A contribution to the ontogenesis of social relations. *Genetic Psychological Monograph,* 1946, **34,** 67–125.

Standing, E. M. *Maria Montessori: Her life and work.* Fresno, Calif.: Academy Library Guild, 1957.

Stoddard, G. D., and Beth L. Wellman. Environment and the IQ. *Yearbook of National Social Studies Education,* 1940, **39** (1), 405–442.

Taylor, D. W. "Toward an information processing theory of motivation." In M. R. Jones (ed.), *Nebraska symposium on motivation.* Lincoln: University of Nebraska Press, 1960, 51–79.

Thompson, W. R. and W. Heron. The effects of restricting early experience on the problem-solving capacity of dogs. *Canadian Journal of Psychology,* 1954, **8,** 17–31.

Thorndike, E. L. *Educational psychology.* Vol. II. *The psychology of learning.* New York: Columbia University Press, 1913.

————, and R. S. Woodworth. The influence of improvement in one mental function upon the efficiency of other functions, *Psychological Review,* 1901, **8,** 247–261, 384–395, 553–564.

Uzgiris, Ina C., and J. McV. Hunt. *An instrument for assessing infant psychological development.* Urbana: Psychological Development Laboratory, University of Illinois (mimeographed progress report to be revised and published as "Ordinal Scales of Infant Psychological Development"), 1966.

———— and ————. *Ordinal scales of infant psychological development:* Sound cinemas depicting scales of (1) object permanence, (2) development of means, (3) imitation: gestural and vocal, (4) operational causality, (5) object relations in space, (6) development of schemas. Urbana: University of Illinois Motion Picture Service, 1967.

Walker, A. E. and T. A. Weaver, Jr. Ocular movements from the occipital lobe in the monkey. *Journal of Neurophysiology,* 1940, **3,** 353–357.

Watson, J. B. *Psychology from the standpoint of a behaviorist.* Philadelphia: Lippincott, 1919.

————. *Psychological care of infant and child.* New York: Norton, 1928.

————, and R. Rayner. *Conditioned emotional reactions. Journal of Experimental Psychology,* 1920, **3,** 1–14.

Weiskrantz, L. Sensory deprivation and the cat's optic nervous system. *Nature,* 1958, **181** (3), 47–105.

White, R. W. Motivation reconsidered: The concept of competence. *Psychological Review,* 1959, **66,** 297–333.

Wiener, N. *Cybernetics.* New York: Wiley, 1948.

Wolf, A. The dynamics of the selective inhibition of specific functions in neuroses. *Psychosomatic Medicine,* 1943, **5,** 27–38.

Woodworth, R. S. Heredity and environment: A critical study of recently published material on twins and foster children. *Social Science Research Council Bulletin,* 1941 (47).

CHAPTER NINE

A Nonpsychological Approach to Early Compensatory Education

CARL BEREITER[1]

Many graduate students in education reveal a monstrous educational handicap when they enter their first statistics course. They are baffled, terrified, rigid, forget things as soon as they learn them, and often leave the course with practically no transferrable knowledge. Suppose that a benign college administration decided to give these students some compensatory education, a subsidized eight weeks of experiences aimed at enabling them to start statistics on a more nearly equal footing with those privileged students whose undergraduate backgrounds had not been barren of mathematics. Here is a transcript of discussion in a committee drawn together to plan Project Head Stat.

"Perhaps you're wondering why I've asked such a variety of experts to sit in with us. Well, these are multi-problem kids. . . ."

"The thing that really grabbed me was I noticed a lot of them couldn't even add fractions. . . ."

"How do you know it isn't that they're just not motivated? Their values are different from science students'. They just don't give a damn about the sum of cross-products."

"You've got to develop positive attitudes toward stat. So make it mostly

---

[1] Ontario Institute for Studies in Education.

fun, with a warm accepting teacher and lots of brightly colored calculators around the room."

"You don't realize how deprived most of these students are. Why, half the students in my class last year had never seen a slide rule. They'd never lit a Bunsen burner. They didn't know the difference between mass and weight."

"How can we expect to make up for years of deprivation like that in eight weeks?"

"We can't, but we have to start someplace. Now a trip to the Museum of Science and Industry. . ."

"How about giving them some lessons in algebra?"

"Whoa, there! It's understood this is not to be a downward extension of statistics class. If we started trying to ram algebra down their throats we'd only succeed in teaching them to hate stat eight weeks earlier."

"Let's not forget that we're dealing with individuals and every one is different. I'd suggest a complete battery of aptitude and personality tests. . . ."

"We need a theoretical rationale for what we're doing. Now from a Piagetian point of view the problem can be seen as one of failure to attain the level of formal logical operations."

"It's in the medulla, I think. I'd have to look it up but I believe numerical reasoning is in the medulla."

"We really ought to involve the students' wives in this too. After all, it won't do any good to change their behavior here in school if it's all undone when they get home at night."

I should like to believe that no such interchange would ever take place—that the committee members, being sane and reasonable people, would simply try to find out what were the misconceptions and voids in understanding that gave students trouble in statistics and then put together a meaty little eight-week course that would teach the students what they most needed to know. But I am not too confident, for it is just such people—social scientists and educators—who have engaged in identical dialogue when presented with the closely related problem of designing a preliminary program for children expected to have difficulty learning what is taught in primary school.

In the preschool programs that Siegfried Engelmann and I conduct, we have tried to approach the educational problems of disadvantaged children in the same matter-of-fact way that we think most people would approach other learning deficit problems—like the problem in teaching statistics just cited. It seemed evident that first-grade academic work, like academic work at any other level, has certain prerequisites; and it was also apparent that disadvantaged children were usually weak in prerequisite learnings, their weaknesses tending to lie in the areas of language and reasoning. Although there might be other factors contributing to early school failure among disadvantaged children, it seemed wise strategy to clear away the large known factor first and then see what was left.

The task of designing a remedial course for four-year-olds deficient in language and verbal reasoning proved to be much more difficult— by an order of magnitude at least—than, say, designing a remedial mathematics course for statistics students. The difference is not in the pupils but in the state of the art. Whereas the mathematical requirements of a given statistics course are fairly evident, the requirements of primary-grade instruction in terms of the kinds of statements and reasoning operations a child is expected to grasp are not instantly derivable from a knowledge of what content is presented. Whereas mathematics has been taught for centuries, so that for any given topic there is a goodly supply of methods and materials available, the prerequisites for first grade—whatever they might be—have not been deliberately taught in the past. The child has been expected to learn them at home in some unspecified way. Finally, whereas graduate students have been taught things for as long as there have been graduate students, the deliberate teaching of anything very definite to children below the age of five has been a rarity in schools and virtually unheard of with children from underprivileged homes. In fact, there seemed to be a widespread belief among professional child lovers that it would be impossible or ruinous to the children.

But here is the key point: Although the task of designing such a remedial program for preschool children was more difficult than that of designing other kinds of remedial education for older students, there did not seem to be any reason for putting it on a different conceptual basis. We were mystified that other people working in the area seemed to act as if no analogous problems had ever been dealt with before, and were running off widely and wildly in search of theories to give them some guidance. Faculty psychology was reborn and many people began advocating mental exercises, under the banner of "stimulating psychological processes." Others turned to Piaget who, by offering a theory that managed to deal with learning independently of teaching and cultural transmission, made it possible for them to ignore cultural deprivation altogether, while conjuring up interesting possibilities. Everyone seemed to be avoiding the difficult task of deciding what, specifically, disadvantaged children needed to learn and how it could be taught to them.

DEVELOPMENT OF A BEGINNING LANGUAGE

PROGRAM

The problems in planning a short-term compensatory educational program are of an earthly sort. Had the mythical committee I introduced at the beginning of this paper stayed off the mushrooms for a while, they would eventually have gotten around to considering problems such as these:

1. The mathematical learning which the disadvantaged graduate students have missed out on normally occurs over several semesters of work. Since that much time is not available, it will not do simply to imitate the educational histories of the more privileged students.

2. An inventory of all the things it would be useful for the students to know would be unmanageable. How assign priorities and, especially, how distinguish the necessary from the merely desirable?

3. Assuming that it is out of the question to give students the foundations of mathematical reasoning in so short a time, how does one impart some understanding to them and not just rote memorization?

4. Sophisticated people may well overlook many of the more troublesome misunderstandings of the students because they involve things that have been second nature to the sophisticated person for years. (For instance, it might never occur to a teacher that some students didn't realize subscript numerals served only as identification tags and didn't count as numbers in computation.)

The same or very similar problems occur in planning a program to prepare disadvantaged children for the verbal demands of primary school. Middle-class children learn what they learn about using language through years of informal interaction with literate adults; but even though that method of language learning seems to work fine, something much quicker has to be discovered if the same results are to be achieved in a few hundred hours. The second problem, the assigning of priorities, is especially perplexing in this case. There is so much to language—so many aspects and so much detail—that it seems presumptuous to pick out some things as vital and let the rest go. Analogous to the third point above is the fact that concepts in a first language can't be explained verbally to the learner, and so understanding must be achieved through some other means. Finally, for an adult to anticipate or detect the misconceptions and sources of difficulties, the wrong turns and pitfalls that occur in a child's learning of language and thinking rules, is an unbelievably tricky task.

The first two problems—accomplishing more in less time and assigning priorities—are at once the most difficult and the most critical problems. With only one or two exceptions those experimenters who have developed language programs for disadvantaged children have dealt with these two problems by ignoring them. They have adhered closely to nature's way, relying on informal conversational interchanges to do the job of language teaching and have left the selection of content to chance.

The language program we have used was originated by my colleague, Siegfried Engelmann. His outstanding achievement in this program, I believe, is a bold simultaneous solution to the problem of time, and the problem of priorities. As Engelmann saw it, the child's primary need was for a language that would enable him to be taught. Once the child had that, you could go on and teach him anything else you pleased. Such a language did not have to be distilled from a recording of actual verbal behavior but could be constructed, much as Basic English was constructed, by a consideration of the needs it had to serve. Such a language could be taught to children in a relatively short time (in practice, two to six months), and it would then be possible to add the refinements of complete English and also to teach other things in a more direct and normal manner.

Teaching disadvantaged children a miniature language that someone else has made up for them may sound a bit 1984ish to the doubters among us; but realize that it is regular English, just a stripped-down version of it, and that the principle of starting with a miniature system which is part of, but more easily grasped than, the entire system is a respectable and widely used pedagogical device. Methods of reading instruction that begin with a limited vocabulary that follows a few consistent spelling rules are an example, as are physics lessons that begin with consideration of a homogeneous frictionless environment.

To describe the basic language program briefly, it presumes nothing more of the child at the outset than that he be capable of making some attempt at imitating what is said to him. Only two basic-statement forms are taught, the first being the identity statment, "This is a _____," and "This is not a _____." Once this statement type is mastered (and mastery of the not-statement is a major challenge to many seriously deprived children), the remainder of the beginning language program is devoted to work with the statement form, "This _____ is _____," with its negative and plural variations, introducing several different kinds of concepts that are used in the predicates of these statements: polar sets (big-little, hot-cold, and so on); nonpolar sets, such as the colors and prepositional phrases; and subclass nouns, as in "This animal is a tiger."

Once the basic system has been mastered, it has been found possible to move very rapidly with almost all children through the expansion of the system to include active verbs, the common tenses, and personal pronouns. The remainder of the language program is devoted largely to if-then type statements in which the major problems are logical ones concerning the use of *all, only, some, and,* and *or.* The program, thus, culminates in the use of language for deductive reasoning, all of the more elementary work with statement forms and concept types having been designed to provide the groundwork for this use of language.

The problem of teaching generalizable rules, given that the children cannot understand most explanations, is handled through the use of a kind of pattern drill in which, by repeated application of a form like, "This _____ is not red," they learn through correction where and and on what basis it applies. This is learning rules by analogy, and so to make it work the entire program is structured so as to dramatize significant analogies as much as possible. Rather than grouping concepts on the basis of their thematic associations (concepts related to the school, to the zoo, and so on), they are grouped together on the basis of the rules governing their manipulation. Thus polar sets of diverse content (big-little, hot-cold, boy-girl) are taught as part of a single sequence, so that the child may eventually come to grasp the major principle governing such sets—the principle that saying that something is not one member of the set is equivalent to saying that it is the other member of the set.

The actual teaching consists mainly of variations on five basic "moves":

1. Verbatim repetition:

TEACHER: This block is red. Say it . . .
CHILDREN: This block is red.

2. Yes-no questions:

TEACHER: Is this block red?
CHILDREN: No, this block is not red.

3. Location tasks:

TEACHER: Show me a block that is red.
CHILDREN: This block is red.

4. Statement production:

TEACHER: Tell me about this piece of chalk.
CHILDREN: This piece of chalk is red.
TEACHER: Tell me about what this piece of chalk is *not*.
CHILDREN: (ad lib) This piece of chalk is not green . . . not blue, and so on.

5. Deduction problems:

TEACHER: (with piece of chalk hidden in hand) This piece of chalk is not red. Do you know what color it is?
CHILDREN: No. Maybe it is blue . . . maybe it is yellow . . .

These moves represent a rough hierarchy of task difficulty. In the early stages of the program, large amounts of time have to be devoted to the lowest level—verbatim repetition—and deduction problems can seldom be handled. By the end of the program most of the time is devoted to deduction problems, although at each new step in the program it is necessary to go through all of the moves, if only in very condensed form.

As the above examples suggest, the instruction is carried on in a highly disciplined manner. The pace is fast, all children are required to respond and to put forth continual effort. Guessing and thoughtlessness in responding are discouraged. With the 150 or so children who have been exposed to this kind of teaching, however, we have found few instances of difficulty in maintaining enthusiasm and effort among four- and five-year-old disadvantaged children during twenty-minutes-per-day intensive sessions. So long as the tasks are within their reach, yet difficult enough to be challenging, children seem to take to this kind of instruction very naturally, and with practically no period of breaking in.

SOME EXPERIMENTAL RESULTS

We have run two experimental preschool classes for disadvantaged children to date, both groups starting at age four. Group I consisted of fifteen Negro children coming from households that contained older children who were identified by their teachers as problem children showing effects of cultural deprivation. This group was maintained for two years, through kindergarten, and thirteen of the original children remained to the end. Group II also contained fifteen children, seven white and eight Negro, selected this time according to conventional Project Head Start standards of income and socioeconomic status. This group has had only one year of preschool.

The educational program was much the same for both groups. It consisted of two hours a day, of which three twenty-minute periods were devoted to direct instruction. The language program described in the preceding section occupied one of these periods, and the other two were used for instruction in reading and arithmetic. I will not attempt to describe the latter curricula here.[2] They were similar in conception to the language program—highly verbal, with great emphasis on the learning of generalizable rules through practice on analogous tasks, and embodying as much as possible the principle of minimizing rule complexity and irregularity at the beginning. The other hour of the day was occupied with more informal activities—singing, stories, drawing, and printing—which were nevertheless planned to reinforce the content of the formal instruction. During the second year, for Group

---

[2] All three curricula are presented in full in *Teaching Disadvantaged Children in the Preschool* by Carl Bereiter and Siegfried Englemann (Englewood Cliffs, N. J.: Prentice-Hall, 1966).

I, instruction in basic language gave way to instruction in science concepts, again following the same general approach.

At this writing neither group has entered first grade, and so by the rules of scientific caution I should not make any but the most tentative claims about the program's success in achieving its stated objective— of enabling the children to succeed in primary school. I am, in fact, extremely reluctant to make any claims on the basis of improved psychological test scores, because I don't know of any evidence to show that experimentally induced gains on predictors of academic achievement have any predictive validity themselves.

However, with Group I, who have completed kindergarten, it is possible to claim that a fair number of them have already succeeded, or partly so, in the first grade, by virtue of having already gotten over the most critical hurdles of that grade. On the Wide-Range Achievement Test, ten of the thirteen children in Group I scored at or above the 1.9 grade level in arithmetic (the normal level expected to be attained at the end of first grade). The mean-grade level was 2.6, the lowest, 1.4. In reading, the average was 1.5, three children scoring at 1.9 or above, and only one scoring below 1.0. In spelling, the average was 1.7, with six children scoring at 1.9 or above and the lowest scoring at a grade level of 1.2.

Achievement was notably higher in arithmetic than in reading and spelling. This could easily be passed off as indicating the relatively greater influence of language handicaps on reading than on arithmetic, but that would be begging the question. We are not satisfied that we have yet pinned down what, in particular, disadvantaged children need to be taught that will enable them to catch on to reading more rapidly. The literature is full of suggestions by people who don't know, either. We believe we are on to some important improvements, however, through ideas gained from a comparison of the response of middle-class and lower-class four-year-olds to reading programs using the same introductory approach—a comparison which ended after seven months with the lower-class children scoring at the 1.2 grade level in reading and the middle-class children scoring at 2.4.

In all, however, we have been very gratified by the academic achievements of the disadvantaged children, none of which, incidentally, is achieved by rote memory. The children are not taught multiplication "facts," and so forth, nor are they taught to read or spell words by memory (except for a few high-frequency impossibles like *the*). They are taught to figure these things out. And in doing so they display the verve, agility, and persistence that would ordinarily signal an IQ in the superior range. Thus it is interesting to note that the Stanford-Binet IQs of Group I, although they rose from a mean of 95 (obtained six weeks after the beginning of school) to 105 at the end of kindergarten, do not presage anything more than average performance for their age. The highest final IQs are a 126, earned by a middling performer, and a 117 held by the next-to-lowest achiever. The four all-around highest achievers, who scored at the 1.9 grade level or higher in all three achievement areas, had IQs of 99, 100, 107, and 114.

In Group II, which has completed only its first year of preschool, the IQs rose much more dramatically, from 95 to 112. Yet their achievement-test scores, while quite satisfactory (averaging between 1.1 and 1.2 on all tests), are no better than the first-year scores of Group I, who at that time had a mean IQ of only 102.

What about control groups? We are always a little taken aback when someone who has just watched a kindergarten class solve a page full of linear equations suggests that perhaps disadvantaged children who spent their time playing dress-up in front of a mirror could do just as well. Nevertheless, we do have some comparative data on achievement, which is summarized in Table 9.1.

Group I, the group that has finished kindergarten, is not strictly comparable with any other group. Group II, however, was selected as part of a randomized block-design that included Groups C_1 and C_2 as well and was controlled for IQ, socioeconomic status, and race. Group C_1 consisted of two classes that were given an intensive instructional program, but one that used a variety of educational games rather than sequential teaching. Group C_2 consisted of two other classes that followed a traditional nursery school program. All three groups had the same amount of schooling and the same pupil-teacher ratio of five-to-one. Group II is significantly superior to Group C_2 on all tests and to Group C_1 on everything but arithmetic. This is not so surprising, since the approach taken to arithmetic is one that bears most

TABLE 9.1

Mean Grade-Level Scores on Wide-Range

Achievement Test

| | | | | Achievement Scores | | |
Group	Age	Years in School	N	Reading	Arithmetic	Spelling
I	5–6	2	13	1.5	2.6	1.7
II	4–5	1	15	1.2	1.1	1.2
C_1	4–5	1	26	0.7	0.9	0.8
C_2	4–5	1	26	0.4	0.6	0.6
Ac	4–5	1	18	2.4	1.5	1.7
M	4–5	2	17	1.0	1.2	1.2

of its conventionally measurable fruit in the second year. The first year is highly formal and it is only after the children have acquired sufficient language mastery that an attempt is made to teach them to translate between everyday language statements and mathematical statements.

Groups Ac and M are comparable groups of middle-class children of mostly college-educated parents. Group Ac received instruction paralleling that of the disadvantaged Group II, while Group M attended a private Montessori school, most of them for their second year. The achievement scores of Group M are very similar to those of Group II, whereas Group Ac is significantly superior in all areas to all the other prekindergarten groups. Its scores are more like those of Group I except for the reversal of standing on reading and arithmetic. Interestingly, the distribution of spelling scores for middle-class Group Ac and disadvantaged Group I was almost identical; they attacked the words in the same way and made the same mistakes.

HOW DO YOU KNOW THEY'RE ANY SMARTER?

There is one line of response to our preschool program which goes, "All right, so they can add and subtract and read a little. But how do you know they're any smarter than they were before?" This is one of those naive questions that hits a profound point.

The same question could be asked of any preschool program: "All right, the children have learned to fit cuisenaire rods together (or solve alphabet puzzles, or arrange objects according to size, or carry on conversations with a puppet)—but how do you know they're any smarter than they were before?"

There is no satisfactory answer in any case. It does no good to appeal to IQ gains. They merely indicate that the children have also learned to answer some questions on an intelligence test. The most formidable theoretical claims topple before this question. "All right, so the children have acquired conservation of substance. But how do you know . . .?" Alas, Piaget never said a child would become any smarter for having been taught how to pass one of his tests—and if he had said so, someone could have asked him how he knew.

The question, then, is unanswerable and must ultimately be rejected. But what it does is strip away all superfluous claims, leaving only the bald declarative, "All right, we taught them such-and-such." There is nothing left but to defend what was taught as being useful. This, as I see it, is the sensible starting point for compensatory education.

CHAPTER TEN

Environmental Intervention in Infancy and Early Childhood

CELIA B. STENDLER-LAVATELLI [1]

Recently *The New York Times* ran a story on the progress of two hundred students admitted to Harvard College on a special basis. The students, both Negro and white, reared in poverty and graduates of slum and even unaccredited high schools, were unqualified by conventional standards for admission to Harvard. Yet 85 percent of those selected graduated, some with honors and one with a Rhodes scholarship. This happy outcome plus encouraging results from other kinds of educational intervention ranging from special preschool to youth programs reinforce the conviction of many that education is a most effective weapon in the fight against poverty. This conviction is evidenced in the mushrooming of programs in compensatory education over the past few years, a phenomenal growth that will surely increase in magnitude in the years to come.

But what form should educational intervention take? What *are* effective ways of overcoming the intellectual and educational disadvantages of poverty? When should intervention begin? For years, public

---

[1] University of Illinois.

schools that enrolled large numbers of children from deprived back-grounds solved the problem simply but ineffectually; they planned a curriculum for the disadvantaged that was one or more grades below the norm. Thus "slow-learning" fifth-graders would study subject matter normally mastered in third grade, with no expectation on the school's part that the children would do more than a year's work in the academic year. Under this too-typical pattern, not only did the children not catch up, but they appeared to lose ground, so that the gap in performance between middle and lower classes increased with school grade. It is this kind of solution that writers like Kenneth Clark have railed against.

Today there is a strong tendency to begin educational intervention earlier than public-school entrance, and to base the nature of the intervention on the special intellective and motivational deficits revealed by research on the disadvantaged. For example, the language patterns of the disadvantaged are being analyzed, and experimental preschool programs devised to counteract specific disabilities that reflect the child's social background. In the affective realm, certain deficits in achievement motivation are being identified, and special efforts made to influence the drive to do well in school. It is the aim of this paper to analyze contemporary approaches to educational intervention from a child-development point of view; this analysis will begin with the infancy period, where some believe intervention ought to be initiated.

THE INFANCY PERIOD AND ENVIRONMENTAL

INTERVENTION

A number of writers have proposed that the impact of cultural disadvantage begins during the period of infancy. (We define infancy here as extending to eighteen months.) They argue that to begin intervention at three years is too late; counteracting disadvantage ought to begin in infancy as it is during that period that structures of intelligence begin to emerge. Such intervention, the argument goes, ought to take the form of training mothers to interact with their babies so that a proper foundation for cognitive and affective development is laid, or of providing prenursery schools like the Russian crèches, or a modified Israeli kibbutz.

The case for early intervention is made considerably stronger by a recent study of mental-test scores for infants from one month of age through fifteen months. Bayley (1965) found no difference in scores of Negro and white infants during the first fifteen months of life on the

Mental Scale of the Bayley Infant Scales of Development;[2] yet we know from IQ scores reported in the literature that culturally disadvantaged preschool children test significantly lower than do advantaged children. In the Deutsch project in New York City, one group of Negro children tested at 93.21 IQ at four years of age (Goldstein, 1965); Kennedy (Kennedy *et al.,* 1963) has reported an IQ of 86 for five-year-old Negro children in five southeastern states, as compared with the Terman and Merrill data of a mean IQ of 101.8. While there are differences in the populations being compared here, the trend toward lower IQs in *all* the studies supports the thesis of a decline for culturally disadvantaged Negroes, if we accept the validity of infant scales of intelligence.

The notion of infancy as having an important impact upon later development is relatively new in man's intellectual history. Not until Freud postulated a theory of psychosexual development beginning in infancy, and ethologists like Lorenz and Tinbergen showed the impact of early experiences upon emerging behaviors of animals, did man begin to study seriously the possible consequences of infantile experience. This study has been given considerable impetus by the work of Piaget on the origins and development of human intelligence. His careful description of the step-by-step emergence of intellective structures during the infancy period makes clear why this hitherto neglected period is important.

Intellective Developments in Infancy

Piaget (1952) traces the development of intelligence from the exercise of certain motor reflexes immediately after birth. The infant is born with two kinds of reflexes, those like the knee-jerk, which are not changed by experience, and others like sucking and grasping, which are modified by functioning and the functioning of which creates a need for further functioning. Exercising those reflexes that are modifiable initiates feedback which regulates future action and leads to the acquisition of new behavior patterns. During the first few months of life the infant through his own activity discovers combinations of reflexes; look-

---

[2] The interpretation of Bayley's data presented here is one that a number of scholars dispute. They argue that infant scales are tests of perceptual-motor development, and that this area of development is not highly correlated with abstract conceptual ability associated with intelligence at later ages. While this author recognizes the lack of correlation, nevertheless, she also is persuaded by Piaget's contention that the origins of intelligence can be traced to the infancy period, and that mental structures developing during the sensorimotor stage of intelligence form the basis upon which later structures are built.

ing and grasping, for example, become coordinated and lead to the emergence of more complex behavior patterns. Thus a doll hanging from the hood of the bassinet may first be an object to be looked at, grasped, or sucked, but then at six months becomes something the infant can pull in order to make the hood shake. He can act upon the external environment to make an interesting event happen, by co-ordinating certain separate patterns of behavior involving both grasping and pulling that he has practiced upon other objects.

One of the most important intellective developments during infancy is the acquisition of the notion of permanence of object. As a result of cumulative sensorimotor experiences with objects, there develops an image of absent things and their displacement; the object continues to exist even when it is out-of-sight. The infant can then represent the object mentally without the object being actually in sight. As Piaget (1963) puts it, it is then possible for the child to represent "the data offered to his sight otherwise than he perceives them directly. In his mind he corrects the things he looks at; that is to say, he evokes po-sitions, displacements or perhaps even objects without actually con-templating them in his visual field. . . " (p. 351). Representative thought is taking the place of sensorimotor intelligence.

Stimulation and Interaction

Piaget sees notions of space, time, matter, and causality developing in this early, sensorimotor stage of intellective growth, but these de-velopments are not the result of some innate maturational process; they depend upon a facilitating environment. If the infant at eighteen months finds himself with a problem that is new to him and can invent new means to solve the problem, it is because he has available to him schemata acquired earlier through *transactions he has been carrying on upon objects in the environment.* The infant must be actively engaged in transactions from which feedback can be derived and fed into the next transaction. And, because of his helplessness, the infant is de-pendent upon others to make available objects and events that will stimulate him to activity. Only as others do something to the infant or make some form of stimulation available to him does the mind grow optimally.

Learning-theorists, psychoanalysts, and other strange bedfellows agree that it is the nature of the child to need stimulation. Erikson (1963) notes that the prevailing mode of behavior during the first stage of de-velopment is one of incorporation; not just the oral zone, but also other zones, including the whole skin surface, the sense organs and the skin, are "receptive and increasingly hungry for proper stimulation"

(p. 74). And Hunt, whose *Intelligence and Experience* (1961) triggered the contemporary concern with early experience and later development, concludes from his study of how intelligence develops that "the counsel from experts on child-rearing during the third and much of the fourth decades of the twentieth century to let children be while they grow and to avoid excessive stimulation was highly unfortunate" (p. 362).

We need to be clear, however, as to what constitutes stimulation, or what will provoke an infant to activity. A cursory glance at a disadvantaged home might lead one to believe that there is much in the way of stimulation to activity available within. Homes are active and noisy, but as Susan Gray (Gray and Klaus, 1965) points out, "The active noisy home of the culturally deprived child is so full of conflicting stimuli that the child is unable to attend to those stimuli most relevant in terms of increased intellectual development. These homes, for example, are the ones where the television set booms from morning till night, no matter what else people are trying to do" (p. 889). Berlyne's (1960) analysis as to what constitutes stimulation is relevant here. He includes *novelty* as one of the criteria. We cease to attend to that to which we are accustomed; just as the sensory receptors for smell cease to be stimulated by a strong odor that persists in time, so we literally do not "see" or "hear" or sense in other ways stimuli that constantly surround us.

Furthermore, having things happen in one's vicinity does not necessarily lead to interaction; as Piaget points out, being exposed to experience is not enough to guarantee development of mental structures. Many of the children in a University of Illinois project for the disadvantaged had made annual pilgrimages to the South, but it was hard to find evidence in them or older siblings that the trips had contributed to concept development. C. Deutsch (1965) reports the same thing to be true of children of migrant workers; they may have traveled from Florida to Texas to California and back many times, without learning anything of geography en route. Middle-class parents, on the other hand, tend to interact with their children, so as to milk every experience of its educational potentialities; they call attention to things, ask questions, get the child to tell others about his experiences, so that the experience is truly assimilated by the child. They also provide objects and materials to stimulate the child and encourage self-activity; even the bassinet as a vehicle for stimulation has not been neglected, as evidenced by the mobiles dangling within the vision of the modern, middle-class infant, and changing constantly with currents of air. Cradle gyms are within reach, with objects that can be manipulated to produce movements and sound in varying amounts. "Educational" toys of many kinds are available to encourage activity on the part of the baby out of which there will be feedback resulting in a changed pattern of behavior, and perhaps a more complex pattern, available for the next organism-environment transaction. The middle-class infant is involved with things and with people, and not merely surrounded by a confusion of stimuli difficult to assimilate.

Out of twenty-eight homes of young children in a compensatory education project at the University of Illinois, we found at least one half living in homes with minimal stimulation available to infant siblings. While infants spent considerable time on someone's lap during waking hours, thus providing opportunity to take in the visual surroundings, there were none of the traditional infant toys in sight—no rattles, cuddly animals, or other traditional toys, or homely substitutes from the kitchen that would encourage development of prehension and active experimentation that would lead to discovery. Nor did the mothers and the many surrogate mothers living under the same roof play traditional games with the babies. They did not engage babies in "Pat-a-Cake," "Peek-a-Boo," "This Little Pig," or waving good-bye, or any subcultural substitutes. Spitz (1965) notes the infant's growing participation in reciprocal social games during the second half of the first year of life. If a ball is rolled to the child, he rolls it back; if one waves "bye-bye," he waves in return. Psychoanalysts would see such mastery of action patterns through imitation as permitting the infant to achieve increasing autonomy from the mother, but there are cognitive implications also. "Peek-a-Boo" may well help the infant to achieve the concept of permanence of object—that the hidden face continues to exist even when it is no longer visible. There is readiness for one-to-one correspondence in "This Little Pig," as the mother pinches a different toe in succession and recites "This little pig went to market, this little pig stayed at home," and so on. Such games help build the foundation for the important mental operation of reversibility, of being able to return to a starting point in thought as well as in sensorimotor activity. They also contribute to an understanding of social relations and the role of social gestures as a vehicle of reciprocal communication. The dearth of interactions in which the infant in a culturally disadvantaged home engages may be the source of stimulus deprivation.

Effects of Deprivation and Enrichment on
Sensorimotor Intelligence

That deprivation of stimulation in infant animals has an impact upon later development has been well-documented (see Denenberg,

1964, for a discussion of theoretical issues). It is obviously not possible to carry out controlled research on human infants, but studies of babies living in institutions under conditions of deprivation have been reported. One of the most fascinating was the study by Skeels and Dye (1939) of the fate of thirteen babies aged 7.1 months to 35.9 months with IQs from 36 to 89. The babies were transferred from an orphanage with little individual care and stimulation to a school for the feeble-minded, where they received almost individual care from older girls selected as brighter among the feeble-minded inmates. Remarkable gains in IQ were noted, especially from one-and-a-half to two years. (Again we remind the reader that experts disagree as to whether or not the scales measure intelligence.) An average gain of 27 points on the Kuhlmann scale was recorded for the total group after two years time, while a control group that remained in the institution experienced a decrease of 26 points. A follow-up study by Skodak and Skeels (1949) showed that twenty-one years later, the experimental group had grown into self-supporting adults, while one third of the control group were still institutionalized. However, since eleven of the experimental group were adopted in the preschool years, the ultimate fate of individuals in these two groups cannot be attributed solely to the factor of stimulation in *infancy*. What the evidence clearly demonstrates is that there are significant changes in infant IQ scores correlated with differential amounts of environmental stimulation.

Infant tests of intelligence assess sensorimotor intelligence. Can aspects of sensorimotor development be speeded up by enrichment? White (1965) reports results of selectively enriching the early experience of infants being reared in an institution where they received minimal stimulation. The investigators conducted a series of studies on the development of visual regard and prehension in infants during the first five months of life. In separate studies, a number of enrichment conditions were provided, including twenty minutes of extra handling a day for a month, placing infants in a prone position and removing crib liners for a better view, suspending stabiles over the cribs, attaching pacifiers to the sides, using printed sheets and crib bumpers and attaching colorful wrist bands. The investigators found that the course of development of visual exploratory behavior seems to reflect the availability of interesting things to look at. Discovery of the hands occurred earlier in control groups without more interesting things to look at, but reaching and swiping for objects occurred earlier for experimental subjects, and particularly those in whose cribs pacifiers were mounted on colored-patterned discs close to the eyes of the infants.

At this point the skeptic might ask what acceleration of visual-motor development has to do with stimulating growth of intelligence. White's own comment on the meaning of these sensorimotor accomplishments is as follows:

> In Piaget's system, a target, such as a small toy, has no conceptual existence for the newborn infant. It may serve to evoke innately organized responses such as grasping and pursuit, but once these actions cease, there is no reason to assume that the toy "exists" in any conceptual way for the neonate. When, however, the infant develops to the point that he makes a prehensory contact with the toy, something qualitatively new appears. That one toy has elicited visual fixation, appropriate arm movements, and tactual contact followed by grasping. Several previously separate action systems intersect at the toy. The toy acquires the beginnings of an independent conceptual existence in so far as it is no longer merely a part of any single action pattern, but now ties several sub-systems together. True cognitive representation doesn't develop until many months later in Piaget's system, but prehensory efforts such as reaching do constitute the major early vehicle for this achievement (pp. 6–7).

One would not, of course, expect any of the specific developments during the sensorimotor period to be correlated with intelligence-test scores at school age, but the onset of each new behavior like prehension makes possible for the infant new experimentations upon objects and subsequent discoveries. These in turn lead to acquisition of still more complex discoveries, if appropriate stimulation is available. Effects of deprivation in infancy may not be irreversible, but where deficit is sustained, one would expect sensorimotor development to be slowed and the appearance of operational structures which depend upon a sensorimotor underpinning to be delayed.

The infancy period also sees the beginnings of language development. Does lack of stimulation from the environment affect development in the area? Rheingold (1961) found significantly more talking (five to nine times as much) to infants at home than in institutions; she also found that the infants reared at home vocalized more. When reinforcement techniques were used in the institutions, vocalizations by the infants increased. However, Irwin's (1948) research leads to the conclusion that environmental differences begin to make a difference *after* eighteen months. He found no significant differences in number of speech sounds and tokens produced by infants during the initial stages of language development, but upper-status infants surpassed the lower beginning at eighteen months of age and extending to the age limit of his sample (thirty months). The language deficit of the disadvantaged school-age child has been well-documented, but we need more studies before we can trace its roots to specific deprivation in *infancy*.

Impact of a Low Socioeconomic Environment on
Affective Development in Infancy

The school problems of the disadvantaged stem not just from intellective deficit; they also derive from deficits in affective development. Deutsch (1964), and Gray and Klaus (1965) describe the
child from the slums as having difficulty in postponing immediate gratification, and many writers note a low achievement drive and school-
behavior problems that interfere with learning among the disadvantaged.
In Erikson's scheme of ego development, the ego qualities that would
produce achievement in the school-age child begin with the development of basic trust in infancy, a trust deriving from the quality of
maternal care, the manner in which the mother responds to the physiological needs of the infant. We have some descriptions of infant care
among the disadvantaged, but no studies to reveal consistent patterns.
And it may be that there are no consistent patterns in the subgroups
as they are presently delineated. Pavenstedt (1965) describes a very
poor, lower-lower class of disorganized families among whom infant
care was distressingly casual:

> The youngest child usually was found in his crib in a back room. Di-
> apers were changed infrequently. As often as not, a partially full bottle
> was somewhere in the crib beyond the baby's reach. During our visits,
> crying often remained unheeded while the mother discussed her own wor-
> ries and needs, or she would hold the baby with little attention to his com-
> fort. The outstanding characteristic in these homes was that activities were
> impulse-determined; consistency was totally absent. The mother might stay
> in bed until noon while the children also were kept in bed or ran around
> unsupervised. Although families sometimes ate breakfast or dinner to-
> gether, there was no pattern for anything. Until children had learned not to
> mess with food, the mothers fed them and prevented them from holding
> the spoon. Curiously enough, they always dressed their children, who were
> completely passive and expected to be dressed. Most children ran around
> in an undershirt and diapers until they were about two and a half years
> old (p. 94).

On the other hand, in some families under similar conditions of low
income, little education, bad housing, and illegitimacy, babies spend
a great deal of time with adults and older children in the family;
their physiological needs seem to be adequately met, although, as we
have noted, not necessarily their need for stimulation. Undoubtedly
it is true that there are more disorganized families among the lower-
lower class, but not all such families are disorganized, and some seem

to provide the kind of psychological care *at least in infancy* that Erikson and others deem to be so important.

However, affective development may be influenced adversely by the lack of sensory stimulation in the life of the lower-class infant. In fact, one of the interesting very recent developments in research has been the systematic attempt to explore relationships between psychoanalytic theory with its emphasis upon affective processes and sensorimotor theory with its emphasis upon the cognitive. Wolff's (1960) *The Developmental Psychologies of Jean Piaget and Psychoanalysis* with its theoretical exploration of relationships between propositions derived from each school of thought laid the groundwork for such endeavors. Spitz (1965) has published a revision of *The First Year of Life,* and in an appendix, Cobliner continues the theoretical rapprochement. Cobliner sees cognitive processes as "triggered and interlocked with affective processes and experiences," and explores in some detail the way in which affective processes influence the development of the notion of permanence of object. For example, the search for a hidden toy is only successful as frustration and ambiguity are tolerated. The transactions the infant carries on with people and objects in the environment lead not only to knowledge, but also to ego strengths.

Some interesting empirical studies that bridge the two theories are reported by Wolff and White (1965). They have been interested in the relationship between oral satisfaction and attentiveness. Is an infant more alert to his surroundings when oral needs are gratified? The investigators studied visual pursuit in infants, and what factors are related to its development. They considered visual pursuit to be an index of attentive behavior; they hypothesized that there would be less visual pursuit when there were competing excitations within the infant, but that a reduction in such competition would enhance attentive behavior. Specifically they predicted that "sucking on a pacifier increases the range of visual pursuit and, by inference, the capacity for attention" (p. 475). Experimentation with forty-eight neonates disclosed, among other findings, that after sucking the pacifier for at least three minutes, infants pursue a moving object more consistently than right after they begin to suck (p. 483).

The research of investigators like Wolff and White may be significant for work with culturally disadvantaged, for it reveals the outcome of very specific transactions between organism and environment. We do not know the long-range impact of specific transactions, but it is reasonable to assume that an attentive, alert, active infant will be interacting with stimuli from the environment and deriving feedback, thereby accelerating development, and that where environmental conditions exist to discourage or depress self-activity, there would be less feedback and slower development.

Some Proposals for Environmental Intervention during Infancy

Our view of infancy has changed. The notion of this period as important only for physical growth and motor development is dispelled by the analyses done to date, revealing significant developments in affective and cognitive areas. We know that some disadvantaged homes do not provide the environment to support such developments. The question is what kind of environmental interaction will counteract the depressing effects of poor environments.

One possibility would be the development of a corps of psychologically trained home visitors for the express purpose of improving the infant environment in culturally deprived families. Social workers are usually too involved with the enormous economic and social problems of such families to be of much service in this area. Psychologically trained visitors could demonstrate the possibilities of mother-child interaction in behavioral contexts like bathing and feeding the baby, and providing visual-motor stimulation. Older siblings who participate actively in child care would be included in the training. Mothers could be encouraged to get together in small groups to discuss what they have tried, and what the results were; such discussions might make parents more active and involved participants in the processes of infant care.

Environmental intervention of the kind just described might be very effective in families where poor or indifferent care is due to ignorance. Many mothers are "bad" mothers because they do not realize that early experiences have an impact upon later development, and because they do not know the ingredients of good psychological care. They have never seen babies taken care of, except in a haphazard way, and they do not realize that there are other ways of behaving toward babies. Some mothers who are recent migrants from the rural South would fall into this category.

Exactly this kind of intervention is now being tried out experimentally in Washington, D.C. Furfey and others (in process) are attempting to find out whether a program of intellectual stimulation, with emphasis on verbal skills, will foster intellective development in low socioeconomic-status infants. Individual tutors are assigned to homes for one hour a day, five days a week. Emphasis in the training sessions is upon playful, informal interaction centered around household objects, toys, picture books, the child's own body, and clothing. Sessions began with fifteen-month-old infants and will continue until the children are three years of age. Intelligence tests were administered to the fifty experimental and fifty control subjects; retests will be made every six months. Evaluation, including language variables, will continue through the kindergarten. A first report from this promising project of testing at twenty-one months should be available soon.[3]

An interesting research design involving intervention during infancy has been devised by Kirk (in process) at the University of Illinois. Kirk has selected thirty infants between the ages of eight months and two years who have four-year-old siblings in nursery school. The infants will receive one hour of intellectual stimulation each day, five days a week. Areas included in the training program are movement, self-concept, object manipulation, language, symbolic representation, and socialization. The objective of the program is to see whether infants with such training will exceed the levels of cognitive development attained by their older siblings at the onset of the study.

Another type of intervention that has been suggested is the neighborhood crèche where three or four infants would be assigned to one caretaker. Such crèches would provide part-time care for the infant, not to free a mother for a job, but to relieve her of some of the burden of baby-care and free her to provide more adequately for the rest of the family. Trained workers in the crèche would interact with the babies, providing appropriate stimulation. Involvement of mothers in caretaking processes in the crèche would assist the intervention process.[4]

Some argue that under conditions of severe disorganization in the family, full-time care of infants should be provided in the neighborhood crèche, with the infant spending only a few hours each day with the family, as do infants in the kibbutz. Undoubtedly, we will see proposals for even more drastic steps in environmental intervention during the infancy period increasing in the years to come. However, such drastic

---

[3] Intervention projects beginning in infancy have mushroomed since this manuscript was prepared. Most of the projects recognize the importance of the mother as teacher. Typically, a tutor goes into the home on a regular basis primarily to teach the mother the kinds of activities she might carry on with her child. Experimental projects involving various forms of infant stimulation are under way at the Early Childhood Centers at Cornell University, University of Arizona, University of Chicago, and George Peabody College, all under the aegis of the National Laboratory for Early Childhood Education. Also active in the area are the University of Illinois (Drs. Merle Karnes and Queenie Mills), The Durham (N.C.) Education Improvement Program (Dr. Robert L. Spaulding, Director), and the University of Florida (Dr. Ira Gordon). A critical review of infant intervention projects is being prepared by ERIC-PS (preschool) at the National Coordination Center of the National Laboratory for Early Childhood Education, University of Illinois.

[4] An experimental project in group care of infants has been under way for several years at the University of Syracuse under the direction of Dr. Bettye Caldwell. A curriculum of weekly activities has been devised, and a regular program of testing and follow-up is in operation. The new Parent-Child Centers being set up can look to such projects for guidance.

proposals need to be viewed cautiously in the light of past experiences of rearing infants without families. Nor can we copy the Israeli kibbutz, for the societal context in which that institution has prospered is very different from that of a Chicago slum. Intervention for some families ought to begin in the infancy period, but whatever steps are taken to provide a facilitating environment for development must have cultural relevance.

COMPENSATORY PRESCHOOL EDUCATION

The nursery school years have traditionally been regarded as the period when educational intervention into the lives of children of the poor would be most effective. The child is old enough to bear separation from home, yet sufficiently plastic in development so that, with intervention, he can remedy maladaptive behavioral and thought patterns. Left in his deprived environment until entrance to first grade, the disadvantaged child has several years to build up ways of getting along in his environment that may actually interfere with school learning. He develops speech and thinking patterns that are at variance with what he needs to learn, the three R's. The analogy is sometimes made to an adult moving to a new city. Unless he builds a map of the city in his mind, together with names of streets, within the first few weeks, he will find other, less efficient, ways of getting about, and even after several years, will discover that he does not really know the geography of the city. We find, therefore, as a result of the powerful arguments advanced for compensatory training at preschool level, that a considerable amount of interesting experimentation is in progress.

TYPES OF NURSERY SCHOOL CURRICULA

Perhaps the bulk of preschool programs for the disadvantaged are of the community service type, and not experimental programs. Head Start programs initiated in the summer of 1965 and most of the continuing preschool programs financed by the Office of Economic Opportunity are community service programs. They are designed, not to try out experimental approaches to the question of how to educate the disadvantaged, but to provide compensatory experiences based upon a traditional but enriched nursery school curriculum.

There appears to be general agreement that the traditional middle-class nursery school curriculum cannot bring the lower-class child up to the developmental level of the middle-class child. In fact, some investigators, new to the nursery school scene, argue that the traditional preschool is only of limited benefit even to the middle-class child. They speak contemptuously of the emphasis placed upon personal-social adjustment through permissive play to the neglect of the cognitive. However, such criticisms should not blind us to the considerable contribution play activities make to intellective development. Every serious student of the child has pointed out that the play of the child is not "play" in the sense of random activity, but may involve considerable directed experimentation. Balancing a see-saw, building a block tower, floating play toys, putting away play toys by categories, pouring juice into containers of different sizes are examples of play activities from which new information can be assimilated, developing mental structures accommodated, and new behavior patterns adopted. Were all nursery school teachers and psychological investigators as alert to the contribution of play to cognition as Piaget (1951), there might be more exploitation of its educational possibilities. Regardless of one's attitude toward play, however, there is general agreement that compensatory programs must have *structure;* they must include some directed activities especially planned for the disadvantaged to match their specific needs. There is controversy over how much of the preschool day should be devoted to directed activities and also as to what those activities should consist of.

Enrichment Programs: Institute for Developmental Studies (Martin Deutsch)

Enrichment programs are generally planned to add to, or emphasize, the traditional curriculum activities designed to overcome specific deficits in disadvantaged children. Deficits in both cognitive and affective areas are recognized. Unfortunately there are little evaluative data available on most enrichment programs, and where data are reported, the kind of enrichment provided is not described in sufficient detail to be helpful to others. A notable exception is the intervention program of Martin Deutsch and others at the Institute for Developmental Studies in New York City.

In the ongoing research and demonstration programs of the Institute for Developmental Studies (1965), experimental subjects are exposed to an enriched curriculum beginning with two years of pre-first grade, and continuing through third grade. In addition to the experimental subjects, three additional subject groups will be studied over an eight-year span. The first experimental group was admitted to the preschool in 1962, and a control group was selected at the same time from the same "self-selected" population (that is, parents had applied for admission). Two additional samples were set up: one, a group of children who entered regular kindergarten classes with no preschool training; and the other, a group who entered regular first-grade classes with no prior school experience. Most of the children in all groups are Negro, and all share the same socioeconomic background in Harlem.

For the enrichment classes the physical environment of the typical nursery school—with housekeeping, block, art and book centers—has been expanded to include a number of auto-instructional devices. One of these, the Listening Center, accommodates six children at a time; they listen on individual earphones to tapes recorded first in the teacher's voice, and then in a variety of voices and language styles not found in the home environment. Tapes may require only listening on the part of the child, or they may require motor or verbal responses. Each is designed to foster a particular kind of learning and they are sequenced for presentation. There is also a Language Master, a two-track tape recorder with the teacher's voice recorded as a standard on one track to which the child can compare his own recording on the other track. A visual stimulus can be presented at the same time. Additional special materials for visual discrimination include an Alphabet Board with cut-outs in the shape of letters of the alphabet, into which children put the appropriate letter which will fit only the proper slot. A talking typewriter (the Edison Responsive Environment Instrument) is also being used to aid reading acquisition. Emphasis in all the materials is upon orderly sequence of presentation of stimuli.

The enriched curriculum provided for experimental subjects is "a 'therapeutic curriculum' in language, mathematics, science, reading skills and concept formation" (Institute for Developmental Studies, 1965). Language training does not take place in isolated periods; rather, all class activities are used to expose the child to acceptable verbal patterns and to insist upon his using language as a means of social and self-communication. Vocabulary for dealing with concepts of size, shape, color, number, space, time, and temperature is taught as children engage in activities involving these concepts. Special songs taught in the music period teach children to follow directions ("Put your finger in the air") and to discriminate colors. In general, a three-stage sequence of learning is observed. The first is sensorimotor where contact with concrete materials is provided; the second is a perceptual stage where contrasting stimuli (of colors, shapes, sounds, and so on) are presented; the third is the ideational-representational where the child deals with objects and ideas with a minimum of concrete and perceptual support.

The science and mathematics experiences for prekindergarten children have not been described in detail. However, materials from the Educational Services Incorporated are being used, and the schools make extensive use of field trips to parks, zoos, and museums which presumably add to children's store of general information.

Much of the language training contributes, of course, to preparation for reading. Vocabulary and concept development, auditory training, and training in listening are generally considered to aid the learning-to-read process, and are, as we have seen, part of the Institute curriculum. Special devices that might bear a more direct relationship to reading are the Alphabet Board and the computerized typewriter on which experimental work is now being done. The Institute hopes to provide a "sequential development of reading skills that will lead from the beginning auditory and visual discriminations stressed in the preschool curriculum to the alphabet-training program of the kindergarten, and [later] to the actual combination of known sounds into meaningful words and sentences" (Institute for Developmental Studies, 1965).

Evaluation procedures included the use of three standardized tests: the Stanford-Binet, the Peabody Picture Vocabulary Test, and the Columbia Mental Maturity Scale (Goldstein, 1965). These tests were administered to the first experimental and control groups at the beginning of the project and toward the end of the first treatment year. Results on the CMMS are inconclusive. On the Stanford-Binet, no significant differences between groups were found in intelligence-test scores at the beginning of the project; both groups tested at about 99 IQ. Differences *were* significant at the 0.01 level on posttest scores; after a year of schooling, average IQ for the experimental prekindergarten group on the posttest was 102, while that of controls was 93. Tests were repeated during the kindergarten year; the *E*'s now tested at almost 104, while *C*'s had dropped a point to 92.

Essentially the same results were noted for the second groups admitted to the program; children exposed to the enriched curriculum were able to maintain or to increase their achievement level, while mean performance of children left in the poor environment deteriorated. The deterioration at this early age is not significant, but it is worth noting that it *does* become significant after an additional year. Children who entered public school at first-grade level, without any prior schooling, scored significantly lower than the controls with kindergarten experience, lending further evidence to the hypothesis of a cumulative deficit in IQ scores, the longer a child remains in a culturally disadvantaged environment.

Results on the Peabody also favored the enriched curriculum. After one year of prekindergarten enrichment, the mean raw score of the *E*'s was significantly higher than that of the *C*'s (44.9 as compared with 37.9). A year later, scores were 52.8 as compared with 48.2, a difference significant at the 0.05 level.

Additional data on the impact of an enriched curriculum upon language development are available in a study by C. Deutsch (1965) who reported that the experimental group performed at a higher level on the Illinois Test of Psycholinguistic Abilities than did the control. (A complete analysis is forthcoming.) The Kendler concept-formation paradigm (1963) was also used, but revealed no differences between experimental and control groups in use of verbal mediation. Deutsch noted that the question still remains as to whether a language-enriched curriculum will foster this type of mental growth in disadvantaged children without specific training in use of verbal mediation.

The enrichment curriculum also included materials and activities designed to enhance self-concept and help overcome the inferiority feelings and negative self-attitudes that characterize lower-class minority children. The experimental groups were provided with Negro and white dolls and pictures. Stories involving Negro families were read to the children. There were full-length mirrors in the playroom (mirrors are rare in lower-class homes); photographs were taken of the children and became part of individual photograph albums and a larger class album.

So far, only subjective evaluations of changes in behavior that might stem from enhanced self-concept are available. Anecdotal reports by teachers and family members emphasized positive effects of the enriched curriculum. Not only did the children change, but they changed their families. Goldstein (1965) commented,

> The children have brought into the familial setting many of the attitudes which have been shaped in the classroom, incurring a variety of behavioral changes in their parents and siblings. The quality and degree of child-parent and child-sibling interaction has been enhanced. Teachers, not involved in our program, have observed that many of these children are more active, more outgoing, and more vocal than other children of this age and environmental background with whom they have had contact (pp. 10–11).

On the basis of the many investigations carried on at the Institute, Deutsch (1965) has described three progressive goals of intervention at the preschool level. The first goal is to prevent or arrest the cumulative deficit observed in disadvantaged children, so that they will not continue to lose ground. A preschool program that included the kinds of environmental stimulation middle-class families provide for their children would contribute to this goal. These are the kinds of experiences now included in enrichment programs. However, arresting deficit is not enough; because the children have some catching up to do, the second goal emphasizes language and cognitive development. Here Deutsch sees the need for special training in verbal-mediational processes to help children make abstractions and generalizations from their concrete experiences. The third goal is to facilitate maximum growth and utilization of intellectual potential by making it possible for children to "learn to learn" and to be self-motivating. Continuing intervention along all three lines and over a five-year period is necessary, Deutsch believes, if the effects of deprivation are to be reversed.

Early Training Project
(Susan Gray)

Susan Gray (Gray *et al.,* 1965) reports encouraging results from a research-demonstration study based upon a specially developed enriched-curriculum principle. Sixty children were selected from deprived groups, with criteria for selection based upon housing conditions (including house furnishings, and educational and cultural materials present), occupation, education of parents, and income. The first project was unique in that experimental groups attended preschool only in the summer; during the winter a home visitor maintained contact with the families, providing materials and reinforcement of skills and attitudes emphasized in the training program. The preschool program consisted of ten-week sessions for consecutive summers prior to entrance to public school; to date one group has attended for three summers, and a second group two summers, before school entrance. Staff of the school was integrated as to race and sex; there was one staff member for every five children and much of the instruction was in small groups.

Teachers were to emphasize certain attitudes selected as important to school success: achievement motivation, delay of gratification, persistence, interest in school-type activities and identification with achieving role models. For each attitude there were no formal reinforcement schedules to be followed, but guidelines were laid down for teachers to follow. For example, for delay of reward, it was suggested teachers might give children a choice between one stick of candy at the beginning of an activity, or two upon completion of work, with attention being called at the appropriate time to the awarding of the two sticks to the child who chose to delay.

Aptitude variables emphasized in the Early Training Project were perception, concept development, and language. Again, guidelines for teachers were worked out, to be applied as children engaged in small-group activities. A specific small-group activity, like a pegboard game in which children hang cards on pegs according to color and number, was used for perceptual as well as conceptual development. Colored inch cubes were used to teach space relations, the following of directions, and visual discrimination. Activities were related to certain themes such as

Pets and Other Animals, The Farm, Foods, and Transportation; the themes were selected to enlarge the children's background of general information.

Average gain for the first experimental group (three summers of preschool) was 9 IQ points (from 86 IQ to 95 IQ), a modest gain, the investigators (Gray and Klaus, 1965) point out, but one maintained over a period of two-and-one-half years, while two control groups had lost 3 and 6 points respectively. Additional instruments used to evaluate the program included the Peabody Picture Vocabulary Test; experimental groups surpassed the controls at the end of the first summer's training and the gap was widened by the end of the second summer. The city school system administered a battery of tests to all first-grade entrants; again *E*'s surpassed *C*'s. Particularly noteworthy is the fact that they were superior on reading-readiness tests, approximating the performance of advantaged children. Additional evaluation instruments are being developed.

Evaluation of Special Programs

Special programs, at least of the Deutsch and Gray variety, are yielding measurable gains in IQ scores that hold up over at least a few years. Furthermore, these gains are occurring while children with no schooling or with exposure only to conventional kindergartens are losing ground. Exact mental ages cannot be figured from published data, but if the posttest in the Deutsch project was given about nine months after project initiation, then the children gained about thirteen months in mental age during that nine-month time. If children were to continue to progress at that rate, then for roughly every two years of chronological growth they would be gaining approximately three years of mental age. One would, of course, expect rate of gain to slow down after a time; the question is whether the accelerated rate can be continued long enough.

Gains in the Gray project that provided summer school only are of a lesser magnitude. In the three-year period, average gain in mental age was thirteen months a year. In other words, children gained at not appreciably better than the normal rate. These children are, of course, much better off than children without schooling since the latter deteriorate, as we have seen, but such a rate of progress is not fast enough to overcome the original deficit. Given a choice between no schooling and summer session training only, communities should obviously choose the summer session, but the data now available indicate that a 36-week preschool yields appreciably better results, as might be predicted. Whether the rate of gain is as fast as can be expected is open to question; some critics think more efficient ways of working with children are possible.[5]

There is a difficulty inherent in programs where many things are tried for those looking for a model to follow. When a program is "enriched" in many ways, it is never clear which aspects of the curriculum contributed most to the gains, and which are worth very little. If we are to facilitate development of the culturally disadvantaged child to a maximum degree, it becomes necessary to specify the environmental events antecedent to the gains; only as the stimulus is clearly defined can we be confident of our guidelines. Several experimental approaches in which the stimuli *have* been clearly defined will be reviewed next.

PRESCHOOL PROGRAMS WITH SPECIAL EMPHASES

Environmental Assistance to Language Growth

All preschool programs for culturally disadvantaged children put language development high on the list of goals, and all stress the importance of the child's language environment. Written descriptions of curricula include such activities as encouragement of conversation (means not specified), labeling, trips, and other experiences to build concepts and vocabulary, reading and telling of stories, and some special lessons to teach the vocabulary for size, shapes, and color. Investigators have selected these remedial measures because they seem to supply the kind of language environment that is available to the middle-class child but is absent in the life of the lower-class child. But, as Cazden (1965) points out, while it is generally agreed that the quality of the child's language environment is the most important factor in language development, there is little agreement on what the *critical* features of that environment are. The psycholinguist's approach to discovering critical features goes beyond the mere listing of activities involving language. It is not enough to say, for example, that the middle-class child engages in two-way conversations missing in the lower-class child's life; the psycholinguist wants to know what goes on in the two-way conversation to stimulate language development.

One feature that has been suggested as important in the language

---

[5] Since the preparation of this manuscript, the DARCEE (Demonstration and Research Center for Early Education) project at George Peabody under the directorship of Dr. Gray has been considerably expanded. It now includes nursery schools for disadvantaged children, both rural and urban, all of which operate on a 36-week school year, plus a training program for professionals and paraprofessionals, plus a home intervention program where mothers are trained to teach their children.

environment is the expansion of the young child's telegraphic utterances by the mother (or other adults). To the utterance, "Mommy sandwich," the mother says, "Mommy'll have a sandwich"; to, "Pick glove," she says, "Pick the glove up." The child has transformed adult speech by removing functors (auxiliaries, prepositions, articles, pronouns, and inflections). The mother in turn transforms his transformations; she expands his utterances by supplying the functors (Brown and Bellugi, 1964). Any adult who has been around young children very much will be struck with the aptness of this description of a hitherto unrecognized process. Such expansions, conceivably, could be helpful to the child in inducing correct grammatical structure from the comparison of what he has said with his mother's expanded version.

Are such expansions really *necessary* for language learning? Do they aid language growth, or do children learn as well or better just from hearing parents and others make well-formed sentences? It was to answer these questions that Cazden (1965) set up an experimental program within an existing child-care program. Subjects were twelve Negro children, age twenty-eight to thirty-eight months, attending a day-care center in Boston, Massachusetts, assigned to three groups: an expansion group that received forty minutes per day of intensive and deliberate expansions; a modeling group exposed to thirty minutes per day of well-formed sentences; and a control group. In the expansion treatment, the tutor supplied functors; for example, to the child who says, "No he not," the tutor responds. "No, he's not? Yes, I think he is." In the modeling treatment, the tutor supplied models of well-formed utterances; for example, to the child who says, "Das a rabbit," the tutor responds, "Yes, he goes hop, hop, hop." In both treatment sessions, a tutor worked with one child only; increased exposure to language was provided in the context of one-to-one conversation with a warm and attentive adult. Treatment lasted for three months. Tape recordings of children's speech were analyzed for mean length of utterance, noun-phrase index, verb-complexity index, copula index, and sentence-type index.

A word of explanation about some of the measures is in order here, for they may prove to be more helpful in evaluating language growth than existing standardized measures. The noun-phrase index assesses the complexity of noun phrases used by the child ("doggie" as compared with "Andy's big black doggie"). The verb-complexity index assesses perhaps the single most important source of problems for the disadvantaged child—his use of verbs. By his omission of inflections and auxiliaries, he fails to encode the richest possible meaning. When the child says, "My Mommy help me," he is not conveying as much information as if he said "My Mommy helps me," or "helped," or "is helping," or "could help," or any of the other alternatives. The copula index measures use of some form of the verb to be; its omission ("Dat my doll") has been noted as a feature of Negro speech (Loban, 1963; Bailey, 1964). A sentence emulation test was also used because of the close relationship found to exist between what a child can repeat and what he produces spontaneously (Brown and Bellugi, 1964); fourteen sentences having certain characteristics were spoken to the child and he was asked to repeat what he heard.

Contrary to prediction, modeling, not expanding, is the more effective treatment. On all the measures listed above, plus a sentence imitation test, the modeling group gained most, and there was no evidence that expansions aided the acquisition of grammar. Results suggest that the richness-impoverishment dimension is critical in the language environment. In a nonexperimental home or nursery school, it is, of course, possible to use both expansion and modeling; there would be no reason to exclude expansions in adult utterances, even if it were feasible. However, *limiting* utterances to expansions means that one does not use as rich a variety of sentence forms, verb forms, and noun phrases, so the child is exposed to only a very limited selection of grammatical structures.

While investigators are always a bit disappointed when a good, theoretically oriented hypothesis is rejected, there is much to be learned from Cazden's study, and some implications for those who work with young children. One implication is that there be more concern with models supplied for children. Teachers often develop a telegraphic style of their own in conversing with children, and fail to supply "well-formed utterances." Many supply models only of directions or commands with limited grammatical variety. Furthermore, it takes at least two people to carry on a conversation; a very silent child has a quieting effect upon an adult, and some disadvantaged preschool children are almost nonverbal. Such a child may play happily in the doll corner, but unless the teacher makes an effort to initiate and, indeed, bear the burden of conversation, the child will be completely silent. And to make sure that there will be no children who spend half a day in nursery school without saying more than four or five words, or without being personally exposed to adult language models, teachers might schedule each day some individual or small-group work where a child engages in activities conducive to conversation—for example, listening to and discussing stories, looking at picture books, playing with dolls or miniature toys, or playing house, and where the conversation is carried on with the same warm and attentive adult supplying the best possible models.

An Academically Oriented Preschool

At the opposite pole from conventional nursery school is an experimental preschool at the University of Illinois under the direction of Carl

Bereiter (1965). In this preschool, children have directed lessons in three subjects each day—in basic language, reading, and arithmetic. The fifteen four-year-old children are divided into three groups, and each group moves from one room to another for the lessons, which last twenty minutes. There is a separate teacher for each subject. The only equipment essential to the program are chairs for children and teacher, and a chalkboard. The children do not engage in any of the conventional nursery school activities; they do not build with blocks, or play house, or engage in art activities, or look at picture books or listen to stories. The conventional equipment of a Sunday School playroom is used only as props for the lessons. Between classes, juice is served, and then the children go out on the playground for a brief period of undirected activity.[6]

Language training is carried out as if the children were learning English as a second language. The teaching technique is the pattern drill; children learn basic statement patterns and how to answer questions about the pattern. The teacher begins by holding up a block, "This block is big." The children must then repeat, "This block is big," which they shout after a time in unison, with considerable zest and marked rhythm, often clapping hands or stomping feet to mark the rhythm. Then individual children repeat the statement, with the teacher insisting upon correct pronunciation. Eventually another smaller block is shown next to the larger one, or drawn on the board next to a drawing of a large square, and the children learn, "This block is little." A variety of objects other than squares (balls, sticks, chalk, dolls) are introduced, and then work advances to negatives and comparatives. Eight prepositions and two conjunctions (*and, or*) were selected for teaching, using the same technique. Logical distinctions using color names are also taught by rote; the children chant at the top of their voices and in beautiful rhythm, as they see two blocks side by side, "If this one is red, this one is not red."

Approach to the teaching of arithmetic was the same as for teaching language. In fact, arithmetic was treated as a language, and children taught identity statements by rote: "One plus zero equals one, two plus zero equals two," and so on. Then again by rote they were taught non-identity statements: "If $1 + 0 = 1$, $1 + 1$ can't equal 1." Pictures of objects or shapes might occasionally be drawn on the blackboard, or fingers used in counting, but the use of concrete objects to develop sensorimotor referents for number concepts is deemphasized; emphasis

---

[6] The description here is that of the first group of children, who in 1968 were finishing the second grade in public schools. Dr. Bereiter is now with the Ontario Institute for Studies in Education (Toronto), while Mr. Engelmann continues the Bereiter-Engelmann program at the University of Illinois. A full report on their research is contained in *Acceleration of Intellectual Development in Early Childhood,* Final Report, Project No. 2129, U.S.O.E. Bureau of Research, June, 1967.

instead is on the learning of abstract concepts and formal meanings.

Reading instruction began with three-letter words (bat, cat, sat, and so forth) and the teaching of six sets of rules. The first rule was, "A word has a beginning and an end. If it [sic] has a beginning and an end it is a word. The beginning always comes before the end." Five additional rules were taught in a carefully planned sequence. Instruction included, for example, in connection with Rule 5, that rhyming words form a family and that the rhyming principle can be used to figure out unfamiliar words.

After three months of schooling, almost all children had learned color names, and were judged to have mastered prepositions when they were able to respond correctly to such tasks as "Put the scissors in front of the box," and then, "Tell me where the scissors are." Results of additional tests, designed to assess the other language learnings the children had been taught, were also reported as encouraging; children could use the formal grammatical patterns that they had been taught.

To evaluate progress in arithmetic, children were given twelve tasks, ranging from the simple task of rote counting (all but one could count to ten) to one of medium difficulty: "One plus one equals . . . Two plus one equals . . . " and so on, through "Nine plus one equals . . . . " Again results were highly favorable; most of the children were able to respond correctly to easy tasks, and some to more difficult tasks.

Visitors to the program fall into two camps, the wildly enthusiastic and the sharply critical. The enthusiastic are impressed by lessons where the teacher extends the top line of a two-step ladder beyond the vertical, saying, "The top line gets longer; tell me about the bottom line," and the children respond, "The bottom line gets shorter" [sic]. Or they marvel to hear a culturally disadvantaged four-year-old respond clearly to the questions, "What comes after one? What comes after two?" in a complete and grammatical sentence, "Two comes after one." The critical see what they take to be evidence of response learning; they doubt that the patterned drill affects language and thought processes any more effectively than memorizing nursery rhymes and learning to respond, "Dickory comes after Hickory" and, "The mouse ran *down* the clock; the mouse did not run *up* the clock."

Evaluation measures to date have assessed how well children have learned the responses taught them and how well these responses transfer to similar situations. Plans call for additional evaluation after children have had two years of the program, and enter public school. Until there is further evidence, we are left with the question as to whether response learning makes a significant contribution to language and thought processes. Can one generalize that learning to speak certain sentences enables children to " 'unpack' meaning from statements, to convey meanings which they otherwise could not, and to draw inferences which carry them beyond the immediately given facts"? (Bereiter *et al.,* 1965, p.

16). Or do the children learn specific answers to questions which do not have much generality?

There are also questions as to whether such a program underestimates human intelligence. The children in this project are presented with only a very limited variety of models of well-formed sentences. There is a severe restriction of language stimuli; the same few verbs are used over and over again—*is, equals, put, pick up, do,* for example. Restriction is justified on the grounds that the project is designed to teach logical thinking and not social communication. However, almost all statements are in the third person present tense, so that children never hear the complex verb forms that encode considerable meaning and from which the child can infer grammatical and syntactical rules. Both kinds of restriction may interfere with growth in ability to generate new sentences, just as the severely restricted vocabulary in preprimers restricts opportunity to learn. An analysis of the corpus of each child's free speech might be useful in assessing impact of restriction.

There is also the question as to whether one becomes a logical thinker by manipulating statement patterns. Does stating correctly that three plus three equals six make one accept the statement logically?

Anyone who has worked with some of Piaget's conservation tasks knows that it is quite possible for the young child to deny that there are as many objects in one row as in another if the objects in one row are spread out, even though he has counted ten in each row. Piaget himself notes how over and over children hear and use a linguistic structure which implies a logical structure and yet the children do not understand the logic. A child can say, "A hammer is a tool" with no awareness of the logic of the inclusion of a subclass in a class. As Piaget says, "I believe that logic is not a derivative of language. The source of logic is much more profound. It is the total coordination of actions, actions of joining things together, or ordering things, and so on. . . . It is only when they themselves are in firm possession of this logical structure, when they have constructed it for themselves . . . that they succeed in understanding correctly the linguistic expression" (Ripple and Rockcastle, 1964, p. 13).

The deficit of the culturally disadvantaged child is admittedly great. The child has much to learn, but we should not underestimate human intelligence. Given a richer language environment, coupled with special activities to counteract a deficit, it may be that the child can make faster progress in logical thinking than through pattern drill. Naturally occurring activities can be used more advantageously; for example, the teacher may say to the child, "It's time to put away playthings. The play clothing goes in this box, and the doll's bedding in this one." Through his own activity the child learns that the class of play clothing is made up of subclasses of hats, shoes, dresses, and so on, and may develop the notion of class inclusion faster than if he merely learned sentence patterns.

What the conventional school lacks, however, even the "enriched" variety, is the *amount* of linguistic interchange between teacher and child in the two experimental projects described. In the Bereiter project, five children to one adult are actively engaged in language activities for almost two hours a day. Cazden found that thirty minutes of language on a one-to-one basis aided language development. Whatever form the specially designed curriculum takes, provision should be made for children to hear and interact with a good adult model.

Environmental Assistance to Logical Thinking: A Piaget-Derived Model

A number of projects have attempted to build into preschool programs for the disadvantaged special activities to foster the development of thinking processes. Some of these have been based upon Piaget's genetic theory of logical development. Evidence is accumulating that culturally disadvantaged children are retarded in logical thinking. Wei (1966) found that children at five and eight years of age of low socio-economic status, both Negro and white, scored significantly lower on several classification tasks including those involving the formation of classes (putting objects together by category); membership of objects in multiple classes (something can be pink and also square); and class inclusion (red objects may be included together with yellow objects to form a larger class of objects made of plastic). It can be safely predicted that these children will be severely retarded in school learning.

Two studies by Sigel are relevant here. In one report, the investigators (Sigel and Mermelstein, 1966) noted the effects of nonschooling upon performance on certain Piagetian tasks. The experimental group in the study consisted of sixty Negro children, six and nine years of age, from Prince Edward County, Virginia. It will be recalled that Prince Edward County closed its schools in 1959, as an alternative to integration. In 1963, the Prince Edward County Free School was opened to provide schooling for the children who had been deprived of it for four years; the children in the studies conducted by Sigel and Mermelstein were, therefore, completing their first year of formal schooling. These children were tested on conservation and classification tasks and their performance compared with that of Negro academically-experienced children in Flint, Michigan.

Some interesting findings are reported in the Sigel and Mermelstein paper. Deprivation of schooling and the factor of urban-rural milieu did not produce significant differences in performance of the two groups on the conservation tasks, except that more nine-year-old girls than boys in the rural setting had acquired conservation of substance and weight.

However, virtually all of the children in Prince Edward County failed a class-inclusion task comparable to one for which Inhelder and Piaget (1964) report success at nine years. It appears that the disadvantaged milieu contributes differentially to cognitive deficit, and that performance in classification skills is affected more adversely than is performance on conservation tasks. According to Piaget, the same logical operations are involved in both cases, but it may be that the classification tasks demand more symbolic thought.

In the second paper relevant to impact of disadvantaged milieu upon logical thinking, the authors (Sigel *et al.*, 1966) report on a study of classificatory responses of middle- and lower-class preschool children. More lower-class than middle-class children have difficulty in grouping objects according to category. Furthermore, lower-class children find even more difficulty in grouping pictures of objects than they do three-dimensional objects. Middle-class children apparently can transcend the mode of presentation in classifying, while lower-class children appear to have less ability to deal representationally with material.

Cultural disadvantage, then, has an adverse effect upon the development of logical thinking. Operations upon classes in particular appear to be affected. To overcome the deficit, some writers would emphasize perceptual training. Compensatory programs using this approach provide the child with many experiences in finding similarities and differences in pictured objects, in geometric figures and abstract symbols, in sounds and textures, and in perceiving more than one property of an object. Supporters of this approach argue that the culturally disadvantaged child has lacked experiences that sharpen perceptions and make one a good observer, and that to match training to deficit, a curriculum for the culturally disadvantaged should emphasize perceptual training.

For Piaget, the answer to the question of whether a perceptual emphasis will aid the development of logical intelligence is an emphatic "No." In *Les Mécanismes Perceptifs* (Piaget, 1961) and *The Early Growth of Logic in the Child* (Inhelder and Piaget, 1964), Piaget has analyzed the relations between perception and intelligence. He has considered these hypotheses: Is there a direct line from primary perception to operative structures, through the intermediary of perceptual activities? Is knowledge of objects and events *first* perceptual, and then operational, with the perceptual being simply a more elementary form? Or, as an alternate hypothesis, is intelligence an autonomous development, deriving out of the actions of the subject?" To accept or reject these hypotheses, Piaget conducted a searching analysis of the structures of perception and those of intelligence and directed a series of studies, using the genetic method upon classical optical-geometric illusions. His investigations (Piaget, 1961) led him to the conclusion that there are certain fundamental differences between perception and intelligence:

1. Perception is dependent upon the presence of the object, and perceptual knowledge is limited to certain physical characteristics. Perception of a rectangle, for example, is limited to the shape, dimensions and size of the particular rectangle being perceived. Operative structures (intelligence), on the other hand, can evoke the object even in its absence, and in its presence can interpret the rectangle as a particular case of rectangles, or even of quadrilateral figures in general.

2. Perception is bounded by limits of space and time. In viewing a full moon, one can only perceive at the same time its quarter by evoking memory or an operative structure. Intelligence, on the other hand, can consider any element independent of space-time, and can equally as well dissociate neighboring objects and reason about them in complete independence.

3. Perception is essentially egocentric; what is perceived is special to the point of view of a particular person. Furthermore, it is subject to systematic deformations through centration effects (an overvaluation of those elements upon which perception centers). The intelligence of operations, on the other hand, makes possible knowledge of an object apart from self, and from the particular point of view of an individual. Operational structures enable one to view objects or events from viewpoints other than the narrow, restricted one afforded by the perceptual.

4. Perception is limited to that which is cognizable by the senses. In perceiving a box which is closed, for example, one sees only a box in three dimensions with a particular volume and an interior, but other mechanisms are necessary to decide about the contents of the box. Intelligence, on the other hand, can go beyond sensory data and make a deductive guess about what the box contains.

5. Perceptual structures ignore abstractions; they cannot restrict themselves to certain elements of an object or event while making an abstraction of others. It is the province of intelligence to choose which data are necessary to resolve a particular problem and to pass up other data.

A Piaget-derived preschool curriculum would not, then, emphasize perceptual training. For Piaget, the complex structures of operational thought are founded, not upon increasing sophistication of perceptual structures, but upon simpler operational structures growing out of actions upon classes and relations between classes. Through the coordination of the actions of combining, dissociating, ordering, and setting up correspondences, the structures of intelligence are built during the sensorimotor and preoperational stages and rebuilt during the operational. Operational thought is not the result of a cumulative stockpiling of perceptual data previously accumulated; the child comes to view phenomena in a completely different way when he can break the whole into its parts, compare parts, associate parts in different ways, and reverse actions.

Special training activities to foster acquisition of schemas in disadvantaged four-year-old children were developed at the University of Illinois and tried out over a six-month period (Stendler, in press). Additional work has been done at the Oakland Children's Centers. At Illinois, thirty minutes of training was provided each day, in three regularly scheduled, ten-minute periods, interspersed with conventional nursery school activities. As the children's attention span lengthened, two fifteen-minute periods each day were substituted for the three shorter ones. The class of fifteen children was divided into three groups for the special training, with a trained teacher in charge of each group of five. The schemas selected for emphasis included one-to-one correspondence, classification, and seriation. For all three types of schemas, an attempt was made to identify a sequence of skills from simple to complex, each phase of which might contribute to development of the next. The schemas are not mutually exclusive, as we shall see.

ONE-TO-ONE CORRESPONDENCE. The ability to match one-for-one is a basic mental operation that lays the foundation for the more complex. In order to establish the equality of two sets and put two systems in equilibrium, we make a comparison, one-to-one, of each of the parts; hence one-to-one correspondence is basic to conservation. It is basic also to classification; to establish whether or not an object is a member of a particular class we make a one-to-one comparison of the properties that define that class and the properties of the object in question. Activities were planned that involved matching sets of objects that varied in color, size, shape, and number.

A second series of activities involving one-to-one correspondences was developed to lay the foundation for the concept of conservation of number: That number of objects in a set is conserved even when the amount of space occupied by the objects is changed. These exercises take the child beyond the merely perceptual, for in order to solve the task at hand, he must think about the transformation upon the data confronting him, reversing the transformation or performing an identity operation. In each case he first established correspondence between two sets of objects, and then was asked about physical equality of the sets after physical correspondence was destroyed.

The last set of activities in this series involved conservation of continuous quantities. The concept of conservation is dependent upon logical operations of reversibility, associativity, combinativity, or identity. That is, the child must be able to reverse thought processes, or associate parts in different ways to achieve the same result, or combine parts to make a whole, or perform an identity operation, putting parts in one-to-one correspondence. Water, sand, and clay were used to develop the concept. For example, children were given a twelve-ounce juice can filled with water and an empty twelve-ounce coke bottle and were asked to predict water level in the bottle after pouring from the can. Or children might be asked to indicate a preference for a twelve-ounce can of juice or two six-ounce cans before pouring from the large can into the small and back again.

CLASSIFICATION ACTIVITIES.   All programs for disadvantaged children stress so-called classification activities, but many of these are actually perceptual rather than operational in character. That is, the activities provide training in visual or tactile perception, but they do not demand that the child make transformations upon the data. To ask a child to put all objects that are the same color in one pile and all objects that are different in color in another pile simply requires that he make a visual discrimination between two colors. To ask a child, however, to separate geometric shapes that are squares and circles, pink and blue, large and small, into *two* piles, putting the shapes that are alike in some way in one pile and those alike in some other way in another pile, requires that *he* abstract from the shapes the property that will form the basis for a class, and that he be able to keep that property in mind as he searches for other objects in the same class.

To teach the logic of classification, it is necessary to identify the successive phases by which operational classification is achieved. This task has been performed by the Geneva group (Inhelder and Piaget, 1964). They found that the child of two or three years is not able to construct a class; asked to put objects together that are alike in some way, he will proceed to construct a single complex object. He may, for example, put geometric shapes together to form a house, instead of classifying them by size, shape, or color. Gradually during the preschool years, there appears the ability to identify a common property, although the child may have difficulty in keeping the property in mind as he continues to group.

Identification of a common property leads to an awareness of "otherness"—that there exists a complementary class of objects other than the ones possessing the common property. There are robins and other birds not robins. Awareness of others as a complementary class eventually leads to an understanding of all-some relations—that *all* members of the subset *A* may constitute *some* of the members of the set of *B*.

Meanwhile, multiplicative classifications are developing which permit the classifying of an element simultaneously in terms of two additive orders. A robin may be grouped with other robins to form a class of robins, but since robins possess the attributes essential to bird-ness, the robin is also a bird. Additive and multiplicative classification form the combinatorial structure that makes it possible for the older child to form a class on the basis of a single element, and then to construct successive classes on the basis of combinations of elements, or, in other words, to perform hierarchical classification. Exercises based upon the above analysis were planned and carried out, using a variety of materials.

Logical structures have proved singularly resistant to training. However, previous studies have provided some guidelines to procedures that might be effective: activity of the subject; long-term training; a variety of materials; emphasis upon logical operations rather than response learning.

In carrying out activities with the children, teachers emphasized logical operations as they asked questions or made statements about the child's activity: "When you add something, what happens?" "When you take something away, what happens?" "If you don't add and you don't take anything away, what happens?" "If every time I give you one, I give myself one, will we each have the same?" In addition, the children received in the thirty-minute training periods considerable exposure to language modeling from a warm interacting adult who supplied among other things the verbal expressions the children lacked to express the concepts they were acquiring.

Evaluation measures have been developed for each of the successive phases of one-to-one correspondence, classification, and seriation. Preliminary results are encouraging. Of twenty older four-year-old children exposed to twelve weeks of training at the Oakland Children's Centers, all but three were able to solve multiplicative classification tasks and to achieve physical correspondence in buying objects one-for-one. At the onset of training, none of the children had these skills. Four of the children maintained conservation of number when physical correspondence was destroyed, and gave reasons in terms of logical operations. In classification, none of the children mastered all-some relations, but six of the group were able to do the simpler matrix-type puzzles, and nine children were able to carry through a dichotomy started by the tutor. A full-scale evaluation was carried out at the University of California during the summer of 1966 (Lenrow, 1966); results favored the Piaget-trained group as far as performance on tests of logical operations was concerned. None of the groups in the experiment (Piaget-type and other) gained on an average more than five IQ points on the Binet, but this discouraging result might have been due to difficulties in testing procedures. Lenrow raises the question of whether thirty minutes a day of structured training for ten weeks might not interfere with self-initiated activity and create more teacher dependence later on. This question needs to be studied where the teacher variable can be controlled.[7]

SUMMARY

The Deutsch and the Gray projects might be characterized as research of the action type, in which results are fed back into training as they become available. Such projects can serve as models for those communities who want to set up programs, incorporating recent research findings in their preschool curriculums. Meanwhile it is safe to predict that there will be an acceleration of attempts to relate specific training conditions to specific changes in behavior: Federal funds have a way of generating research productivity as clinical psychologists and specialists in mental retardation can attest. Hopefully we can look for more projects where affective as well as cognitive development is emphasized, and where impact of affective upon cognitive is experimentally studied (Lenrow, 1966). Furthermore, while the necessity for structured programs will continue to be recognized, research should clarify the nature of the structure that is most effective, and what kind of population it affects. We also need new evaluation instruments to measure the effects of different kinds of treatment across different projects. Tuddenham's (1966) work on the standardization of the Piaget tasks may provide one such kind of instrument.

References

Bailey, Beryl L. A proposal for the study of the grammar of Negro English in New York City. Ithaca, N. Y.: Cornell University, Project Literacy Reports, 1964 (2), 19–22.

Bayley, Nancy. Comparisons of mental and motor test scores for ages 1–15 months by sex, birth order, race, geographical location, and education of parents. *Child Development,* 1965, **36,** 379–411.

Bereiter, C., Jean Osborn, S. Engelmann, and P. A. Reidford. An academically-oriented preschool for culturally deprived children. Paper presented

---

[7] The whole question of evaluating preschool projects is an exceedingly complicated one. The chief instruments used for evaluation are the Binet and the ITPA (Illinois Test of Psycholinguistic Abilities). In using such instruments, one needs to ask: Were the initial scores for children obtained prior to school entrance and before the child had any exposure to answering questions posed by a stranger? Were the children tested by an examiner of their own race? Did their school curriculum include drill on Binet or ITPA items that might influence postexperiment scores? Did follow-up studies take into account the effects of attending integrated classrooms? A full-scale evaluation of early childhood projects could be very revealing, and perhaps disillusioning for those who have believed that spectacular gains in a short period of time are possible for most children.

at the American Education Research Association, Chicago, February 1965.

Berlyne, D. E. *Conflict, arousal and curiosity.* New York: McGraw-Hill, 1960.

Brown, R., and Ursula Bellugi. Three processes in the child's acquisition of syntax. *Harvard Educational Review,* 1964, **34,** 133–151.

Cazden, Courtney B. *Environmental assistance to the child's acquisition of grammar.* Unpublished doctoral dissertation, Harvard University, 1965.

Denenberg, V. H. Critical periods, stimulus input, and emotional reactivity: A theory of infantile stimulation. *Psychological Review,* 1964, **71,** 335–351.

Deutsch, Cynthia P. Learning in the disadvantaged. Paper presented at Conference of Analyses of Conceptual Learning, Research and Development Center for Learning and Re-Education. Madison: University of Wisconsin, October 1965.

Deutsch, M. Facilitating development in the preschool child: Social and psychological perspectives. *Merrill-Palmer Quarterly,* 1964, **10,** 249–263.

————. Social intervention and the malleability of the child. Fourth Annual School of Education Lecture, Cornell University, May 6, 1965. Revised, November 1965, 3–24.

Erikson, E. H. *Childhood and society.* (Ed. 2.) New York: Norton, 1963.

Furfey, P. H. Intellectual stimulation of culturally deprived infants. Research in progress, Washington, D.C.: Howard University and D.C. Teachers College.

Goldstein, L. S. Evaluation of an enrichment program for socially disadvantaged children. Institute for Developmental Studies, New York University, June 1965 (mimeo).

Gray, Susan W., and R. A. Klaus. An experimental preschool program for culturally deprived children. *Child Development,* 1965, **36,** 887–898.

Gray, Susan W., R. A. Klaus, J. O. Miller, and Betty J. Forrester. *The early training project: A handbook of aims and activities.* Nashville, Tenn., George Peabody College for Teachers, and Murfreesboro, Tenn., City Schools, 1965.

Hunt, J. McV. *Intelligence and experience.* New York: Ronald Press, 1961.

Inhelder, B., and J. Piaget. *The early growth of logic in the child.* New York: Harper & Row, 1964.

Institute for Developmental Studies. *Annual Report 1965.* School of Education, New York University, Washington Square.

Irwin, O. C. Infant speech: The effect of family occupational status and of age on sound frequency. *Journal of Speech and Hearing Disorders,* 1948, **13,** 320–323.

Kendler, Tracy S. "Development of mediating responses in children." In J. C. Wright and J. Kagan (eds.), Basic cognitive processes in children, *Monographs of the Society for Research in Child Development,* 1963, **28** (2).

Kennedy, W. A., V. Van de Riet, and J. C. White, Jr. A normative sample of intelligence and achievement of Negro elementary school children in the southeastern United States. *Monographs of the Society for Research in Child Development,* 1963, **28** (6).

Kirk, S. A. Development of a program of sensory-motor, verbal, and motor integration with eight-month to two-year-old disadvantaged children in the home. 1966, Research in process, Institute for Research on Exceptional Children, University of Illinois, Urbana.

Kofsky, Ellin. A scalogram study of classificatory development. *Child Development,* 1966, **37,** 191–204.

Lenrow, P. Preschool socialization and the development of competence. Berkeley: University of California, 1966 (mimeo).

Loban, W. D. *The language of elementary school children.* Champaign, Ill.: National Council of Teachers of English, 1963.

Pavenstedt, Eleanor. A comparison of the child-rearing environment of upper-lower and very low-lower class families. *American Journal of Orthopsychiatry,* 1965, **35,** 89–98.

Piaget, J. *Play, dreams and imitation in childhood.* New York: Norton, 1951.

————. *The child's conception of number.* London: Routledge & Kegan Paul, 1952.

————. *Les mécanismes perceptifs.* Paris: Presses Université de France, 1961.

————. *The origins of intelligence in children.* New York: Norton, 1963.

———— and Barbel Inhelder. *The Child's conception of space.* London: Routledge & Kegan Paul, 1956.

Rheingold, Harriet L. "The effect of environmental stimulation upon social and exploratory behavior in the human infant." In B. M. Foss (ed.), *Determinants of infant behavior.* London: Methuen, 1961.

Ripple, R., and V. Rockcastle (eds.), *Piaget rediscovered: A report of the conference on cognitive studies and curriculum development.* Ithaca, N. Y.: School of Education, Cornell University, 1964.

Sigel, I. E., L. M. Anderson, with H. Shapiro. Categorization behavior of lower- and middle-class Negro preschool children: Differences in dealing with representation of familiar objects. Detroit: Merrill-Palmer Institute, 1966 (mimeo).

———— and E. Mermelstein. Effects of nonschooling on Piagetian tasks of conservation. Detroit: Merrill-Palmer Institute, 1966 (mimeo).

Skeels, H. M., and H. B. Dye. A study of the effects of differential stimulation on mentally retarded children. *Proceedings of the American Association on Mental Deficiency,* 1939, **44,** 114–136.

Skodak, Marie, and H. M. Skeels. A final follow-up study of one hundred adopted children. *Journal of Genetic Psychology,* 1949, **75,** 85–125.

Spitz, R. A. *The first year of life.* A psychoanalytic study of normal and deviant development of object relations. In collaboration with W. G. Cobliner. New York: International University Press, 1965.

Stendler, Celia B. A Piaget-derived model for the pre-school child. In J. L. Frost (ed.), *Early childhood education rediscovered.* New York: Holt, Rinehart and Winston, in press.

Tuddenham, R. D. Jean Piaget and the world of the child. *American Psychologist,* 1966, **21,** 207–217.

Wei, Tam. *Racial and social class differences on Piaget's classification tasks: Differences at five and seven years of age.* Unpublished doctoral dissertation, University of Illinois, 1966.

White, B. L. Second-order problems in studies of perceptual development. Presented at Institute for Juvenile Research, Chicago, September 1, 1965.

———— and R. Held. "Plasticity of sensorimotor development." In Judy F. Rosenblith and W. Allinsmith (eds.), *Causes of behavior: Readings in child development and educational psychology.* Ed. 2. Boston: Allyn & Bacon, 1966.

Wolff, P. The developmental psychologies of Jean Piaget and psychoanalysis. *Psychological Issues,* 1960, **2** (1), Monograph 5.

Wolff, P. H., and B. L. White. Visual pursuit and attention in young infants. *Journal of American Academy of Child Psychiatry,* 1965, **4** (3).

CHAPTER ELEVEN

Programs
of Compensatory Education

EDMUND W. GORDON[1]

Certain political, economic, and social factors have combined in recent years to bring the condition of underdevelopment in human beings
in all parts of the world to the center of our attention. Nowhere are
the handicaps imposed by deliberate and accidental underdevelopment
of human resources a greater source of embarrassment and concern
than in the United States. In response to our embarrassment we have
looked for someone to blame, and the most convenient someone in this
situation has proved to be the professional educator. This disposition
of blame is not wholly unjustified. Everyone recognizes that the schools
did not create the underlying conditions that lead to social disadvantage
and deprivation. But most people also are aware that professional
educators have done relatively little to change significantly the life
chances of the disadvantaged despite tremendous gains in educational
technology and resources.

[1] Yeshiva University.
Editor's note: This paper is a revision of an earlier paper which appeared in the
July 1965 issue of the *American Journal of Orthopsychiatry,* **XXXX** (4), and it
utilizes material from studies supported by the College Examination Board and
the National Scholarship Service and Fund for Negro Students.

The Zacharias Panel on Educational Research and Development has reported:

> By all known criteria, the majority of urban and rural slum schools are failures. In neighborhood after neighborhood across the country more than half of each age group fails to complete high school, and 5 percent or fewer go on to some form of higher education. In many schools the average measured IQ is under 85, and it drops steadily as the children grow older. Adolescents depart from these schools ill-prepared to lead a satisfying, useful life or to participate successfully in the community (Zacharias, 1964).

Who are the children so poorly served by the most affluent nation in history?

The term "socially disadvantaged" describes a population of children and adults varied in a number of ways but having in common a low economic status, a low social status, low educational achievement, tenuous or no employment, limited participation in community organizations, and limited ready potential for upward mobility. Variously referred to as the "culturally deprived," the "socioeconomically deprived," the "socially and culturally disadvantaged," the "chronically poor," the "poverty stricken," and the "culturally alienated," these people are handicapped by depressed social and economic status. They also are handicapped in too many instances by ethnic and cultural *caste* status. The children whom we refer to as "disadvantaged" are predominantly Negro, Puerto Rican, Mexican, and rural or mountain southern whites. The problems of these youngsters are acute wherever they are found and have come into sharper focus as increasingly large numbers of the children have migrated to our metropolitan centers. In school these children show disproportionately high rates of social maladjustment, behavioral disturbance, physical disability, mental subnormality, and academic retardation. Although there is ample documentation of the *fact* of academic deficiency in a high percentage of this population, the specific nature of this deficiency is not so clearly documented. Psychoeducational appraisal more often has been directed toward the confirmation and quantification of the deficits than toward the determination of their quality and nature.

ACADEMIC AND COGNITIVE CHARACTERISTICS

Available research permits the identification of several categories of behavior which are encountered with great frequency among socially disadvantaged children. First, there are several studies which suggest that children from disadvantaged backgrounds in comparison with middle-class children are less able to make use of conventional verbal symbols in representing and interpreting their feelings, their experiences, and the objects in their environment. It is important to note that the apparent deficiency is in the use of such conventional verbal symbols—there is no definitive evidence that such children suffer from an underlying deficiency in symbolic representation.

Available evidence suggests that depressed language function can be the result of a variety of circumstances which make for disadvantaged status. Kellner *et al.* (1958) found in a group of children of comparable economic level, age, sex, and IQ differences on all quantitative measures of language function, differences which consistently favored children raised in their own homes as opposed to children raised in institutions. The authors suggested that children raised in the institutions studied were disadvantaged by an insufficient language stimulation resulting in restricted capacity for language development. Other investigators have been concerned with language development in different economic groups. Davis (1937) found a considerably higher percentage of children with good articulation among upper occupational groups than among lower. Beckey (1942) reported finding significantly more children with retarded speech among lower socioeconomic groups. Templin (1953) found a significant difference between children of upper- and lower-economic groups on tests of articulation, the difference being in favor of the higher-economic group. Her data indicate that children of the lower socioeconomic group take about a year longer to reach essentially mature articulation than do those of the upper group. Irwin (1948) reported that children after the age of one-and-one-half showed significant differences in their mastery of speech sounds according to their father's occupational status—with the advantage in the direction of the higher-occupational groups.

Anastasi (1952) compared Negro and Caucasian children and found among the Caucasians a greater frequency of mature-sentence types, more complex construction, and better elaborated concepts. Hilliard (1957), approaching the questions inferentially, found that children with rich information backgrounds were better equipped for reading than were pupils whose previous experience had been meager. In studies by Thomas (1962) and Templin (1957) in which the variable studied was number of words used per remark, Thomas' subjects drawn from a low socioeconomic group showed a mean of 5.6 words used, while Templin's subjects drawn from a middle-class population showed a mean of 6.9 words per remark.

In an interesting, though limited, study of linguistic behavior in lower- and middle-class subjects, Bernstein (1961) reported that the language of lower-class youth tends to be "restricted" in form. He characterized this language as serving to communicate signals and direction and to confine thinking to a relatively low level of repetitiveness. On the other hand, he described the language of the middle and upper classes as "elaborated" and serving to communicate ideas, relationships, feelings, and subjective states. These works suggest that symbolic representation is present in both classes, but also that important qualitative differences exist in the form and utilization of the symbol or language systems. These differences may have important implications for learning. However, since these studies have not included analysis of learning facility or lack of it in terms of language forms and vernacular peculiar to the population, the data do not enable us to determine accurately the specific nature of the learning disabilities involved.

But the inferential conclusions drawn from these studies, relating school failure to differences in language development in disadvantaged children, gain some support from studies of concept development in this population. Reissman (1962) has described concept formation among the disadvantaged as content-centered rather than form-centered, their reasoning as inductive rather than deductive. Such a conceptual style has been viewed as limiting the child's ability to make accurate generalizations and to transfer knowledge utilizing previously learned concepts (Gordon, 1964).

Deutsch (1963) and Hilliard (1957) have noted that increasing age amplifies the difference in the quality of language usage between classes; and Deutsch has suggested that if the acquisition of language is a prerequisite of concept-formation and problem-solving, then these evidences of relatively increasing language deficiency would indicate a tremendous lower-class deficit in conceptual function. Deutsch (1963) found that his subjects, drawn from a disadvantaged population, were relatively proficient on motor tasks, on tasks which required a short time span, and on tasks which could be most easily related to concrete objects and services; but, as he later reported (1964) he found lower-class children generally inferior in abstract conceptualization and in the categorizing of visual stimuli. Ausubel (1963) concluded that when there was a delay in the acquisition of certain formal language forms, there was a resultant difficulty in making the transition from concrete to abstract modes of thought.

In a cross-cultural inventory of the arithmetic concepts of kindergartners, Montague (1964) found significant differences between social classes in favor of the higher *SES* group; but Deutsch (1960) found that arithmetic scores were higher than reading scores among a population of lower-class children, even though both were depressed below national norms. In interpreting this finding, the investigator suggested that the difference might be accounted for by a hypothesis that reading involves motivations arising from specific value systems not shared by the disadvantaged society, while arithmetic may involve concrete acts, such as marketing, which are common to the society. In the work of this author (Gordon, 1965) in Prince Edward County, Virginia, arithmetic scores were similarly found to be less depressed than reading scores in the seven- to ten-year-old age groups. These children who had been deprived of formal education for four years are thought to have developed simple arithmetic skills in their everyday chore experiences, which experiences did not, however, provide a basis for the casual or incidental acquisition of reading skills.

If these assumptions about the experience-based distinctions between acquisition of reading and arithmetic skills are correct, then the Montague, Deutsch, and Gordon data would seem to support the observation that disadvantaged children tend to depend more on concrete than symbolic experience in dealing with concepts. In a study by Siller (1957), however this view is subjected to closer examination. Studying 181 white sixth-graders he found that higher-status children (a) scored higher than lower-status children on all tests of conceptual ability; (b) showed a significantly greater tendency toward abstraction in making choices between types of definitions than lower-status children; and (c) when matched with lower-status subjects on nonverbal tests, scored higher than their counterparts on tests of verbal concepts. Had Siller stopped there, his findings would confirm the impressions of others. When, however, the groups were matched on the basis of IQ scores, none of the above differences between children of high social status and children of low social status remained. Instead, these differences in style appeared to be related to differences in level of intellectual function. Suggested by these findings is the possibility that what has been referred to as a stylistic-response preference for concrete as opposed to abstract stimuli may be related more to level of intellectual function than to social class. Siller's data for low-status children may be accounted for by the presence of more low-scoring pupils in the lower-status group. Thus, while there is a considerable body of evidence to support the statement that lower-status children tend to show preference for concrete as opposed to abstract frames of reference in concept formation, the origin and nature of this style dominance and its relationship to intelligence and the teaching-learning process are yet to be established.

Among other disadvantageous characteristics, disadvantaged children have been noted by several investigators and observers to demonstrate perceptual styles and perceptual habits which are either inadequate or irrelevant to the demands of academic efficiency. Although high levels of perceptual sensitization and discrimination are often present, these skills tend to be better developed in physical than in visual behavior and in visual than in aural behavior (Reissman, 1962). Probably the most significant characteristic in this area is the extent to which these children fail to develop a high degree of dependence on the verbal- and written-language forms of academicians for learning cues. Many of the children simply have not adopted the modes of reception and expression which are traditional to, and necessary for, success in school.

The extent to which styles of perception and expression differ among children of different backgrounds is well-documented. In his study of retarded, average, and gifted children, Jensen (1963) concluded that many children viewed as retarded have merely failed to learn the verbal mediators which facilitate school learning. Earlier Carson (1960) found white children superior to Negroes, and northern Negroes superior to southern Negroes, when it came to understanding the meanings of words used in communication. In a study of children's use of time in their own stories, LeShan (1952) found that time orientation varies with social class and that middle- and upper-class children told stories involving a more prolonged period of time than those of lower-class children. Reissman (1962) includes slowness as a feature of the cog- nitive functioning of disadvantaged youngsters, a conclusion arrived at by Davidson some ten years earlier (1950) on finding differences in speed of response to be primarily responsible for racial differences in IQ estimated by timed performance tests. Deutsch (1964) found lower- class children relatively poorer in auditory discrimination, in recog- nizing perceptual similarities, and in the syntactical manipulation of language. Earlier (1960) he had found them inferior to a control group on tasks requiring concentration and persistence.

In fact, many of the children with whom we are concerned show a marked lack of involvement with, attention to, and concentration on the content of their academic experiences. There are few academic tasks which commit them to deep involvement. Their work habits are fre- quently insufficiently developed. Because of the high-interest demands of nonacademic experiences and the relatively low-interest demands of academic experiences, they are limited in their ability to inhibit re- sponses to those stimuli which are extraneous to academic learning and to disinhibit responses which are pertinent to academic learning. Deutsch reported that lower-class children tend to ignore difficult problems with a "so what" attitude and that as a result over a period of time their learning is decreased proportionately. Ausubel (1964) found that lower-class children depend more on external as opposed to internal control than do children from the middle class.

AFFECTIVE AND SOCIAL CHARACTERISTICS

Moreover, socially-disadvantaged children have generally been thought to be less highly motivated and to have lower aspiration for academic and vocational achievement than do their middle- and upper-class school peers. However, research findings relative to the aspirations of Negro children are contradictory. Data on these students probably best support the conclusion that educational aspirations (for example, interest in attending college) are as high for Negro youngsters as they are for comparable youngsters from middle-class backgrounds, but vocational aspirations are somewhat lower for the Negro group. The degrees of motivation and the direction which it takes among many of these children are often inconsistent with both the demands and the goals of formal education. It is the judgement of this investigator that although the quality of aspiration is often depressed, it is usually consistent with the child's perceptions of the opportunities and rewards available to him. As Reissman (1962) has observed, symbolic rewards appear to have little value as positive motivators of achievement. Similarly, achievement is not sustained in the presence of delayed gratification. For these children, goals tend to be self-centered, immediate, and utilitarian, as are the goals of the dominant culture. However, children growing up under more privileged circumstances have available many sources of immediate satisfaction and immediate feedback as well as many more evidences of the utilitarian value of academic effort. The differences between the privileged and the disadvantaged in this area are not so much differences in values as differences in the circumstances under which the values are called into play. Although the values from which motivation is derived in the disadvantaged child seem to reflect the dominant-culture concern with status, material possessions, in-group morality, Judeo-Christian ethics, competition, and so on, there is usually lacking a concern with the esthetics of knowledge, symbolization as an art form, introspection, and competition with one's self. In other words, dominant societal goals and values are operative, but their direction and context may not be complementary to academic achievement.

Rosen (1956), observing a relationship between high motivation and high grades, postulated that middle-class children are more likely to be taught the motives and values which make achievement possible. Similarly, in Gould's study (1941), only sons who internalized their parents' values and aspirations were sufficiently motivated to overcome obstacles which faced them in school. Bernstein (1960) found achievement-strivings arising from parental demands for success to be a more central motivational factor among middle-class than among lower-class children.

Closely related to these motivational factors are attitudinal factors, and these too are often a source of problems in educational planning for disadvantaged children. Hieronymus (1951) found that higher socioeconomic status was correlated with a high level of aspiration and positive attitudes toward school, while negative attitudes toward school and lower levels of aspiration were more frequently encountered in lower socioeconomic status groups. Sewell's (1957) findings that educational aspirations tend to be greatly influenced by class values in a manner favoring the middle and upper classes is consistent with the earlier work. Among other characteristics which have been referred to in this population are utilitarian attitudes toward knowledge and negative attitudes toward the pure pursuit of knowledge. Many of these children and their parents view education primarily in terms of its job-market value and their orientation is toward achieving the minimum level of education commensurate with employability. Carroll (1945) sees the lower-class ideal self as characterized by personal beauty and fame, not the moral and intellectual qualities which characterize the ideal self of middle-class children.

As important as these attitudes toward school and learning may be, it is in the area of attitude toward self and others that the crucial determinants of achievement and upward mobility may lie, and it is in these areas that our data are least clear. It has been observed by some that disadvantaged children show affinity for in-group members and demonstrate a sense of distance from, or even hostility toward, representatives of out-groups, whether in peer or nonpeer relationships. Contrastingly, other observers have noted the high degree of respect and awe in which these children hold selected out-group status persons or idealized models. Tendencies toward self-depreciation and depressed self-concepts have been noted by several observers (Dreger, 1960; Keller, 1963; Silverman, 1963). Goff (1954) found that lower-class children have more feelings of inadequacy in school than do children from the middle class. On the other hand, some recent findings (Gordon, 1965) suggest that depressed self-concept is not so prevalent a condition, and that even where present it may have little negative bearing on achievement. In fact, it is entirely possible that positive or negative feelings of self-worth may operate respectively to depress or accelerate achievement. Furthermore, it is in this area that the rapidly changing national and world situations involving underdeveloped peoples are likely to be most influential, and it is difficult to predict the ultimate effect of these altered situations on self-perception and behavioral change. Our knowledge and even our researchable hunches are as yet limited. But it is around these changing situations that the school may yet find a fulcrum on which to raise motivation, aspiration, and involvement. There is growing empirical evidence to support the view that young people actively associated with the current civil rights struggle draw from their involvement in that effort a new source of motivation and an enhanced view of themselves (Coles, 1963). The impression is gained that such experiences are reflected in greater application of effort to, and greater achievement in, academic endeavors.

The evidence for such improvement is less clear, yet there can be little doubt that attitudes toward self and toward the environment in relation to self are crucial variables in academic, as well as in social and emotional, learning situations.

It is noteworthy that much of the work done on characteristics of disadvantaged children has focused on their weaknesses, deficits, or limitations. With the notable exception of Reissman (1962) attempts at identification of positives or strengths in this population are hard to find. However, even in Reissman's treatment there is a tendency to romanticize these characteristics, which may be a more serious error than to ignore them. Among the several positives which may be identified are those behaviors and conditions which can be utilized and built upon for the purposes of educational improvement. It is extremely important to recognize that *selective* motivation, creativity, and proficiency are present in this population, and, as Reissman has consistently stressed, if we look for these characteristics in their traditional form and along traditionally academic dimensions, we shall merely ensure that they not be found. These children, like others, *are* motivated by *some* factors in the field. They show creativity in *some* situations. They are proficient at *some* tasks and under *some* conditions.

Reference has earlier been made to problems in language development and use. In contrast to the colloquially accepted concept that language is inadequate in this population is the proposition that there exist in disadvantaged populations quite complex languages. The form in which the language is expressed may not be verbal nor may the specific symbols be consistent with those normative to the dominant culture. But the presence of a language system or a system of symbolic representation adequate to the needs of the culture in which it has developed should not be ignored. The important question then becomes not whether language exists, but to what extent a given language system may be utilized in understanding and managing advanced conceptual problems. If the facts and integrative relationships of science, or the conceptual explorations of philosophy cannot be expressed in symbols capable of incorporation into the language system in question, then that language, though it may be adequate for the culture in which it exists, is inadequate to the demands of contemporary educational processes. To date, investigations into the utilitarian dimensions of divergent language patterns have not been conducted. Our research has established the fact of language differences (Deutsch, 1963, 1964; Jensen, 1963; John and Goldstein, 1964), and in addition we know something of the nature of these differences. The Bernstein work (1960, 1961, 1962) referred to earlier characterized lower-class language as restricted and middle-class language as elaborated. Strodtbeck (1964) has described a mechanism by which such language systems may develop and be perpetuated. He identifies this mechanism in the context of intrafamilial decision-theory where the elaborative characteristic of middle-class language is a product of parity (and thus conflict) in the decision-making process in the middle-class home. Restricted language on the other hand develops as a product of unilateral decision making in the lower-class home. In a situation involving equality and conflict of ideas the learner (child) early develops sensitivity to language as a vehicle for the elaboration of ideas. Where the opposite situation obtains, the child early develops sensitivity to language as a vehicle for the communication of signals or directions. Some findings of C. Deutsch (1964), that there are significant class differences in the time spent in parent-child communication, are not unrelated. Her data indicate that the length of such communication is considerably shorter for lower-class than for middle-class subjects. This difference has been viewed as a handicap, but it may be that given a different instructional method this proclivity for brief verbal communicative contact could be an advantage to the learner.

Much of our knowledge concerning children from socially disadvantaged backgrounds has been drawn by inference from the wide literature on juvenile delinquency. Sensitive analysis of this literature leads to an awareness of several other characteristics of this population. One can not study the literature on boys' gangs or juvenile offenders without coming to the conclusion that these youngsters show ingeniousness and resourcefulness in pursuing self-selected goals and in coping with very difficult and complex conditions of life. Such coping behavior reflects accuracy of perception and generalization around a variety of social, psychological, and physical phenomena. It is at once obvious that these children are capable of meaningful and loyal personal relationships and operate with an in-group morality that surpasses that of some more privileged segments of society. In many situations where the problems flow from the experiences and are important for the self-selected goal, such operations as memory, recall, computation, and representation have been demonstrated to be functionally adequate.

Now all these studies concerned with disadvantaged children have stressed the delineation of characteristics thought to be peculiar to this group. Considerable attention has been given to the projection of "needed" changes in this population with the research effort more often directed at the question of whether the change can be made and measured rather than to such questions as: Is a change needed? If so, what is the nature of that change? What is its relevance to the learning process? By what mechanisms are such changes achieved? In an earlier period, our studies of disadvantaged children followed the example of much of the research relating to children in general, that of emphasizing affective or personal social development. This fairly unsophisticated work has been replaced by studies emphasizing cognitive development.

In both cases less attention is given to developmental sequences than is devoted to comparing the status of affective or cognitive development in the disadvantaged child with that in more privileged children. But the nature of these functions, their idiosyncratic patterns, and the courses and mechanisms by which they develop have largely been ignored. This research is also limited in concern for the study of the affective-cognitive dimensions of learning as a nondichotomous process. Noteworthy exceptions are the investigations of academic performance of Negroes under varying conditions by Katz (1964) and the very sensitive study of education in an American Indian Community by M. and R. Wax (1964).

The second area to which research attention has been directed is the environment. Studies referrable to environmental concern have consisted largely of a cataloging of the factors, in homes and communities from which disadvantaged children come, which may interfere with normal school achievement. Such studies have often been conducted with the ultimate aim of incorporating knowledge obtained from them in the training of school personnel so that they may "understand" the culture and values of their pupils. The concurrence between certain conditions of life, certain population characteristics, and poor school adjustment has been interpreted as indicating a causal relationship, though the evidence supports only the conclusion that these phenomena are correlated. Such studies, while they may have social-anthropological value, are of questionable use in planning educational programs for these children. It is probably true that adverse conditions of life do not facilitate academic achievement in most children, but we have no firm evidence that such conditions preclude academic success. In fact, there are sufficient cases of success despite adverse conditions to make untenable the conclusion that difficult life circumstances prevent success in school. Insufficient attention has been given to the fact that many "normal" and functioning individuals have such adverse circumstances in their lives. There are many good reasons for improving the living conditions of the disadvantaged, and there is certainly no good excuse for an affluent society to fail to do so, but a concern on the part of the school for conditions of life should not substitute for a primary concern with the teaching-learning process as it relates to the individual. It is the individual, his potential for learning, and the sources of his behavior as a learner that represent the third focus of research attention.

THEORETICAL AND SOCIAL ORIGINS OF COMPENSATORY EDUCATION

The theoretical basis for such research is skimpy. Serious concern with the problems of individual differences in intelligence and learning ability is a relatively recent phenomenon. Around the turn of the century, Binet advanced the position that several aspects of intellectual function could be trained. His concern with the trainability of intelligence led him to argue for special instructional procedures designed to strengthen aspects of intellectual function which seemed less well-developed than others. The then emerging need for classificatory procedures by which children could be grouped in school and, later, men could be selected and grouped for military training purposes, led to the subversion or neglect of Binet's earlier concerns. Following World War I, psychologists in the United States become so preoccupied with the problems of classification and treatment within the narrow confines of psychoanalytic theory that this earlier concern with the trainability of intelligence continued to be ignored. Despite the parallel and prophetic model reflected in Montessori's work with slum children, these ideas, born more of optimistic and humanitarian attitudes than of science lay almost dormant until very recent years.

Resurgence of interest in the trainability of intellect and the graduated sequential development of perceptual and conceptual functions grew out of serious concern with the educational problems of mentally, physically and/or neurologically handicapped persons. With the strongest push coming from the works of Strauss and Kephart (1955), Kirk (1958), Gallagher (1958), Haeussermann (1958), and Birch (1964), educators began to be sensitive to the possibility that subnormal intellectual function did not necessarily reflect subnormal potential. In fact, these special educational efforts with handicapped children produced results which in large measure began to change some of our concepts of intellectual function and the function of educational experience.

Given the special education model, and some success in its application to brain-injured and cerebral-palsied children, some educators have begun to build compensatory education for the disadvantaged child on learning experiences designed to compensate for, or circumvent, certain identifiable or alleged deficiencies in function. Persons utilizing this model have not bothered to argue the origins of the functional state but have set about to develop experiences by which that state may be improved. Still others, sensitive to the political implications of accepting a deficits theory, have made a major point of the deficiencies which exist in the schools, and insist that differential achievement is but a reflection of these school-based inadequacies. Both of these positions are reflected in the programs and practices which have been hastily organized to serve socially disadvantaged children.

Most available evidence on the impact of intervention in the developmental process comes from studies involving educational and environmental change. The Klineberg (1963) studies support the view that intelligence-test scores can be changed by changes in the environment such as migration, acculturation, and adequate educational programs. In a study of Negro children migrating from the southern United States to Philadelphia, Lee (1961) found that intelligence-test scores improved significantly and steadily with length of residence in that northern metropolis, where the quality of education was superior. Clark (1954) reports the reverse of these findings when Negro children moved from schools in the South to a northern city where *de facto* segregation and other problems resulted in their exposure to educational experiences of poorer quality in the north than those which had been available to them in the south. Davis (1963) attributed a 10-point increase in measured IQ of Negro children in Chicago and Philadelphia over a five-year period simply to acculturation. The intelligence and reading-readiness scores of a group of Negro children in Tennessee are reported by Terrell and Brazziel (1962) to have been raised to national norms as a result of a six-week enrichment program consisting of exposure to readiness materials, and training in perceptual discrimination, vocabulary building, verbal reasoning, and direction following for the children, together with a series of informational and supportive conferences with parents. As a limited number of systematic evaluations of programs of compensatory education show, many forms of environmental and educational intervention appear to be accompanied by generally improved functioning for some of the children served (Wilkerson, 1965). Unfortunately, the gains obtained tend to be modest and, in some instances, are more apparent than real (Wrightstone *et al.,* 1964).

The work of Pasamanick and Knoblock (1958) suggests further that environmental conditions less conducive to wholesome physical development are not only reflected in impaired health, but in behavioral sequela as well. It is not unexpected that they find that where maternal health and prenatal care are poor, where obstetrical service is inadequate, where postnatal care is deficient and provision for child care precarious, the incidence of neurologic defects, of childhood illnesses and disorders, of behavior disorders, and of learning disabilities or inefficiencies is high. Implicit in these findings is the assumption that if the social and physical conditions of life were improved, intellectual and social function would improve as well. At the most obvious levels, then, we have evidence supportive of the position that interventional efforts directed at modified environmental encounters or improved organismic conditions result in behavioral changes which would not have been predicted by the assumption that quality of function is intrinsically determined. To balance this judgment, however, are the findings of a few studies and numerous programs which seem to result in no demonstrable change in behavior or achievement as a result of what may appear to have been massive interventions. It is likely that many of these efforts do not speak to the crucial determinants of behavior, are applied in insufficient concentrations, or represent inappropriate combinations of remedial services. Evidence mounts to support the view that in many situations in which *necessary* or *essential* behavioral determinants are present and available, these determinants may not produce conditions *sufficient* for the achievement of certain behavioral results.

It is out of the anticipation that improved educational opportunity and circumstances of parity with respect to the availability of education will result not only in improved school achievement, but in improved social development and upward mobility that the civil rights struggle has focused so sharply on education. Keppel (1964) has pointed to the contribution to the advancement of education made by the national human rights effort. Although Negro children do not constitute the largest segment of the poverty-stricken population in this country, they have come to represent one of the major foci of attention in the antipoverty and compensatory-education efforts. It is from our experience with educational efforts directed at Negro children, particularly in recently desegregated settings, that we also get encouraging but sobering findings which face us with some of the most challenging problems in compensatory education. Systematic study of the impact of desegregation and improved educational opportunity is limited. While one is encouraged by reported gains on the part of Negro students with no loss on the part of white students (*Southern School News,* 1960), it is in these improved situations that the difference between conditions which are desirable, necessary, and even essential, and those which are sufficient is highlighted.

In the few available studies it is clear that improved opportunities for education which have paralleled school desegregation efforts have resulted in improved school achievement for Negro pupils. In his study of school achievement in the Louisville public schools, Stallings (1959) found gains in median scores for all grades tested. The degree of improvement of achievement levels over the year prior to school desegregation was greater for Negro pupils than for white pupils. However, the Negro pupils' *level* of achievement did not equal that of the white pupils. The analysis of academic progress in schools in the District of Columbia following desegregation (Hansen, 1960) shows consistent gains for the Negro pupils, some initial decline for white pupils, followed by return to previous rates of academic achievement, and, again, an achievement level for white pupils somewhat in advance of that for Negro pupils. Reporting on experiences in a North Carolina school system, Day (1963) indicated that Negro pupils in the desegregated schools of that system had failed to keep pace with their white classmates. The picture is one of achievement gain following improved opportunity, but it is not at all clear that such gains result from the simple act of desegregation, since in most instances covered by these reports, Negro pupils remained in largely segregated settings. In fact, Stallings (1959) found greater gains when Negro pupils remained with Negro teachers and, incidentally, in segregated class groupings. Of even greater significance to those concerned with equality of educational achievement is the fact that, as groups, Negro pupils continue to be academically outdistanced by their white counterparts despite improvements in educational opportunities and desegregation efforts.

When selected populations are studied, results of improved opportunity are more encouraging. The original Demonstration Guidance Project findings suggest that improved educational opportunity even under conditions of *de facto* segregation results in gains for Negro pupils chosen from the upper 50 percent of the classes studied. Similarly, the carefully selected beneficiaries of services from the National Scholarship Service and Fund for Negro Students were found to far exceed norms for completion of college and were effective in competition with other students in predominantly white institutions. If one is willing to accept success (completion of high school or college) rather than excellence as the criterion, it is clear that, given improved opportunity, many disadvantaged youths can make the grade in academic achievement.

The presence in our schools of children whose backgrounds of experience and whose readiness for traditional school demands differ significantly from that of middle-class white, United States nationals is not a new phenomenon. In the past we have had large numbers of such children, particularly during the period of great migrations to this country. History reveals that the schools were challenged at that time just as they are today. It also is clear that the schools failed in their attempt to provide for the educational needs of many of these children. The schools' failures in previous years, however, had far less serious consequences for pupils and for society than do our failures today.

In the nineteenth and early twentieth centuries the uneducated, endowed only with strong backs or skillful hands, were eagerly sought by an economy which required manual strength and dexterity. In contrast, the economy of the late twentieth century requires trained minds, educated judgment, and conceptual skill. We have arrived at a period in human history in which man is increasingly required to manage vast categories of knowledge, to identify and solve highly complicated interdisciplinary problems, and to arrive at infinitely complex conceptualizations and judgments in order to maintain control of, and to advance the technological and social organization by which we live. Students with the quality of intellect, the adequacy of conceptual competence, and the depth of human understanding and compassion required of those who must man that organization are not routinely produced in today's schools. In fact, we school people are constantly embarrassed by the large numbers of young people whom we have failed to prepare for much less complex intellectual, academic, vocational, and social functioning. We also are under attack in many quarters for our failure to prepare adequately even many of those who *seem* to succeed in our system. Witness the large number of "successful" people who read inefficiently and without pleasure. Think of those among us whose skills in arithmetic are limited to simple computation. Consider the large number of high school and college graduates who have difficulty in recognizing a concept and are practically incapable of producing a clear one. Professional education has a long history and is not without some successes, but it has had many failures. In its present state it is hardly ready to meet the demands of this crucial period in the management of knowledge and technology.

Our nation has faced crises before. Following the Great Depression of the early thirties, we were confronted with the incongruities produced by high-level industrial potential and low-level socioeconomic organization. Organizing workers led a social revolution which produced new concepts of governmental responsibility for the promotion of the general welfare. New ideas, new techniques, and new approaches to socioeconomic organization were introduced and accepted as *social necessity* in a modern industrialized society. These innovations primarily enabled this nation to meet the domestic and international challenges of midcentury.

Now another social revolution has emerged. This revolution is not unrelated to the growing crisis in the use of intellectual resources and the management of knowledge. This time the battle is being waged by Negroes and their allies for civil or, more correctly, for human rights. Soon, no doubt, the poverty-stricken will join them. What they are demanding is nothing less than total and meaningful integration into the mainstream of our society. *Equality of educational achievement* (together with equal opportunity to share in the nation's wealth) is looked upon as a major means of attaining such integrated status.

This human rights revolution and the simultaneous explosion in knowledge pose challenges for society in general and for education in particular. To meet these challenges school systems and other responsible agencies in many parts of the country have begun to mobilize both concern and talent. The research of Clark and Clark (1939), Davis (1963), Deutsch (1964), Havighurst (1957), Pettigrew (1964), Smilansky (1064), Strodtbeck (1959), and others, and the ideas of leaders in the field like Bloom (1964), Jenkins (1964), Liddle (1962), Plaut (1957), Riessman (1962), Schreiber (1964), and Shepard (1962), have initiated special programs to upgrade education and to increase the life chances of disadvantaged children and youth.

Contemporary programs date back to work with Mexican-American and American Indian children in the Southwest where a project, focused on remedial work in reading and language usage and on inculcation of middle-class values, seems to have met with little success. The landmark project was the Demonstration Guidance Program, first initiated in the New York public schools in 1956. The primary purpose of the program was the identification and upgrading of students from backgrounds of limited cultural experience. This experimental program provided both remedial academic instruction and individual counseling for the top 50 percent of students in two New York City junior high schools. Integrated with the curriculum was a program of cultural enrichment which included visits to art galleries, plays, concerts, operas, and college campuses. In addition, attempts were made to involve parents and to help them understand, encourage, and assist the children in their pursuits. Subsequently the Demonstration Guidance Program was expanded and incorporated into the regular structure of the New York City public schools under the title, "Higher Horizons." Although the expanded program seems to have had little measurable effect in the enhancement of school functioning in the target population and has been discontinued, it none the less became the model for much of the work throughout the country directed toward the rehabilitation of disadvantaged youth.

Impetus toward the development of compensatory programs has come from other sources as well. At least three deserve mention. The National Defense Education Act, passed under the pressures of international competition and concern for national security, made special provision for the discovery and encouragement of youth with latent or undiscovered talent. With funds made available through this legislation, state departments of education and local school districts were able to initiate programs providing increased opportunities and services for this population.

A second major contribution was developed entirely outside the public schools as an outgrowth of the research programs of the Institute for Developmental Studies at New York Medical College and the Peabody College for Teachers. These programs, which have been investigating the use of a variety of enrichment experiences and stimulational work in language development at the preschool level, have attracted sufficient interest to encourage a number of private agencies and public school systems to institute special nursery programs as supplements to or as a part of the regular school program. The idea of intervention at the preschool level was so logically appealing and politically attractive that, under the banner "Project Head Start," it became one of the central components of the War on Poverty.

Probably the most influential growth force in programs for the disadvantaged has been the Ford Foundation's Great Cities Project. By providing sizable grants to a number of the nation's larger cities, the Foundation has encouraged massive and integrated attacks upon the problem of education in depressed urban areas. Typically these projects have mobilized a wide range of school and community resources, but they have had no single programmatic emphasis. What they have had in common is a concern for concentrating a wide variety of special services on the education problems of disadvantaged children and their families.

With the passage of the Elementary and Secondary Education Act of 1965 and the legislation establishing Project Head Start, the influence and support of the federal government was committed to special educational services for disadvantaged children. The relatively large amount of financial support made available to local communities through these programs has resulted in an unprecedented focus of attention on educational innovation designed to enhance the educational development of the target population. So pervasive has been this influence that there is hardly a state in the union which has not experienced some addition to its educational services. By fall 1967, except for those school systems which refuse to pay even lip-service to racial desegregation, the United States will have an almost universally applied national effort directed at educational uplift for the disadvantaged.

A constellation of forces has raised to the level of national concern the issue of providing special educational and social projects for disadvantaged children. These forces are the struggle of the disadvantaged and segregated for improvement in their life chances, society's growing demand for competence in the conceptualization and use of knowledge, new insights growing out of pilot demonstration and research programs, and, finally, the allocation of federal funds and support which is unprecedented in the history of education in the United States.

COMPENSATORY PROGRAMS AND PRACTICES

Although existing programs of compensatory education vary widely in size and scope throughout the country, they have in common the dual goals of remediation and prevention. They are remedial in that they attempt to fill gaps—social, cultural, or academic—in the child's total education. They are preventive in that they try to forestall either initial or contributing failure in school and later life.

Despite the mulitplicity of programs which share these goals it is possible to identify common strands in the fabric of compensatory education. Recognizing the arbitrariness of such a dissection, I nevertheless have chosen to tease apart these strands in order to deal understandably with the wide variety of current programs. Following a brief description of these eight identified areas of approach and some types of programs which employ them all, I shall take a more critical look at the question of how well these various practices meet the problems.

The principal focus of fundamental curricular change in compensatory programs has been *reading and language development*. New reading methods and materials, the training of teachers to use them, and the extensive use of such special personnel as remedial reading teachers or reading specialists all are evidence of the primacy of reading in the hierarchy of school learning. The assumed relationship between the quality of oral language and skill in reading has led to increased emphasis in some projects on practice in speaking and listening. Where youngsters do not speak English there are special methods and materials for developing bilingualism. Some projects have made significant strides in developing primers featuring racially integrated characters and naturalistic speech patterns which reflect inner-city life. Thanks to one of the provisions of Title I of the Elementary and Secondary Education Act, such a simple innovation as the providing of books for fledgling libraries is made possible in disadvantaged area schools where, in some instances, none had existed before.

In addition to new practices in reading, a number of other *curricular innovations* affecting both structure and content have been inaugurated in various project schools with the dual aim of individualizing instruction and increasing the relevance of classroom materials. Two major types of structural modification, team-teaching and ungraded classes, have been widely used, as have transitional classes, to ease children's entry into school or to facilitate their shift from one school situation to another. Various programs have provided time for classroom teachers to offer individual instruction and generally function with greater flexibility. These programs include employment of extra classroom teachers; use of specialists in such areas as music, science, art, or mathematics; and use of volunteer aides to assume routine classroom burdens.

Certain practices taken for granted in more privileged neighborhoods (such as providing movable desks, special art classes, or student government activities) have been introduced as innovations in disadvantaged schools. New textbooks, emphasizing low reading skills and high interest level, have been purchased or developed in various school systems. A new emphasis has emerged, particularly in the area of social studies, on texts which recognize minority group contributions. Through field trips and guest speakers as well as through a number of new curriculum materials which emphasize the role of minority groups in American life, disadvantaged children are introduced to the wider world and helped to recognize that there are alternatives to the limited roles their parents and neighbors have been permitted to play in society.

A number of projects have become involved in what might best be called *extracurricular innovation,* an umbrella phrase for a number of efforts to extend the school's influence into nonschool time. Afterschool or Saturday study centers are widely used as are clubs organized around such areas as sports, science, music, or reading for pleasure. Often paid or volunteer tutors are in attendance. Cultural events, hobby groups, picnics, and camping trips are some of the activities which have been used to enlarge the experience of disadvantaged children during the afternoon, evening, and weekend hours. Where project schools have continued their programs into the summer, both the children and the schools often have benefited from summer-school experimentation in remediation and enrichment.

Almost every sizable program of compensatory education now includes some effort to increase *parental involvement* in project goals as more and more schools serving disadvantaged neighborhoods have moved toward breaking down the barrier that has separated school and home. Recognizing the need for more aggressive methods of breaching the wall than a trumpet call from the traditional PTA, project schools have used home visits by teachers, community aides, or social workers. In addition to simply "getting in touch," these visitors interpret the school program to families, provide information about school events, suggest ways parents may assist the school program, counsel them about behavioral or school problems, or put them in contact with appropriate community-assistance agencies. When meetings with parents *are* held at school, they tend to be small, social, and informal and often are conducted by the staff persons responsible for home visits or for augmenting school-family contacts. Increased involvement of parents in the school has been achieved through such activities as adult education courses, clubs, and hobby groups and by enlisting their services in such activities as decorating classrooms or costuming school plays.

The question of *community involvement* has concerned a number of project schools as they have reached out beyond the parents into the total surrounding community both to offer and to seek help. Resources have been shared with other community agencies. School doors have been opened to adult education classes. Various community groups have made use of school facilities for their meetings. In return schools have benefited from community volunteer help for tutorial services such as English instruction or remediation, from community financial help for enrichment programs, and from the help of the business community in providing widened vocational opportunities. In many project communities the school has found it useful to employ a school-community agent to organize wide-ranging programs for children and adults. Often such a coordinator functions as a liaison person not only between school and community but also between the school and such governmental agencies as the local departments of public welfare.

Concerning *teacher recruitment and training,* schools have made use of a wide variety of practices designed to attract teachers to disadvantaged schools and to modify favorably their attitudes toward low-income families and communities. Internships at problem schools for teacher trainees or education majors in local colleges increase the number of teachers competent to work in disadvantaged areas. Orientation programs which include home visits and community field trips are conducted to dispel new teachers' fears and uncertainties concerning low-income neighborhoods. Extra consultative personnel or specially qualified teachers help train new faculty, conduct demonstration classes, provide special instructional materials, or reduce the regular teacher's load either by directly assisting her in the classroom or by taking students out of class for remedial or enrichment activities. In-service training courses and workshops emphasize programs to increase teacher understanding of low-income children. Seminars and discussion periods give teachers an opportunity to share experiences and to discuss problems.

Guidance, together with remedial reading, is the one approach almost universally included in projects for the disadvantaged. Although guidance personnel are unfortunately still hampered by their traditional preoccupation with the misfit, increasing emphasis is being placed on providing counseling and guidance to all students in a project school. In these guidance-oriented programs less emphasis is placed on changing the school than on changing the student through individual and group counseling designed to increase his self-understanding, to enhance his self-concept and to improve his motivation and attitudes toward school. In addition to expanding its personal counseling role, guidance also has enlarged its informational role, particularly in regard to vocational and educational opportunities. A typical compensatory guidance program will combine individual counseling, vocationally oriented group guidance and, not infrequently, extensive enrichment activities to widen the student's view of the world.

Special personnel (many of whose roles have been described above) usually fall into three categories: special instructional personnel, special service personnel, and nonprofessional personnel. Special instructional personnel include classroom teachers, specially trained in work with the disadvantaged, whose employment may result in reduced class size for all the other teachers. In addition such special staff as curriculum specialists (in language arts, science, mathematics, and the like) both train teachers and conduct classes themselves. Additions to the school staff for special services occur principally in the areas of guidance and health. Guidance counselors, psychologists, psychiatrists, social workers, physicians, nurses, and dental technicians are the most frequent new additions in this area. A major innovation in school personnel is the greatly expanding use of nonprofessionals. Often referred to as "subprofessionals" when paid and drawn from persons indigenous to the disadvantaged community ("volunteers" when unpaid and drawn from persons of more advantageous backgrounds), these new school-workers serve in community liaison roles, function as teacher-aides and work as tutors, study-hall supervisors, recreation and lunchroom monitors, record clerks, and monitors in a variety of small-group situations.

These then are the eight areas in which innovation has taken place in current compensatory programs. Many of the specific approaches just described function as parts of complex programs covering more than one phase of the relationship between the school, the child, and the community. Indeed, where resources permit, school districts have initiated "total" programs which have aimed at altering the entire school experience of the children involved in them. Sometimes these broad-scale programs, including the whole battery of compensatory practices, serve thousands of students. In other instances a variety of techniques are combined in a small program aimed at only a few youngsters.

Two familiar types of programs in which a variety of techniques often are combined are the early-admission or prekindergarten programs for children under conventional school age. At the other end of the educational continuum are programs for dropouts.

The problem of school dropouts is not a new one. But the demands of modern life have made dropout a momentous and tragic event. Years ago the dropout, entering a thirsty labor market, could fill a productive social and economic role. Today he automatically is relegated to an economically perilous life in which finding a job will become increasingly difficult as the need for unskilled labor continues its precipitate decline. Concern for the dropout has therefore intensified. New approaches have been sought for coping with this crucial problem. Adult education programs to provide technical training and to combat widespread functional illiteracy have been instituted by large companies, by boards of education, and by the government. A number of businesses and industries have conducted job-upgrading projects for their employees. Daytime programs for recent dropouts have been established by the school systems in several cities. For high school students on the verge of dropping out there are work-study programs designed to hold them or, failing that, to give them better preparation for employment.

Programs like these, although they are important and helpful, can only try to ameliorate an existing educational failure. To deal with the problem most effectively, *preventive,* more potent, more fundamental measures also are being tried. These are the programs aimed at broadening the experiences of children as young as three and four years to equip them better for school learning. These preschool programs have added to the best of the traditional nursery school activities directed at language development and enrichment, sharpened socioperceptual discrimination, broadened and amplified encounters with the environment, and accelerated socialization in directed learning situations.

The fact that so many attempts have been made to renovate, enrich, and extend school programs for the benefit of disadvantaged children is an important step forward. But our enthusiasm should not blind us to their shortcomings.

I think it is significant that so much of the current work in the education of the disadvantaged has been directed either at preschool children or at youngsters who have dropped out of high school. So little attention has been given to investigating the over-all appropriateness of contemporary educational processes. If school people were not such a decent lot, one would think that these two emphases have been so widely accepted simply because they require the least change in the school itself. It often is easier to add extensions than to change the basic structure of institutions.

There is, of course, some evidence to support the preschool emphasis. There is no question that children who grow up under different life conditions are likely to show different developmental patterns. Unless experiential input has been designed to produce the same learning-readiness end, such readiness will vary. Consequently, it is not inappropriate to assume that children coming from privileged homes enter school with skills and competencies different from those of children from less privileged homes. And since all these children, despite the differences present upon entry, must meet common academic standards, it is argued that the disadvantaged child needs special remedial or enrichment experiences in order to better cope with the traditional school requirements. As a firm advocate of expanded public educational opportunities, I welcome this downward extension of public education to include the three- to five-year-olds. However, I am unprepared to accept this downward extension as a substitute for new, different, and greater effort in the traditional school grades. I also find it difficult in the light of some of the work of Piaget and Hunt to settle for intervention at the third year of life rather than at the eighteenth month or during the first year of life. If we are serious about the importance of early encounters with the environment, it may be that we must take greater collective responsibility for influencing life experience from birth and even for influencing the quality of the physical environment before birth. It is unlikely, however, that our society will be ready for the revolutionary social changes involved in such a commitment for a good many years to come.

It would seem as if we have been equally unready to accept the degree to which our traditional methods for altering the behaviors of older children have failed. Despite considerable evidence that counseling is not the most effective instrument of behavioral change, programs for disadvantaged children all across the United States have included a major counseling and guidance component. I do not want to demean the role that information, understanding, insight, and support play in human adjustment. But I submit that significant changes in behavior are products of significant changes in life experiences. It certainly is true that the counselor can help a student to feel better about a difficult situation. He may even help him to find a better solution. But the student's attitude and behavior with respect to that situation are more likely to be significantly altered by changes in that situation itself, particularly if he has had a hand in effecting those changes.

Probably the most interesting thing about the programs studied is the absence of really "new" or radical innovation in pedagogy. Most of the programs use common sense procedures which are, or should be, part of any good educational program. It is, in fact, something of an indictment that we have not introduced these practices earlier. What is missing, however, is the introduction of truly new approaches. Such innovational timidity reflects that, although a good deal has been discovered about human beings and how they learn, much basic research simply has not been done. Such research is needed in order to make fundamental changes.

For example, although considerable effort has been invested in improving teacher competence and teacher behavior, designers of in-service and preservice training programs have had their problems. Neither research nor practice has provided definite guidelines as to what should be emphasized in such training. When Kconigsberg studied teachers who were thought by their administrators to be successful with the disadvantaged, she found no objective evidence of their superiority in this area. Some programs stress the human relations approach, but in our own investigation of this area we have observed allegedly good teachers who, judged by colloquial standards, seemed to be lacking in warmth, support, and sympathy. Other programs stress understanding the culture and values of the poor. Yet we know that a good bit of this "awareness of the child's background" gets distorted into gossip about the children's parents' "lack of morals" and is seldom reflected in significantly changed teacher attitudes or behaviors.

Probably the most productive approach to changed teacher behavior and attitudes is that which emphasizes provision of new and improved tools for teachers. Taking a cue from the experience with the new math curriculum, the Zacharias Commission has stressed the importance of new instruments and of workable methods in achieving behavioral change in teachers. It is easy for teachers to slip into attitudes of defeat and indifference when they see little return for their efforts. But it is difficult for them to remain indifferent and unchallenged when their efforts begin to meet with success. A weakness of our teacher-training programs and of our over-all programs of education for the disadvantaged is our failure to match the informational, technological, and social revolutions of the present with a revolution in the teaching-learning process. We have not yet removed the burden of proof from the shoulders of the learner and placed the responsibility for the success of the academic venture where it belongs—on the shoulders of those of us who teach.

In no area is this misplaced responsibility more obvious than in the area of curriculum innovation. Remedial education programs have been developed, teacher-pupil ratio has been reduced, new materials have been produced, classroom grouping has been modified. All are sensible and appropriate changes, but they represent no basic alteration in the teaching-learning process. They are likely to result in an increasing number of children who succeed, but they are unlikely to meet the real challenge of our time to the schools—that of ensuring that all children except those with significant neurologic defects achieve conceptual competence as well as mastery of the basic academic skills. If the school cannot do this, it is dysfunctional in modern technological societies.

To meet this challenge, curricular innovation will need to give greater attention to the effective dynamics of intragroup interaction on the learning process. It would be well to explore the relationship of variations in receptor readiness and in the hierarchical organization of sensory modalities to differential patterns of learning experience. Further, we might give attention to experimentation with peer-group instructors, with modified sequential arrangement of curriculum content, and with manipulation of the social, psychological, and physical environments in which learning occurs. Although we recognize the school's deficiencies here, let us not exempt from blame the behavioral scientists who, as we suggested earlier, have failed to provide to educational practitioners sufficiently convincing and comprehensible theories with which to mount such a revolution.

If the flood of interest and activity currently being poured into work with the disadvantaged were based upon substantial research findings or reflected considered, empirically-derived evidence, one could have greater hope that this effort would result in greatly improved life chances for the target populations. Although one must appreciate the fact that human and material resources are being directed at this long neglected problem, we simply will be helping to compound the disadvantaged status and to reinforce old prejudices if we fail to recognize the limitations of these efforts. Given the present level of knowledge and work, five or ten years from now many of our disadvantaged youngsters may still be at the bottom of the academic heap. Such a result could give renewed popularity to the now more dormant concepts of inherent inadequacy. This retreat to a theory of innate deficiency would be defended on the grounds that during the sixties this nation poured resources into helping these children and achieved relatively little despite all efforts. It may not readily be remembered that enriched diet did little to conquer tuberculosis, not because this measure was applied with insufficient diligence, but because the inappropriateness of this treatment modality was less evident before the nature of the disaese was better understood.

Such may well be the outcome of our effort if we fail to keep in mind the fact that inappropriate motivation, depressed levels of aspiration, dysfunctional patterns of conceptualization, academic disenchantment, and underdeveloped intellect are all too frequently products of poverty, social disorganization, lack of opportunity, social isolation, and prejudicial discrimination. To correct the functional limitations caused by such social pathology, we also must correct the conditions which have produced them. The burden of responsbility for the identification of these causative factors and approaches to their correction falls on the behavioral and political scientists. But the final responsibility for their manipulation, control, and elimination falls on each of us—as professional, as scientist, and as citizen. However, this concern with the social origins of the handicaps identified must not blind us to the possibility that changes in the social factors we view as causative are necessary, but may not remedy the resulting behavior. Innovations needed to provide the extra margin of sufficiency fall largely in the area of professional services—social, educational, psychological, and medical.

References

Anastasi, Anne, and Rita Y. D'Angelo. A comparison of Negro and white preschool children in language development and Goodenough Draw-A-Man IQ. *Pedagogical Seminary and Journal of Genetic Psychology (Journal of Genetic Psychology)*, **81,** December 1952, 147–165.

Ausubel, David P. How reversible are the cognitive and motivational effects of cultural deprivation? Implications for teaching the culturally deprived child. *Urban Education,* **I** (1), Autumn 1964, 16–38.

———— and Pearl Ausubel. "Ego development among segregated Negro children." In A. Harry Passow (ed.), *Education in depressed areas.* New York: Bureau of Publications, Teachers College, Columbia University, 1963, 109–141.

Beckey, Ruth Elizabeth. A study of certain factors related to retardation of speech. *Journal of Speech Disorders,* **7,** September 1942, 223–249.

Bernstein, Basil. Language and social class. *British Journal of Sociology,* **II,** September 1960, 271–276.

————. Social class and linguistic development: A theory of social learning. In A. H. Halsey, J. Floud, and C. A. Anderson (eds.), *Education, economy and society*. New York: Free Press, 1961.

Bernstein, Basil. Social class, linguistic codes and grammatical elements. *Language and Speech*, **5**, 1962, 221–240.

Birch, Herbert G. *Brain damage in children: Biological and social aspects*. Baltimore, Md.: Williams & Wilkins Co., 1964.

Bloom, B. S. *Stability and change in human characteristics*. New York: Wiley, 1964.

Carroll, Rebecca Evans. Relation of social environment to the moral ideology and personal aspirations of Negro boys and girls. *School Review*, **53**, January 1945, 30–38.

Carson, Arnold S., and A. I. Rabin. Verbal comprehension and communication in Negro and white children. *Journal of Educational Psychology*, **51**, April 1960, 47–51.

Clark, K., and M. K. Clark. The development of consciousness of the self and the emergence of racial identification in Negro preschool children. *Journal of Social Psychology*, **10**, 1939, 591–599.

Clark, K. B. Segregated schools in New York City. Paper read at conference, "Child Apart," North Side Center for Child Development, New Lincoln School, April 1954.

Coles, Robert. *The desegregation of southern schools: A psychiatric study*. New York: Anti-Defamation League, July 1963.

Davidson, Kenneth S., *et al.* A preliminary study of Negro and white differences on form I of the Wechsler Bellevue Scale. *Journal of Consulting Psychology*, **14**, October 1950, 489–492.

Davis, Allison. "The future education of children from low socio-economic groups." In Stanley Elam (ed.), *New Dimensions for Educational Progress*. Bloomington, Ind.: Phi Delta Kappa, 1963, 27–54.

Davis, Edith A. *The development of linguistic skill in twins, singletons with siblings and only children from age five to ten years*. Institute of Child Welfare Monograph Series, No. 14. Minneapolis: University of Minnesota Press, 1937.

Day, R. E. *Civil rights U.S.A.; Public schools, southern states, 1963: North Carolina*. Staff report submitted to the United States Commission on Civil Rights. Washington, D.C.: Government Printing Office.

Deutsch, Cynthia. Auditory discrimination and learning: Social factors. *Merrill-Palmer Quarterly*, **10**, July 1964, 277–296.

Deutsch, Martin. *Minority group and class status as related to social and personality factors in scholastic achievement*. Society for Applied Anthropology, Monograph No. 2. Ithaca, N. Y.: Cornell University, 1960.

——. "The disadvantaged child and the learning process." In A. Harry Passow (ed.), *Education in Depressed Areas*. New York: Bureau of Publications, Teachers College, Columbia University, 1963.

—— and Bert Brown. Social influences in Negro-white intelligence differences. *Journal of Social Issues*, **20**, April 1964, 24–35.

Dreger, Ralph Mason, and Kent S. Miller. Comparative psychological studies of Negroes and whites in the United States. *Psychological Bulletin*, **57**, September 1960, 361–402.

Gallagher, J. J. Social status of children related to intelligence, propinquity and social perception. *Elementary School Journal*, **58**, January 1958, 225–231.

Goff, Regina M. Some educational implications of the influence of rejection on aspiration levels of minority group children. *Journal of Experimental Education,* **23,** December 1954, 179–183.

Gordon, Edmund W. "Counseling socially disadvantaged children." In Frank Riessman, Jerome Cohen, and Arthur Pearl (eds.), *Mental health of the poor.* New York: Free Press, 1964.

———. *Educational achievement in the Prince Edward County Free School, 1963–64.* New York: Ferkauf Graduate School of Education, Yeshiva University, 1965 (mimeo).

Gould, Rosalind. Some sociological determinants of goal strivings. *Journal of Social Psychology,* **13,** May 1941, 461–473.

Haeussermann, Else. *Developmental potential of preschool children. An evaluation of intellectual, sensory and emotional functioning.* New York: Grune & Stratton, Inc., 1958.

Hansen, Carl F. The scholastic performances of Negro and white pupils in the integrated public schools of the District of Columbia. *Harvard Educational Review,* **30,** No. 3, Summer 1960, 216–236.

Havighurst, R. J. Conditions favorable and detrimental to the development of talent. *School Review,* **65,** 1957, 20–26.

Hieronymus, A. N. Study of social class motivation: Relationships between anxiety for education and certain socio-economic and intellectual variables. *Journal of Educational Psychology,* **42,** April 1951, 193–205.

Hilliard, George H., and Eleanor Troxwell. Informational background as a factor in reading readiness and reading progress. *Elementary School Journal,* **38,** December 1957, 255–263.

Irwin, Orvis C. Infant speech: The effect of family occupational status and of age on use of sound types. *Journal of Speech and Hearing Disorders,* **13,** September 1948, 224–226.

Jenkins, M. D. *The Morgan State College Program—An adventure in higher education.* Baltimore: Morgan State College Press, 1964.

Jensen, Arthur R. Learning ability in retarded, average, and gifted children. *Merrill-Palmer Quarterly,* **9,** April 1963, 123–140.

John, Vera P., and Leo S. Goldstein. The social context of language acquisition. *Merrill-Palmer Quarterly,* **10,** July 1964, 265–276.

Katz, Irwin. Review of evidence relating to effects of desegregation on the intellectual performance of Negroes. *American Psychologist,* **19,** June 1964, 381–399.

Keller, Suzanne. The social world of the urban slum child: Some early findings. *American Journal of Orthopsychiatry,* **XXXIII,** October 1963, 823–831.

Keppel, Francis. In the battle for desegregation what are the flanking skirmishes, what is the fundamental struggle? *Phi Delta Kappan,* **46,** September 1964, 3–5.

Kirk, Samuel A. *Early education of the mentally retarded: An experimental study.* Urbana: University of Illinois Press, 1958.

Klineberg, Otto. Negro-white differences in intelligence test performance: A new look at an old problem. *American Psychologist,* **18,** April 1963, 198–203.

Lee, Everett S. "Negro intelligence and selective migration." In James J. Jenkins and Donald S. Paterson (eds.), *Studies in individual differences.* New York: Appleton-Century-Crofts, 1961, 669–676.

LeShan, Lawrence L. Time orientation and social class. *Journal of Abnormal and Social Psychology,* **47,** July 1952, 589–592.

Liddle, G. P. Modifying the school experience of culturally handicapped children in the primary grades. *Programs for the Educationally Disadvantaged, report of a conference in Washington, D.C., May 21–23.* Washington, D.C.: United States Office of Education, 1962.

Montague, David O. Arithmetic concepts of kindergarten children in contrasting socioeconomic areas. *Elementary School Journal,* **64,** April 1964, 393–397.

Pasamanick, Benjamin, and Hilda Knobloch. The contribution of some organic factors to school retardation in Negro children. *Journal of Negro Education,* **27,** February 1958, 4–9.

Pettigrew, T. F. *A profile of the Negro American.* Princeton, N. J.: Van Nostrand, 1964.

Plaut, Richard L. *Blueprint for talent searching: America's hidden manpower.* New York: National Scholarship Service and Fund for Negro Students, 1957.

Pringle, M., L. Kellmer, and Margaret Tanner. The effects of early deprivation on speech development: A comparative study of four year olds in a nursery school and in residental nurseries. *Language and Speech,* **I,** October-December 1958, 269–287.

Riessman, Frank. *The culturally deprived child.* New York: Harper & Row, 1962.

Rosen, Bernard C. "The achievement syndrome: A psychocultural dimension of social stratification." *American Sociological Review,* **21,** April 1956, 203–211.

Schreiber, Daniel. "An introduction to the school dropout." In *Guidance and the School Dropout.* Washington, D.C.: National Education Association of the United States, 1964.

Sewell, William H., Archie O. Haller, and Murray A. Strauss. Social status and educational and occupational aspiration. *American Sociological Review,* **22,** February 1957, 67–73.

Shepard, S., Jr. "A program to raise the standard of school achievement (St. Louis, Mo.)." In *Programs for the educationally disadvantaged, report of a conference in Washington, D.C., May 21–23.* Washington, D.C.: United States Department of Education, 1962.

Siller, Jerome. Socioeconomic status and conceptual thinking. *Journal of Abnormal and Social Psychology,* **55,** November 1957, 365–371.

Silverman, Susan B. *Self-images of upper-middle class and working class young adolescents.* Unpublished M.A. thesis, University of Chicago, 1963.

Smilansky, S. *A program to demonstrate ways of using a year of kindergarten to promote cognitive abilities.* Jerusalem, Israel: Henrietta Szold Institute, 1964.

Southern School News, Untitled. *Southern School News,* **7** (2), Columns 1–2, August 1960.

Stallings, Frank H. A study of the immediate effects of integration on scholastic achievement in the Louisville Public Schools. *Journal of Negro Education,* **28,** Fall 1959, 439–444.

Strauss, Alfred A., and N. C. Kephart. *Psychopathology and education of the brain-injured child. Vol. 2, Progress in Theory and Clinic.* New York: Grune & Stratton, Inc., 1955.

Strodtbeck, Fred L. *Talent and society.* Princeton, N.J.: D. Van Nostrand, 1959.

————. "The Hidden Curriculum of the Middle Class Home." In C. W. Hunnicutt (ed.), *Urban education and cultural deprivation.* Syracuse, N.Y.: Syracuse University Press, 1964, 15–31.

Templin, Mildred C. Norms on screening test of articulation for ages three through eight. *Journal of Speech and Hearing Disorders,* **18,** December 1953, 323–331.

————. *Certain language skills in children; Their development and inter-relationships.* Institute of Child Welfare Monograph Series, No. 26. Minneapolis: University of Minnesota Press, 1957.

Terrell, Mary, and William F. Brazziel. An experiment in the development of readiness in a culturally disadvantaged group of first grade children. *Journal of Negro Education,* **31,** Winter 1962, 4–7.

Thomas, Dominic Richard. *Oral language, sentence structure and vocabulary of kindergarten children living in low socioeconomic urban areas.* Doctoral thesis. Detroit, Mich.: Wayne State University, 1962. (Abstract: Dissertation Abstracts, **23** (3), 1962, 1014.)

Wax, Murray L., Rosalie H. Wax, and Robert V. Dumont. *Formal education in an American Indian community.* Society for the Study of Social Problems Monograph, Spring 1964.

Wilkerson, Doxey A. School integration, compensatory education and the Civil Rights Movement. *The Journal of Negro Education,* **34,** No. 3, Summer 1965, 300–309.

Wrightstone, J. Wayne, *et al. Evaluation of the Higher Horizons program for underprivileged children.* New York: Board of Education, Bureau of Educational Research, 1964. (Cooperative Research Project No. 1124.)

Zacharias, J. "Innovation and experiment in education." In *A progress report of the Panel on Educational Research and Development.* Washington, D.C.: United States Government Printing Office, 1964.

Name Index

Allen, G., 32
Allison, A. C., 23
Allport, Gordon, 183, 220
Anastasi, Anne, 25, 32, 42, 43, 383
Anderson, L. M., 373
Anderson, Rose G., 296
Applezweig, M. H., 268
Asbell, B., 219
Asch, S. E., 69
Atkinson, J. W., 258, 267, 276–277, 278
Ausubel, David P., 200, 203, 204, 207–208, 384, 386
Ausubel, P., 200, 203, 204, 207–208

Baker, P. T., 24
Barker, R., 269
Barnicot, N. A., 24
Bavelas, Alex, 229
Bayley, Nancy, 117, 348, 349 n.
Bayton, J. A., 267
Beach, F. A., 313
Becker, H. S., 219
Becker, W. C., 302
Beckley, Ruth E., 383
Bellugi, Ursala, 367, 368
Benjamin, L., 267, 272
Bereiter, Carl S., 5, 292, 329, 337–346, 369
Berlyne, D. E., 313, 316, 321, 351
Bernard, Jessie, 208
Bernstein, Basil, 3, 102, 118, 323 n., 325, 326, 383, 387, 389
Bettelheim, Bruno, 1, 209
Bexton, W. H., 318
Bialer, I., 134
Binet, Alfred, 392
Birch, Herbert G., 392
Birdsell, J. B., 12
Bloom, B., 88, 111, 396
Blumberg, B. S., 18, 19, 23
Blumenbach, J. F., 12, 13
Boring, E. G., 63, 296
Bousfield, W. A., 151
Bovard, E. W., 256, 269, 270
Boyd, G. F., 198
Boyd, W., 12, 13
Brackbill, Yvonne, 27
Brattgård, S. O., 301
Brazier, Mary A. B., 67
Brazziel, William F., 393

Brodbeck, A. J., 117
Brown, B., 192, 206, 209–210, 325
Brown, R., 367, 368
Bruner, J. S., 63, 249
Bühler, K., 313
Burt, Sir Cyril, 8, 35, 36–37, 38, 42
Butler, R. A., 313–314

Caldwell, Bettye, 358 n.
Callaway, E., 269
Campbell, D. T., 77 n., 78
Carmichael, L., 298, 300
Carroll, Rebecca Evans, 388
Carter, C. O., 45
Carter, H. D., 149
Casler, L., 34
Castle, P., 72
Cattell, J. McKeen, 295
Cattell, R. B., 42
Cayton, H. R., 204
Cazden, Courtney B., 366, 367, 368, 372
Chein, I., 68, 213
Chevalier, J. A., 309, 311
Child, I. L., 270
Chos, K. L., 301
Clark, Ann D., 80
Clark, Kenneth B., 1, 184, 186, 187, 189, 191, 209, 219, 249, 396
Clark, M. P., 184, 187, 189, 191, 209
Clarke, A. D. B., 393
Coghill, G. E., 298, 300
Cohen, Barbara, 86 n.
Cohen, M., 272
Coleman, James S., 1, 177, 206, 260–261
Coles, Robert, 189, 195, 263, 388
Collier, H. L., 258
Conger, J. J., 270
Converse, P. E., 182
Coon, C. S., 12
Cooper, A. J., 18, 19, 23
Cooper, R., 30
Criswell, Joan H., 211, 257, 263
Cruze, W. W., 300

Darlington, C. D., 35
Darwin, Charles, 294–295, 296, 297, 303,
Dashiell, J. F., 313
Davidson, H. H., 210
Davidson, Kenneth S., 258, 270, 386
Davidson, R. E., 158

Subject Index

417